BATMAN
LAST KNIGHT ON EARTH

BATMAN
LAST KNIGHT ON EARTH

Scott Snyder writer
Greg Capullo penciller

Jonathan Glapion inker
FCO Plascencia colorist
Tom Napolitano letterer
Greg Capullo with **FCO Plascencia**
collection cover artists

Batman created by Bob Kane with Bill Finger

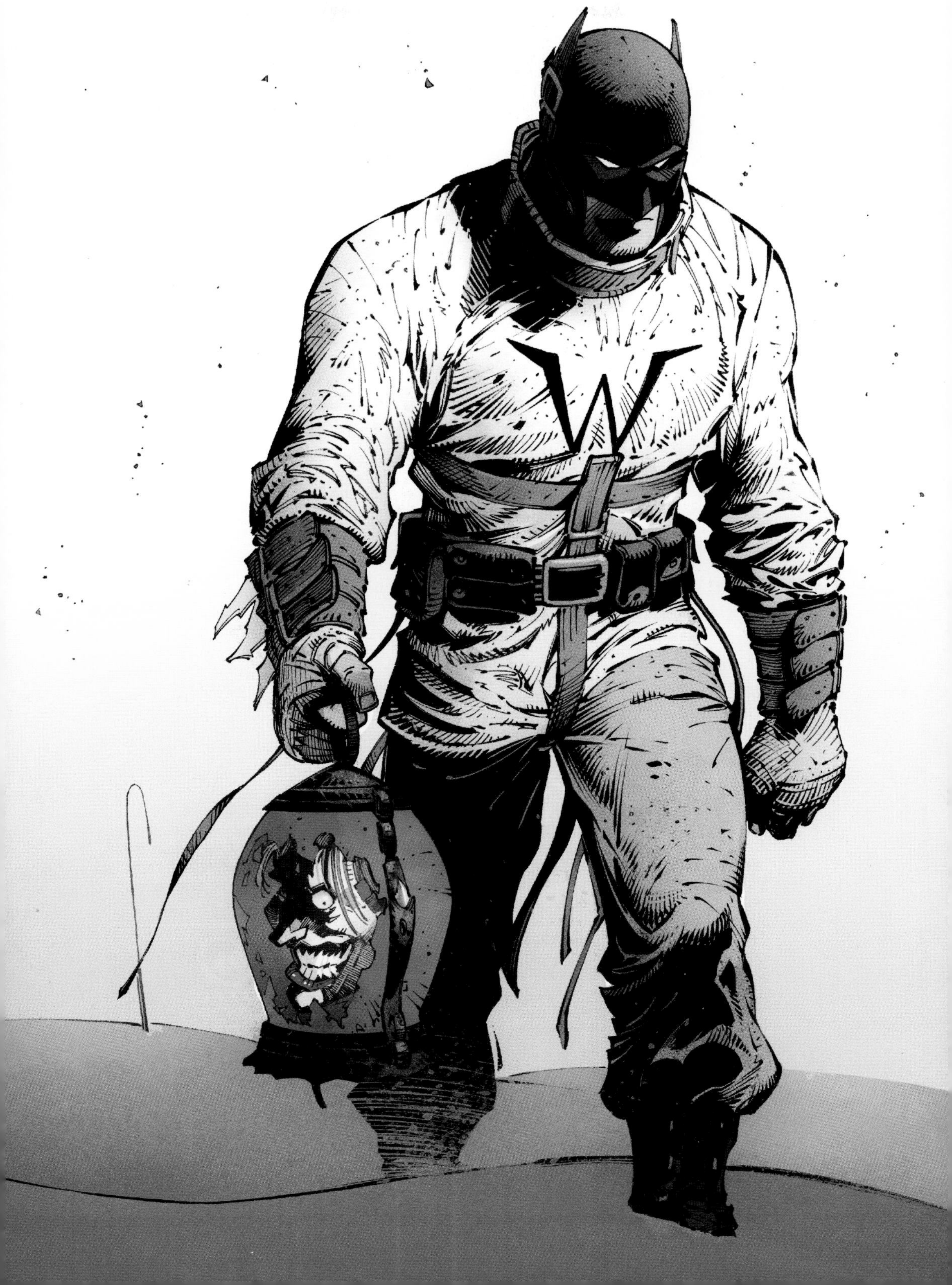

MARK DOYLE — Editor – Original Series
AMEDEO TURTURRO — Associate Editor – Original Series
JEB WOODARD — Group Editor – Collected Editions
ROBIN WILDMAN — Editor – Collected Edition
STEVE COOK — Design Director – Books & Publication Design
SUZANNAH ROWNTREE — Publication Production

BOB HARRAS — Senior VP – Editor-in-Chief, DC Comics

DAN DiDIO — Publisher
JIM LEE — Publisher & Chief Creative Officer
BOBBIE CHASE — VP – New Publishing Initiatives & Talent Development
DON FALLETTI — VP – Manufacturing Operations & Workflow Management
LAWRENCE GANEM — VP – Talent Services
ALISON GILL — Senior VP – Manufacturing & Operations
HANK KANALZ — Senior VP – Publishing Strategy & Support Services
DAN MIRON — VP – Publishing Operations
NICK J. NAPOLITANO — VP – Manufacturing Administration & Design
NANCY SPEARS — VP – Sales
MICHELE R. WELLS — VP & Executive Editor, Young Reader

BATMAN: LAST KNIGHT ON EARTH

Published by DC Comics. Compilation and all new material Copyright © 2020 DC Comics. All Rights Reserved. Originally published in single magazine form in *Batman: Last Knight on Earth* 1-3. Copyright © 2019, 2020 DC Comics. All Rights Reserved. All characters, their distinctive likenesses, and related elements featured in this publication are trademarks of DC Comics. The stories, characters, and incidents featured in this publication are entirely fictional. DC Comics does not read or accept unsolicited submissions of ideas, stories, or artwork. DC – a WarnerMedia Company.

DC Comics, 2900 West Alameda Ave., Burbank, CA 91505
Printed by Transcontinental Interglobe, Beauceville, QC, Canada. 2/28/20 First Printing.
ISBN: 978-1-4012-9496-0
Barnes & Noble Exclusive Edition ISBN: 978-1-77950-543-9

Library of Congress Cataloging-in-Publication Data is available.

PEFC Certified

This product is
from sustainably
managed forests and
controlled sources

PEFC/01-31-106   www.pefc.org

PART ONE:
THE CAVE

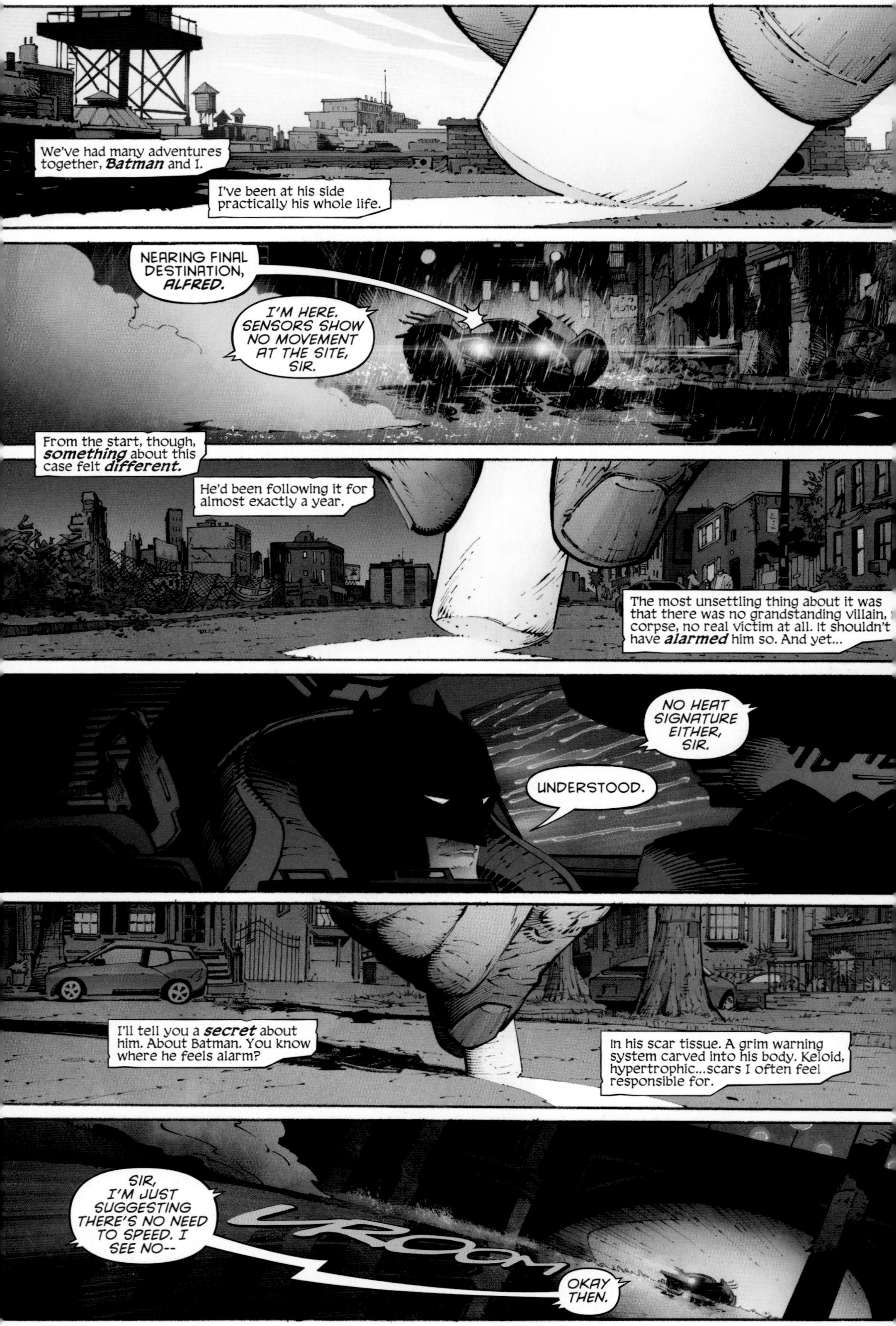
We've had many adventures together, Batman and I.
I've been at his side practically his whole life.
NEARING FINAL DESTINATION, ALFRED.
I'M HERE. SENSORS SHOW NO MOVEMENT AT THE SITE, SIR.
From the start, though, something about this case felt different.
He'd been following it for almost exactly a year.
The most unsettling thing about it was that there was no grandstanding villain, corpse, no real victim at all. It shouldn't have alarmed him so. And yet...
NO HEAT SIGNATURE EITHER, SIR.
UNDERSTOOD.
I'll tell you a secret about him. About Batman. You know where he feels alarm?
In his scar tissue. A grim warning system carved into his body. Keloid, hypertrophic...scars I often feel responsible for.
SIR, I'M JUST SUGGESTING THERE'S NO NEED TO SPEED. I SEE NO--
VROOOM
OKAY THEN.

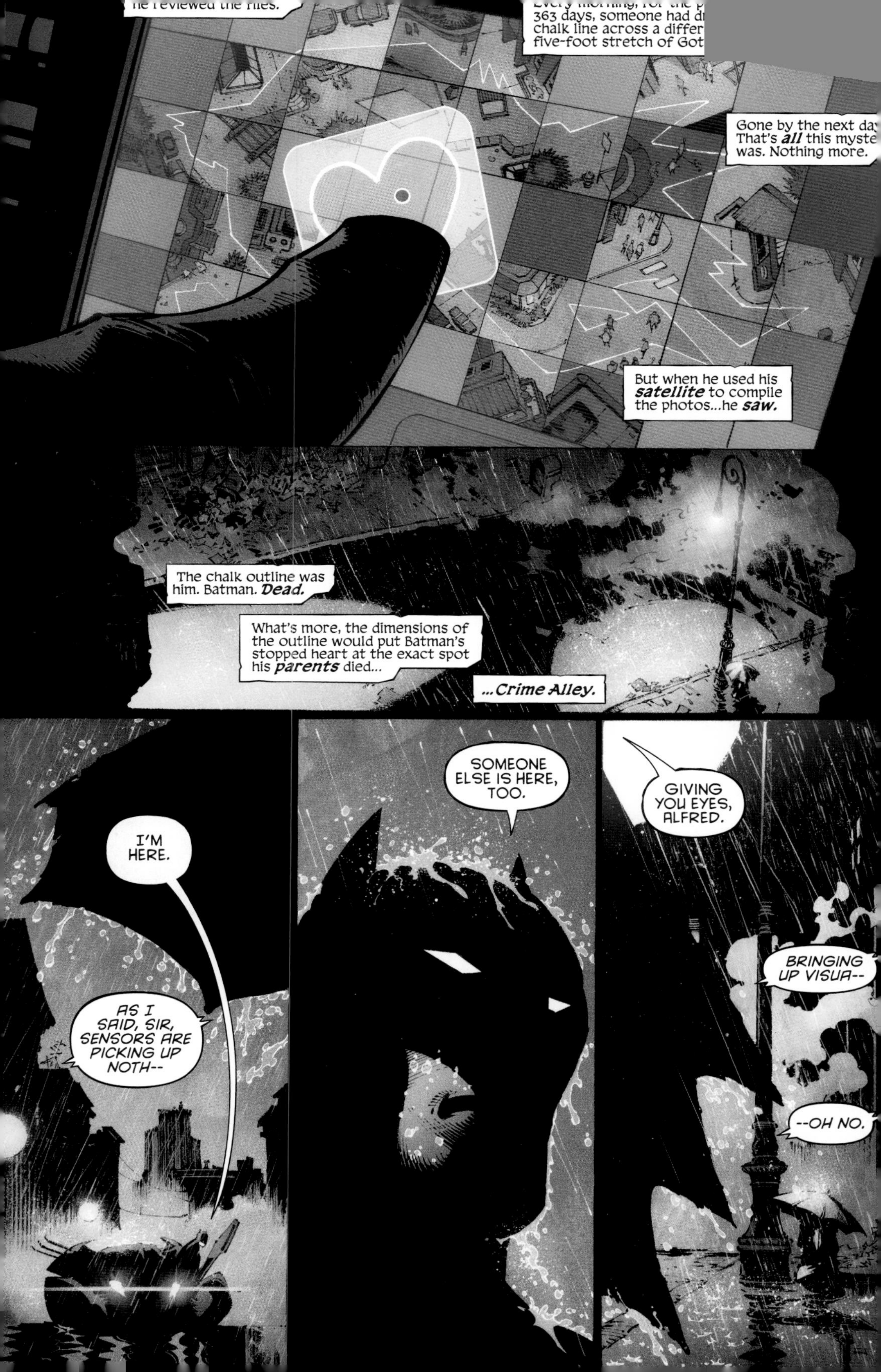

he reviewed the files.
363 days, someone had dr
chalk line across a differ
five-foot stretch of Got
Gone by the next da
That's all this myste
was. Nothing more.
But when he used his satellite to compile the photos...he saw.
The chalk outline was him. Batman. Dead.
What's more, the dimensions of the outline would put Batman's stopped heart at the exact spot his parents died...
...Crime Alley.
I'M HERE.
AS I SAID, SIR, SENSORS ARE PICKING UP NOTH--
SOMEONE ELSE IS HERE, TOO.
GIVING YOU EYES, ALFRED.
BRINGING UP VISUA--
--OH NO.

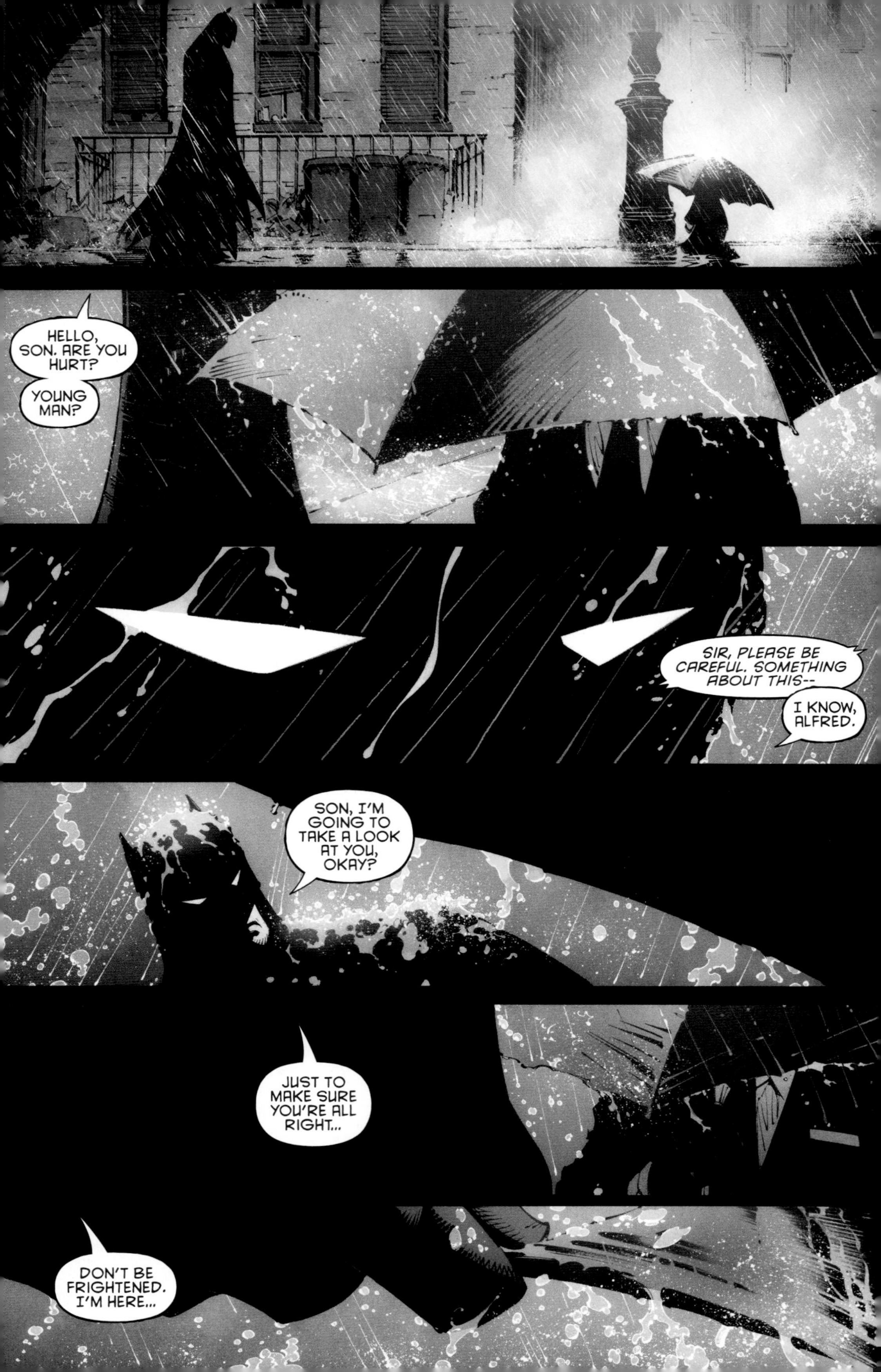
HELLO, SON. ARE YOU HURT?
YOUNG MAN?
SIR, PLEASE BE CAREFUL. SOMETHING ABOUT THIS--
I KNOW, ALFRED.
SON, I'M GOING TO TAKE A LOOK AT YOU, OKAY?
JUST TO MAKE SURE YOU'RE ALL RIGHT...
DON'T BE FRIGHTENED. I'M HERE...

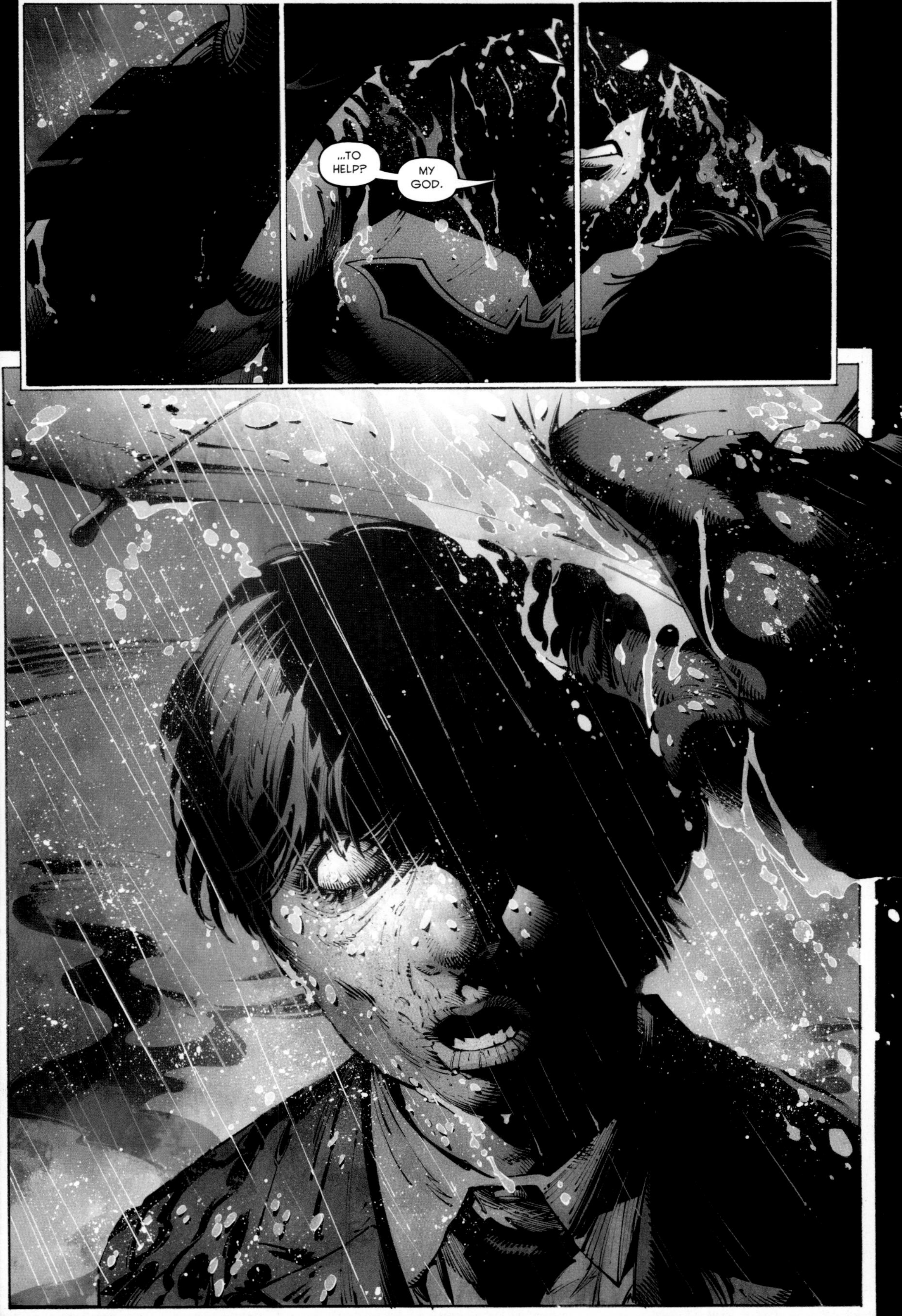
...TO HELP?
MY GOD.

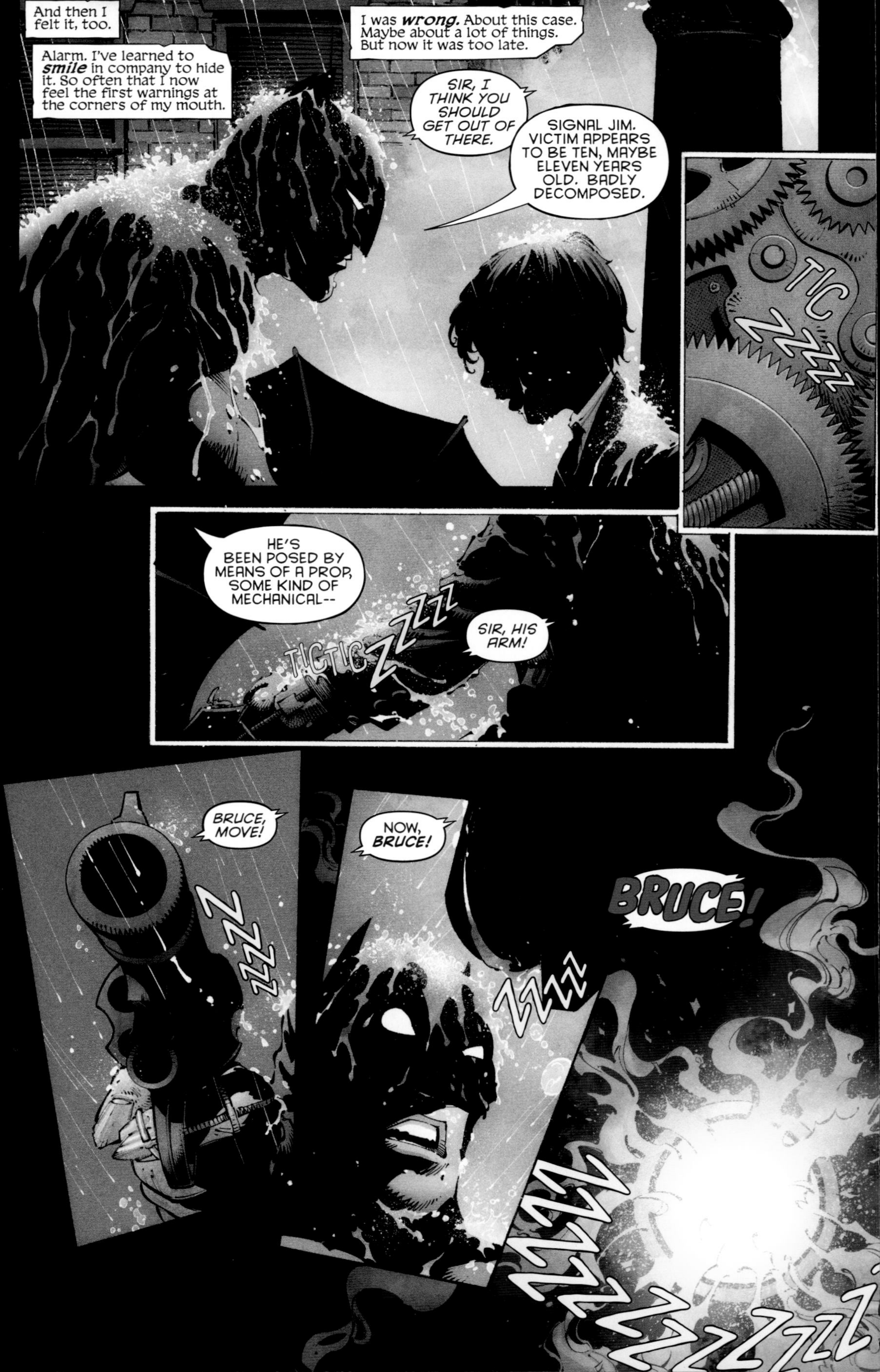
And then I felt it, too.
Alarm. I've learned to *smile* in company to hide it. So often that I now feel the first warnings at the corners of my mouth.
I was *wrong.* About this case. Maybe about a lot of things. But now it was too late.
SIR, I THINK YOU SHOULD GET OUT OF THERE.
SIGNAL JIM. VICTIM APPEARS TO BE TEN, MAYBE ELEVEN YEARS OLD. BADLY DECOMPOSED.
TIC
ZZZZZ
HE'S BEEN POSED BY MEANS OF A PROP, SOME KIND OF MECHANICAL--
TICTIC
ZZZZZ
SIR, HIS ARM!
BRUCE, MOVE!
ZZZZZ
NOW, **BRUCE!**
ZZZZZ
BRUCE!
ZZZZZZZZZZ

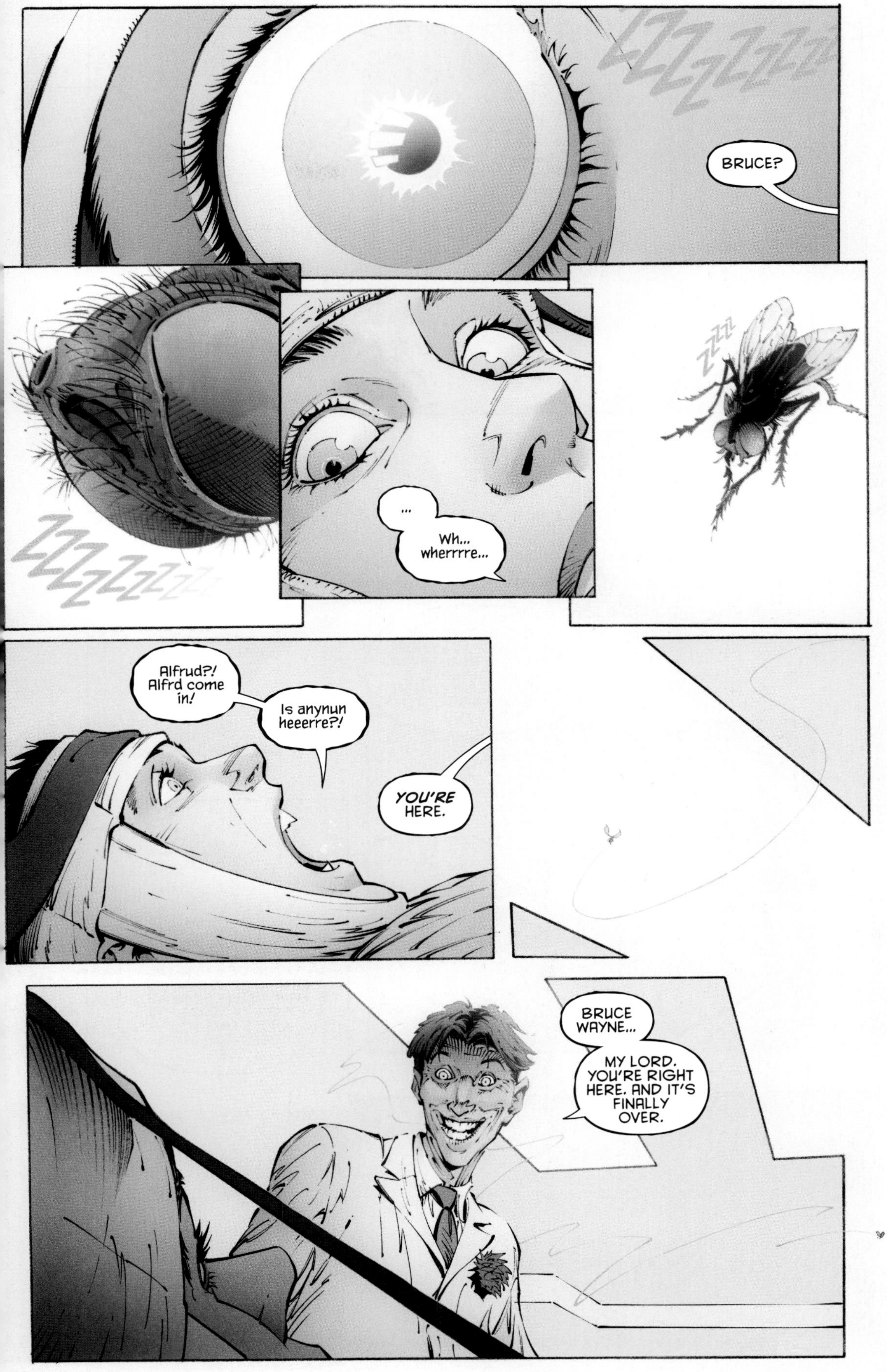
BRUCE?
...
Wh... wherrrre...
Alfrud?! Alfrd come in!
Is anynun heeerre?!
YOU'RE HERE.
BRUCE WAYNE...
MY LORD. YOU'RE RIGHT HERE. AND IT'S FINALLY OVER.

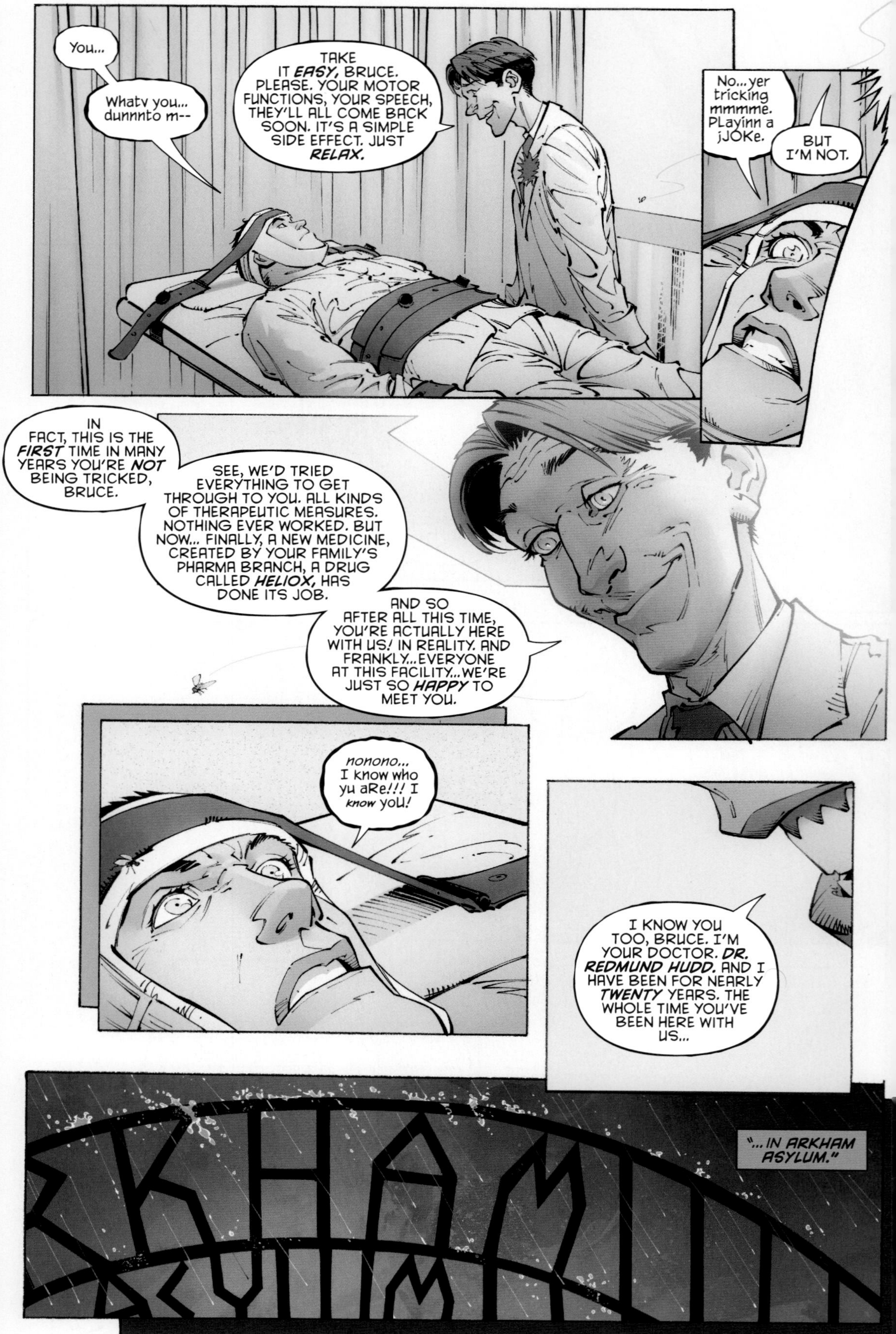
You...
Whatv you... dunnnto m--
TAKE IT EASY, BRUCE. PLEASE. YOUR MOTOR FUNCTIONS, YOUR SPEECH, THEY'LL ALL COME BACK SOON. IT'S A SIMPLE SIDE EFFECT. JUST RELAX.
No...yer tricking mmmme. PLayinn a jJOKe.
BUT I'M NOT.
IN FACT, THIS IS THE FIRST TIME IN MANY YEARS YOU'RE NOT BEING TRICKED, BRUCE.
SEE, WE'D TRIED EVERYTHING TO GET THROUGH TO YOU. ALL KINDS OF THERAPEUTIC MEASURES. NOTHING EVER WORKED. BUT NOW... FINALLY, A NEW MEDICINE, CREATED BY YOUR FAMILY'S PHARMA BRANCH, A DRUG CALLED HELIOX, HAS DONE ITS JOB.
AND SO AFTER ALL THIS TIME, YOU'RE ACTUALLY HERE WITH US! IN REALITY. AND FRANKLY...EVERYONE AT THIS FACILITY...WE'RE JUST SO HAPPY TO MEET YOU.
nonono... I know who yu aRe!!! I know yoU!
I KNOW YOU TOO, BRUCE. I'M YOUR DOCTOR. DR. REDMUND HUDD. AND I HAVE BEEN FOR NEARLY TWENTY YEARS. THE WHOLE TIME YOU'VE BEEN HERE WITH US...
"...IN ARKHAM ASYLUM."

Nononono... no...

LETT ME OUTTT!

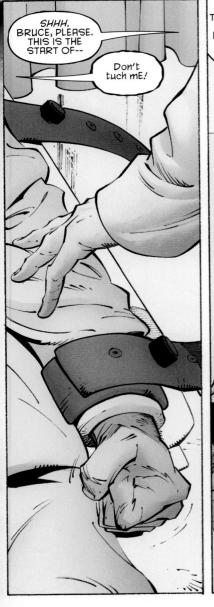

SHHH. BRUCE, PLEASE. THIS IS THE START OF--

Don't tuch me!

LOOK, I UNDERSTAND THIS IS A LOT. WE *ALL* DO. AND BEHIND THAT DOOR ARE A LOT OF PEOPLE WHO'VE BEEN *WAITING* TO MEET YOU-- THE *REAL* YOU--FOR A VERY LONG TIME.

BUT FIRST... YOU SHOULD MEET THE PERSON WHO'S BEEN WAITING *LONGEST* OF ALL.

HERE, LET ME GET YOU UP.

BRUCE?

...no.

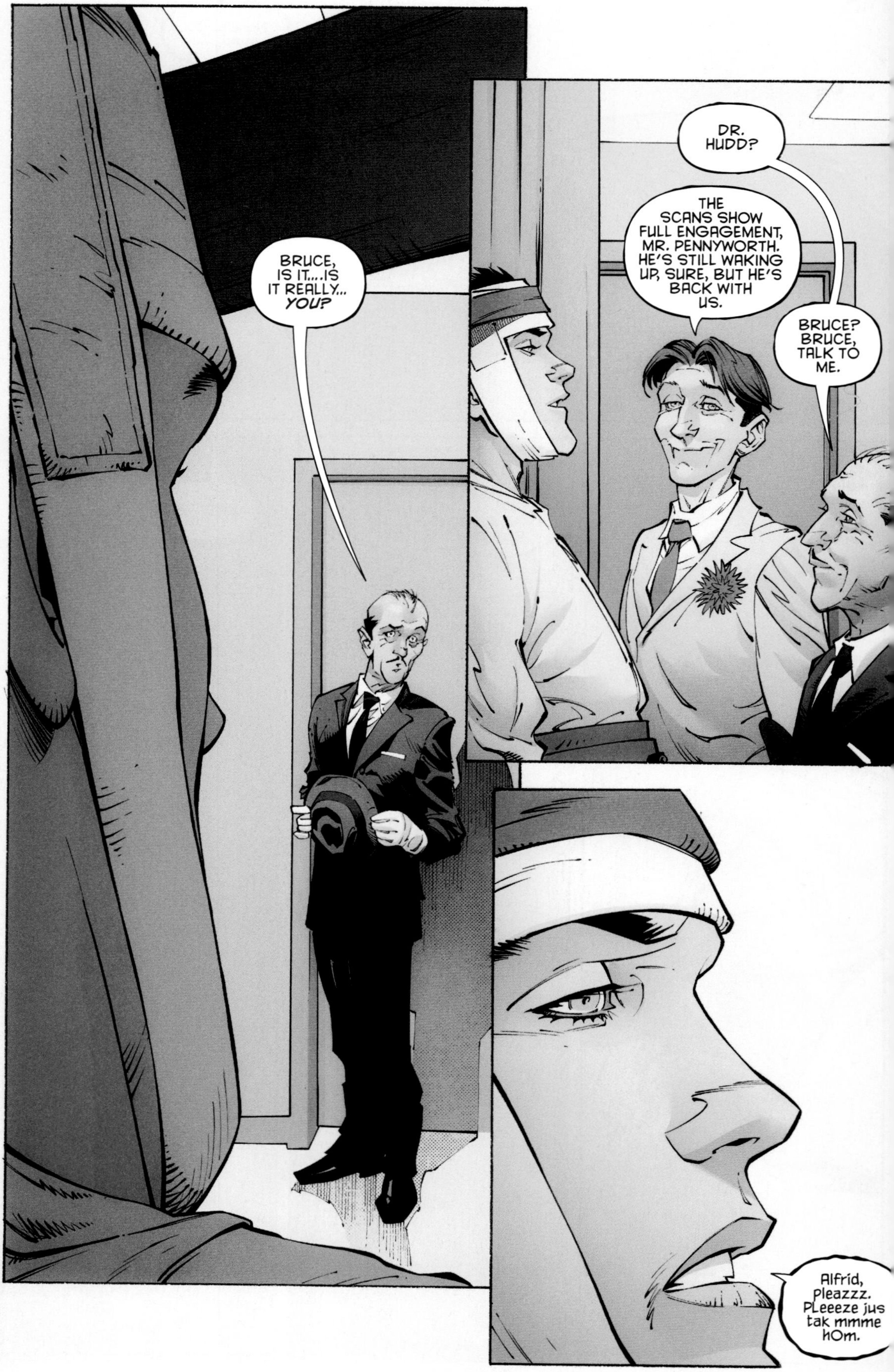
BRUCE, IS IT....IS IT REALLY... YOU?
DR. HUDD?
THE SCANS SHOW FULL ENGAGEMENT, MR. PENNYWORTH. HE'S STILL WAKING UP, SURE, BUT HE'S BACK WITH US.
BRUCE? BRUCE, TALK TO ME.
Alfrid, Pleazzz. PLeeeze jus tak mmme hOm.

I WILL, MY BOY. I WILL. I PROMISE I'LL TAKE YOU HOME AS SOON AS I CAN. AND I WANT YOU TO *KNOW*--AS THE FIRST THING YOU UNDERSTAND WHILE YOU EMERGE FROM THIS *LONG* NIGHTMARE-- THAT YOU ARE FORGIVEN.

NO ONE *BLAMES* YOU, BRUCE. NO ONE. NOT YOUR DOCTORS, NOT THE CITY, AND CERTAINLY NOT ME. *NEVER* ME. EVERYONE KNOWS YOU WEREN'T IN YOUR RIGHT MIND THOSE YEARS AGO. WHEN YOU...WHEN YOU *DID* WHAT YOU DID.

Forgivnnn? When I did wut...

I'M SO SORRY, BRUCE. I...I THOUGHT YOU UNDERSTOOD THIS MUCH.

Alfrrrid...did *wwwut...?!*

...WELL, WHEN YOU...

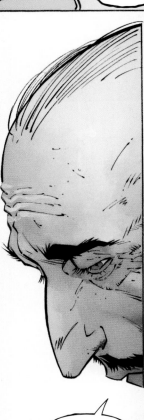

WHEN YOU *KILLED* YOUR PARENTS IN THAT ALLEY.

NONONO NNNNOOO!

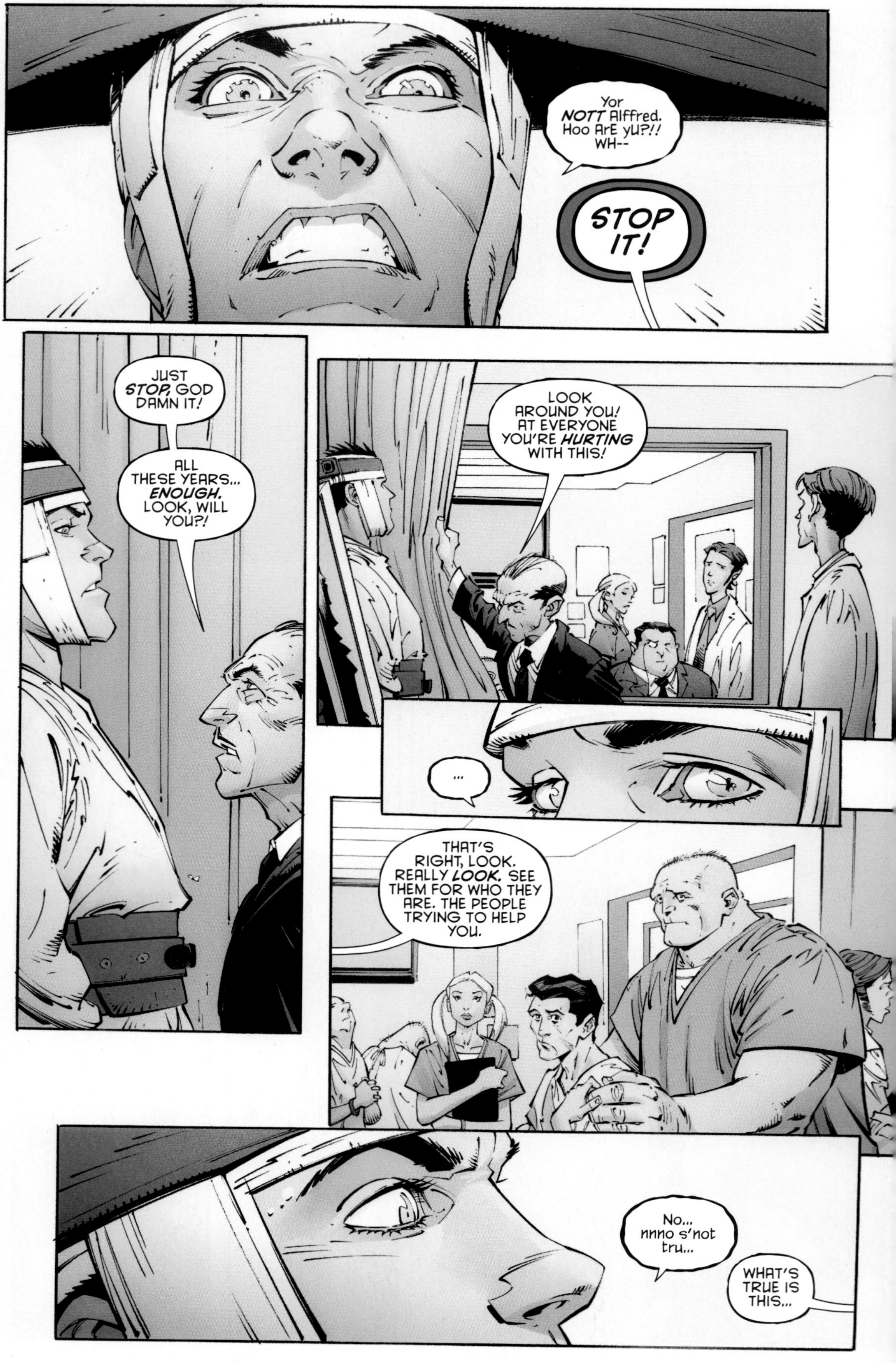
Yor NOTT Alffred. Hoo ArE yU?!! WH--
STOP IT!
JUST STOP, GOD DAMN IT!
ALL THESE YEARS... ENOUGH. LOOK, WILL YOU?!
LOOK AROUND YOU! AT EVERYONE YOU'RE HURTING WITH THIS!
...
THAT'S RIGHT, LOOK. REALLY LOOK. SEE THEM FOR WHO THEY ARE. THE PEOPLE TRYING TO HELP YOU.
No... nnno s'not tru...
WHAT'S TRUE IS THIS...

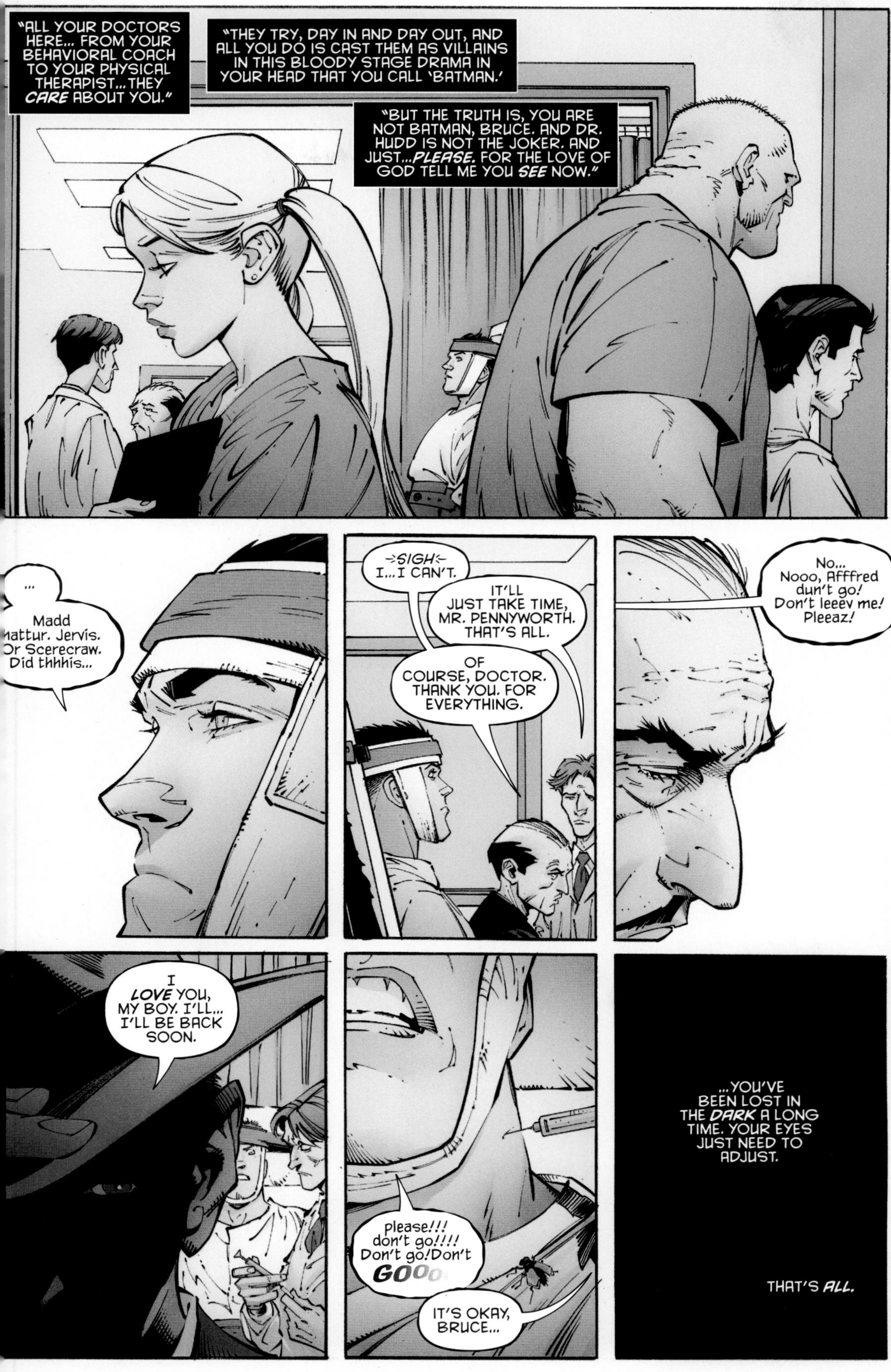
"ALL YOUR DOCTORS HERE... FROM YOUR BEHAVIORAL COACH TO YOUR PHYSICAL THERAPIST...THEY *CARE* ABOUT YOU."
"THEY TRY, DAY IN AND DAY OUT, AND ALL YOU DO IS CAST THEM AS VILLAINS IN THIS BLOODY STAGE DRAMA IN YOUR HEAD THAT YOU CALL 'BATMAN.'
"BUT THE TRUTH IS, YOU ARE NOT BATMAN, BRUCE. AND DR. HUDD IS NOT THE JOKER. AND JUST...*PLEASE.* FOR THE LOVE OF GOD TELL ME YOU *SEE* NOW."
...
Madd Hattur. Jervis. Or Scerecraw. Did thhhis...
-SIGH- I...I CAN'T.
IT'LL JUST TAKE TIME, MR. PENNYWORTH. THAT'S ALL.
OF COURSE, DOCTOR. THANK YOU. FOR EVERYTHING.
No... Nooo, Afffred dun't go! Don't leeev me! Pleeaz!
I *LOVE* YOU, MY BOY. I'LL... I'LL BE BACK SOON.
please!!! don't go!!!! Don't go!Don't GOOO
IT'S OKAY, BRUCE...
...YOU'VE BEEN LOST IN THE *DARK* A LONG TIME. YOUR EYES JUST NEED TO ADJUST.
THAT'S *ALL.*

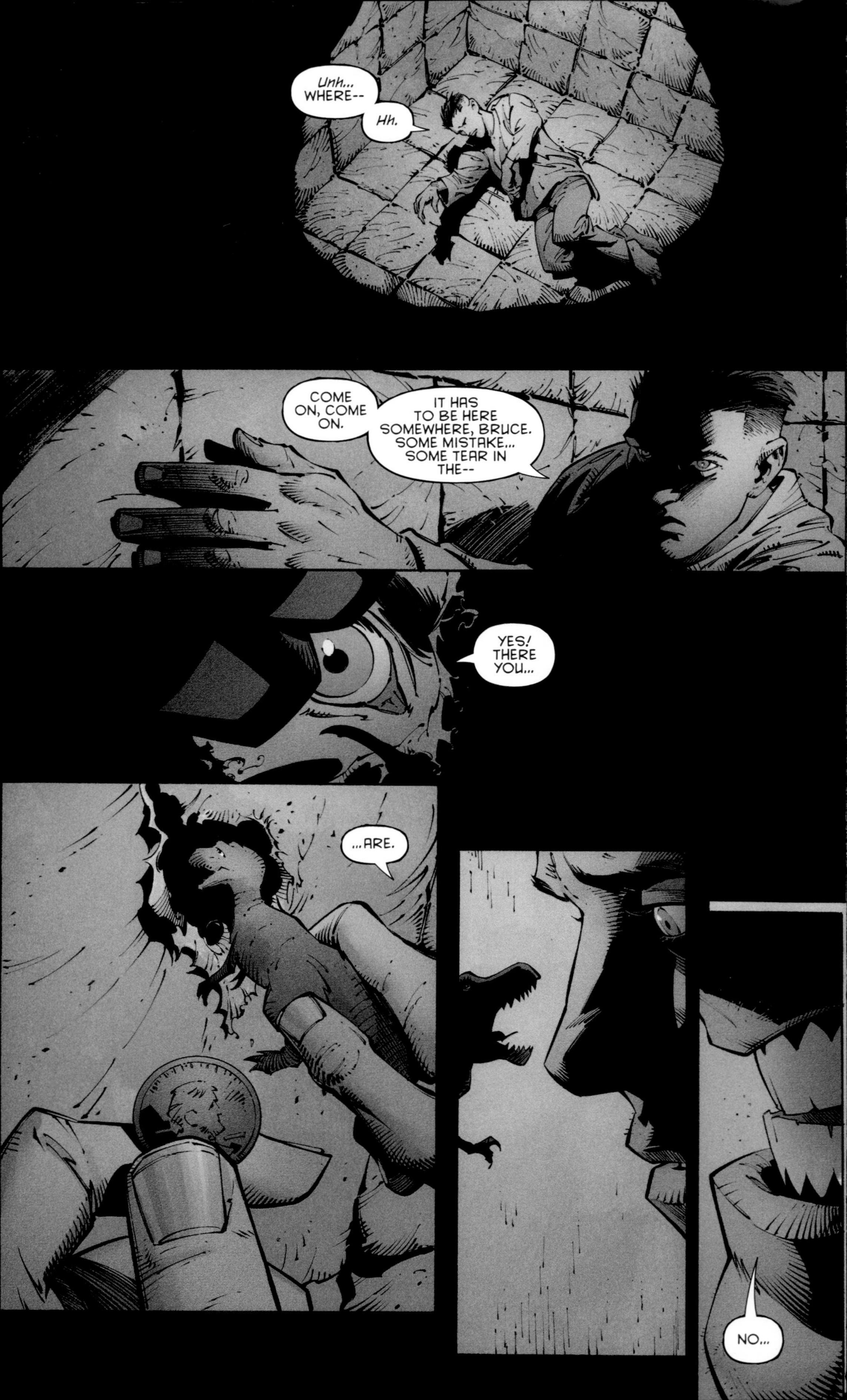
Unh... WHERE--
Hh.
COME ON, COME ON.
IT HAS TO BE HERE SOMEWHERE, BRUCE. SOME MISTAKE... SOME TEAR IN THE--
YES! THERE YOU...
...ARE.
NO...

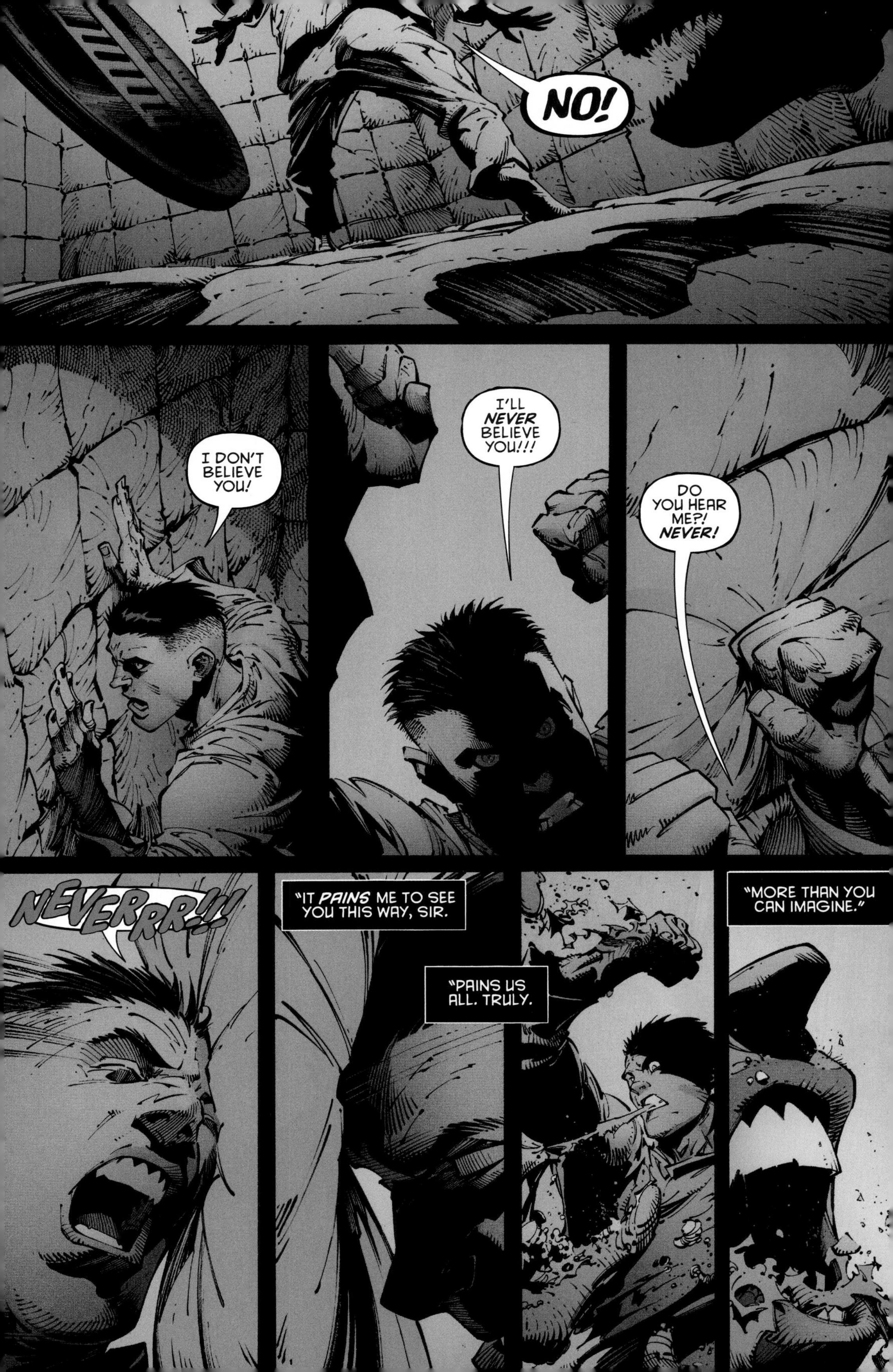
NO!
I DON'T BELIEVE YOU!
I'LL NEVER BELIEVE YOU!!!
DO YOU HEAR ME?! NEVER!
NEVERRRR!!!
"IT PAINS ME TO SEE YOU THIS WAY, SIR.
"PAINS US ALL. TRULY.
"MORE THAN YOU CAN IMAGINE."

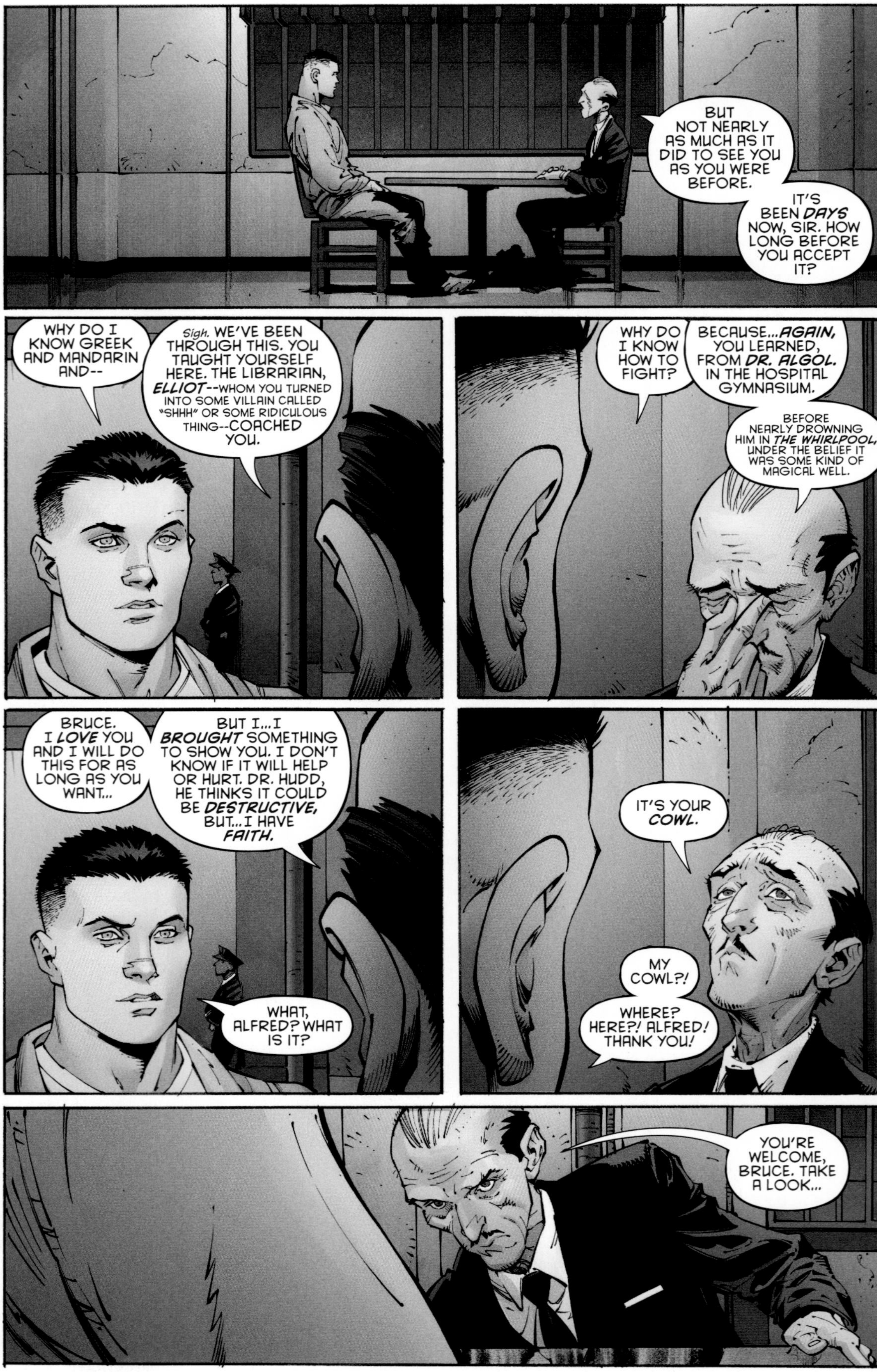

BUT NOT NEARLY AS MUCH AS IT DID TO SEE YOU AS YOU WERE BEFORE.
IT'S BEEN DAYS NOW, SIR. HOW LONG BEFORE YOU ACCEPT IT?
WHY DO I KNOW GREEK AND MANDARIN AND--
Sigh. WE'VE BEEN THROUGH THIS. YOU TAUGHT YOURSELF HERE. THE LIBRARIAN, ELLIOT--WHOM YOU TURNED INTO SOME VILLAIN CALLED "SHHH" OR SOME RIDICULOUS THING--COACHED YOU.
WHY DO I KNOW HOW TO FIGHT?
BECAUSE...AGAIN, YOU LEARNED, FROM DR. ALGOL. IN THE HOSPITAL GYMNASIUM.
BEFORE NEARLY DROWNING HIM IN THE WHIRLPOOL, UNDER THE BELIEF IT WAS SOME KIND OF MAGICAL WELL.
BRUCE. I LOVE YOU AND I WILL DO THIS FOR AS LONG AS YOU WANT...
BUT I...I BROUGHT SOMETHING TO SHOW YOU. I DON'T KNOW IF IT WILL HELP OR HURT. DR. HUDD, HE THINKS IT COULD BE DESTRUCTIVE, BUT...I HAVE FAITH.
WHAT, ALFRED? WHAT IS IT?
IT'S YOUR COWL.
MY COWL?!
WHERE? HERE?! ALFRED! THANK YOU!
YOU'RE WELCOME, BRUCE. TAKE A LOOK...

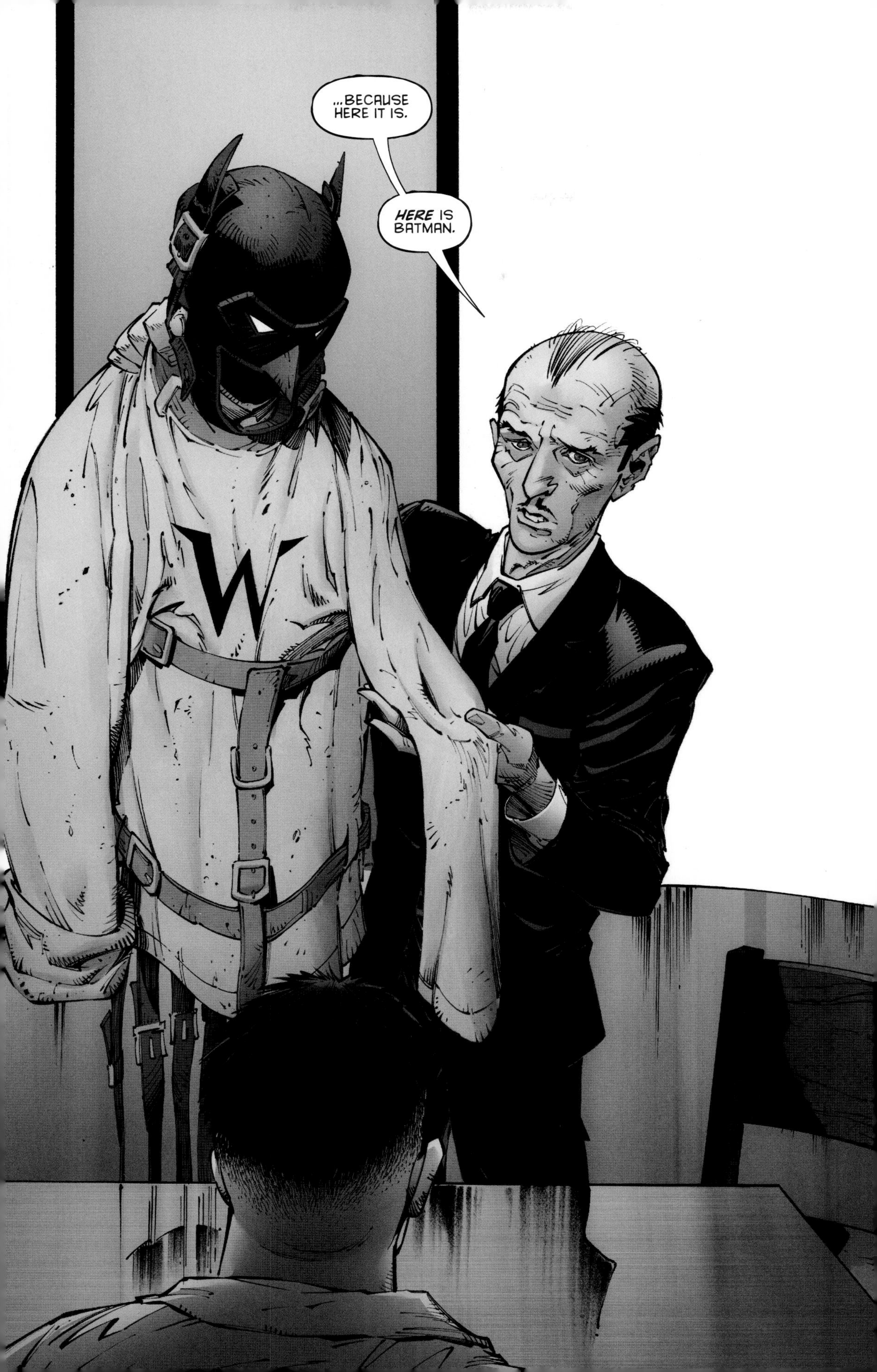
...BECAUSE HERE IT IS.
HERE IS BATMAN.

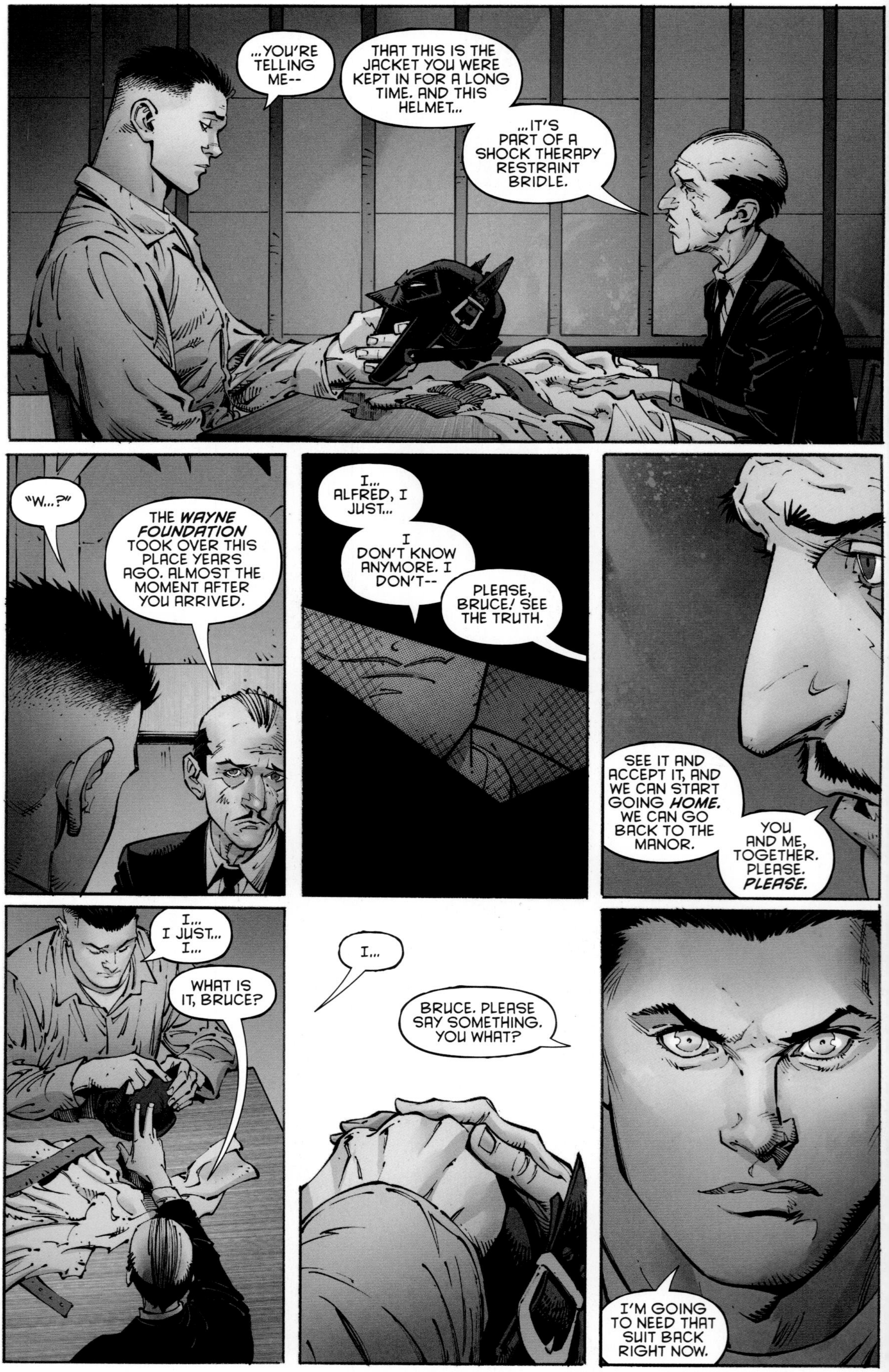
...YOU'RE TELLING ME--
THAT THIS IS THE JACKET YOU WERE KEPT IN FOR A LONG TIME. AND THIS HELMET...
...IT'S PART OF A SHOCK THERAPY RESTRAINT BRIDLE.
"W...?"
THE WAYNE FOUNDATION TOOK OVER THIS PLACE YEARS AGO. ALMOST THE MOMENT AFTER YOU ARRIVED.
I... ALFRED, I JUST...
I DON'T KNOW ANYMORE. I DON'T--
PLEASE, BRUCE! SEE THE TRUTH.
SEE IT AND ACCEPT IT, AND WE CAN START GOING HOME. WE CAN GO BACK TO THE MANOR.
YOU AND ME, TOGETHER. PLEASE. PLEASE.
I... I JUST... I...
WHAT IS IT, BRUCE?
I...
BRUCE. PLEASE SAY SOMETHING. YOU WHAT?
I'M GOING TO NEED THAT SUIT BACK RIGHT NOW.

PART TWO:
THE RIGHT HAND

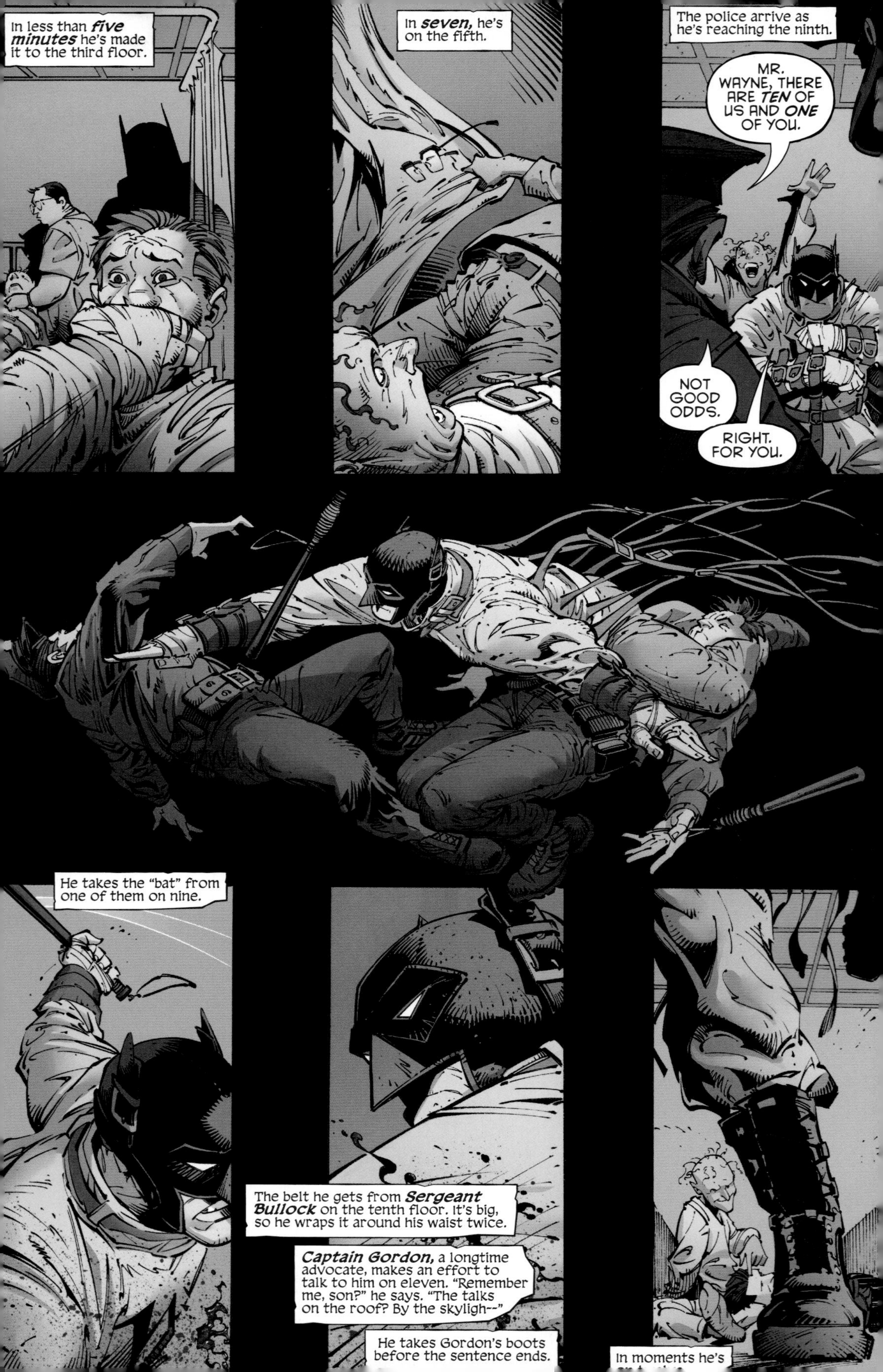

In less than *five minutes* he's made it to the third floor.
In *seven,* he's on the fifth.
The police arrive as he's reaching the ninth.
MR. WAYNE, THERE ARE *TEN* OF US AND *ONE* OF YOU.
NOT GOOD ODDS.
RIGHT. FOR YOU.
He takes the "bat" from one of them on nine.
The belt he gets from *Sergeant Bullock* on the tenth floor. It's big, so he wraps it around his waist twice.
Captain Gordon, a longtime advocate, makes an effort to talk to him on eleven. "Remember me, son?" he says. "The talks on the roof? By the skyligh--"
He takes Gordon's boots before the sentence ends.
In moments he's

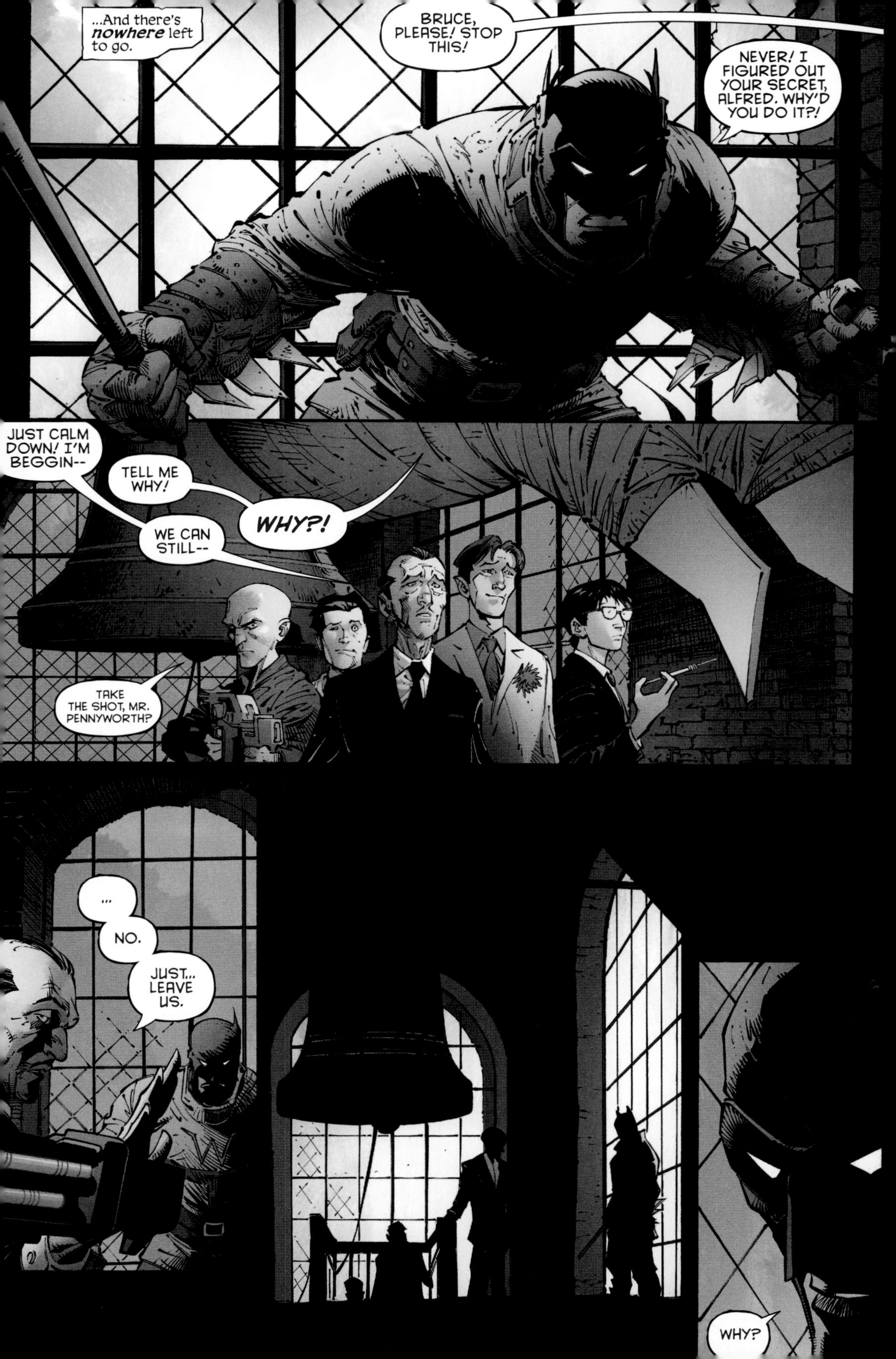
...And there's ***nowhere*** left to go.
BRUCE, PLEASE! STOP THIS!
NEVER! I FIGURED OUT YOUR SECRET, ALFRED. WHY'D YOU DO IT?!
JUST CALM DOWN! I'M BEGGIN--
TELL ME WHY!
WHY?!
WE CAN STILL--
TAKE THE SHOT, MR. PENNYWORTH?
...
NO.
JUST... LEAVE US.
WHY?

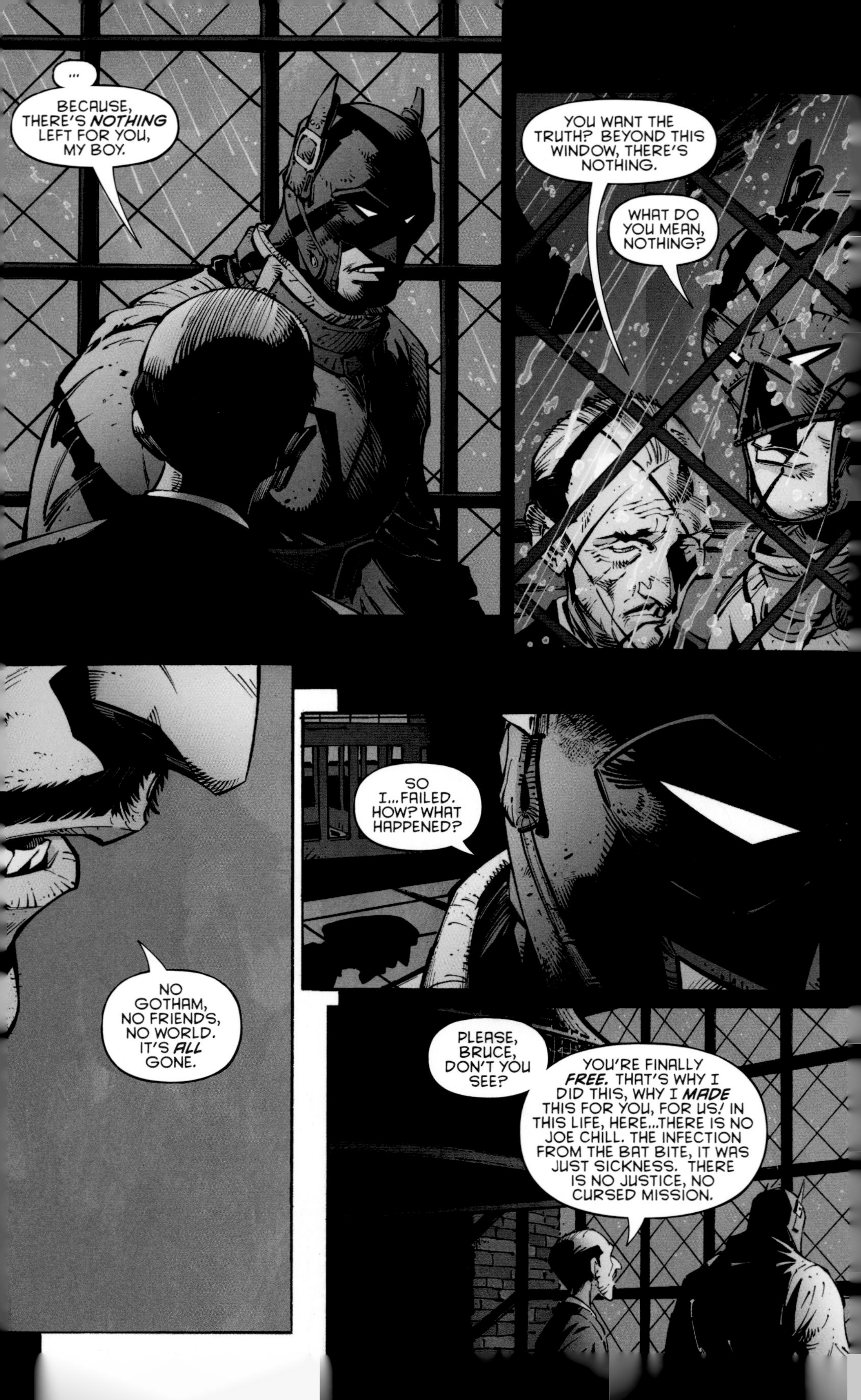
...
BECAUSE, THERE'S NOTHING LEFT FOR YOU, MY BOY.
YOU WANT THE TRUTH? BEYOND THIS WINDOW, THERE'S NOTHING.
WHAT DO YOU MEAN, NOTHING?
NO GOTHAM, NO FRIENDS, NO WORLD. IT'S ALL GONE.
SO I...FAILED. HOW? WHAT HAPPENED?
PLEASE, BRUCE, DON'T YOU SEE?
YOU'RE FINALLY FREE. THAT'S WHY I DID THIS, WHY I MADE THIS FOR YOU, FOR US! IN THIS LIFE, HERE...THERE IS NO JOE CHILL. THE INFECTION FROM THE BAT BITE, IT WAS JUST SICKNESS. THERE IS NO JUSTICE, NO CURSED MISSION.

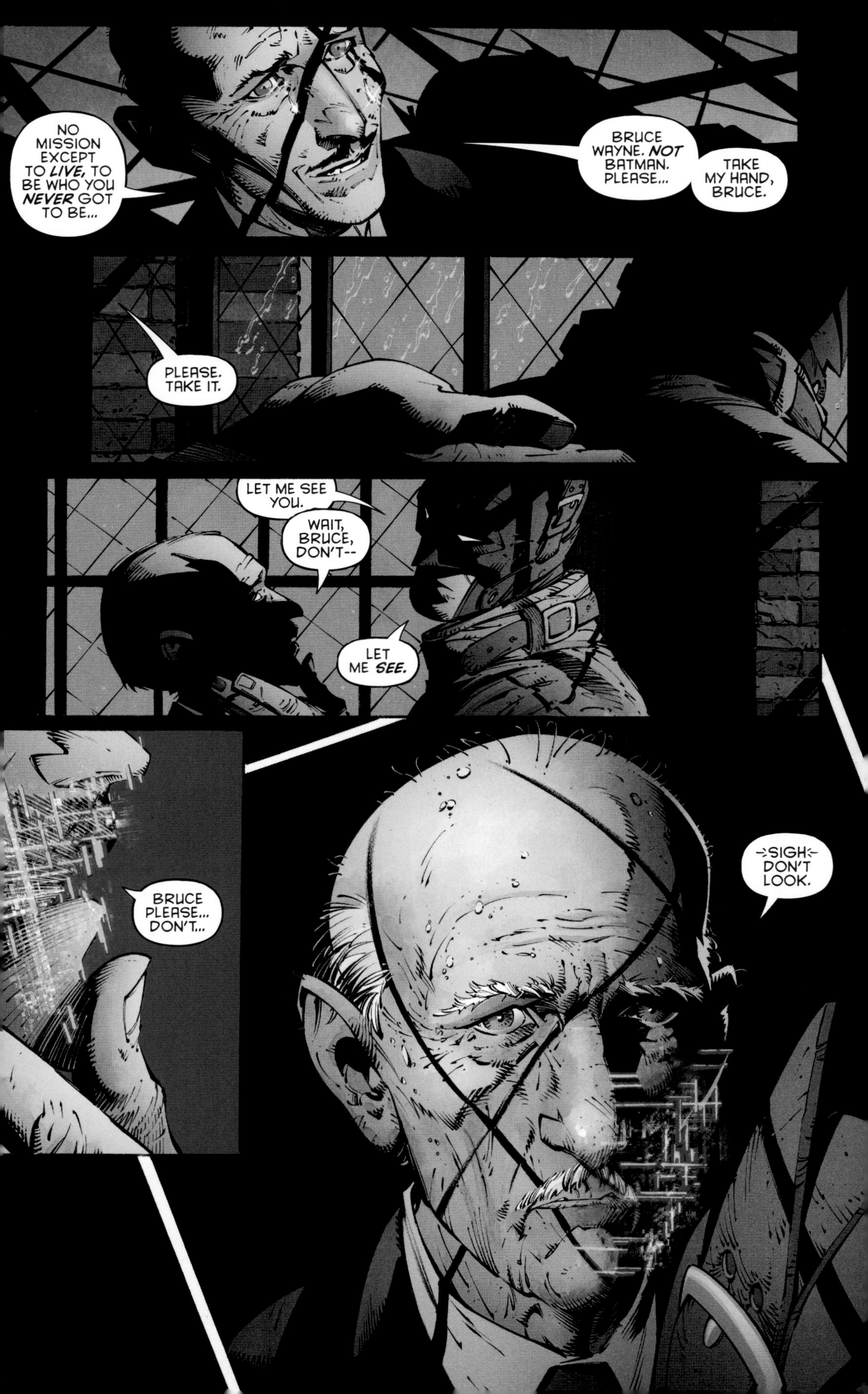
NO MISSION EXCEPT TO *LIVE,* TO BE WHO YOU *NEVER* GOT TO BE...
BRUCE WAYNE. *NOT* BATMAN. PLEASE...
TAKE MY HAND, BRUCE.
PLEASE. TAKE IT.
LET ME SEE YOU.
WAIT, BRUCE, DON'T--
LET ME *SEE.*
BRUCE PLEASE... DON'T...
-SIGH- DON'T LOOK.

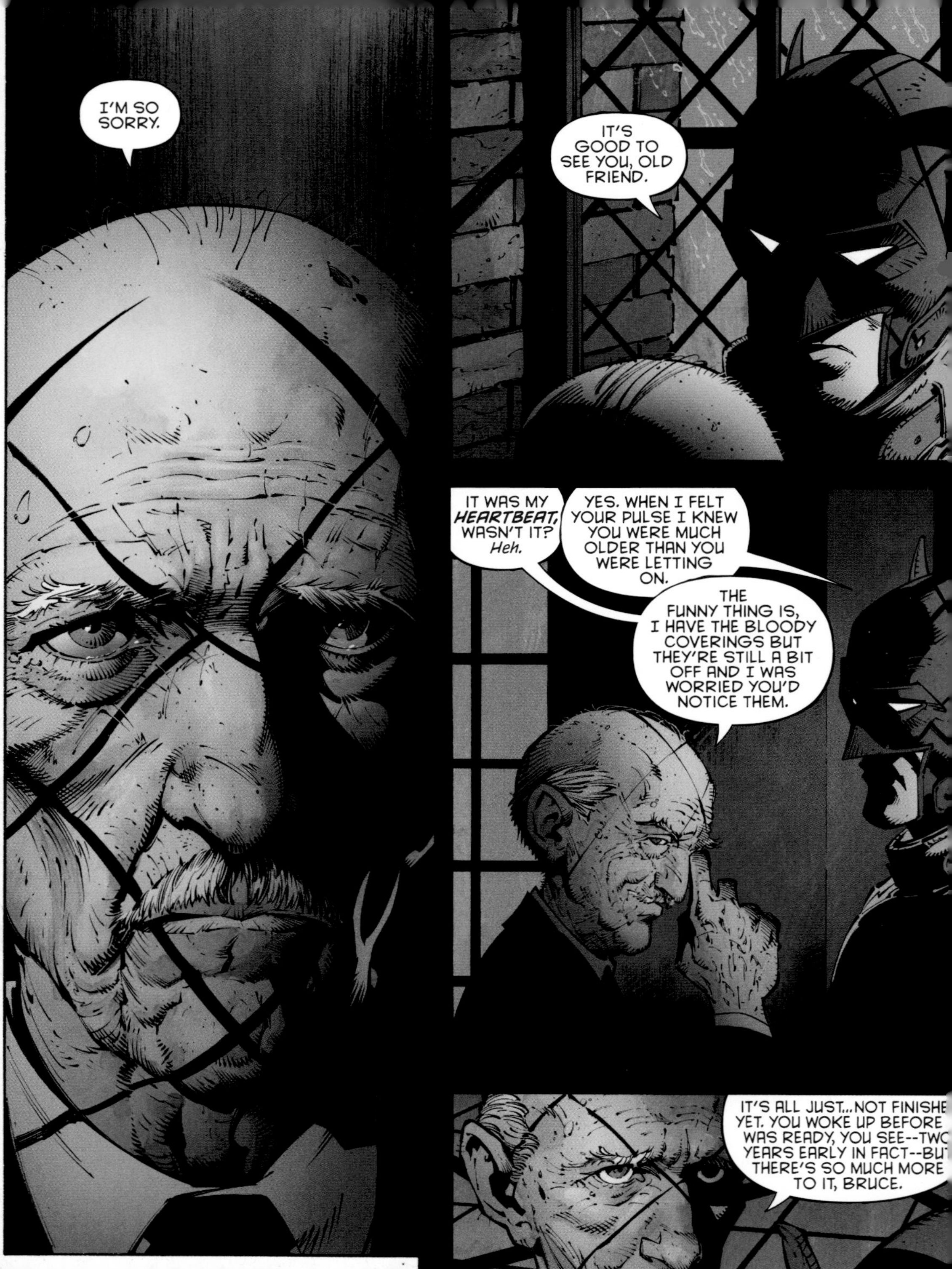
I'M SO SORRY.
IT'S GOOD TO SEE YOU, OLD FRIEND.
IT WAS MY *HEARTBEAT,* WASN'T IT? *Heh.*
YES. WHEN I FELT YOUR PULSE I KNEW YOU WERE MUCH OLDER THAN YOU WERE LETTING ON.
THE FUNNY THING IS, I HAVE THE BLOODY COVERINGS BUT THEY'RE STILL A BIT OFF AND I WAS WORRIED YOU'D NOTICE THEM.
IT'S ALL JUST...NOT FINISHE YET. YOU WOKE UP BEFORE WAS READY, YOU SEE--TWO YEARS EARLY IN FACT--BUT THERE'S SO MUCH MORE TO IT, BRUCE.

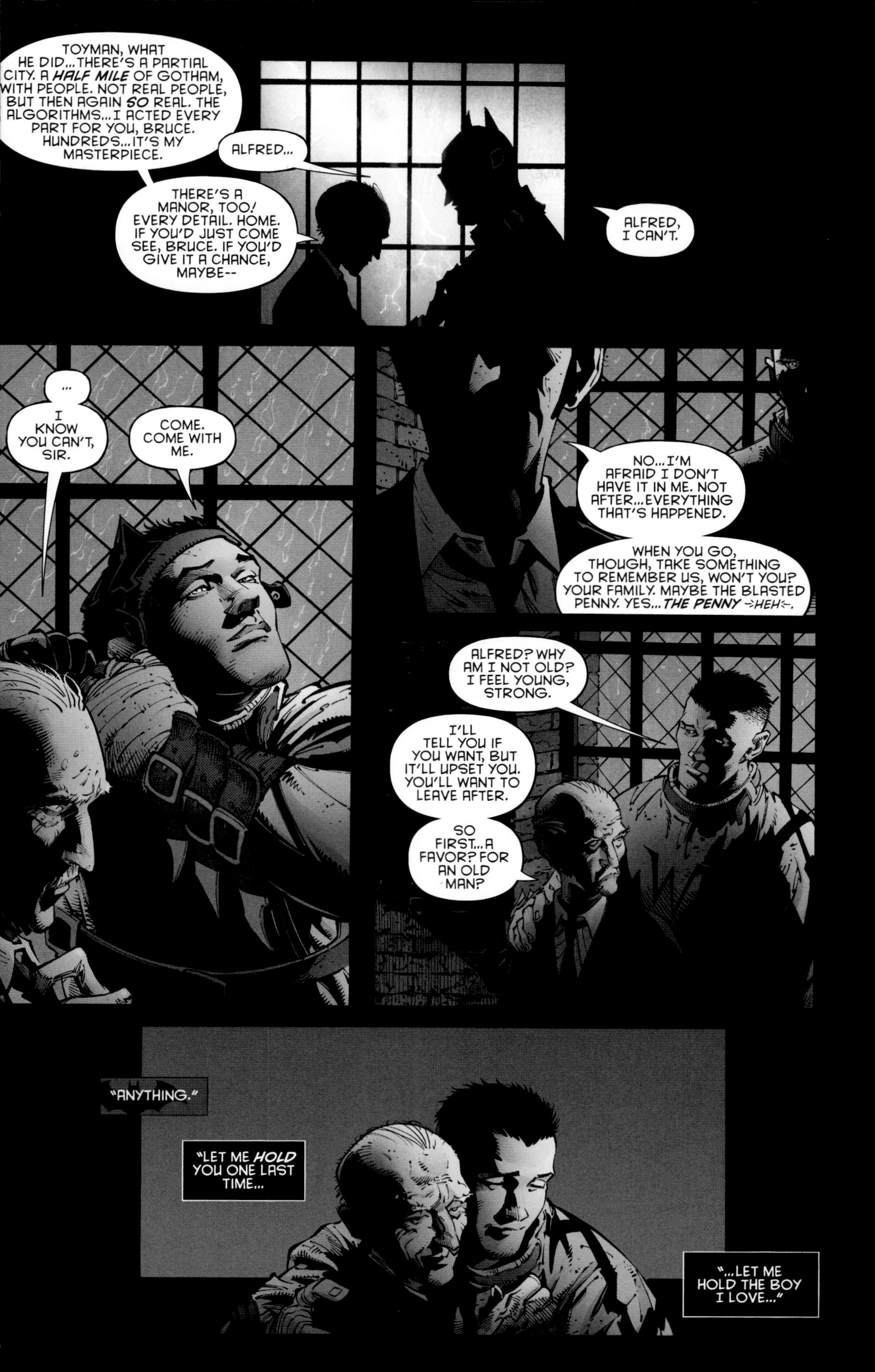
TOYMAN, WHAT HE DID... THERE'S A PARTIAL CITY. A HALF MILE OF GOTHAM, WITH PEOPLE. NOT REAL PEOPLE, BUT THEN AGAIN SO REAL. THE ALGORITHMS... I ACTED EVERY PART FOR YOU, BRUCE. HUNDREDS... IT'S MY MASTERPIECE.
ALFRED...
THERE'S A MANOR, TOO! EVERY DETAIL. HOME. IF YOU'D JUST COME SEE, BRUCE. IF YOU'D GIVE IT A CHANCE, MAYBE--
ALFRED, I CAN'T.
...
I KNOW YOU CAN'T, SIR.
COME. COME WITH ME.
NO... I'M AFRAID I DON'T HAVE IT IN ME. NOT AFTER... EVERYTHING THAT'S HAPPENED.
WHEN YOU GO, THOUGH, TAKE SOMETHING TO REMEMBER US, WON'T YOU? YOUR FAMILY. MAYBE THE BLASTED PENNY. YES... THE PENNY -HEH-.
ALFRED? WHY AM I NOT OLD? I FEEL YOUNG, STRONG.
I'LL TELL YOU IF YOU WANT, BUT IT'LL UPSET YOU. YOU'LL WANT TO LEAVE AFTER.
SO FIRST... A FAVOR? FOR AN OLD MAN?
"ANYTHING."
"LET ME HOLD YOU ONE LAST TIME...
"...LET ME HOLD THE BOY I LOVE..."

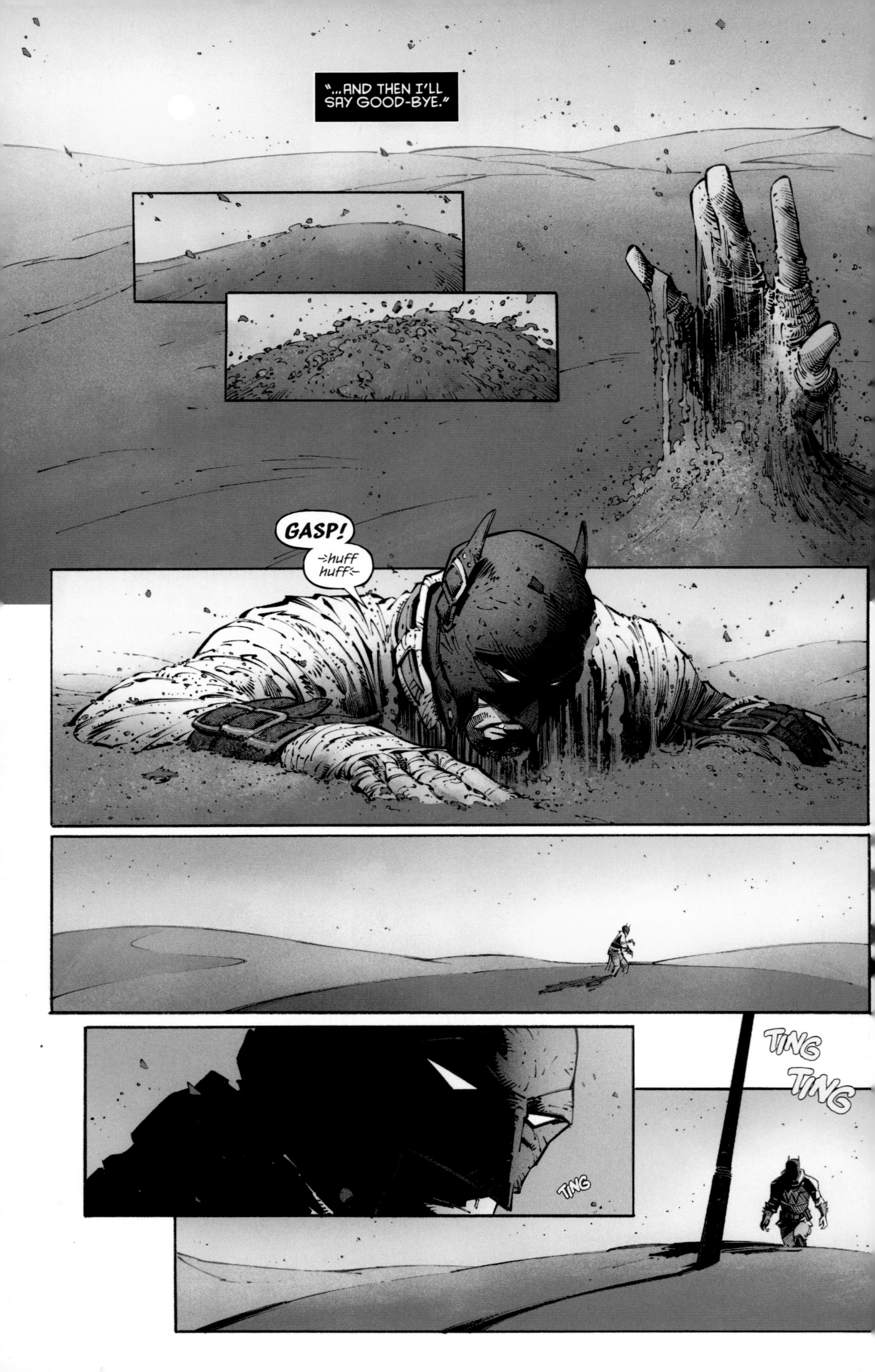
"...AND THEN I'LL SAY GOOD-BYE."
GASP!
huff huff
TING
TING
TING

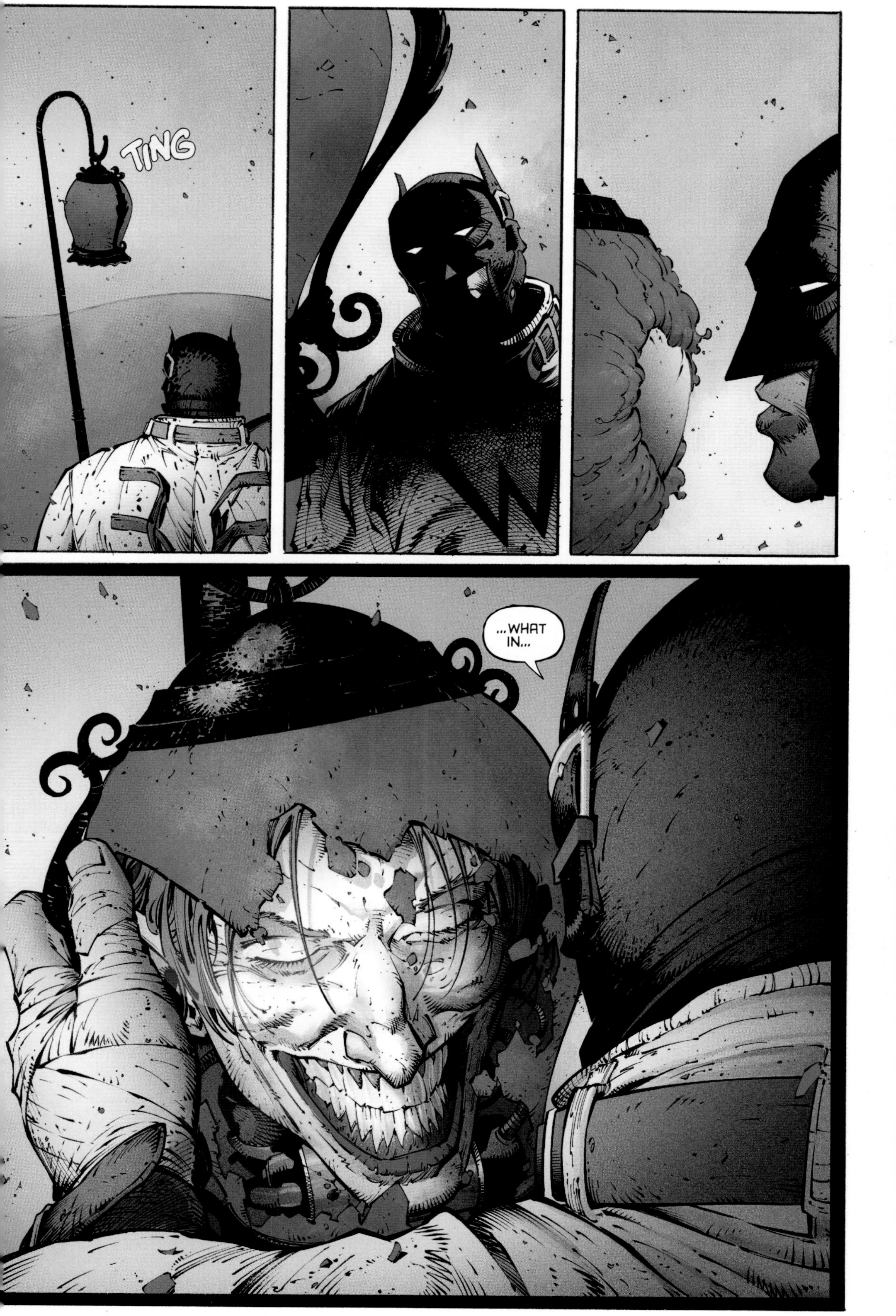
TING
...WHAT IN...

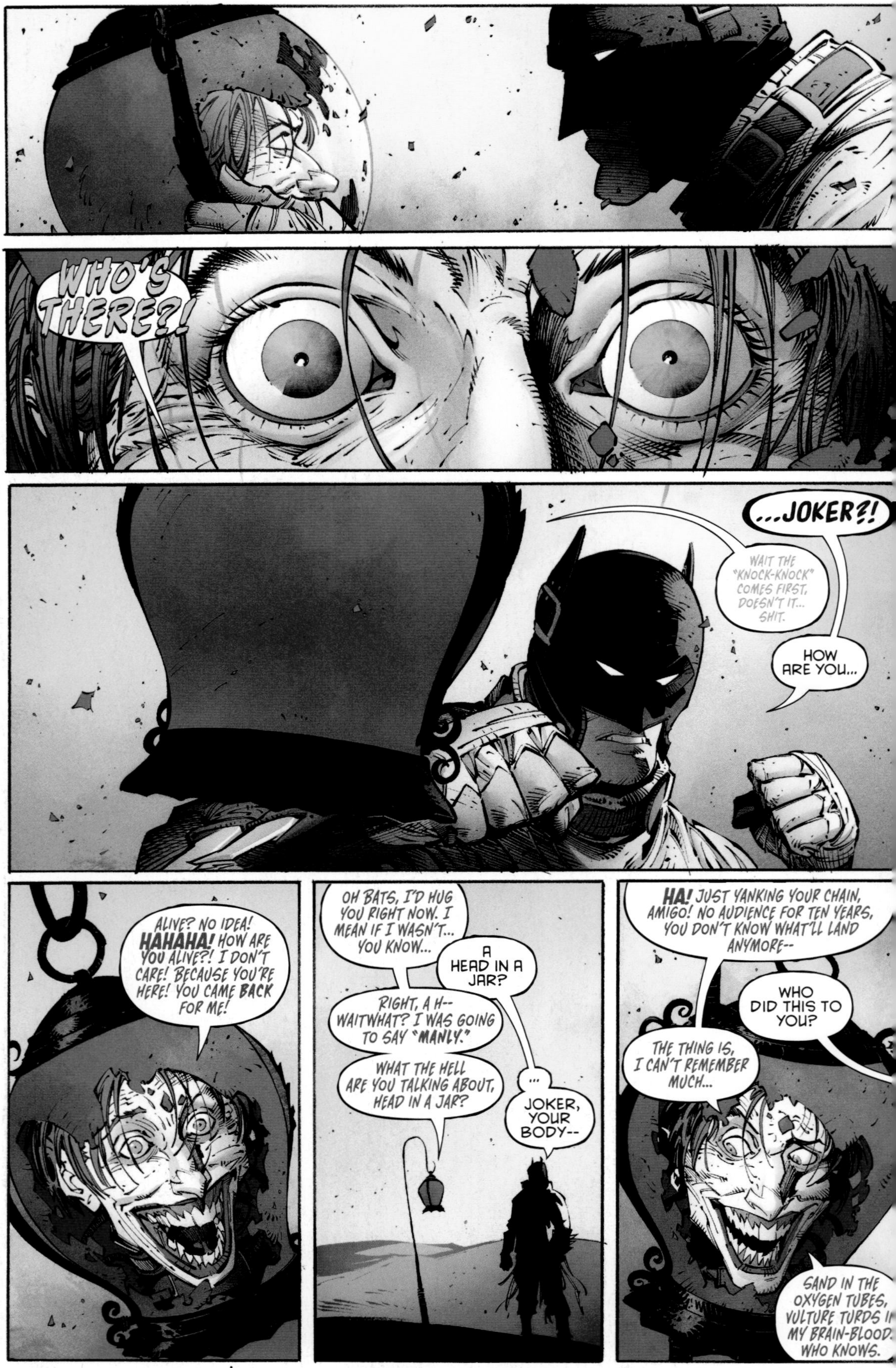
WHO'S THERE?!
...JOKER?!
WAIT THE "KNOCK-KNOCK" COMES FIRST, DOESN'T IT... SHIT.
HOW ARE YOU...
ALIVE? NO IDEA! HAHAHA! HOW ARE YOU ALIVE?! I DON'T CARE! BECAUSE YOU'RE HERE! YOU CAME BACK FOR ME!
OH BATS, I'D HUG YOU RIGHT NOW. I MEAN IF I WASN'T... YOU KNOW...
A HEAD IN A JAR?
RIGHT, A H-- WAITWHAT? I WAS GOING TO SAY "MANLY."
WHAT THE HELL ARE YOU TALKING ABOUT, HEAD IN A JAR?
...
JOKER, YOUR BODY--
HA! JUST YANKING YOUR CHAIN, AMIGO! NO AUDIENCE FOR TEN YEARS, YOU DON'T KNOW WHAT'LL LAND ANYMORE--
WHO DID THIS TO YOU?
THE THING IS, I CAN'T REMEMBER MUCH...
SAND IN THE OXYGEN TUBES, VULTURE TURDS IN MY BRAIN-BLOOD. WHO KNOWS.

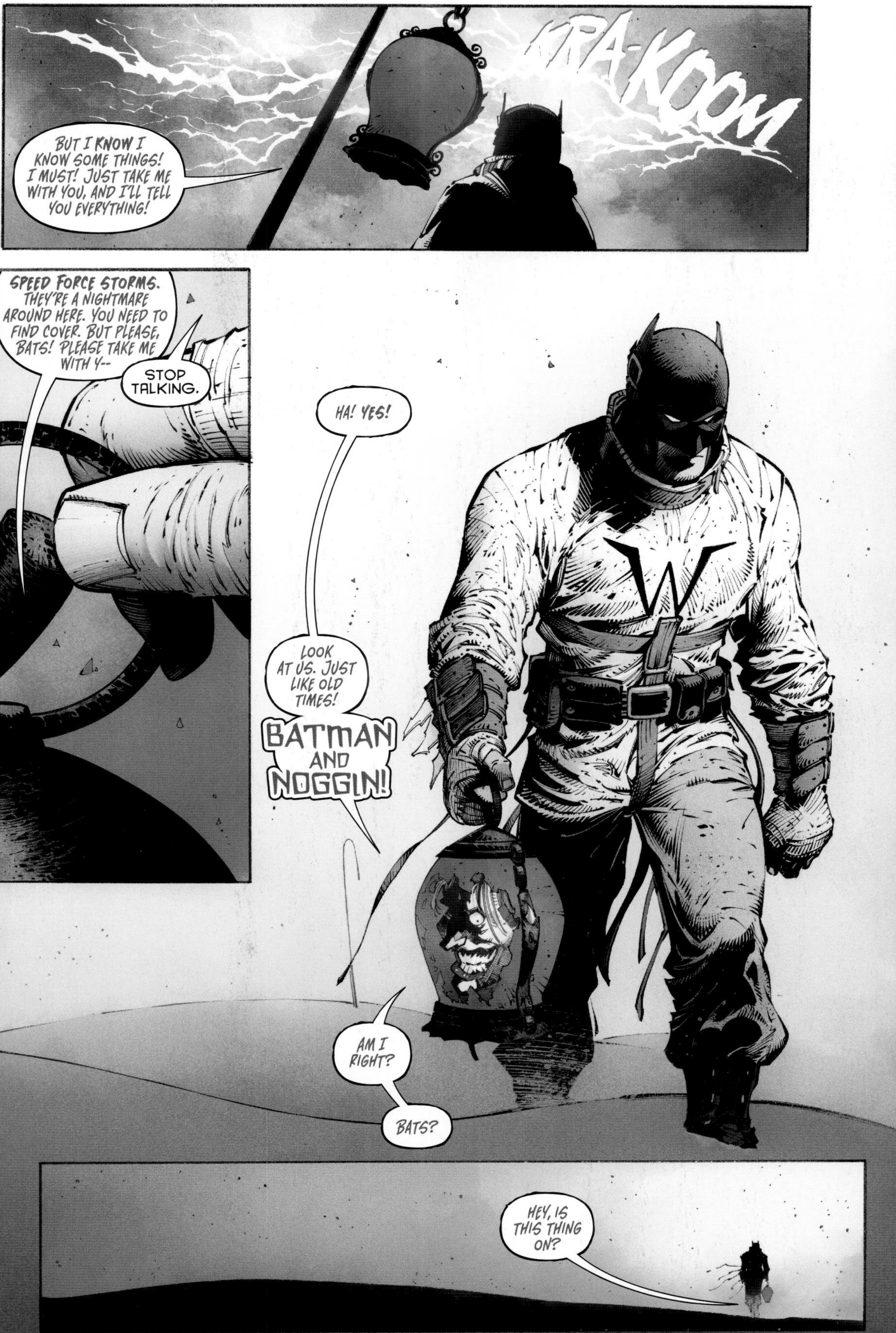
KRA-KOOM
BUT I KNOW I KNOW SOME THINGS! I MUST! JUST TAKE ME WITH YOU, AND I'LL TELL YOU EVERYTHING!
SPEED FORCE STORMS. THEY'RE A NIGHTMARE AROUND HERE. YOU NEED TO FIND COVER. BUT PLEASE, BATS! PLEASE TAKE ME WITH Y--
STOP TALKING.
HA! YES!
LOOK AT US. JUST LIKE OLD TIMES!
BATMAN AND NOGGIN!
AM I RIGHT?
BATS?
HEY, IS THIS THING ON?

PART THREE:
THE ASYLUM

"It was two days' journey
to Coast City..."

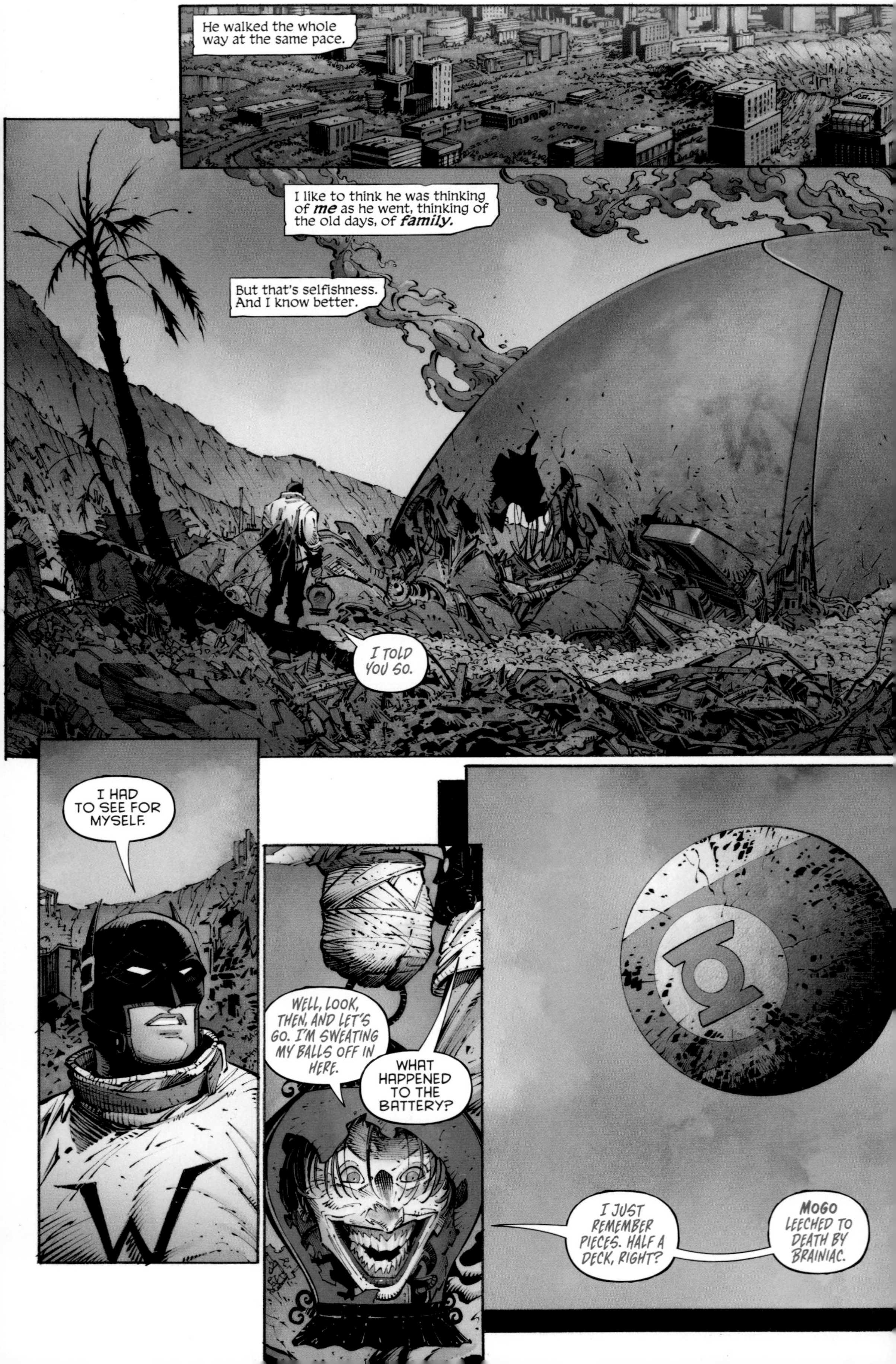

He walked the whole way at the same pace.
I like to think he was thinking of *me* as he went, thinking of the old days, of *family.*
But that's selfishness. And I know better.
I TOLD YOU SO.
I HAD TO SEE FOR MYSELF.
WELL, LOOK, THEN, AND LET'S GO. I'M SWEATING MY BALLS OFF IN HERE.
WHAT HAPPENED TO THE BATTERY?
I JUST REMEMBER PIECES. HALF A DECK, RIGHT?
MOGO LEECHED TO DEATH BY BRAINIAC.

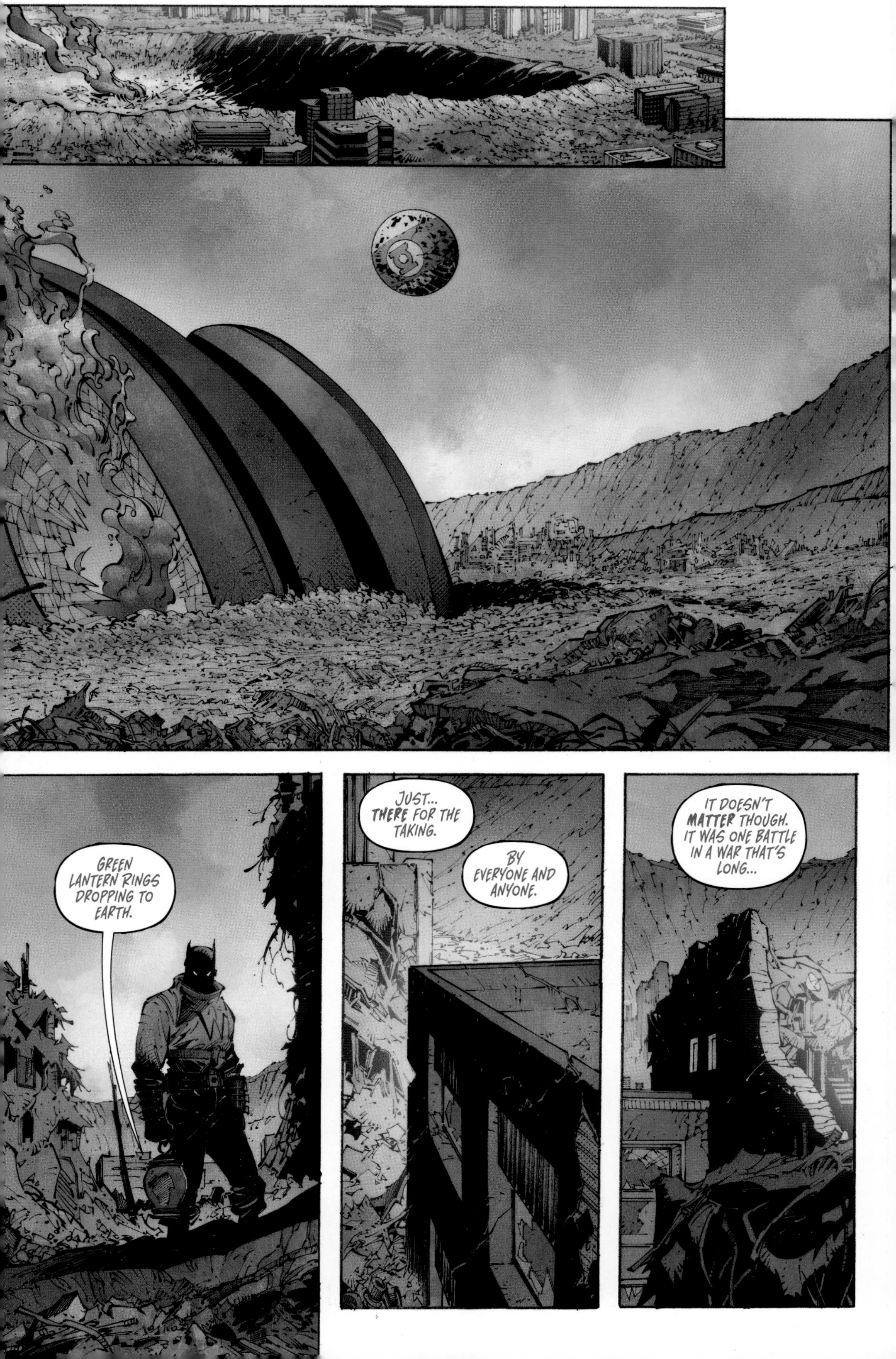
GREEN LANTERN RINGS DROPPING TO EARTH.
JUST... THERE FOR THE TAKING.
BY EVERYONE AND ANYONE.
IT DOESN'T MATTER THOUGH. IT WAS ONE BATTLE IN A WAR THAT'S LONG...

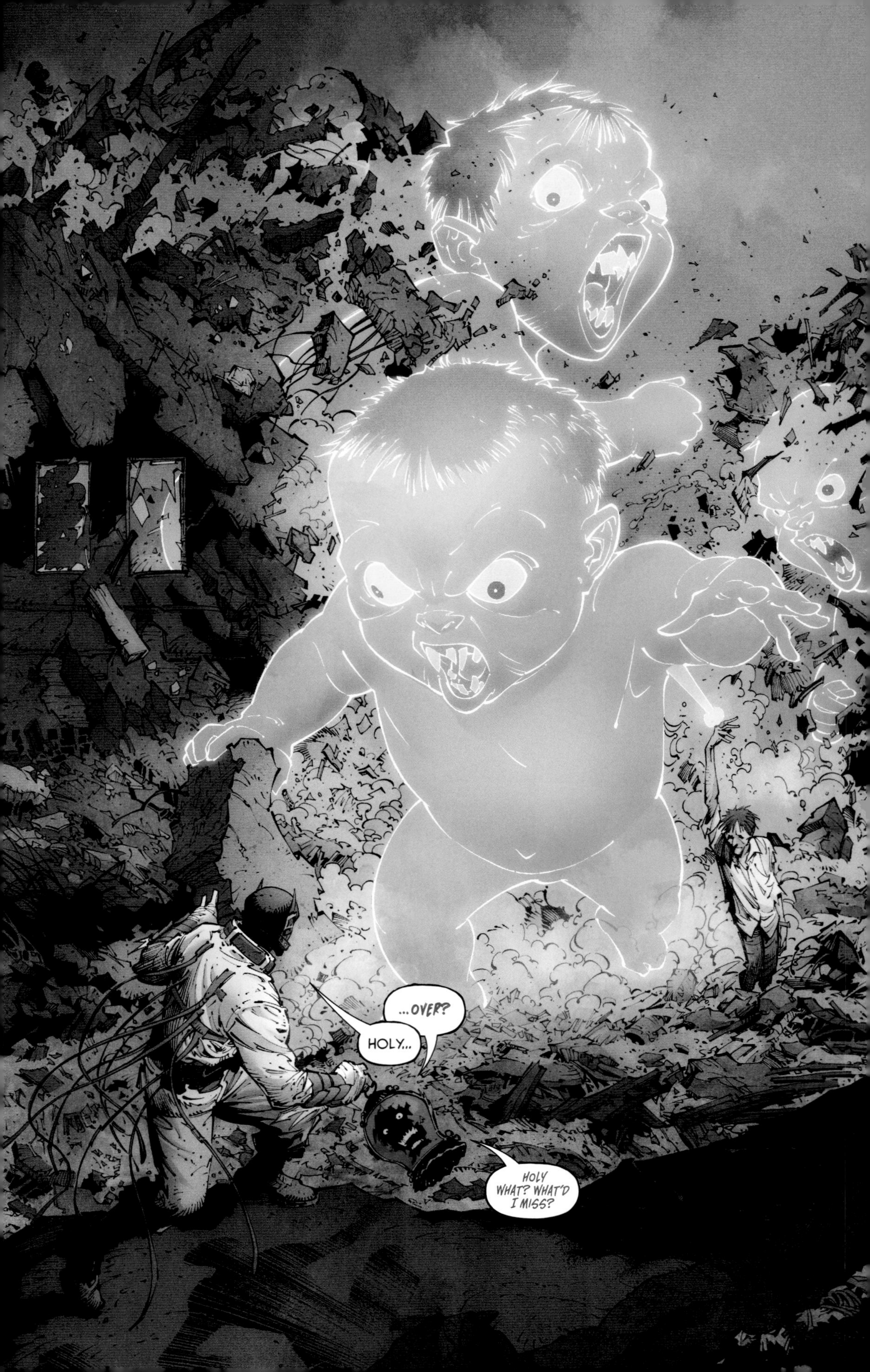
HOLY...
...OVER?
HOLY WHAT? WHAT'D I MISS?

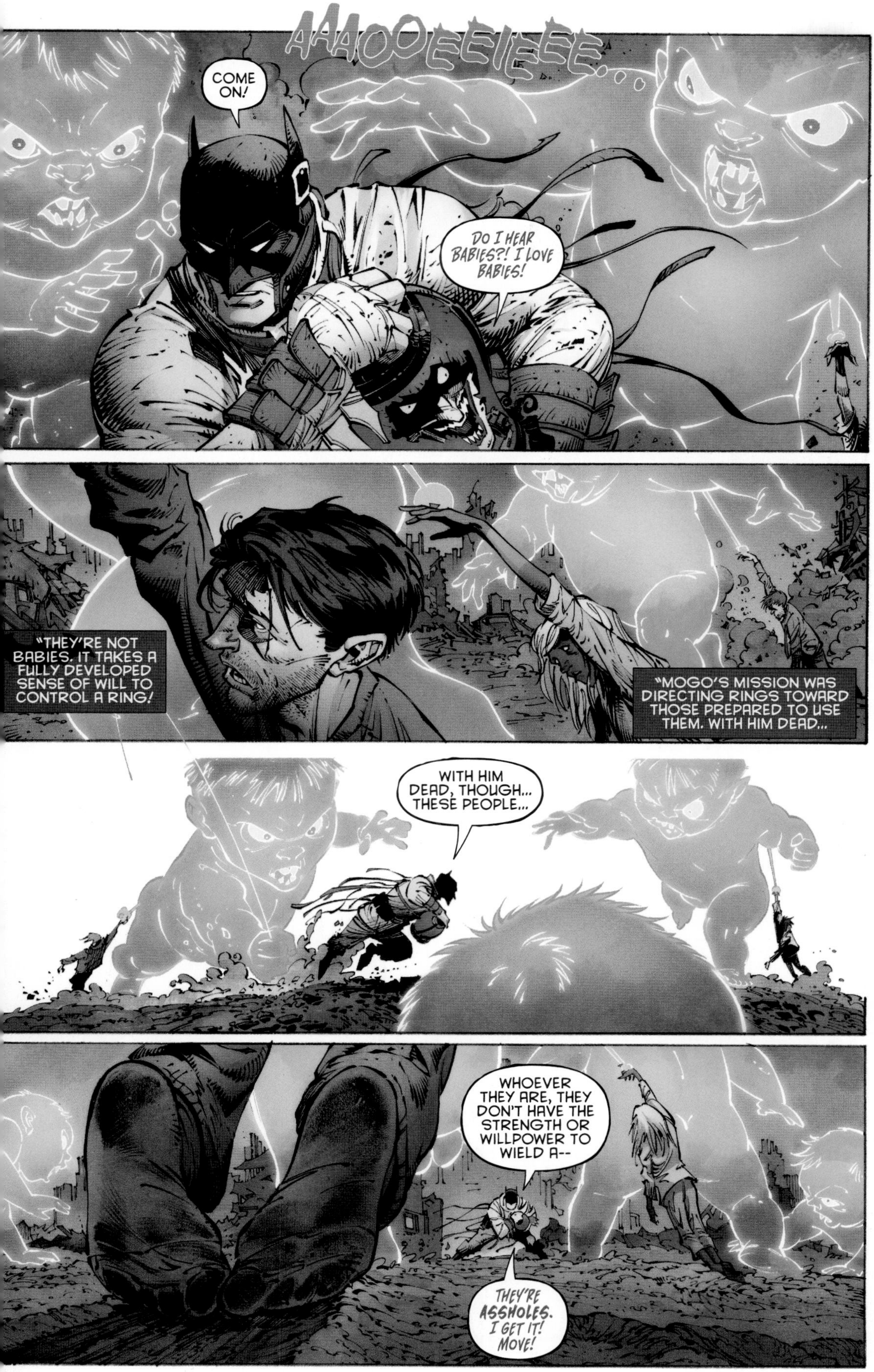
AAAOOEEIEEEE...
COME ON!
DO I HEAR BABIES?! I LOVE BABIES!
"THEY'RE NOT BABIES. IT TAKES A FULLY DEVELOPED SENSE OF WILL TO CONTROL A RING!
"MOGO'S MISSION WAS DIRECTING RINGS TOWARD THOSE PREPARED TO USE THEM. WITH HIM DEAD...
WITH HIM DEAD, THOUGH... THESE PEOPLE...
WHOEVER THEY ARE, THEY DON'T HAVE THE STRENGTH OR WILLPOWER TO WIELD A--
THEY'RE ASSHOLES. I GET IT! MOVE!

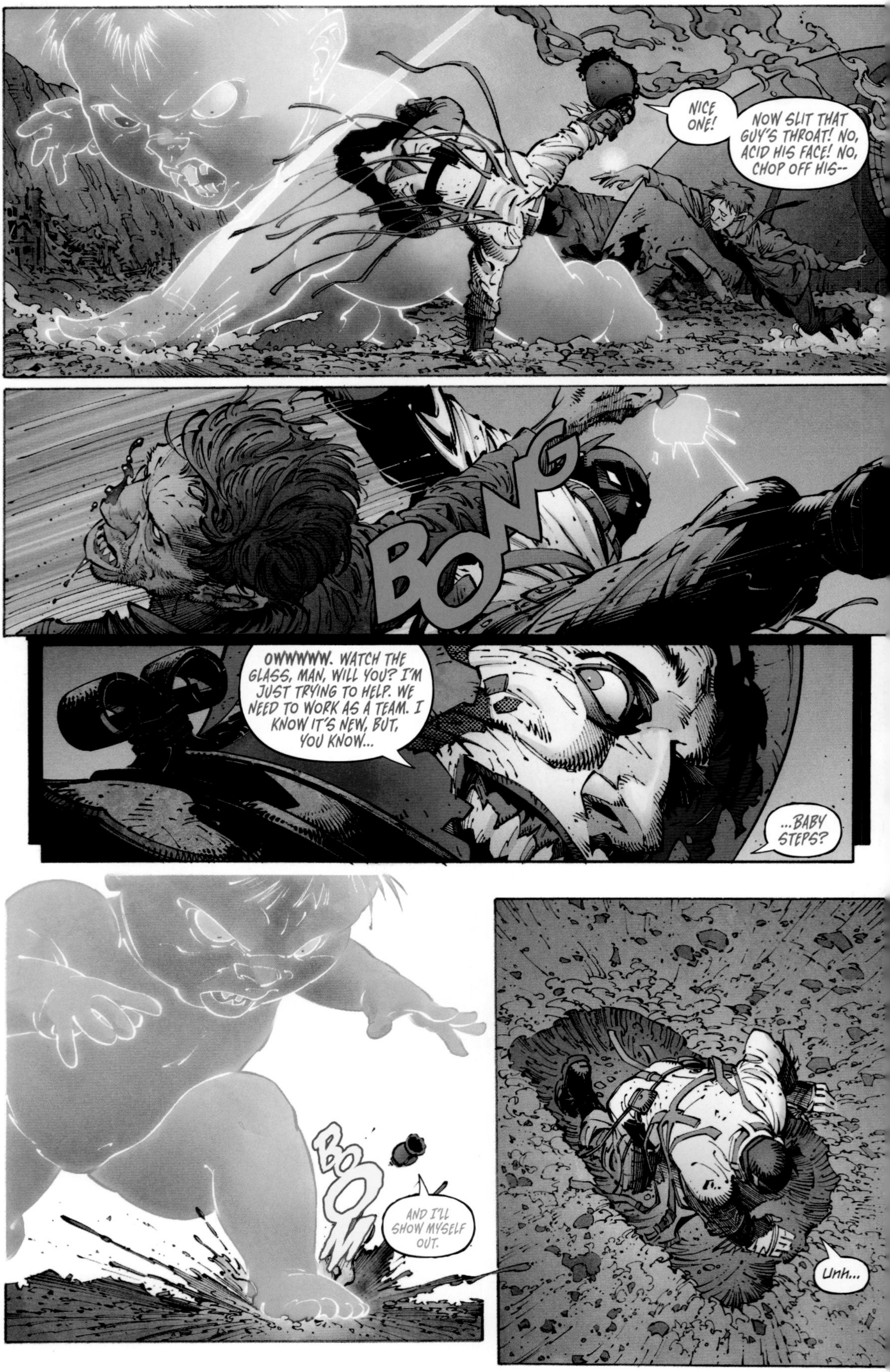
NICE ONE!
NOW SLIT THAT GUY'S THROAT! NO, ACID HIS FACE! NO, CHOP OFF HIS--
BONG
OWWWWW. WATCH THE GLASS, MAN, WILL YOU? I'M JUST TRYING TO HELP. WE NEED TO WORK AS A TEAM. I KNOW IT'S NEW, BUT, YOU KNOW...
...BABY STEPS?
BOOM
AND I'LL SHOW MYSELF OUT.
Unh...

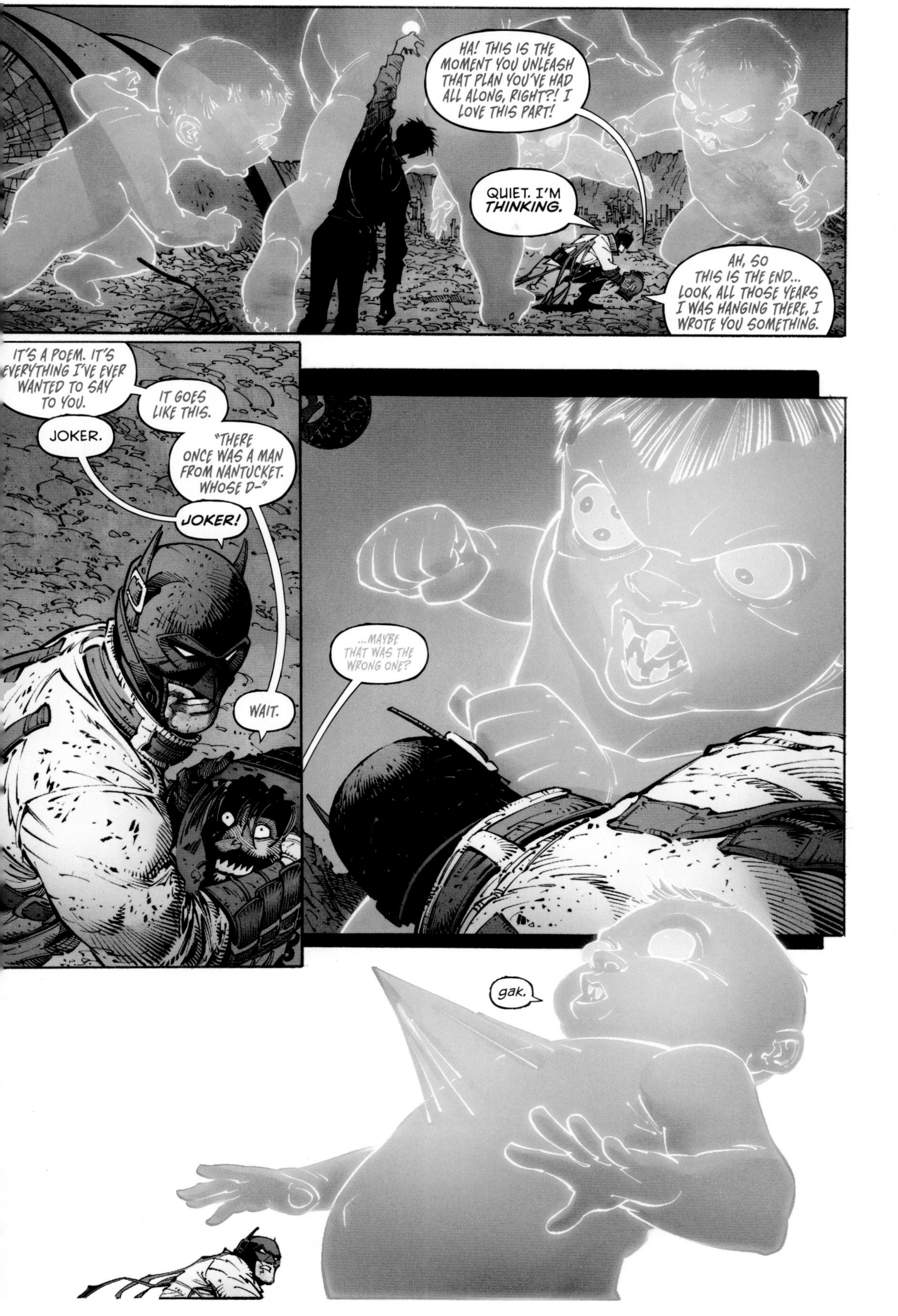
HA! THIS IS THE MOMENT YOU UNLEASH THAT PLAN YOU'VE HAD ALL ALONG, RIGHT?! I LOVE THIS PART!
QUIET. I'M THINKING.
AH, SO THIS IS THE END... LOOK, ALL THOSE YEARS I WAS HANGING THERE, I WROTE YOU SOMETHING.
IT'S A POEM. IT'S EVERYTHING I'VE EVER WANTED TO SAY TO YOU.
IT GOES LIKE THIS.
JOKER.
"THERE ONCE WAS A MAN FROM NANTUCKET. WHOSE D-"
JOKER!
WAIT.
...MAYBE THAT WAS THE WRONG ONE?
gak.

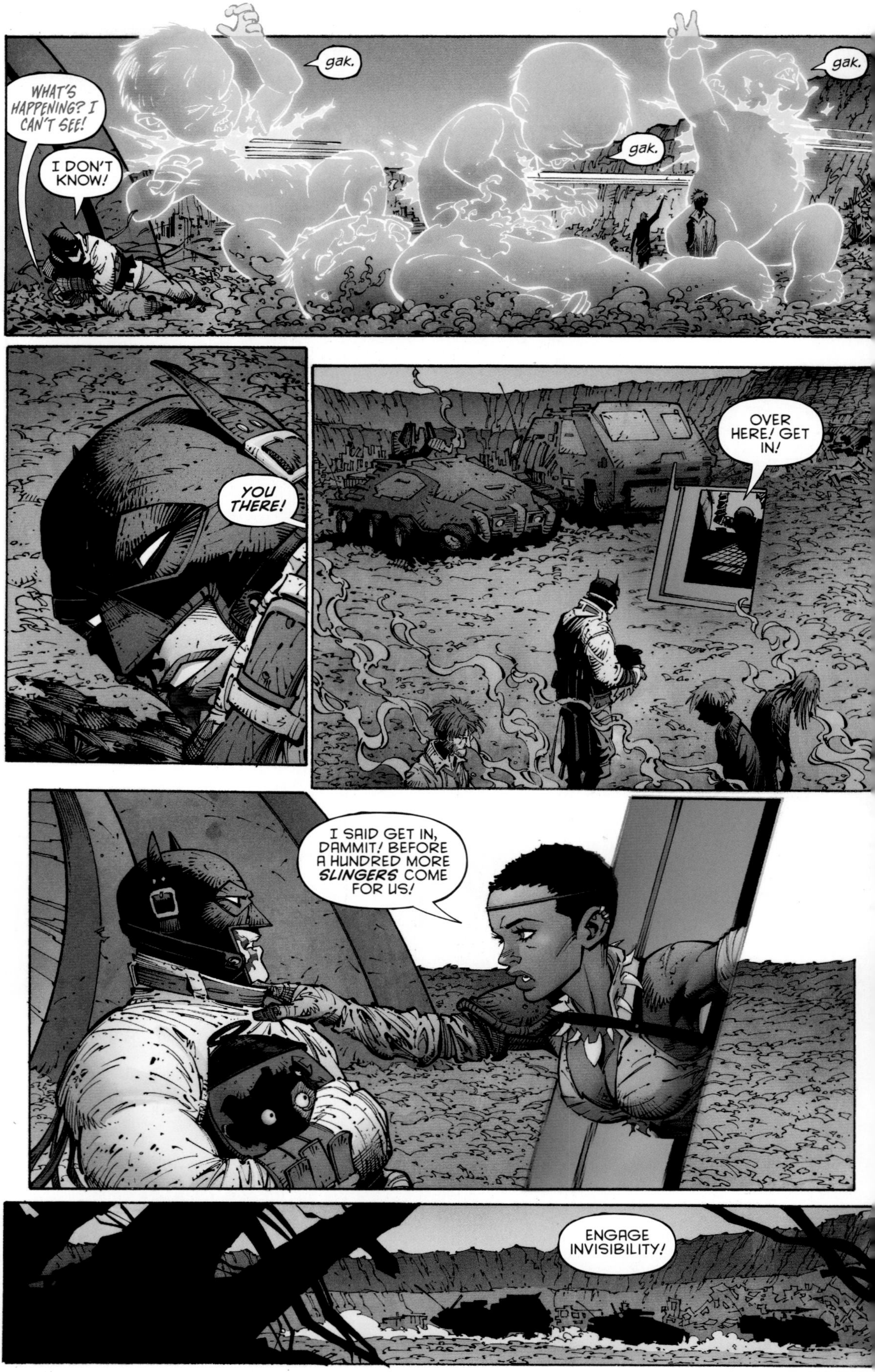
gak.
WHAT'S HAPPENING? I CAN'T SEE!
I DON'T KNOW!
gak.
gak.
YOU THERE!
OVER HERE! GET IN!
I SAID GET IN, DAMMIT! BEFORE A HUNDRED MORE SLINGERS COME FOR US!
ENGAGE INVISIBILITY!

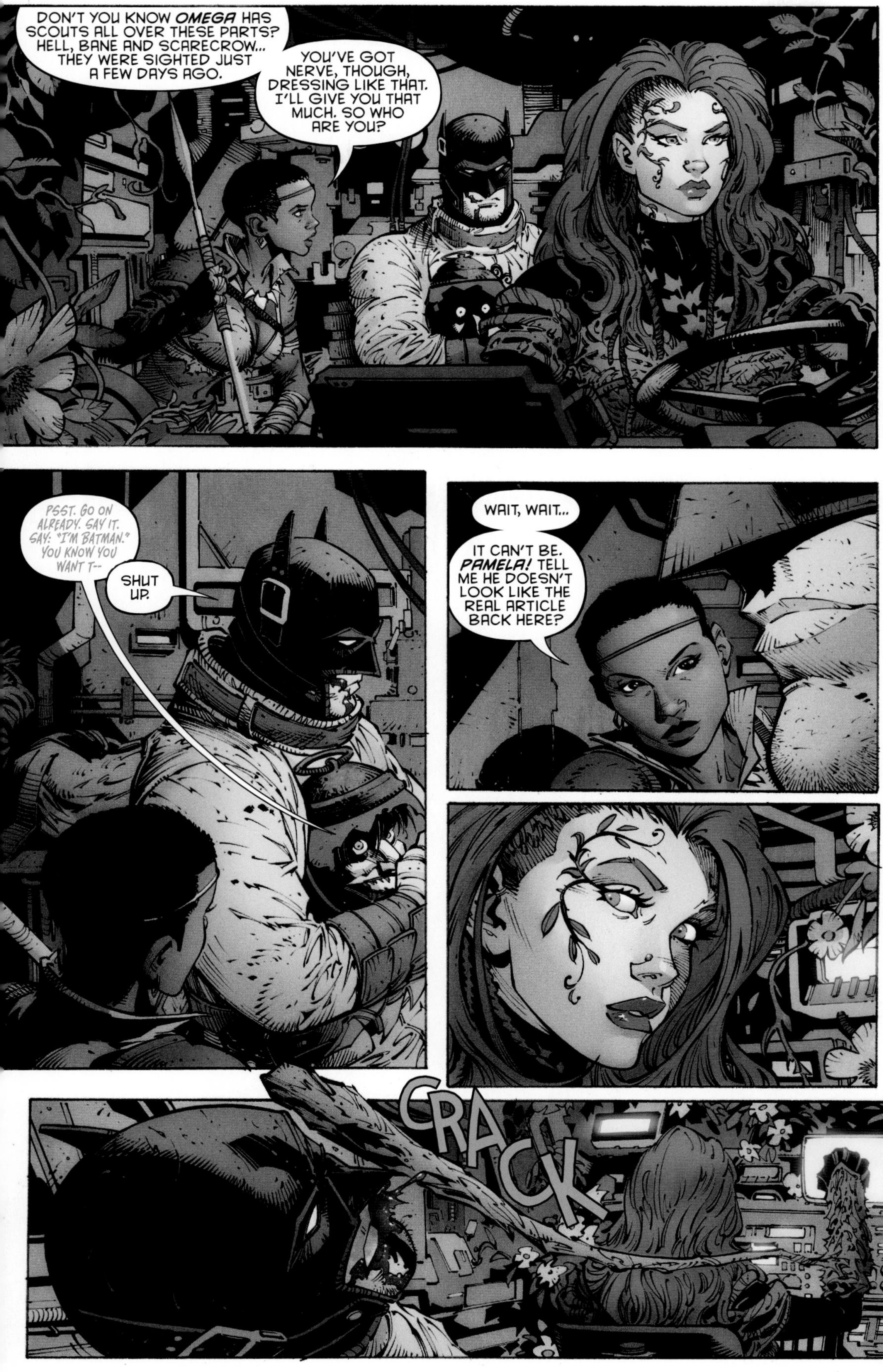
DON'T YOU KNOW OMEGA HAS SCOUTS ALL OVER THESE PARTS? HELL, BANE AND SCARECROW... THEY WERE SIGHTED JUST A FEW DAYS AGO.
YOU'VE GOT NERVE, THOUGH, DRESSING LIKE THAT. I'LL GIVE YOU THAT MUCH. SO WHO ARE YOU?
PSST. GO ON ALREADY. SAY IT. SAY: "I'M BATMAN." YOU KNOW YOU WANT T--
SHUT UP.
WAIT, WAIT...
IT CAN'T BE. PAMELA! TELL ME HE DOESN'T LOOK LIKE THE REAL ARTICLE BACK HERE?
CRACK

PART FOUR:
ECHOLOCATION

"There's no going back,
people..."

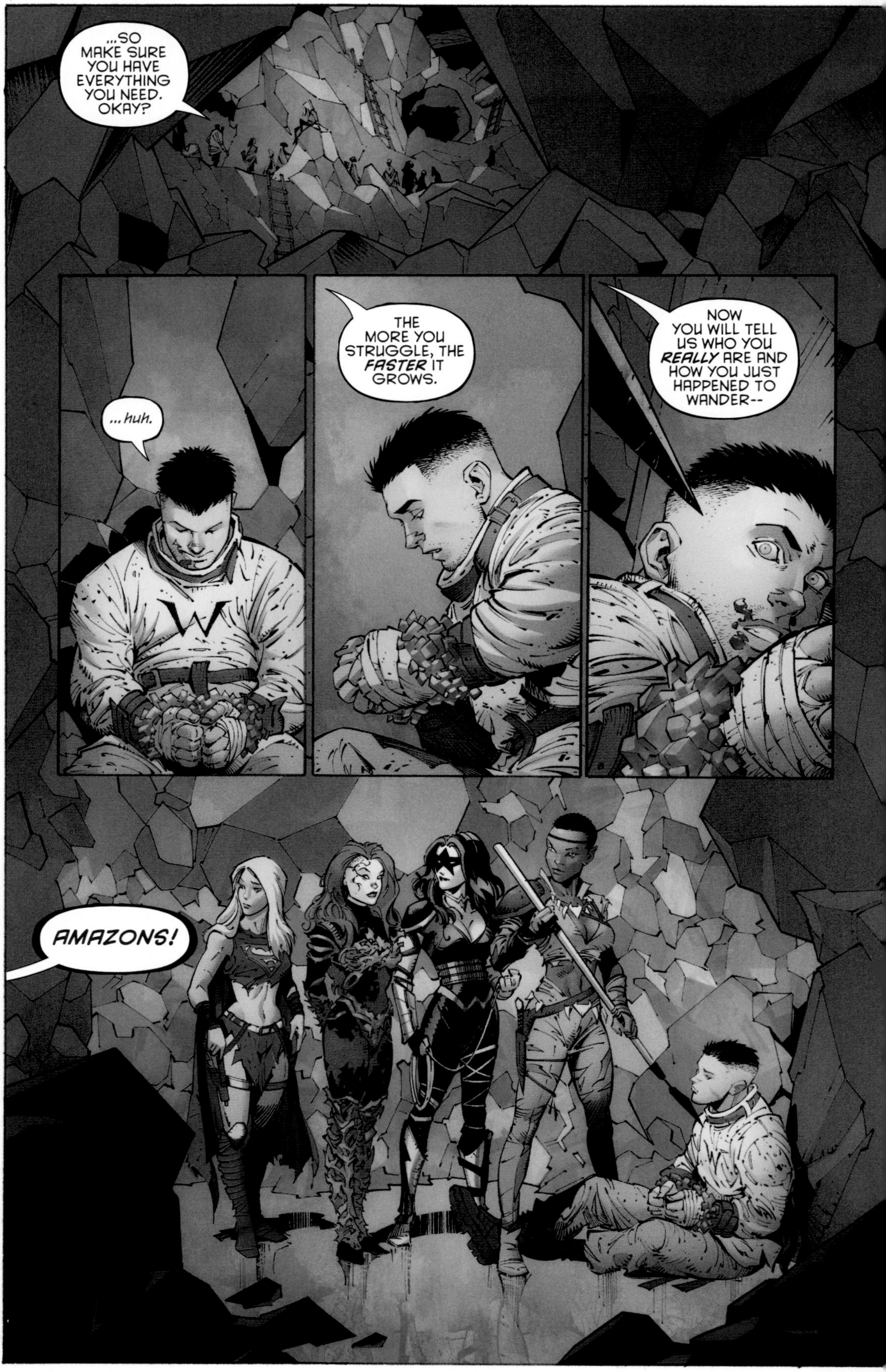

...SO MAKE SURE YOU HAVE EVERYTHING YOU NEED. OKAY?
...huh.
THE MORE YOU STRUGGLE, THE FASTER IT GROWS.
NOW YOU WILL TELL US WHO YOU REALLY ARE AND HOW YOU JUST HAPPENED TO WANDER--
AMAZONS!

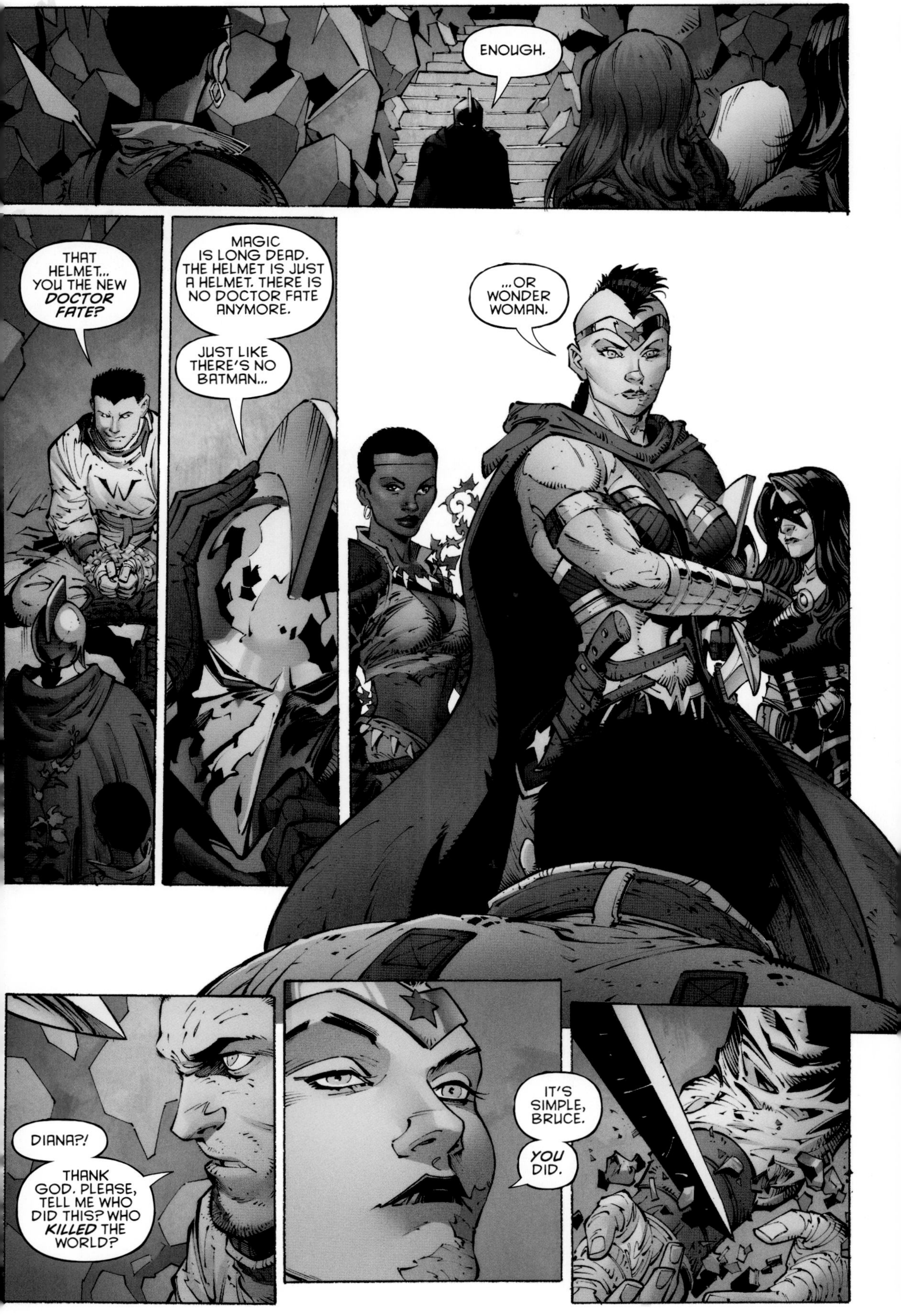
ENOUGH.
THAT HELMET... YOU THE NEW DOCTOR FATE?
MAGIC IS LONG DEAD. THE HELMET IS JUST A HELMET. THERE IS NO DOCTOR FATE ANYMORE.
JUST LIKE THERE'S NO BATMAN...
...OR WONDER WOMAN.
DIANA?!
THANK GOD. PLEASE, TELL ME WHO DID THIS? WHO KILLED THE WORLD?
IT'S SIMPLE, BRUCE.
YOU DID.

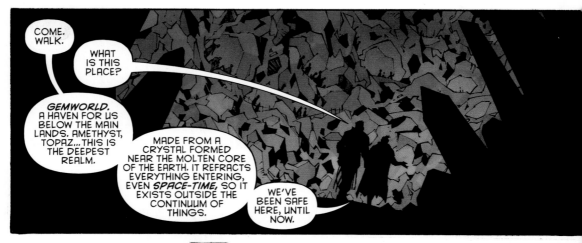

COME. WALK.

WHAT IS THIS PLACE?

GEMWORLD. A HAVEN FOR US BELOW THE MAIN LANDS. AMETHYST, TOPAZ... THIS IS THE DEEPEST REALM.

MADE FROM A CRYSTAL FORMED NEAR THE MOLTEN CORE OF THE EARTH. IT REFRACTS EVERYTHING ENTERING, EVEN *SPACE-TIME*, SO IT EXISTS OUTSIDE THE CONTINUUM OF THINGS.

WE'VE BEEN SAFE HERE, UNTIL NOW.

DIANA, I DON'T UNDERSTAND WHAT HAPPENED OUT THERE, DIANA.

IT'S SIMPLE, BRUCE. WHAT HAPPENED IS WE LOST. IT'S OVER.

LOST HOW? WHY CAN'T WE--

STOP. IT DOESN'T MATTER.

WHAT *DOES* MATTER IS YOU'RE HERE AND YOU CAN COME WITH US.

YOU CAN HELP US *PROTECT* THEM.

PROTECT *WHO?*

THE ONES LEFT, BRUCE.

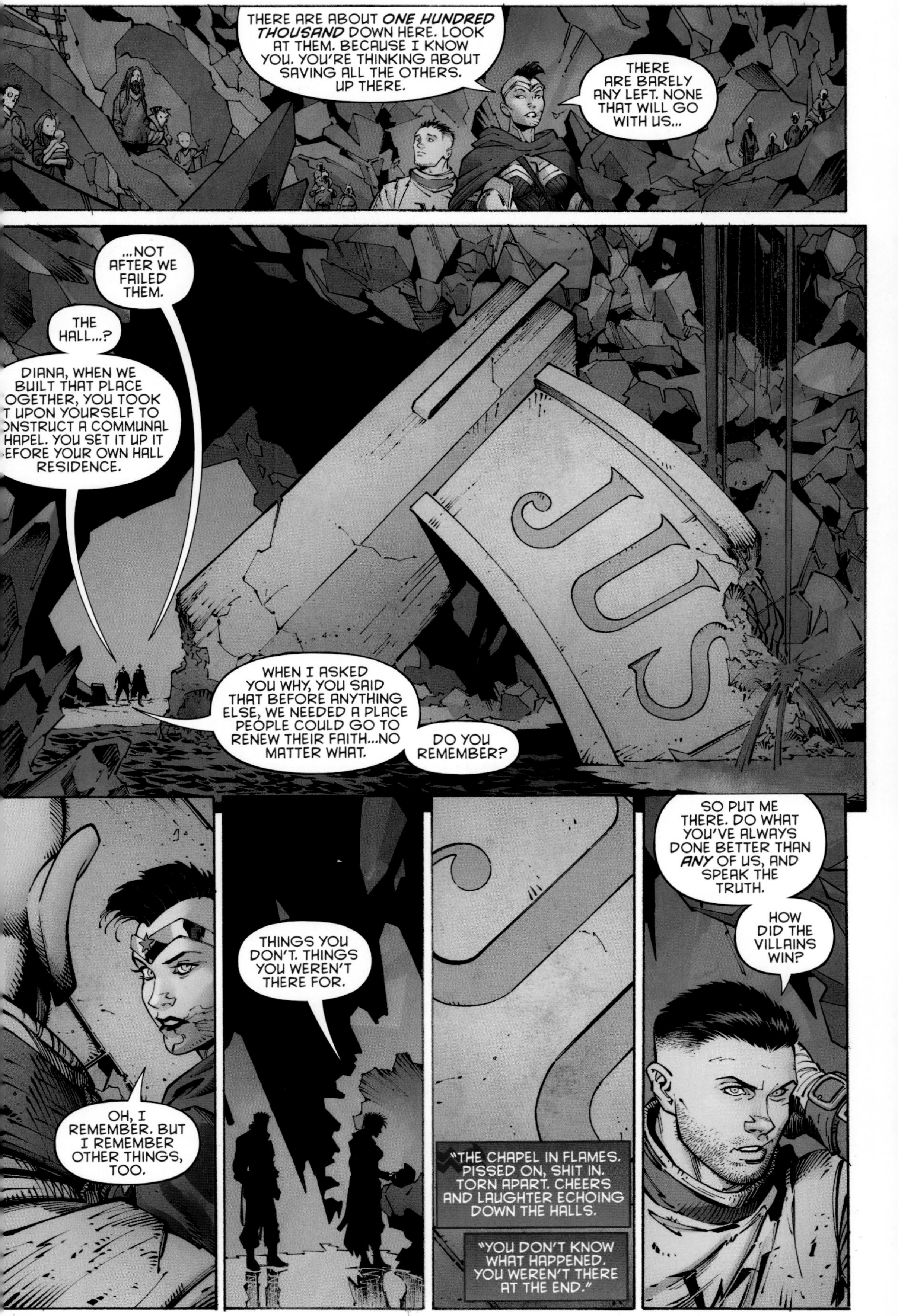
THERE ARE ABOUT ONE HUNDRED THOUSAND DOWN HERE. LOOK AT THEM. BECAUSE I KNOW YOU. YOU'RE THINKING ABOUT SAVING ALL THE OTHERS. UP THERE.
THERE ARE BARELY ANY LEFT. NONE THAT WILL GO WITH US...
...NOT AFTER WE FAILED THEM.
THE HALL...?
DIANA, WHEN WE BUILT THAT PLACE TOGETHER, YOU TOOK IT UPON YOURSELF TO CONSTRUCT A COMMUNAL CHAPEL. YOU SET IT UP IT BEFORE YOUR OWN HALL RESIDENCE.
JUS
WHEN I ASKED YOU WHY, YOU SAID THAT BEFORE ANYTHING ELSE, WE NEEDED A PLACE PEOPLE COULD GO TO RENEW THEIR FAITH...NO MATTER WHAT.
DO YOU REMEMBER?
OH, I REMEMBER. BUT I REMEMBER OTHER THINGS, TOO.
THINGS YOU DON'T. THINGS YOU WEREN'T THERE FOR.
"THE CHAPEL IN FLAMES. PISSED ON, SHIT IN. TORN APART. CHEERS AND LAUGHTER ECHOING DOWN THE HALLS.
"YOU DON'T KNOW WHAT HAPPENED. YOU WEREN'T THERE AT THE END."
SO PUT ME THERE. DO WHAT YOU'VE ALWAYS DONE BETTER THAN ANY OF US, AND SPEAK THE TRUTH.
HOW DID THE VILLAINS WIN?

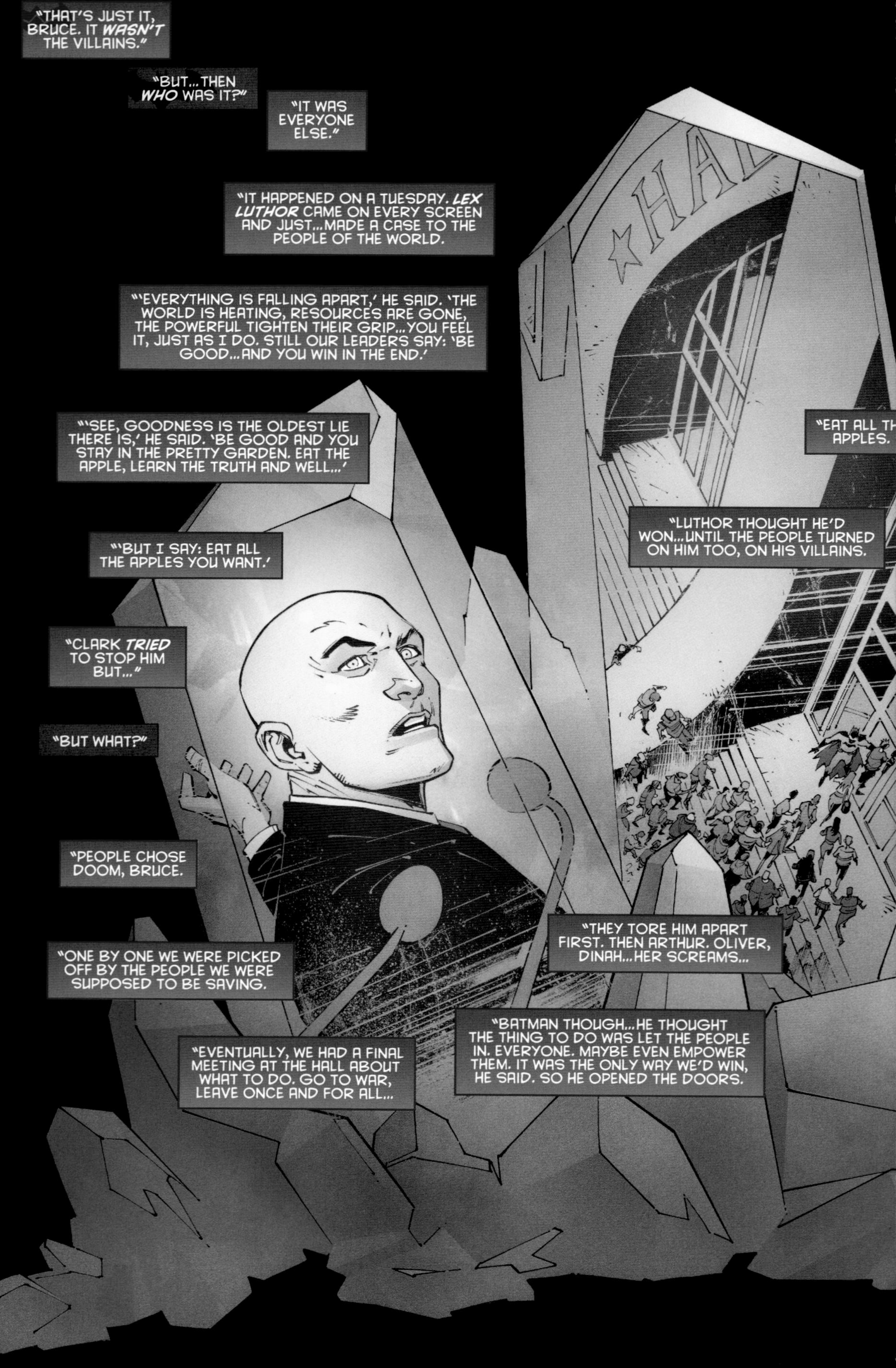
"THAT'S JUST IT, BRUCE. IT *WASN'T* THE VILLAINS."
"BUT... THEN *WHO* WAS IT?"
"IT WAS EVERYONE ELSE."
"IT HAPPENED ON A TUESDAY. *LEX LUTHOR* CAME ON EVERY SCREEN AND JUST... MADE A CASE TO THE PEOPLE OF THE WORLD.
"'EVERYTHING IS FALLING APART,' HE SAID. 'THE WORLD IS HEATING, RESOURCES ARE GONE, THE POWERFUL TIGHTEN THEIR GRIP... YOU FEEL IT, JUST AS I DO. STILL OUR LEADERS SAY: 'BE GOOD... AND YOU WIN IN THE END.'
"'SEE, GOODNESS IS THE OLDEST LIE THERE IS,' HE SAID. 'BE GOOD AND YOU STAY IN THE PRETTY GARDEN. EAT THE APPLE, LEARN THE TRUTH AND WELL...'
"'BUT I SAY: EAT ALL THE APPLES YOU WANT.'
"EAT ALL TH APPLES.
"LUTHOR THOUGHT HE'D WON... UNTIL THE PEOPLE TURNED ON HIM TOO, ON HIS VILLAINS.
"CLARK *TRIED* TO STOP HIM BUT..."
"BUT WHAT?"
"PEOPLE CHOSE DOOM, BRUCE.
"THEY TORE HIM APART FIRST. THEN ARTHUR. OLIVER, DINAH... HER SCREAMS...
"ONE BY ONE WE WERE PICKED OFF BY THE PEOPLE WE WERE SUPPOSED TO BE SAVING.
"EVENTUALLY, WE HAD A FINAL MEETING AT THE HALL ABOUT WHAT TO DO. GO TO WAR, LEAVE ONCE AND FOR ALL...
"BATMAN THOUGH... HE THOUGHT THE THING TO DO WAS LET THE PEOPLE IN. EVERYONE. MAYBE EVEN EMPOWER THEM. IT WAS THE ONLY WAY WE'D WIN, HE SAID. SO HE OPENED THE DOORS.
HAL

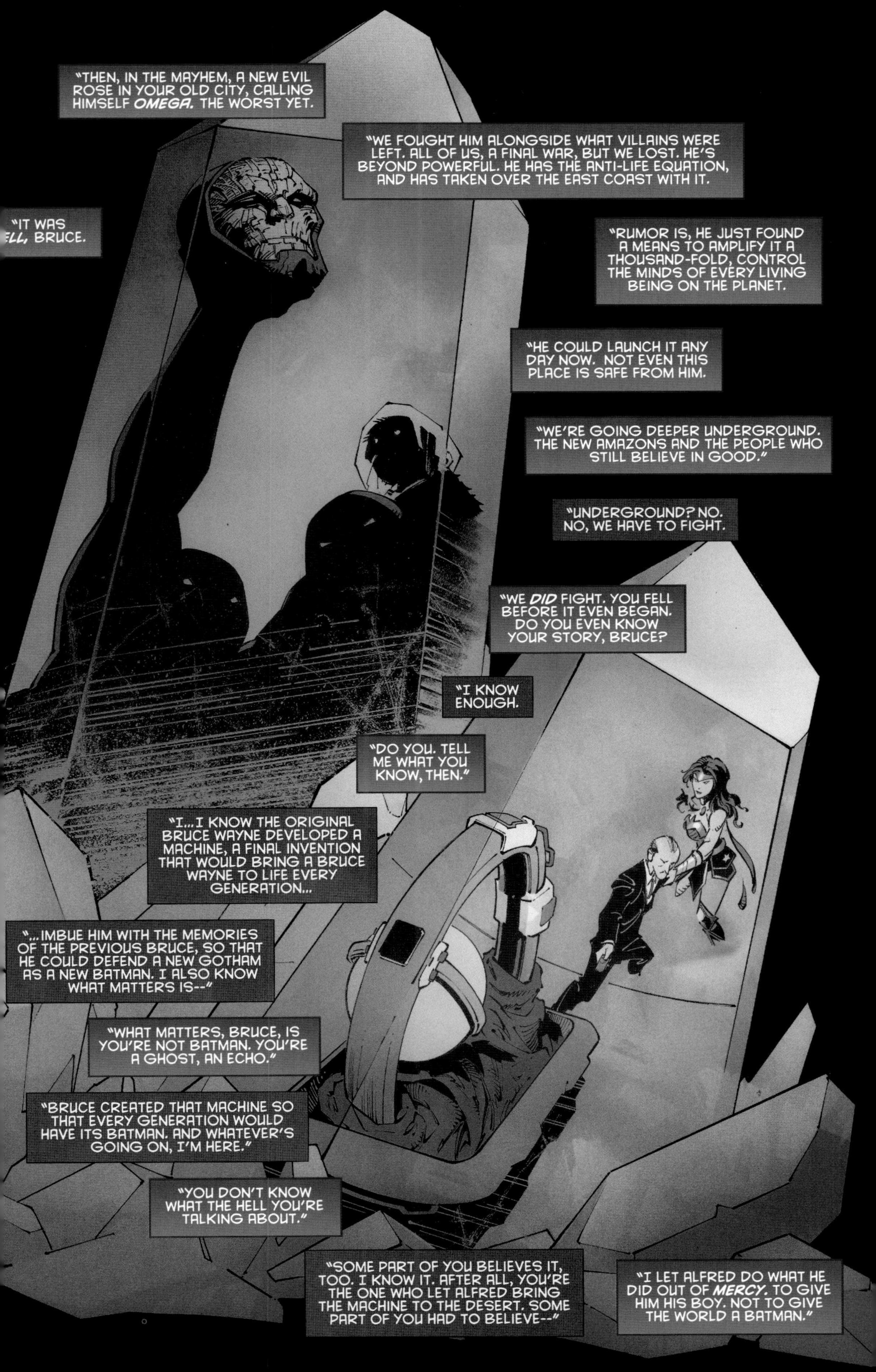
"THEN, IN THE MAYHEM, A NEW EVIL ROSE IN YOUR OLD CITY, CALLING HIMSELF OMEGA. THE WORST YET.
"WE FOUGHT HIM ALONGSIDE WHAT VILLAINS WERE LEFT. ALL OF US, A FINAL WAR, BUT WE LOST. HE'S BEYOND POWERFUL. HE HAS THE ANTI-LIFE EQUATION, AND HAS TAKEN OVER THE EAST COAST WITH IT.
"IT WAS ELL, BRUCE.
"RUMOR IS, HE JUST FOUND A MEANS TO AMPLIFY IT A THOUSAND-FOLD, CONTROL THE MINDS OF EVERY LIVING BEING ON THE PLANET.
"HE COULD LAUNCH IT ANY DAY NOW. NOT EVEN THIS PLACE IS SAFE FROM HIM.
"WE'RE GOING DEEPER UNDERGROUND. THE NEW AMAZONS AND THE PEOPLE WHO STILL BELIEVE IN GOOD."
"UNDERGROUND? NO. NO, WE HAVE TO FIGHT.
"WE DID FIGHT. YOU FELL BEFORE IT EVEN BEGAN. DO YOU EVEN KNOW YOUR STORY, BRUCE?
"I KNOW ENOUGH.
"DO YOU. TELL ME WHAT YOU KNOW, THEN."
"I...I KNOW THE ORIGINAL BRUCE WAYNE DEVELOPED A MACHINE, A FINAL INVENTION THAT WOULD BRING A BRUCE WAYNE TO LIFE EVERY GENERATION...
"...IMBUE HIM WITH THE MEMORIES OF THE PREVIOUS BRUCE, SO THAT HE COULD DEFEND A NEW GOTHAM AS A NEW BATMAN. I ALSO KNOW WHAT MATTERS IS--"
"WHAT MATTERS, BRUCE, IS YOU'RE NOT BATMAN. YOU'RE A GHOST, AN ECHO."
"BRUCE CREATED THAT MACHINE SO THAT EVERY GENERATION WOULD HAVE ITS BATMAN. AND WHATEVER'S GOING ON, I'M HERE."
"YOU DON'T KNOW WHAT THE HELL YOU'RE TALKING ABOUT."
"SOME PART OF YOU BELIEVES IT, TOO. I KNOW IT. AFTER ALL, YOU'RE THE ONE WHO LET ALFRED BRING THE MACHINE TO THE DESERT. SOME PART OF YOU HAD TO BELIEVE--"
"I LET ALFRED DO WHAT HE DID OUT OF MERCY. TO GIVE HIM HIS BOY. NOT TO GIVE THE WORLD A BATMAN."

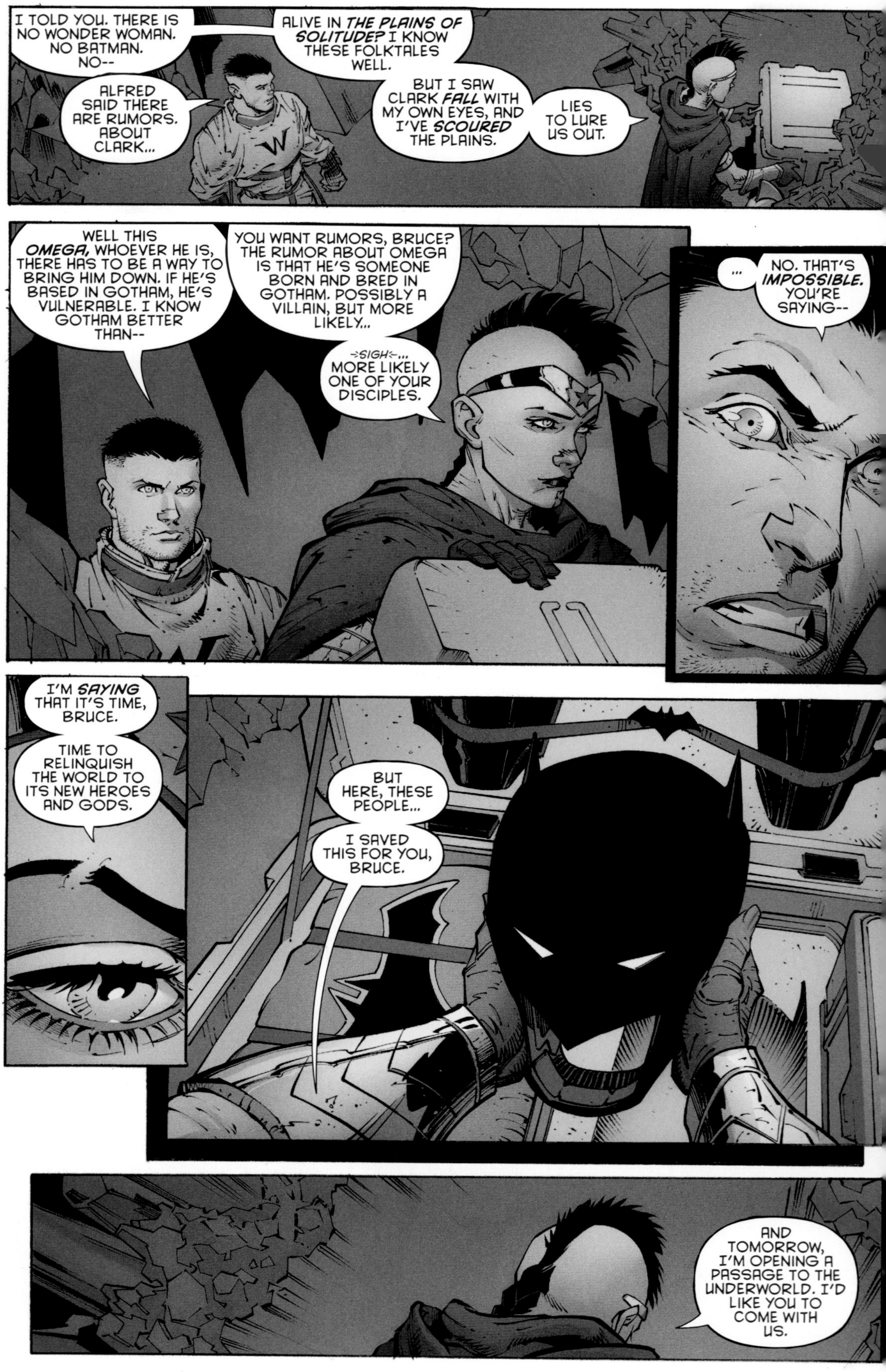
I TOLD YOU. THERE IS NO WONDER WOMAN. NO BATMAN. NO--
ALFRED SAID THERE ARE RUMORS. ABOUT CLARK...
ALIVE IN *THE PLAINS OF SOLITUDE?* I KNOW THESE FOLKTALES WELL.
BUT I SAW CLARK *FALL* WITH MY OWN EYES, AND I'VE *SCOURED* THE PLAINS.
LIES TO LURE US OUT.
WELL THIS *OMEGA,* WHOEVER HE IS, THERE HAS TO BE A WAY TO BRING HIM DOWN. IF HE'S BASED IN GOTHAM, HE'S VULNERABLE. I KNOW GOTHAM BETTER THAN--
YOU WANT RUMORS, BRUCE? THE RUMOR ABOUT OMEGA IS THAT HE'S SOMEONE BORN AND BRED IN GOTHAM. POSSIBLY A VILLAIN, BUT MORE LIKELY...
SIGH... MORE LIKELY ONE OF YOUR DISCIPLES.
...
NO. THAT'S *IMPOSSIBLE.* YOU'RE SAYING--
I'M *SAYING* THAT IT'S TIME, BRUCE.
TIME TO RELINQUISH THE WORLD TO ITS NEW HEROES AND GODS.
BUT HERE, THESE PEOPLE...
I SAVED THIS FOR YOU, BRUCE.
AND TOMORROW, I'M OPENING A PASSAGE TO THE UNDERWORLD. I'D LIKE YOU TO COME WITH US.

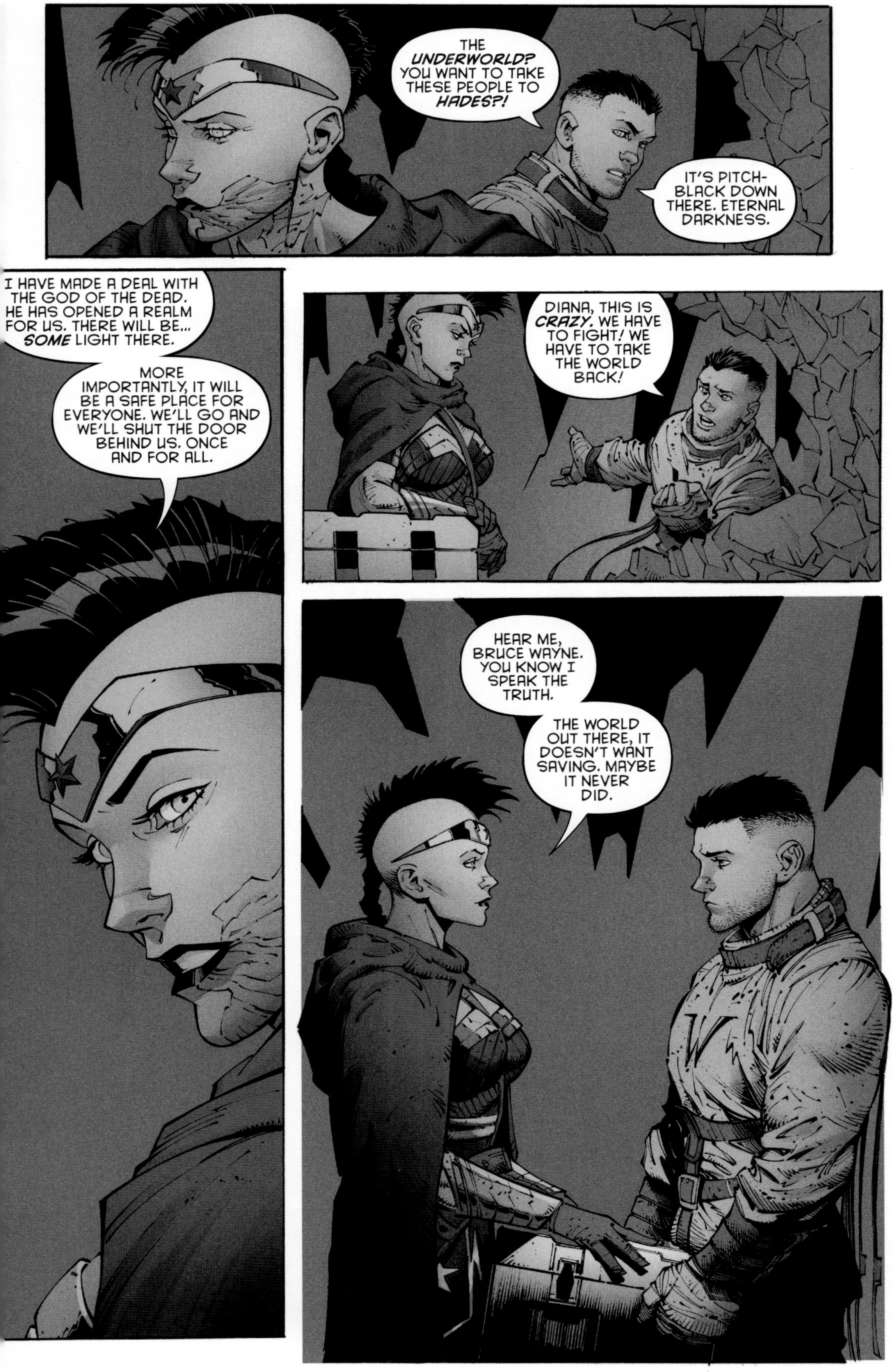
THE UNDERWORLD? YOU WANT TO TAKE THESE PEOPLE TO HADES?!
IT'S PITCH-BLACK DOWN THERE. ETERNAL DARKNESS.
I HAVE MADE A DEAL WITH THE GOD OF THE DEAD. HE HAS OPENED A REALM FOR US. THERE WILL BE... SOME LIGHT THERE.
MORE IMPORTANTLY, IT WILL BE A SAFE PLACE FOR EVERYONE. WE'LL GO AND WE'LL SHUT THE DOOR BEHIND US. ONCE AND FOR ALL.
DIANA, THIS IS CRAZY. WE HAVE TO FIGHT! WE HAVE TO TAKE THE WORLD BACK!
HEAR ME, BRUCE WAYNE. YOU KNOW I SPEAK THE TRUTH.
THE WORLD OUT THERE, IT DOESN'T WANT SAVING. MAYBE IT NEVER DID.

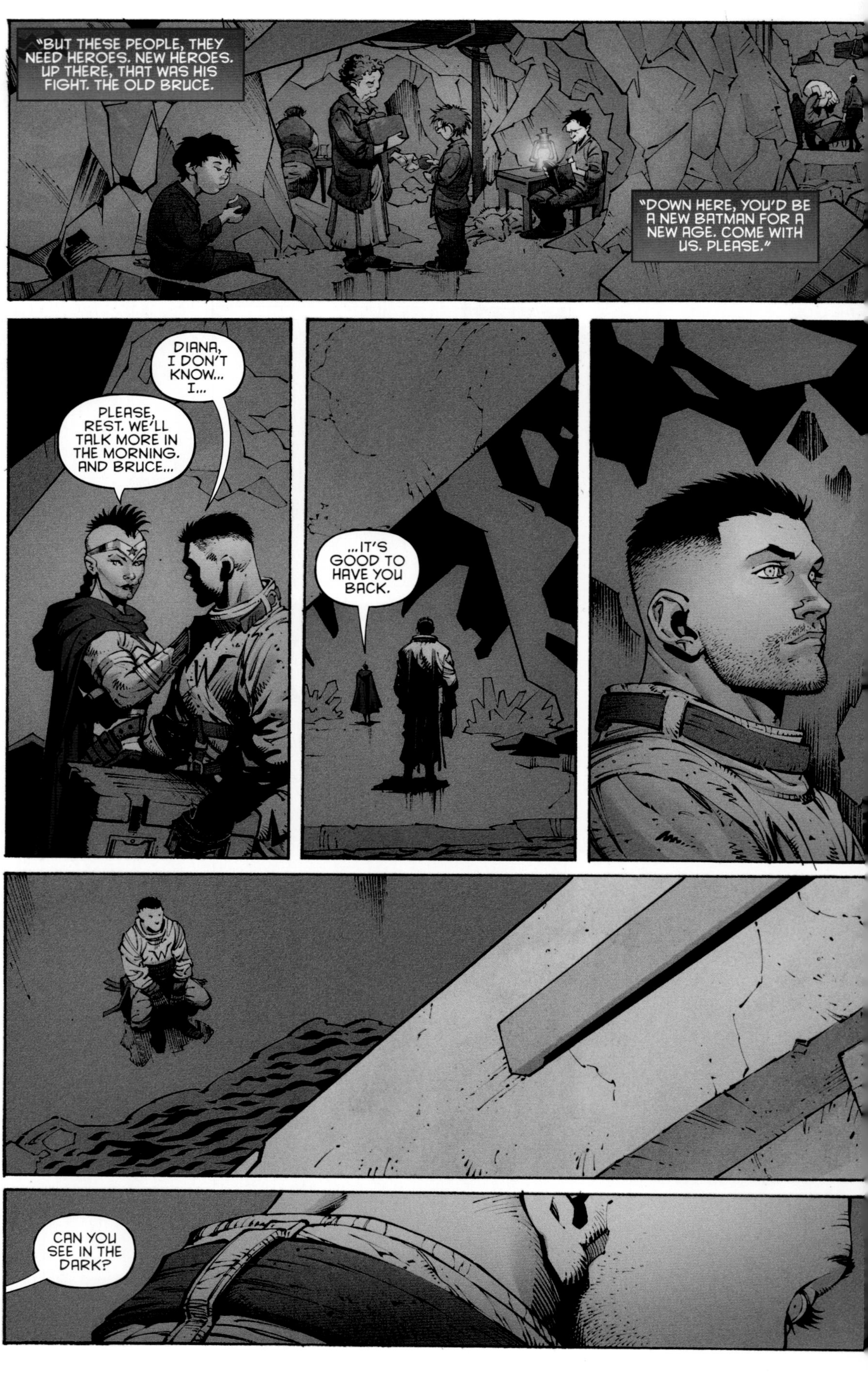
"BUT THESE PEOPLE, THEY NEED HEROES. NEW HEROES. UP THERE, THAT WAS HIS FIGHT. THE OLD BRUCE.
"DOWN HERE, YOU'D BE A NEW BATMAN FOR A NEW AGE. COME WITH US. PLEASE."
DIANA, I DON'T KNOW... I...
PLEASE, REST. WE'LL TALK MORE IN THE MORNING. AND BRUCE...
...IT'S GOOD TO HAVE YOU BACK.
CAN YOU SEE IN THE DARK?

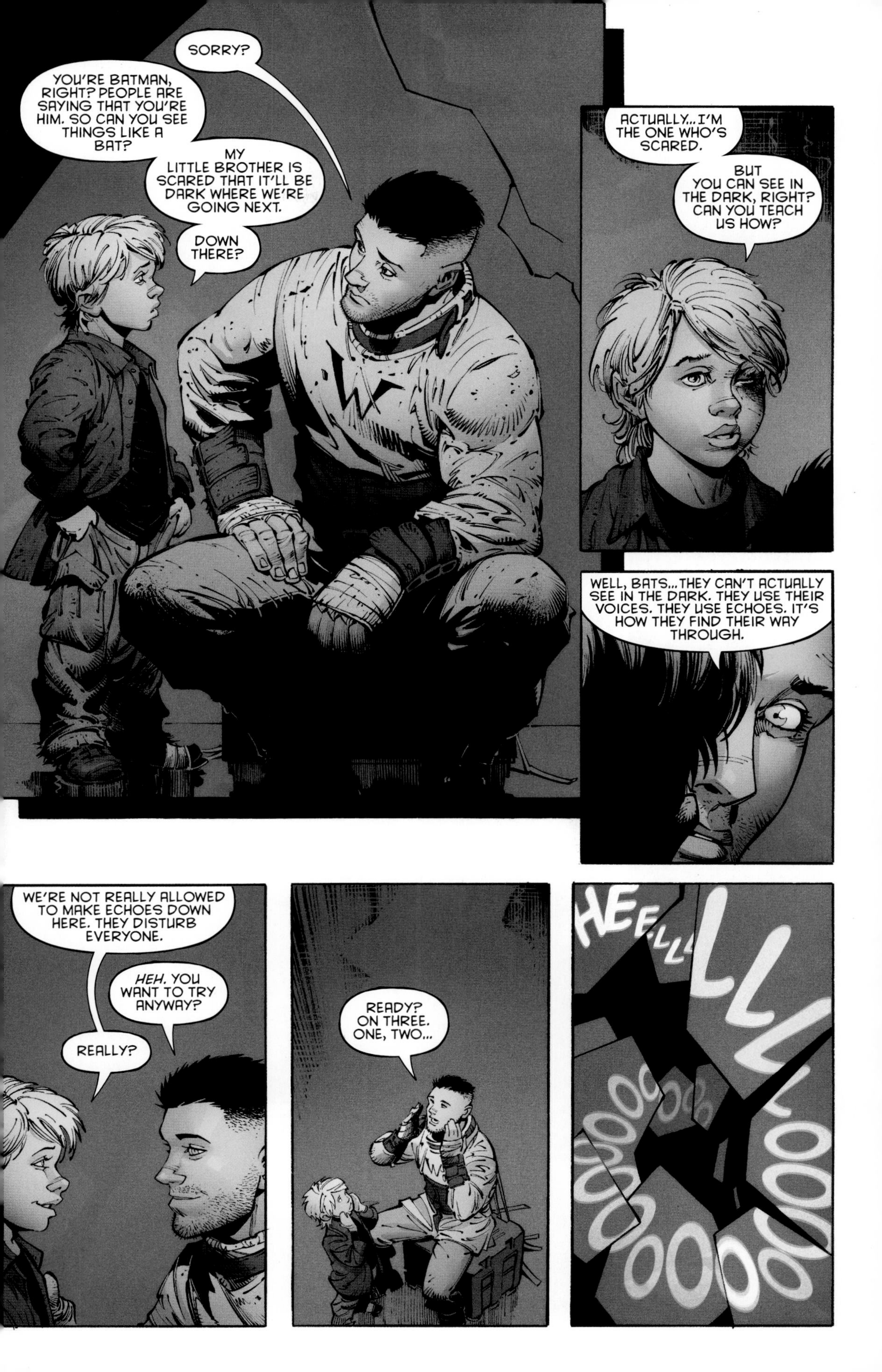
SORRY?
YOU'RE BATMAN, RIGHT? PEOPLE ARE SAYING THAT YOU'RE HIM. SO CAN YOU SEE THINGS LIKE A BAT?
MY LITTLE BROTHER IS SCARED THAT IT'LL BE DARK WHERE WE'RE GOING NEXT.
DOWN THERE?
ACTUALLY... I'M THE ONE WHO'S SCARED.
BUT YOU CAN SEE IN THE DARK, RIGHT? CAN YOU TEACH US HOW?
WELL, BATS... THEY CAN'T ACTUALLY SEE IN THE DARK. THEY USE THEIR VOICES. THEY USE ECHOES. IT'S HOW THEY FIND THEIR WAY THROUGH.
WE'RE NOT REALLY ALLOWED TO MAKE ECHOES DOWN HERE. THEY DISTURB EVERYONE.
HEH. YOU WANT TO TRY ANYWAY?
REALLY?
READY? ON THREE. ONE, TWO...
HEELLLLLLLOOOOOOOOOOOOO

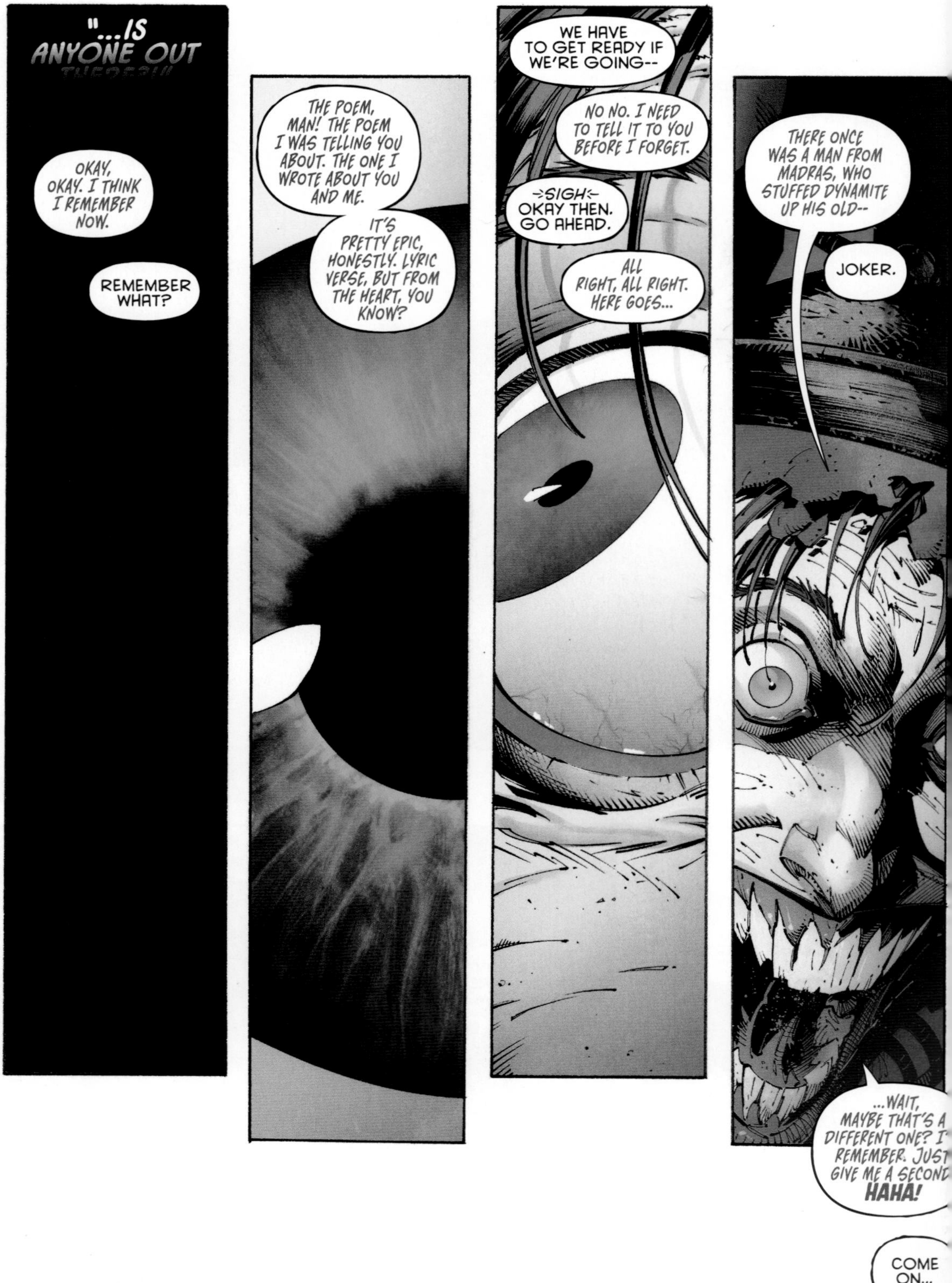
"...IS ANYONE OUT
OKAY, OKAY. I THINK I REMEMBER NOW.
REMEMBER WHAT?
THE POEM, MAN! THE POEM I WAS TELLING YOU ABOUT. THE ONE I WROTE ABOUT YOU AND ME.
IT'S PRETTY EPIC, HONESTLY. LYRIC VERSE, BUT FROM THE HEART, YOU KNOW?
WE HAVE TO GET READY IF WE'RE GOING--
NO NO. I NEED TO TELL IT TO YOU BEFORE I FORGET.
SIGH OKAY THEN. GO AHEAD.
ALL RIGHT, ALL RIGHT. HERE GOES...
THERE ONCE WAS A MAN FROM MADRAS, WHO STUFFED DYNAMITE UP HIS OLD--
JOKER.
...WAIT, MAYBE THAT'S A DIFFERENT ONE? I REMEMBER. JUST GIVE ME A SECOND HAHA!
COME ON...

"...IT'S TIME TO GO."

BRUCE.

ARE YOU AWAKE? I WANT TO SHOW YOU...

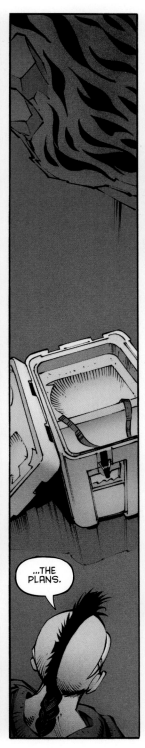

...THE PLANS.

DAMMIT.

GOOD-BYE, BRUCE.

We've had many *adventures* together, he and I.

I've been at his side practically his whole life. Through the bad times, and the good.

This case, like I said, it felt *different* from the start.

We both sensed it. That this one was...stranger. Darker...

But there was no turning back now. It was too late...

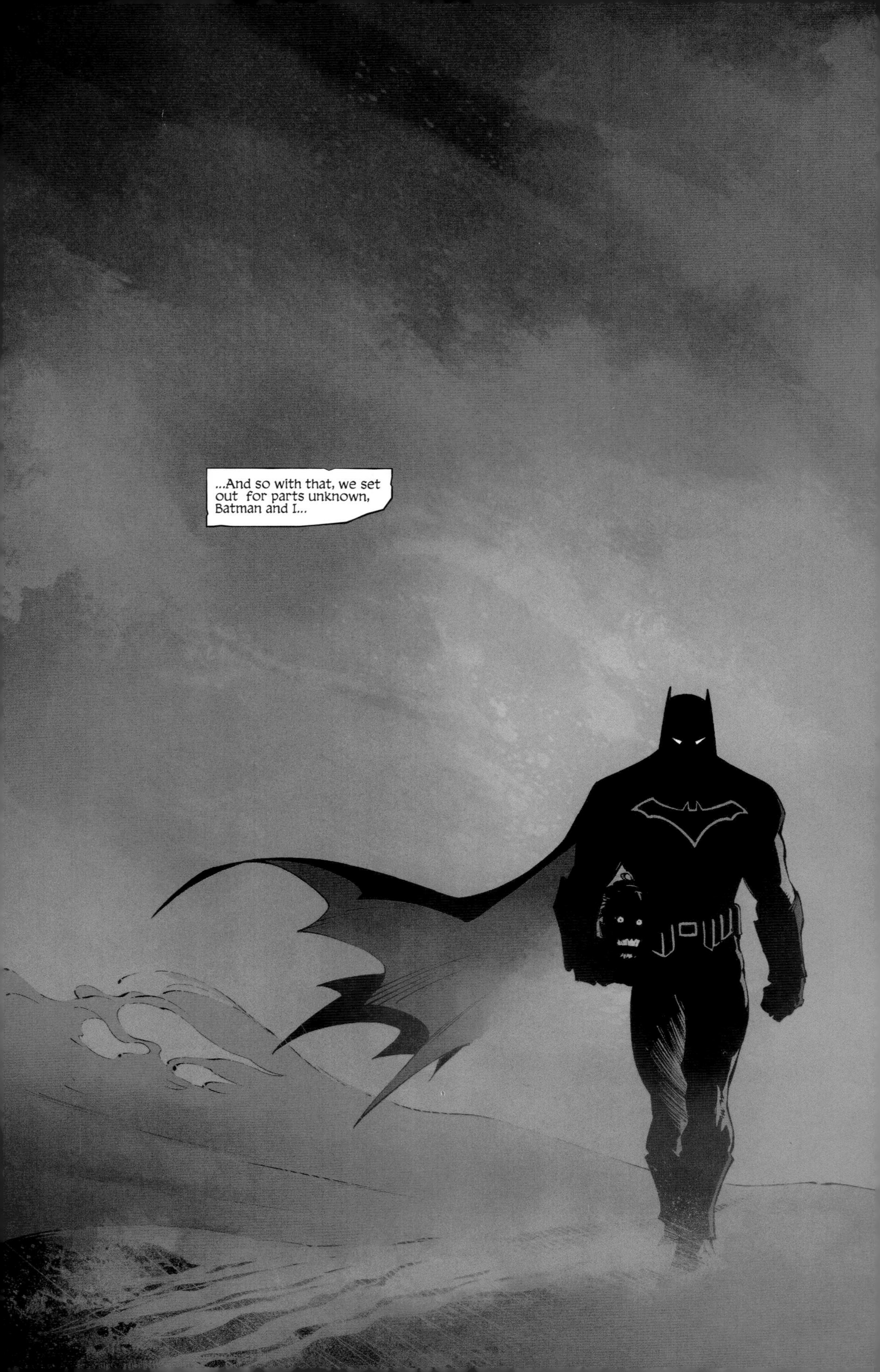
...And so with that, we set out for parts unknown, Batman and I...

"...on one last adventure together..."

PART FIVE:
WHO'S
THERE?

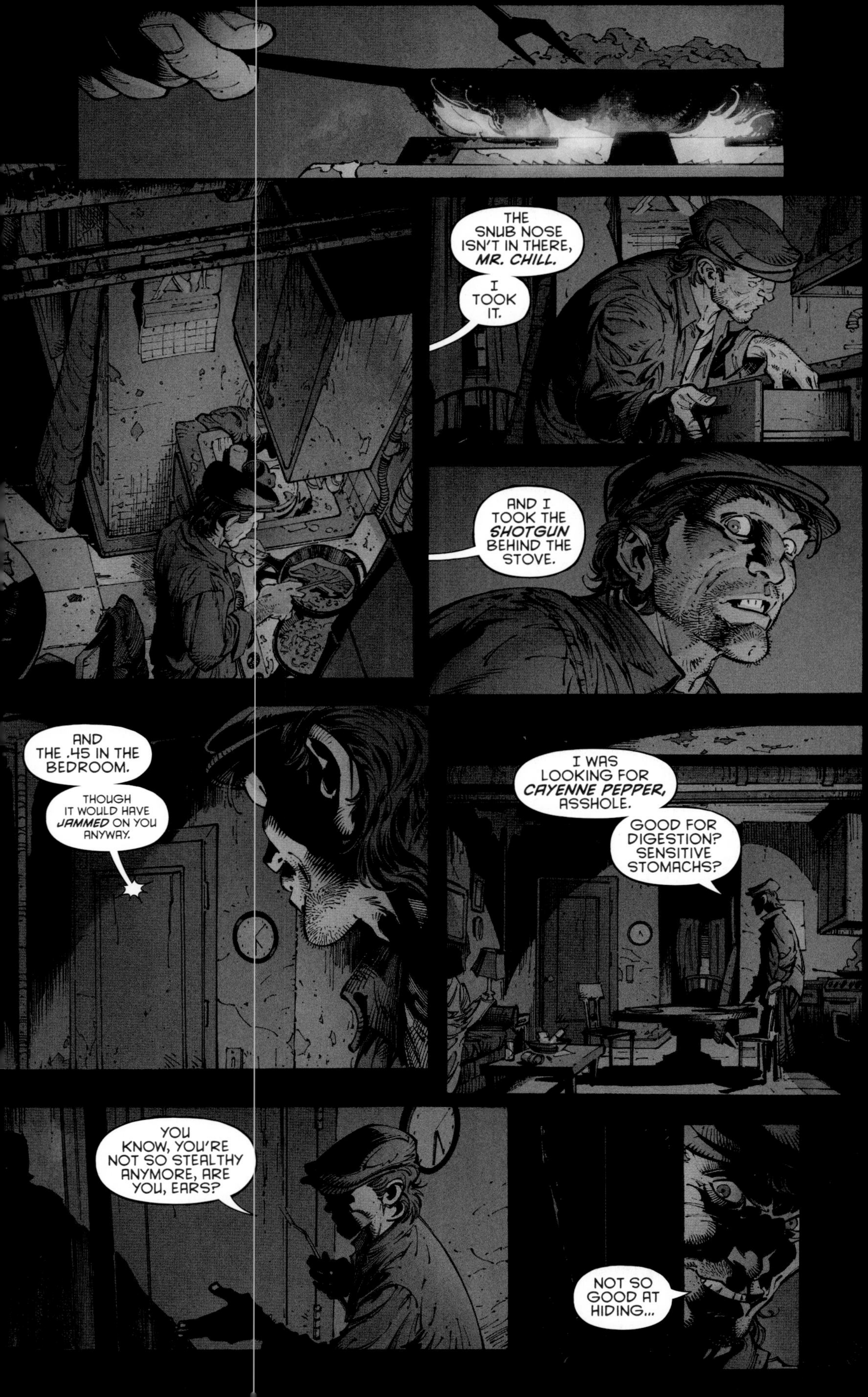
THE SNUB NOSE ISN'T IN THERE, MR. CHILL.
I TOOK IT.
AND I TOOK THE SHOTGUN BEHIND THE STOVE.
AND THE .45 IN THE BEDROOM.
THOUGH IT WOULD HAVE JAMMED ON YOU ANYWAY.
I WAS LOOKING FOR CAYENNE PEPPER, ASSHOLE.
GOOD FOR DIGESTION? SENSITIVE STOMACHS?
YOU KNOW, YOU'RE NOT SO STEALTHY ANYMORE, ARE YOU, EARS?
NOT SO GOOD AT HIDING...

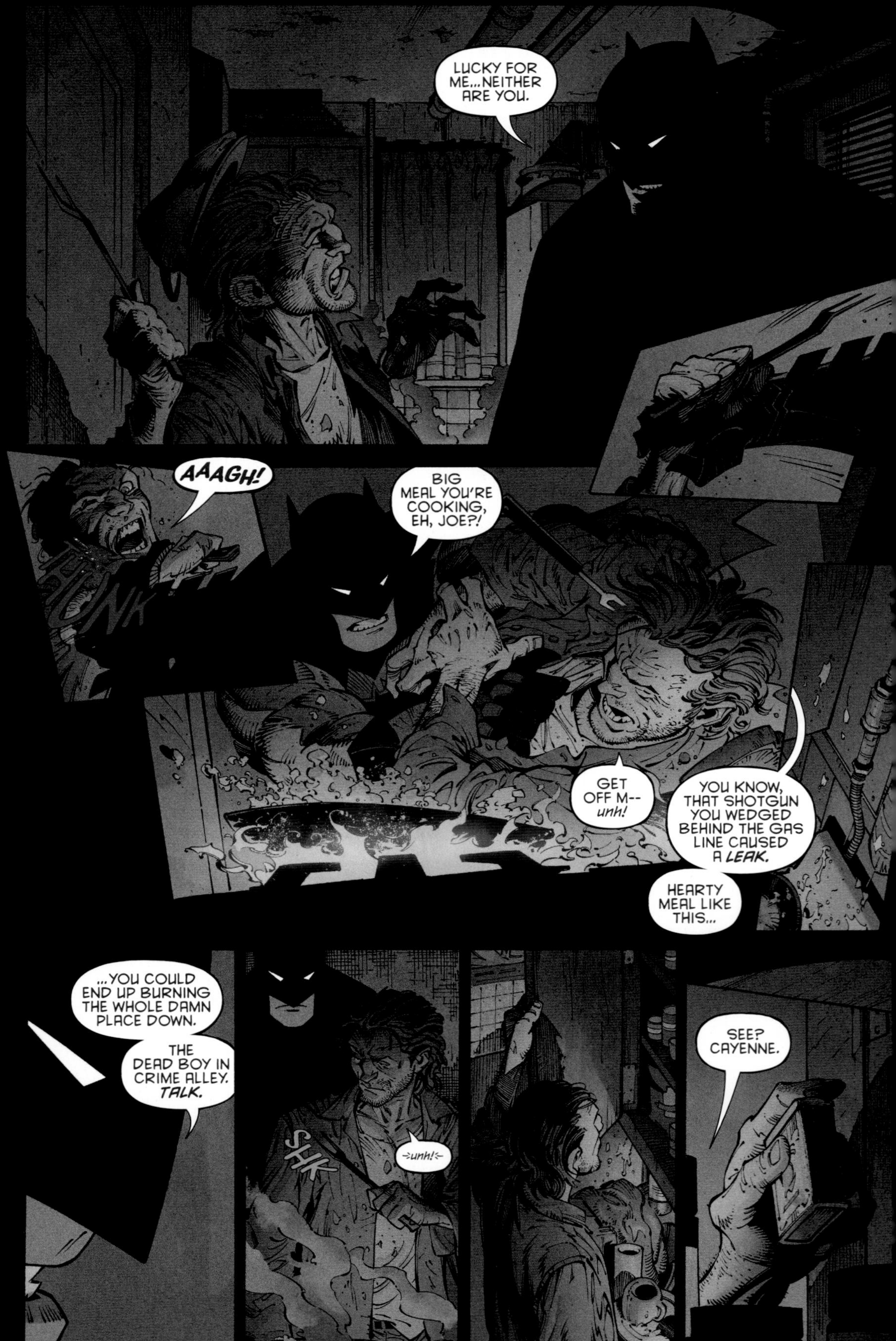

LUCKY FOR ME...NEITHER ARE YOU.
AAAGH!
BIG MEAL YOU'RE COOKING, EH, JOE?!
GET OFF M-- *unh!*
YOU KNOW, THAT SHOTGUN YOU WEDGED BEHIND THE GAS LINE CAUSED A *LEAK.*
HEARTY MEAL LIKE THIS...
...YOU COULD END UP BURNING THE WHOLE DAMN PLACE DOWN.
THE DEAD BOY IN CRIME ALLEY. *TALK.*
SHK
unh!
SEE? CAYENNE.

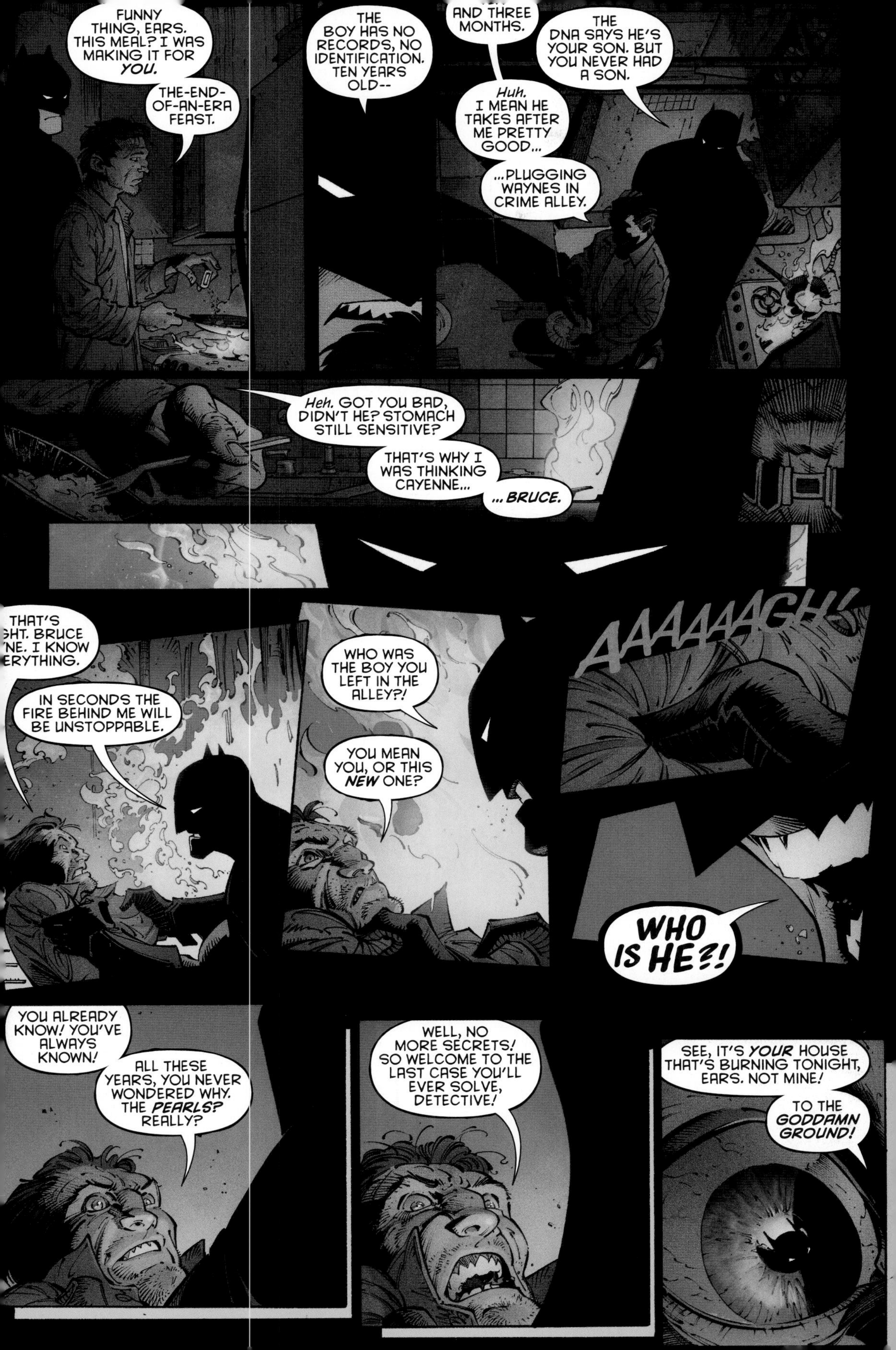
FUNNY THING, EARS. THIS MEAL? I WAS MAKING IT FOR *YOU.*
THE-END-OF-AN-ERA FEAST.
THE BOY HAS NO RECORDS, NO IDENTIFICATION. TEN YEARS OLD--
AND THREE MONTHS.
THE DNA SAYS HE'S YOUR SON. BUT YOU NEVER HAD A SON.
Huh. I MEAN HE TAKES AFTER ME PRETTY GOOD...
...PLUGGING WAYNES IN CRIME ALLEY.
Heh. GOT YOU BAD, DIDN'T HE? STOMACH STILL SENSITIVE?
THAT'S WHY I WAS THINKING CAYENNE...
...BRUCE.
THAT'S GHT. BRUCE NE. I KNOW ERYTHING.
IN SECONDS THE FIRE BEHIND ME WILL BE UNSTOPPABLE.
WHO WAS THE BOY YOU LEFT IN THE ALLEY?!
YOU MEAN YOU, OR THIS *NEW* ONE?
AAAAAAGH!
WHO IS HE?!
YOU ALREADY KNOW! YOU'VE ALWAYS KNOWN!
ALL THESE YEARS, YOU NEVER WONDERED WHY. THE *PEARLS?* REALLY?
WELL, NO MORE SECRETS! SO WELCOME TO THE LAST CASE YOU'LL EVER SOLVE, DETECTIVE!
SEE, IT'S *YOUR* HOUSE THAT'S BURNING TONIGHT, EARS. NOT MINE!
TO THE *GODDAMN GROUND!*

"Knock, knock!"

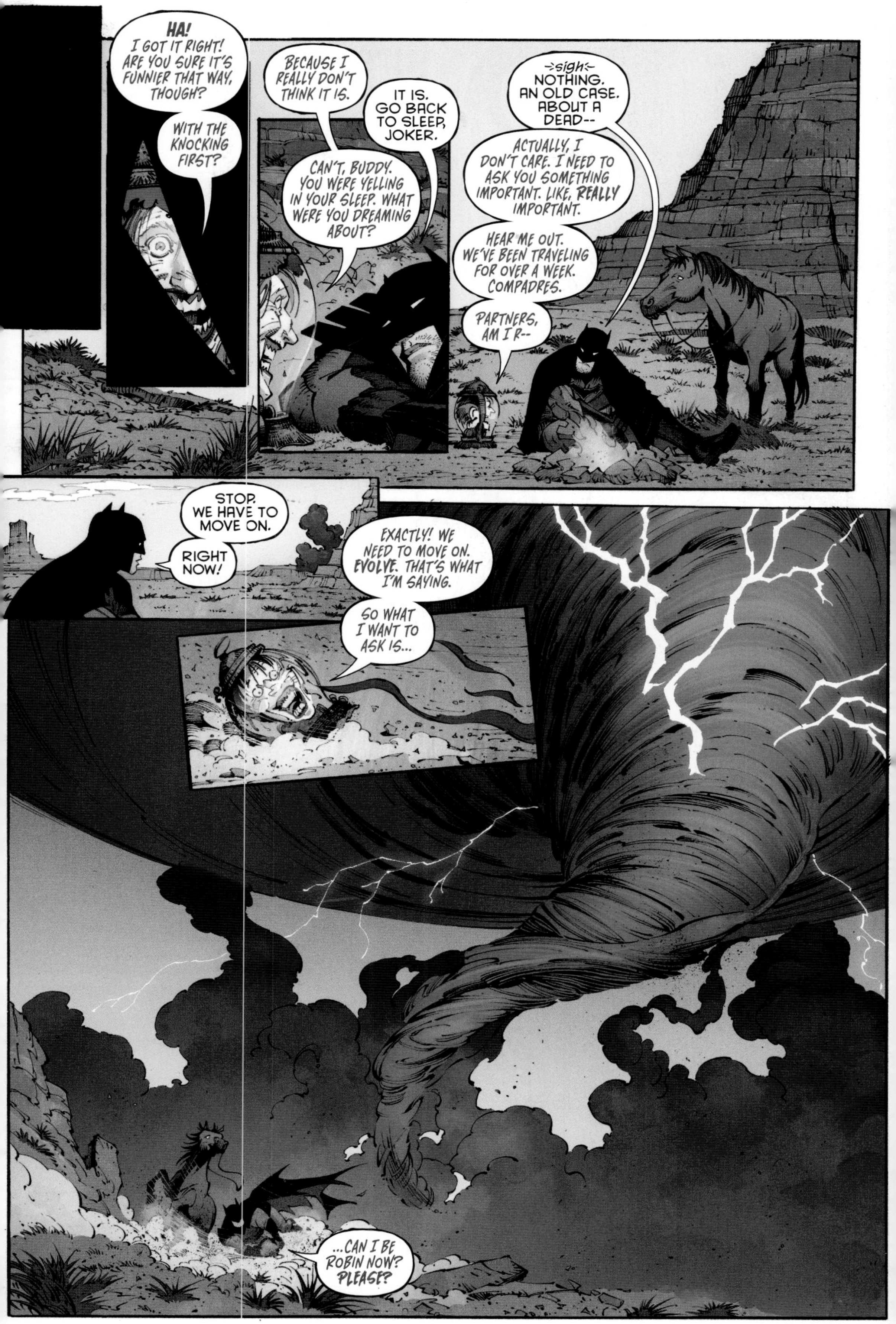
HA! I GOT IT RIGHT! ARE YOU SURE IT'S FUNNIER THAT WAY, THOUGH?
WITH THE KNOCKING FIRST?
BECAUSE I REALLY DON'T THINK IT IS.
IT IS. GO BACK TO SLEEP, JOKER.
CAN'T, BUDDY. YOU WERE YELLING IN YOUR SLEEP. WHAT WERE YOU DREAMING ABOUT?
sigh
NOTHING. AN OLD CASE. ABOUT A DEAD--
ACTUALLY, I DON'T CARE. I NEED TO ASK YOU SOMETHING IMPORTANT. LIKE, REALLY IMPORTANT.
HEAR ME OUT. WE'VE BEEN TRAVELING FOR OVER A WEEK. COMPADRES.
PARTNERS, AM I R--
STOP. WE HAVE TO MOVE ON.
RIGHT NOW!
EXACTLY! WE NEED TO MOVE ON. EVOLVE. THAT'S WHAT I'M SAYING.
SO WHAT I WANT TO ASK IS...
...CAN I BE ROBIN NOW? PLEASE?

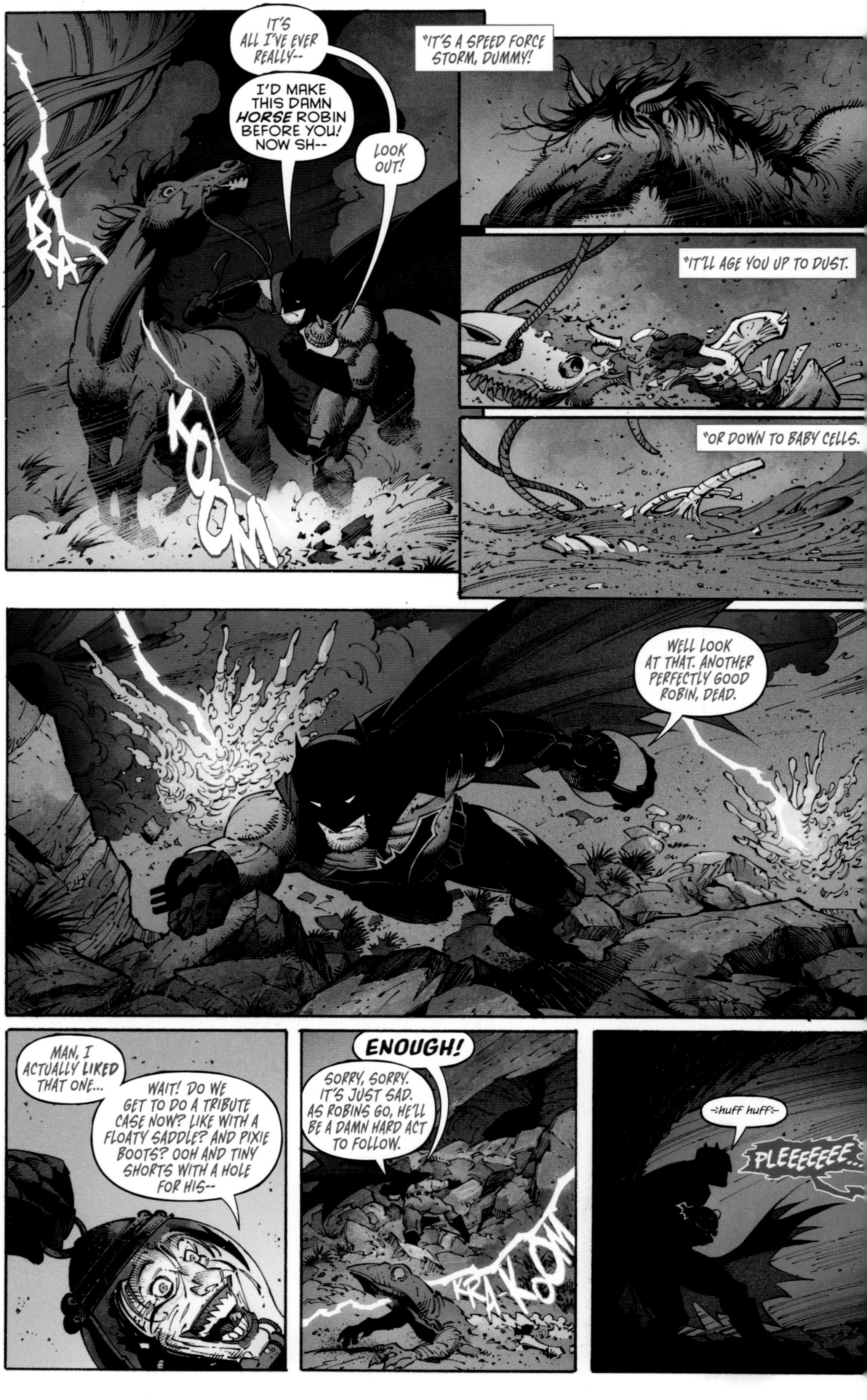
IT'S ALL I'VE EVER REALLY--
I'D MAKE THIS DAMN HORSE ROBIN BEFORE YOU! NOW SH--
LOOK OUT!
KRA-
KOOOM
"IT'S A SPEED FORCE STORM, DUMMY!
"IT'LL AGE YOU UP TO DUST.
"OR DOWN TO BABY CELLS.
WELL LOOK AT THAT. ANOTHER PERFECTLY GOOD ROBIN, DEAD.
MAN, I ACTUALLY LIKED THAT ONE...
WAIT! DO WE GET TO DO A TRIBUTE CASE NOW? LIKE WITH A FLOATY SADDLE? AND PIXIE BOOTS? OOH AND TINY SHORTS WITH A HOLE FOR HIS--
ENOUGH!
SORRY, SORRY. IT'S JUST SAD. AS ROBINS GO, HE'LL BE A DAMN HARD ACT TO FOLLOW.
KRA-KOOM
huff huff
PLEEEEEEE...

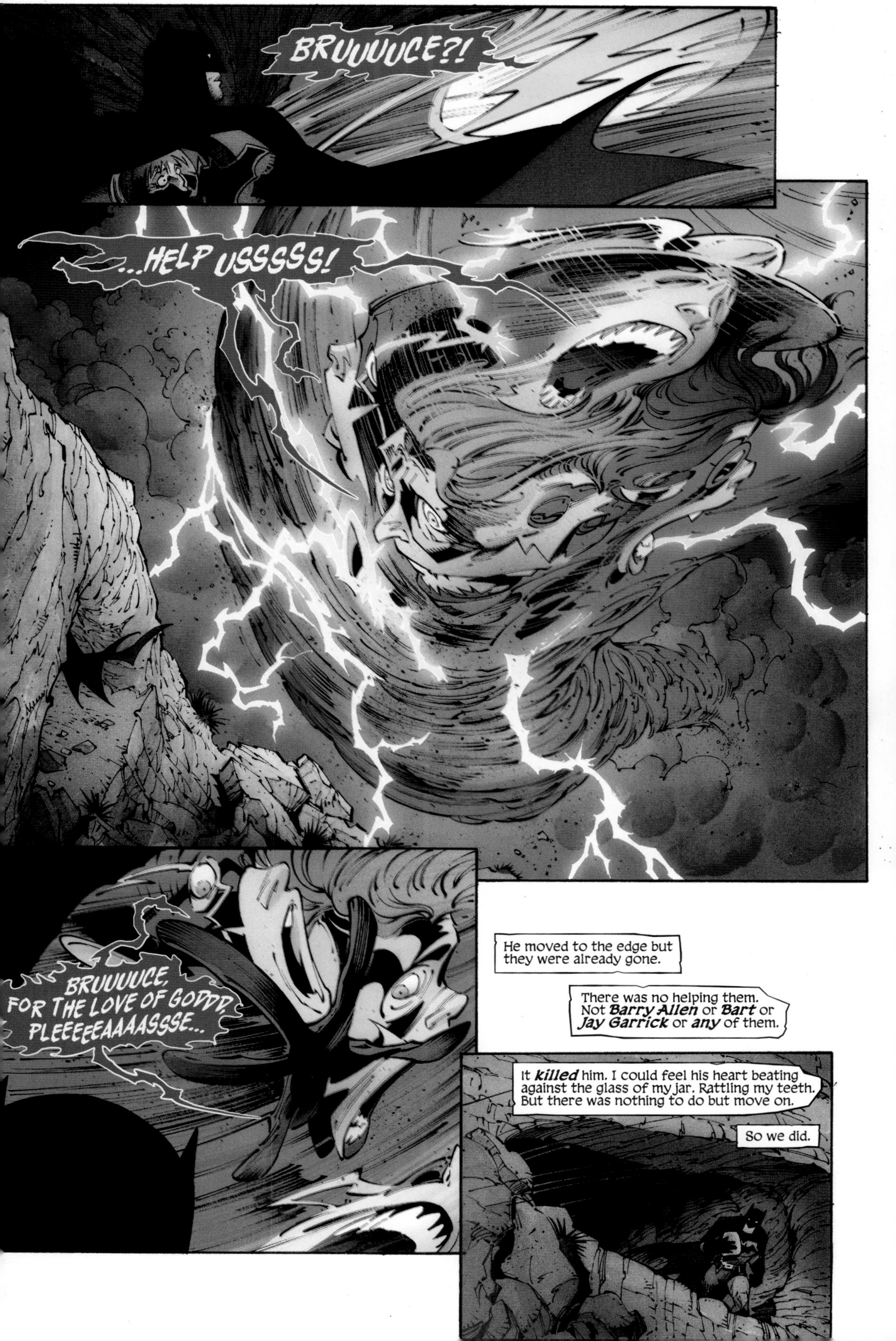
BRUUUUCE?!
...HELP USSSSS!
BRUUUUCE, FOR THE LOVE OF GODDD, PLEEEEEAAAASSSE...
He moved to the edge but they were already gone.
There was no helping them. Not **Barry Allen** or **Bart** or **Jay Garrick** or **any** of them.
It **killed** him. I could feel his heart beating against the glass of my jar. Rattling my teeth. But there was nothing to do but move on.
So we did.

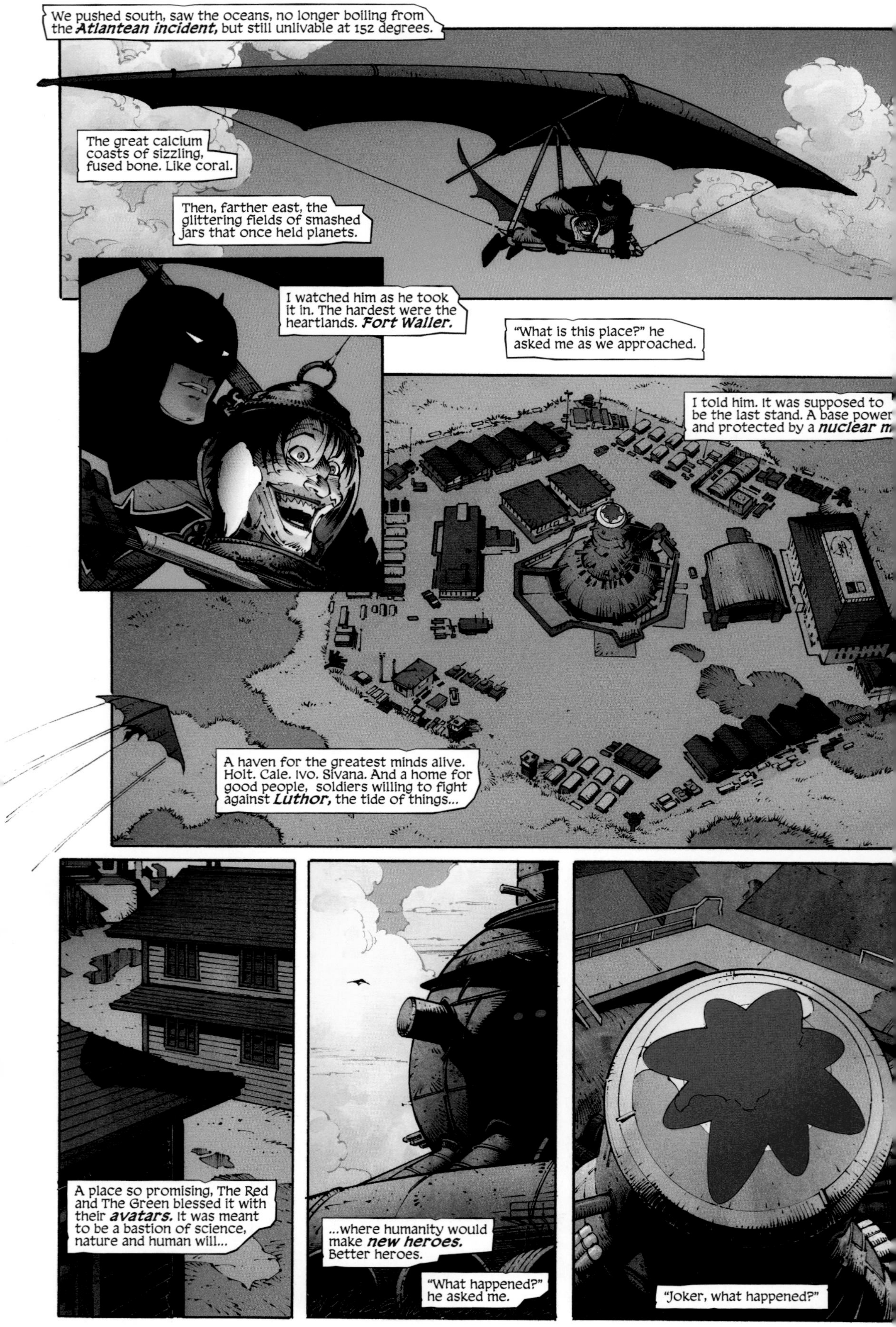
We pushed south, saw the oceans, no longer boiling from the Atlantean incident, but still unlivable at 152 degrees.
The great calcium coasts of sizzling, fused bone. Like coral.
Then, farther east, the glittering fields of smashed jars that once held planets.
I watched him as he took it in. The hardest were the heartlands. Fort Waller.
"What is this place?" he asked me as we approached.
I told him. It was supposed to be the last stand. A base power and protected by a nuclear
A haven for the greatest minds alive. Holt. Cale. Ivo. Sivana. And a home for good people, soldiers willing to fight against Luthor, the tide of things...
A place so promising, The Red and The Green blessed it with their avatars. It was meant to be a bastion of science, nature and human will...
...where humanity would make new heroes. Better heroes.
"What happened?" he asked me.
"Joker, what happened?"

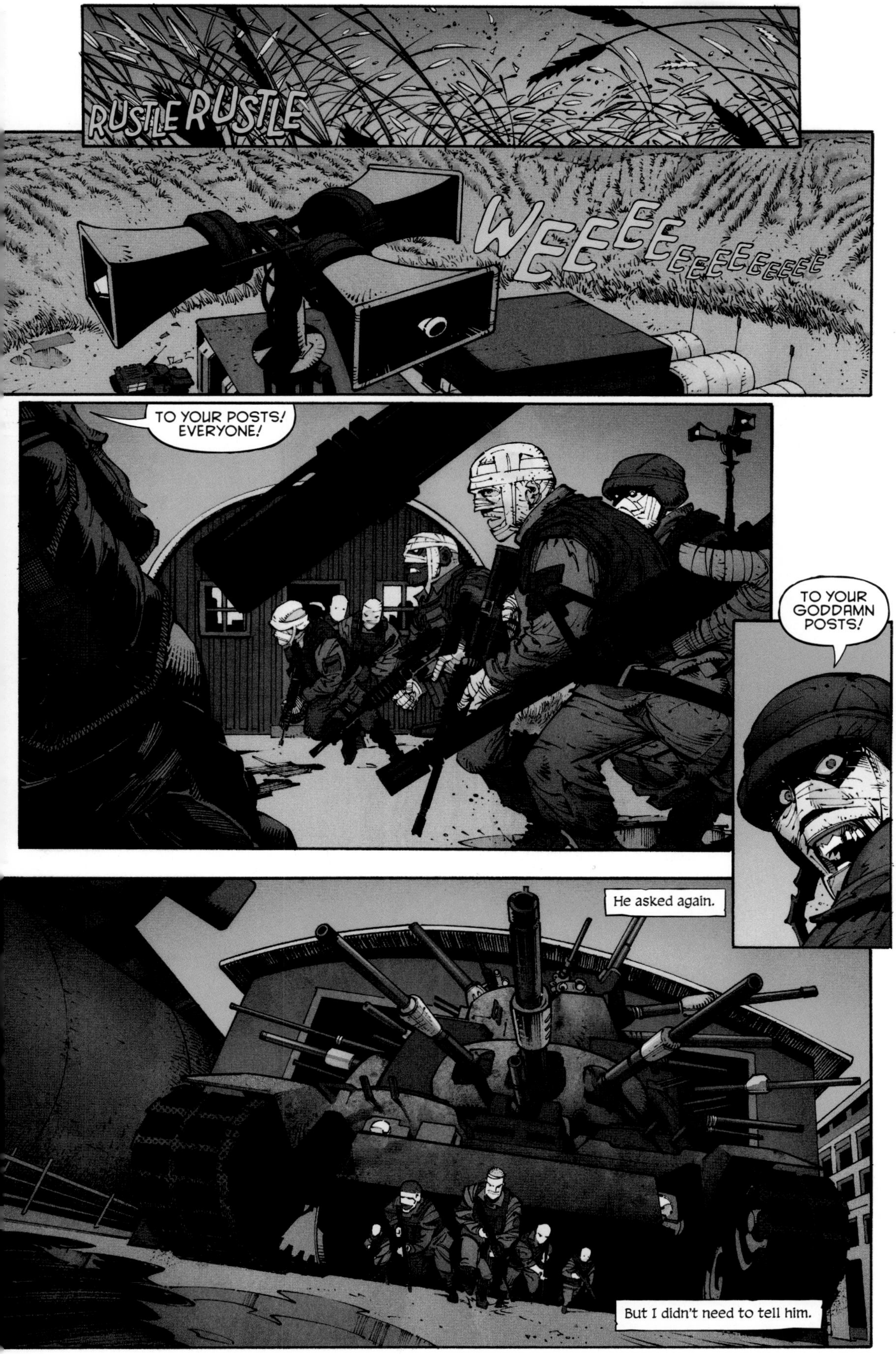
RUSTLE RUSTLE
WEEEEEEEEEEEEE
TO YOUR POSTS! EVERYONE!
TO YOUR GODDAMN POSTS!
He asked again.
But I didn't need to tell him.

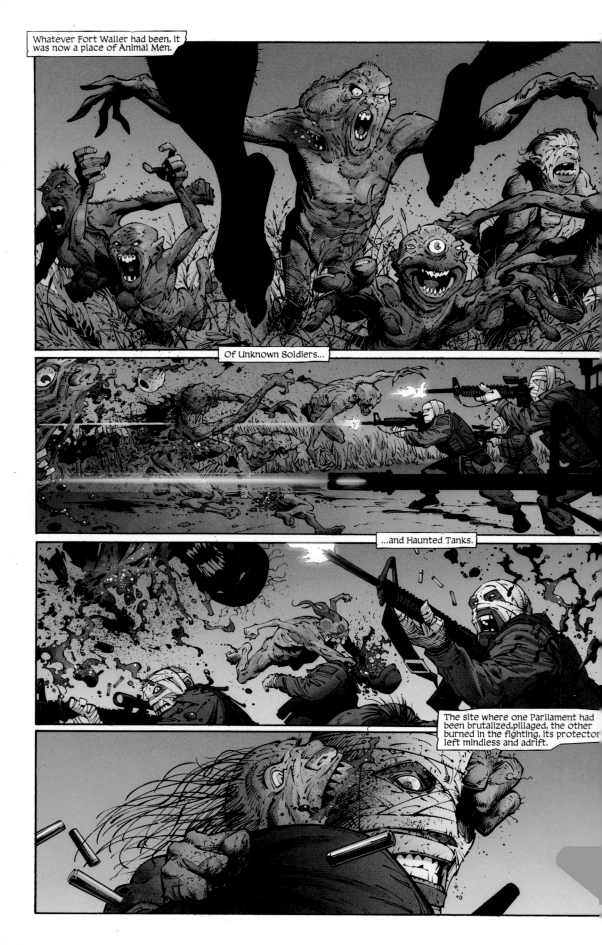

Whatever Fort Waller had been, it was now a place of Animal Men.

Of Unknown Soldiers...

...and Haunted Tanks.

The site where one Parliament had been brutalized, pillaged, the other burned in the fighting, its protector left mindless and adrift.

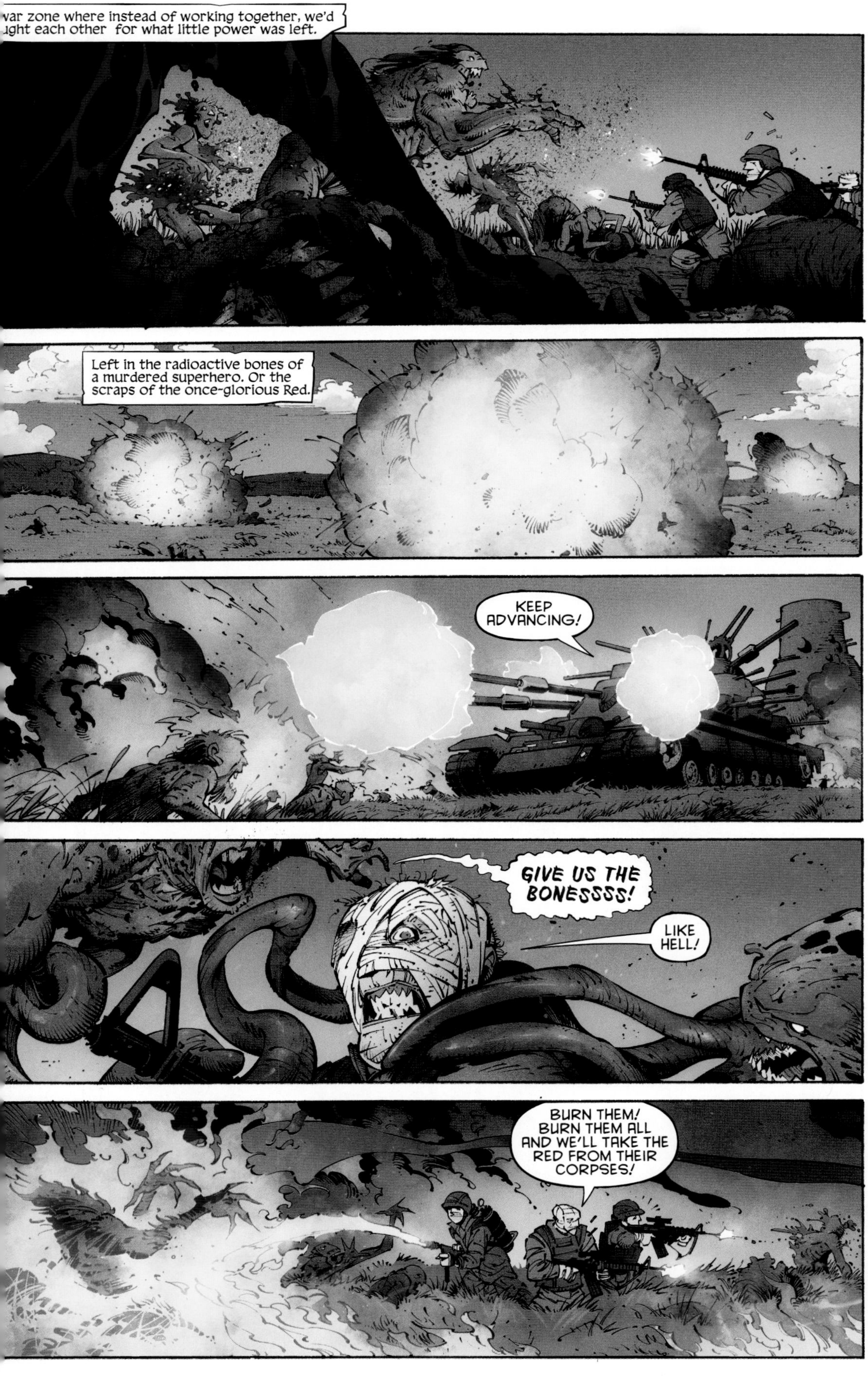

...var zone where instead of working together, we'd ...ught each other for what little power was left.
Left in the radioactive bones of a murdered superhero. Or the scraps of the once-glorious Red.
KEEP ADVANCING!
GIVE US THE BONESSSS!
LIKE HELL!
BURN THEM! BURN THEM ALL AND WE'LL TAKE THE RED FROM THEIR CORPSES!

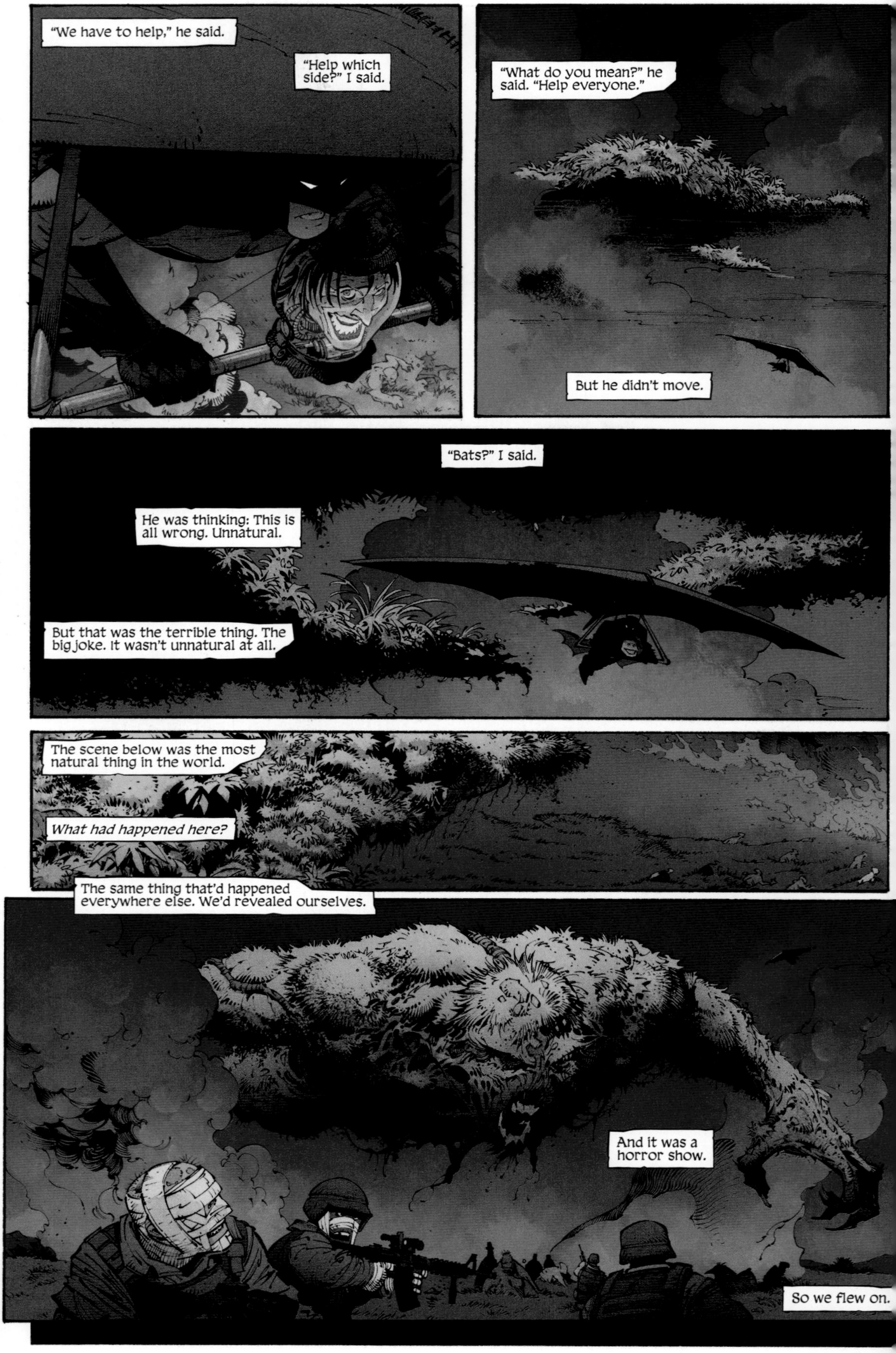
"We have to help," he said.
"Help which side?" I said.
"What do you mean?" he said. "Help everyone."
But he didn't move.
"Bats?" I said.
He was thinking: This is all wrong. Unnatural.
But that was the terrible thing. The big joke. It wasn't unnatural at all.
The scene below was the most natural thing in the world.
What had happened here?
The same thing that'd happened everywhere else. We'd revealed ourselves.
And it was a horror show.
So we flew on.

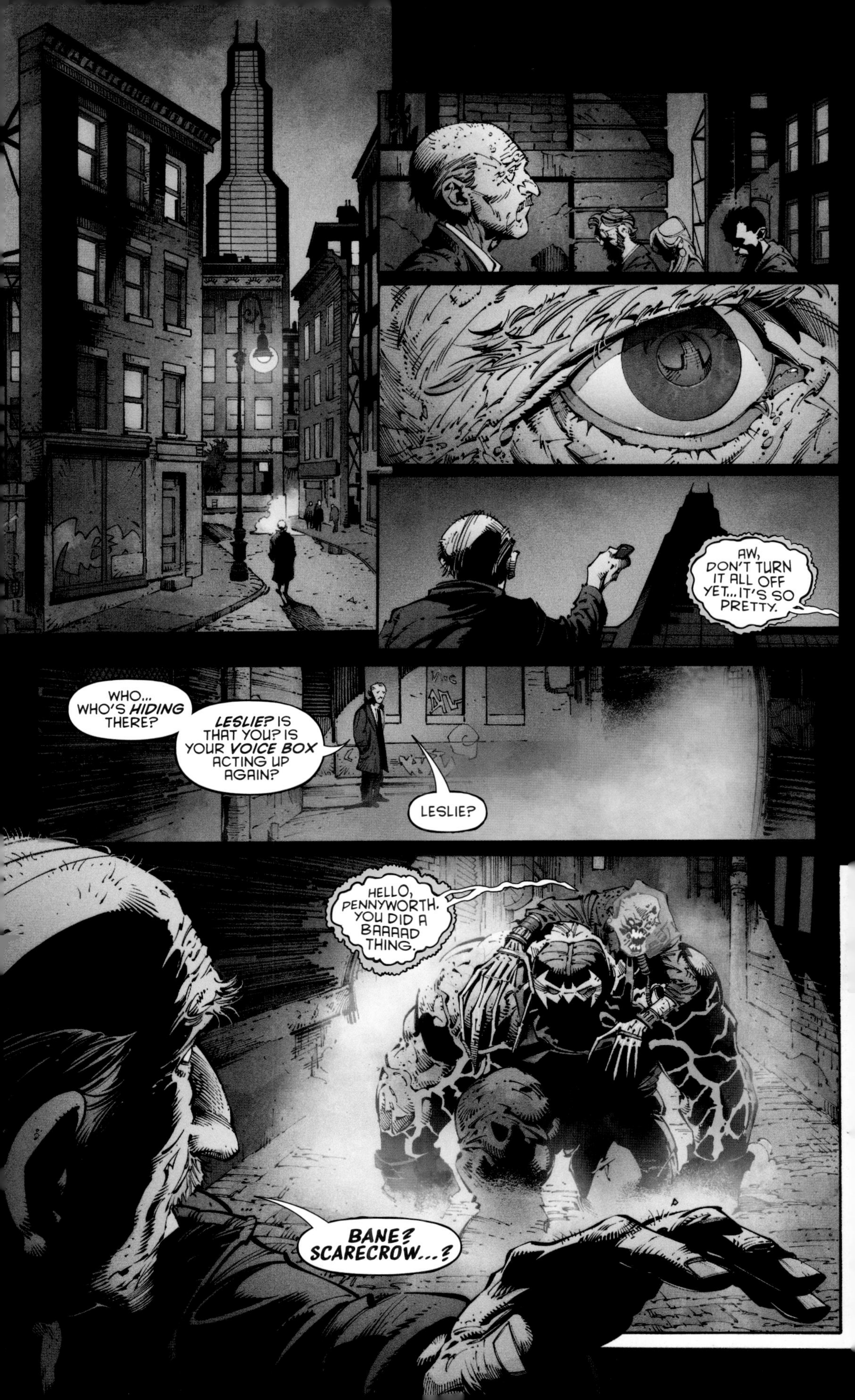
AW, DON'T TURN IT ALL OFF YET...IT'S SO PRETTY.
WHO... WHO'S HIDING THERE?
LESLIE? IS THAT YOU? IS YOUR VOICE BOX ACTING UP AGAIN?
LESLIE?
HELLO, PENNYWORTH. YOU DID A BAAAAD THING.
BANE? SCARECROW...?

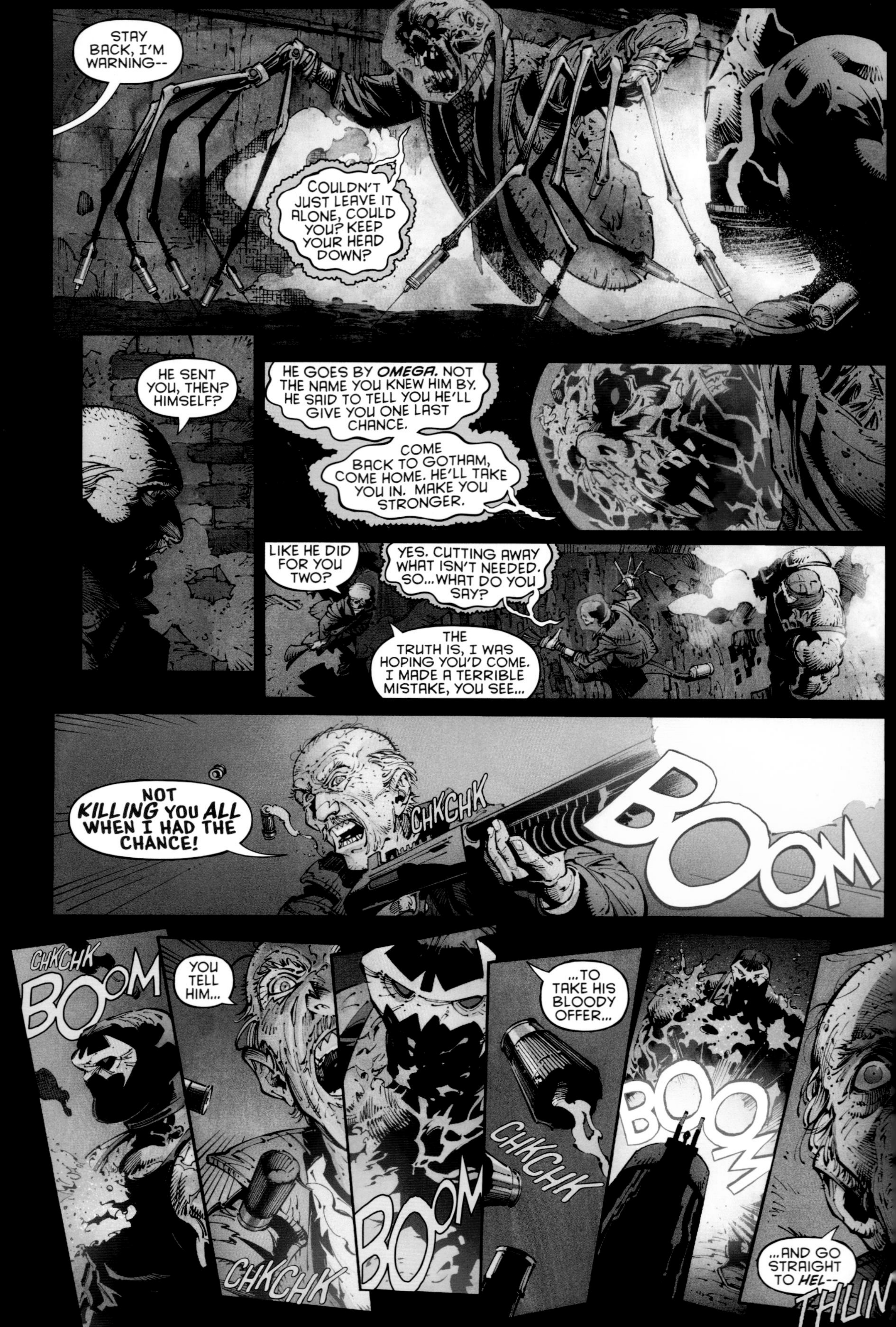
STAY BACK, I'M WARNING--
COULDN'T JUST LEAVE IT ALONE, COULD YOU? KEEP YOUR HEAD DOWN?
HE SENT YOU, THEN? HIMSELF?
HE GOES BY OMEGA. NOT THE NAME YOU KNEW HIM BY. HE SAID TO TELL YOU HE'LL GIVE YOU ONE LAST CHANCE.
COME BACK TO GOTHAM, COME HOME. HE'LL TAKE YOU IN. MAKE YOU STRONGER.
LIKE HE DID FOR YOU TWO?
YES. CUTTING AWAY WHAT ISN'T NEEDED. SO...WHAT DO YOU SAY?
THE TRUTH IS, I WAS HOPING YOU'D COME. I MADE A TERRIBLE MISTAKE, YOU SEE...
NOT KILLING YOU ALL WHEN I HAD THE CHANCE!
CHKCHK
BOOM
CHKCHK
BOOM
YOU TELL HIM...
CHKCHK
BOOM
...TO TAKE HIS BLOODY OFFER...
CHKCHK
BOOM
...AND GO STRAIGHT TO HEL--
THUN

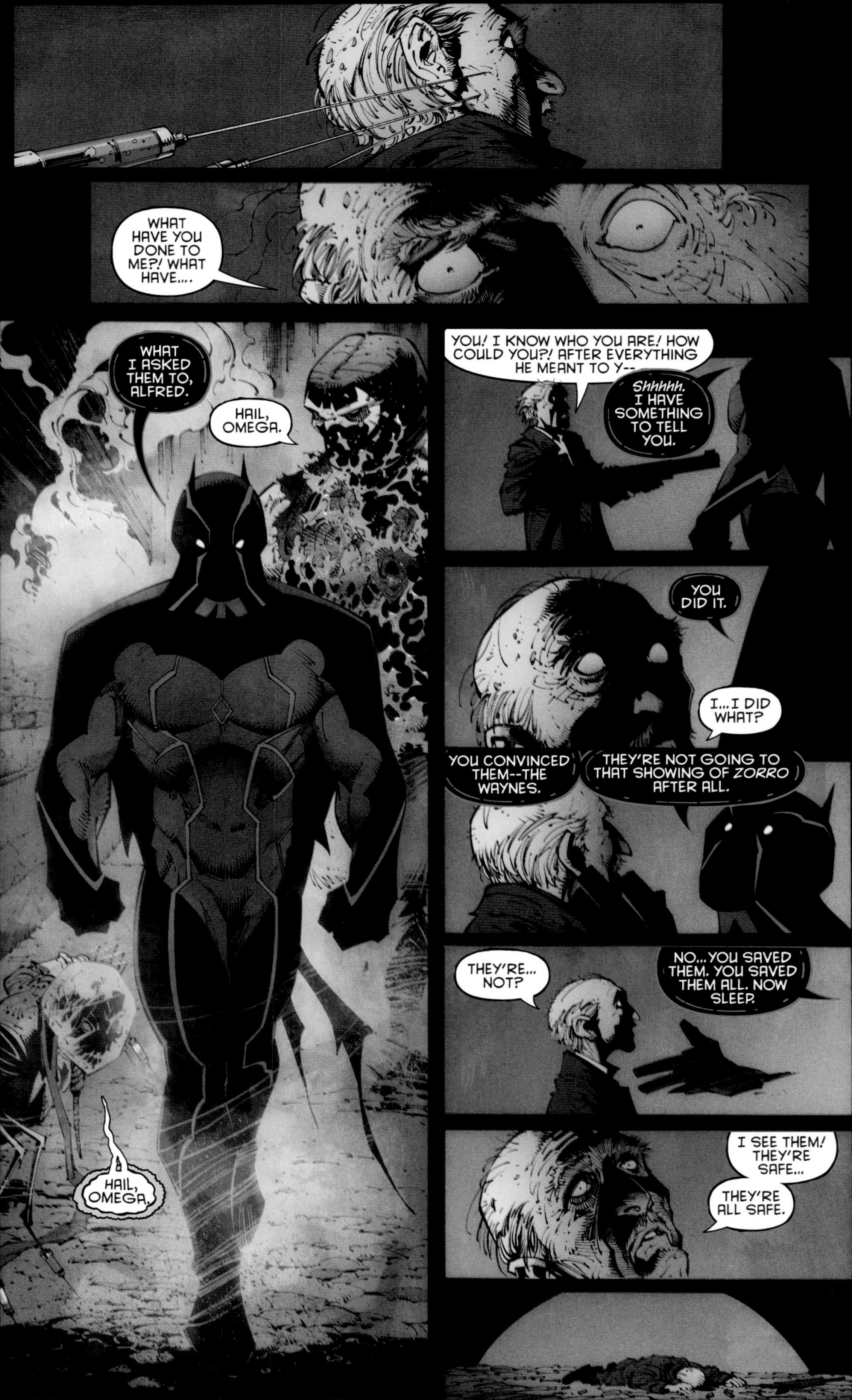

WHAT HAVE YOU DONE TO ME?! WHAT HAVE....
WHAT I ASKED THEM TO, ALFRED.
HAIL, OMEGA.
HAIL, OMEGA.
YOU! I KNOW WHO YOU ARE! HOW COULD YOU?! AFTER EVERYTHING HE MEANT TO Y--
Shhhhh. I HAVE SOMETHING TO TELL YOU.
YOU DID IT.
I...I DID WHAT?
YOU CONVINCED THEM--THE WAYNES.
THEY'RE NOT GOING TO THAT SHOWING OF ZORRO AFTER ALL.
THEY'RE... NOT?
NO...YOU SAVED THEM. YOU SAVED THEM ALL. NOW SLEEP.
I SEE THEM! THEY'RE SAFE...
THEY'RE ALL SAFE.

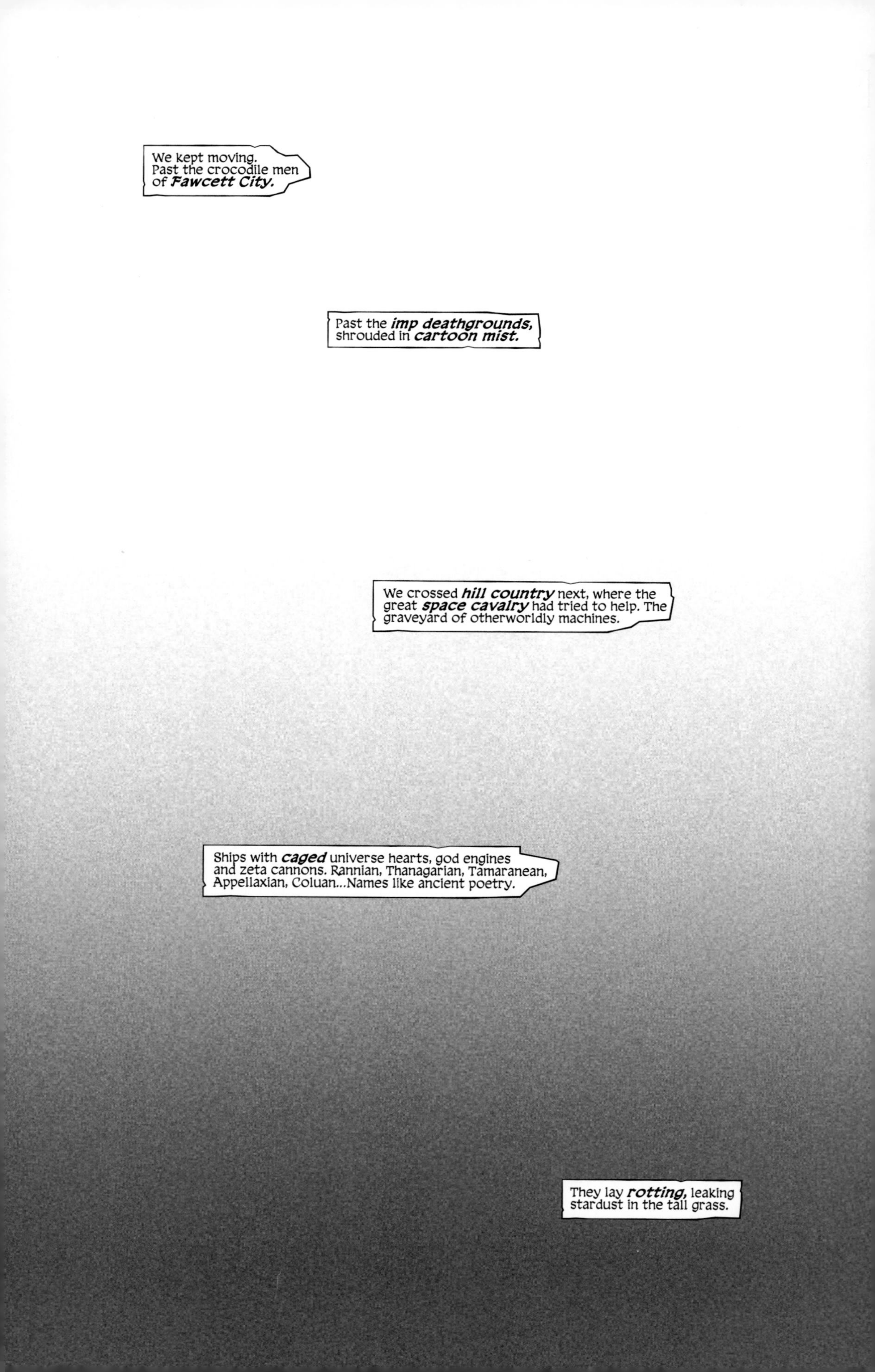
We kept moving. Past the crocodile men of ***Fawcett City.***
Past the ***imp deathgrounds,*** shrouded in ***cartoon mist.***
We crossed ***hill country*** next, where the great ***space cavalry*** had tried to help. The graveyard of otherworldly machines.
Ships with ***caged*** universe hearts, god engines and zeta cannons. Rannian, Thanagarian, Tamaranean, Appellaxian, Coluan...Names like ancient poetry.
They lay ***rotting,*** leaking stardust in the tall grass.

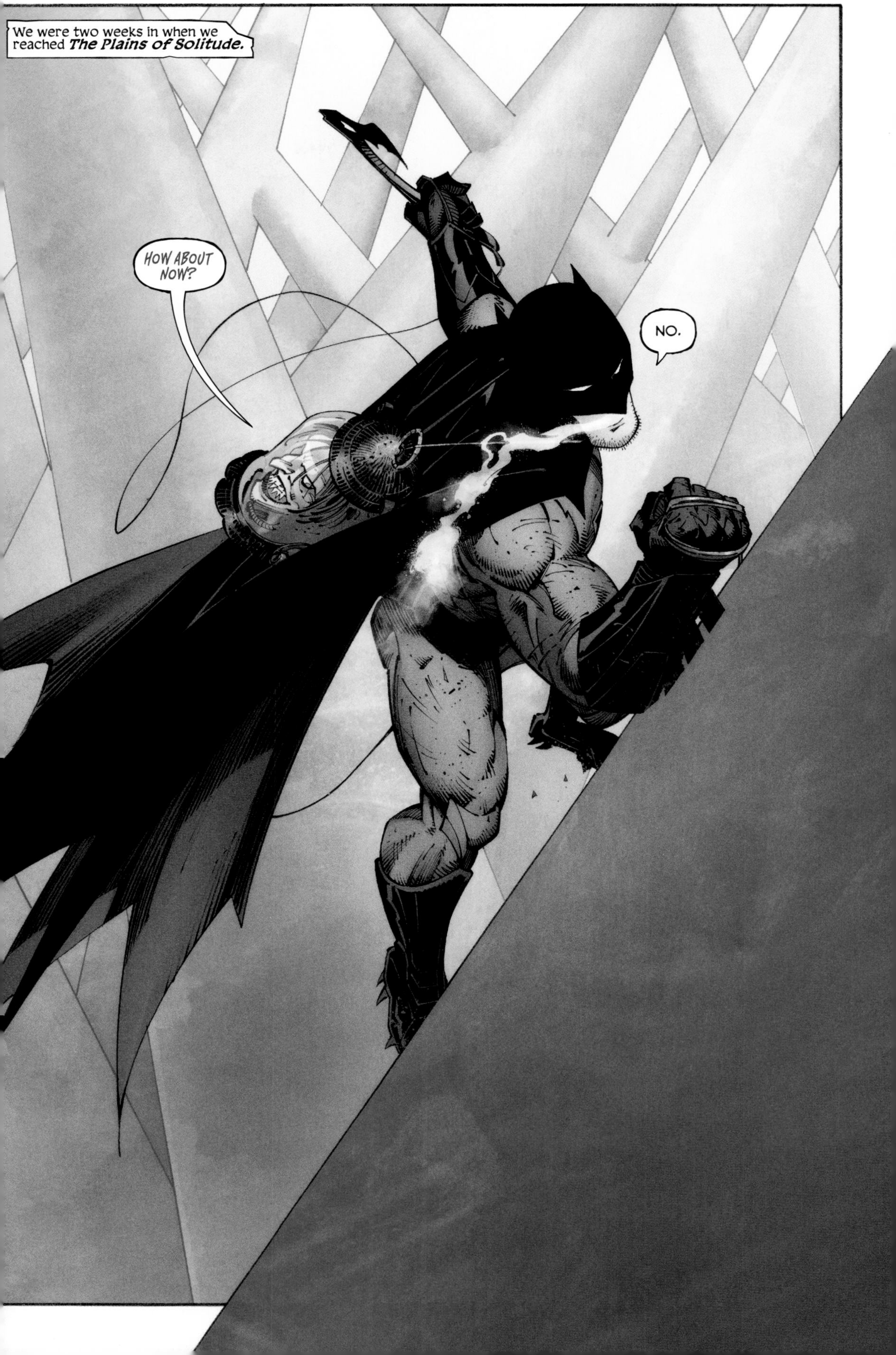
We were two weeks in when we reached *The Plains of Solitude.*
HOW ABOUT NOW?
NO.

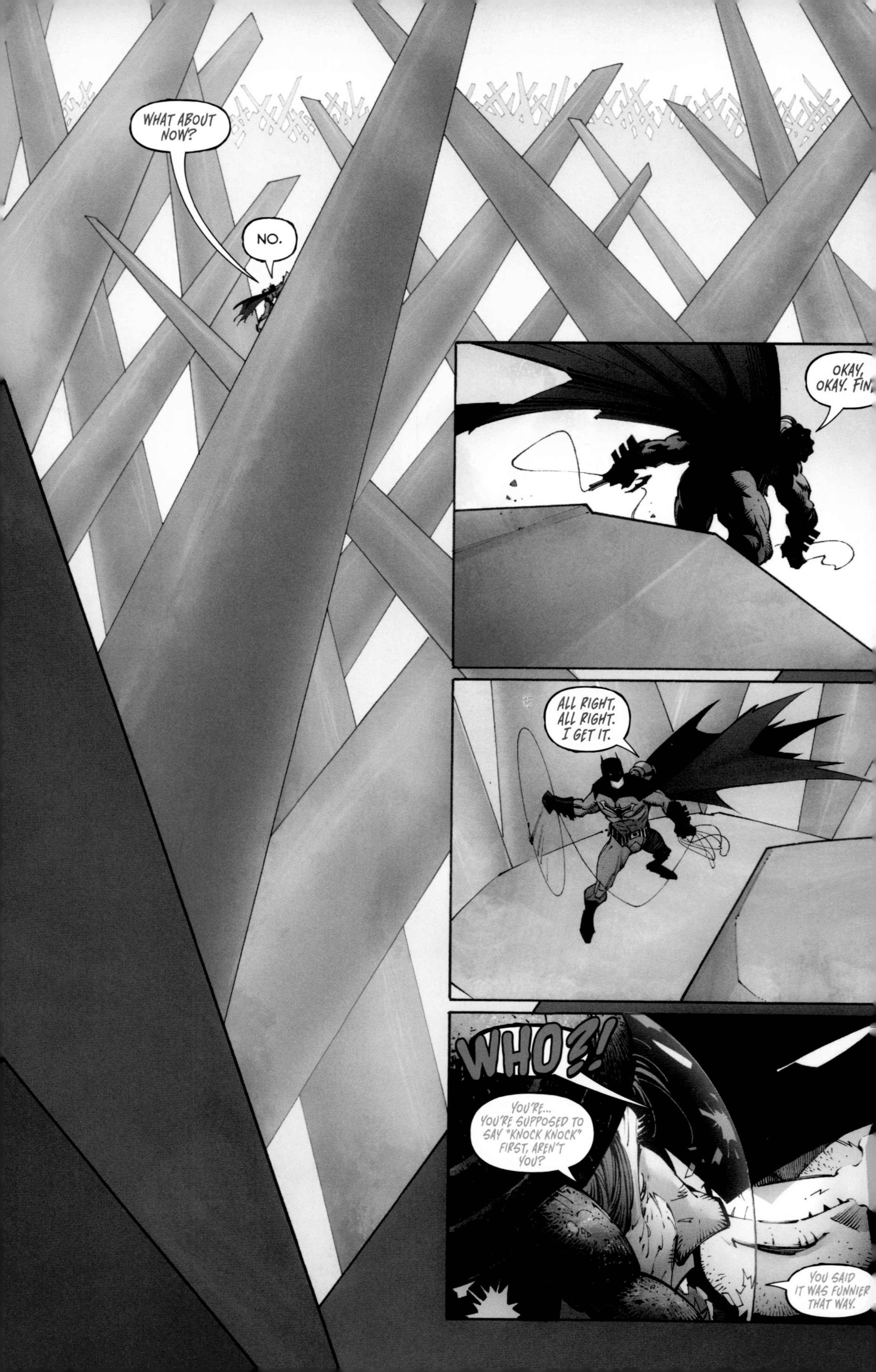
WHAT ABOUT NOW?
NO.
OKAY, OKAY. FIN
ALL RIGHT, ALL RIGHT. I GET IT.
WHO?!
YOU'RE... YOU'RE SUPPOSED TO SAY "KNOCK KNOCK" FIRST, AREN'T YOU?
YOU SAID IT WAS FUNNIER THAT WAY.

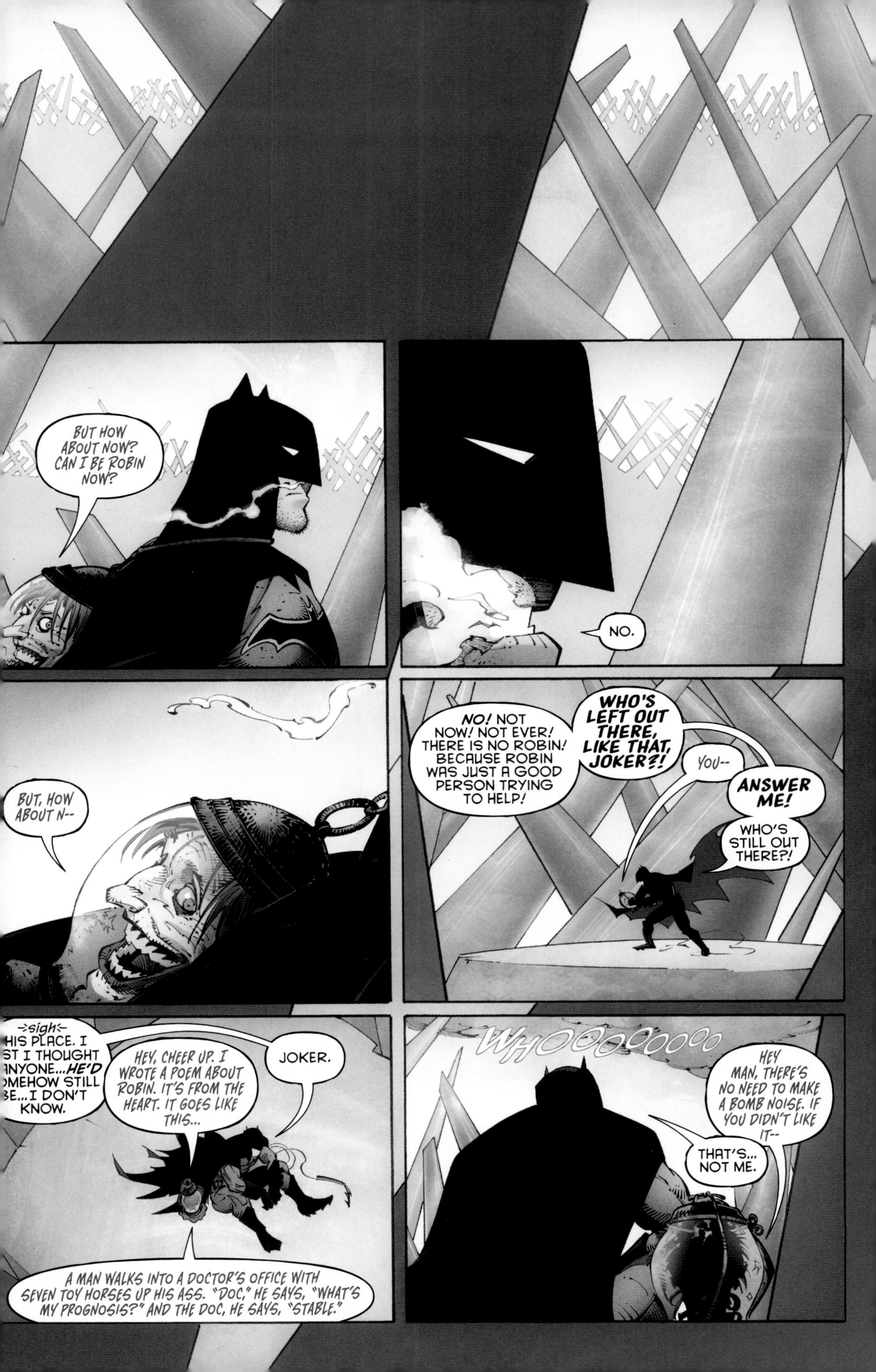
BUT HOW ABOUT NOW? CAN I BE ROBIN NOW?
NO.
BUT, HOW ABOUT N--
NO! NOT NOW! NOT EVER! THERE IS NO ROBIN! BECAUSE ROBIN WAS JUST A GOOD PERSON TRYING TO HELP!
WHO'S LEFT OUT THERE, LIKE THAT, JOKER?!
YOU--
ANSWER ME!
WHO'S STILL OUT THERE?!
-sigh-
HIS PLACE. I ST I THOUGHT NYONE...HE'D OMEHOW STILL BE...I DON'T KNOW.
JOKER.
HEY, CHEER UP. I WROTE A POEM ABOUT ROBIN. IT'S FROM THE HEART. IT GOES LIKE THIS...
A MAN WALKS INTO A DOCTOR'S OFFICE WITH SEVEN TOY HORSES UP HIS ASS. "DOC," HE SAYS, "WHAT'S MY PROGNOSIS?" AND THE DOC, HE SAYS, "STABLE."
WHOOOOOOOOO
HEY MAN, THERE'S NO NEED TO MAKE A BOMB NOISE. IF YOU DIDN'T LIKE IT--
THAT'S... NOT ME.

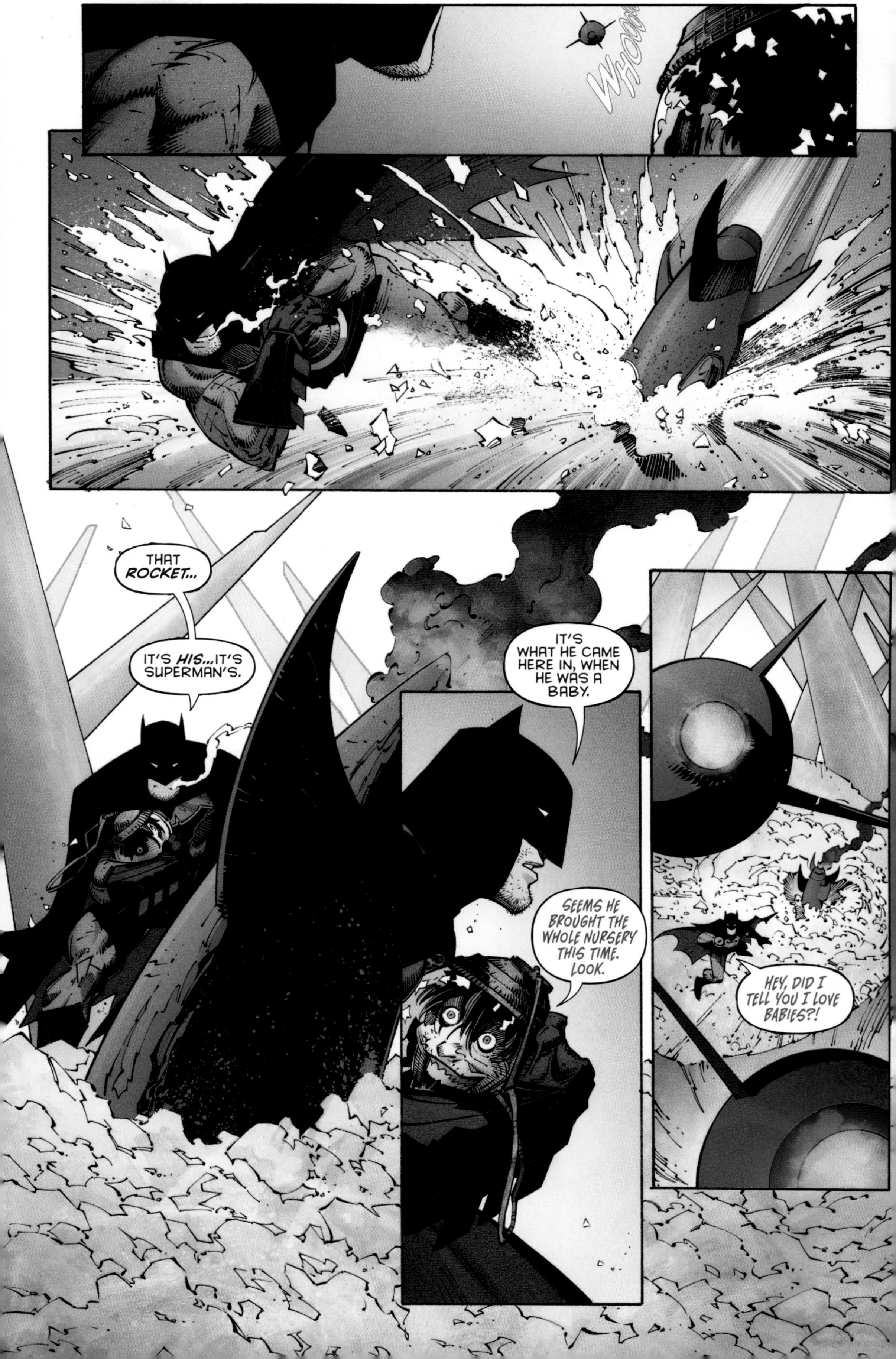
WHOOOM
THAT ROCKET...
IT'S HIS...IT'S SUPERMAN'S.
IT'S WHAT HE CAME HERE IN, WHEN HE WAS A BABY.
SEEMS HE BROUGHT THE WHOLE NURSERY THIS TIME. LOOK.
HEY, DID I TELL YOU I LOVE BABIES?!

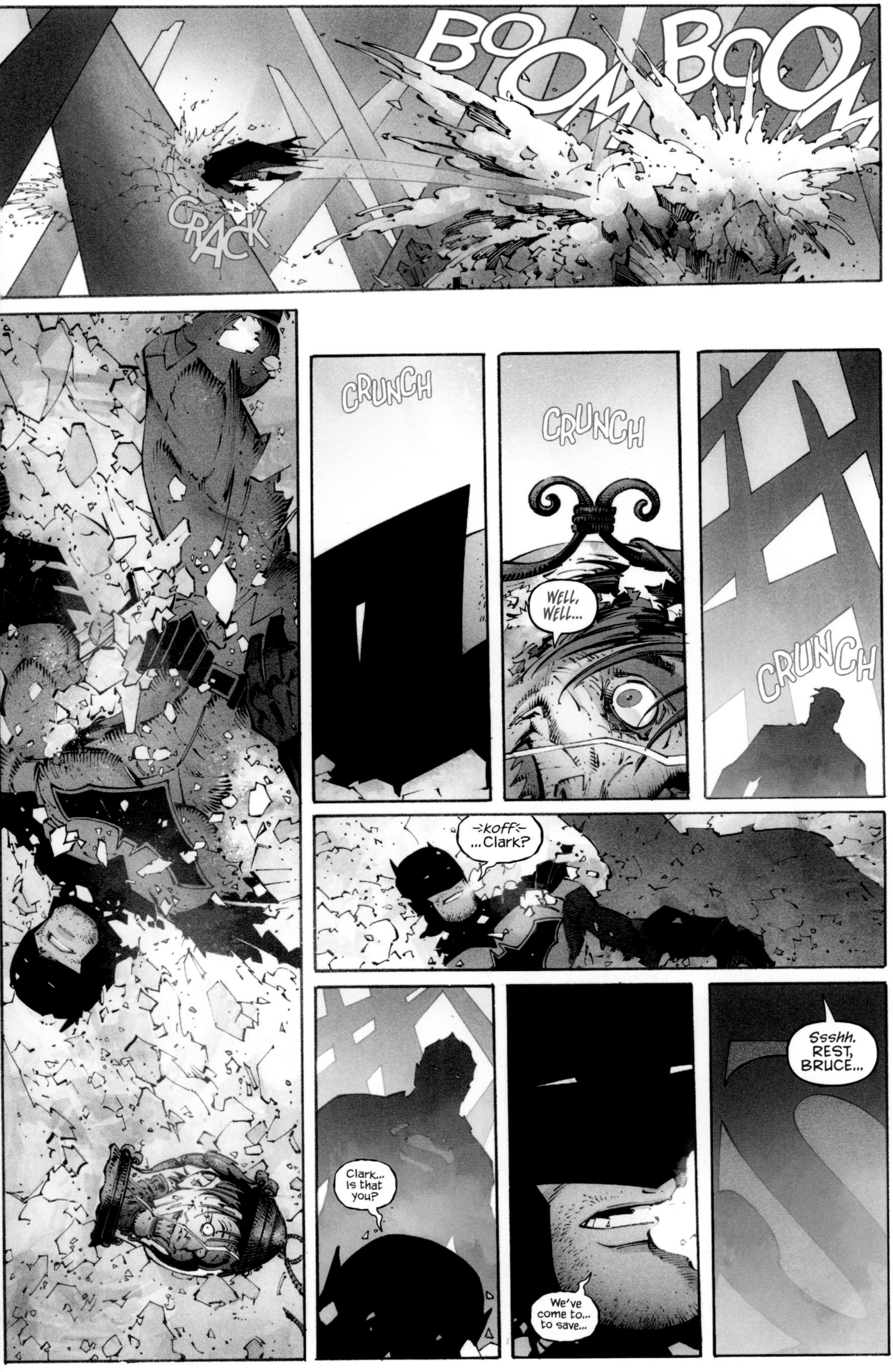
BOOM BOOM
CRACK
CRUNCH
CRUNCH
WELL, WELL...
CRUNCH
-koff- ...Clark?
Clark... Is that you?
We've come to... to save...
Ssshh. REST, BRUCE...

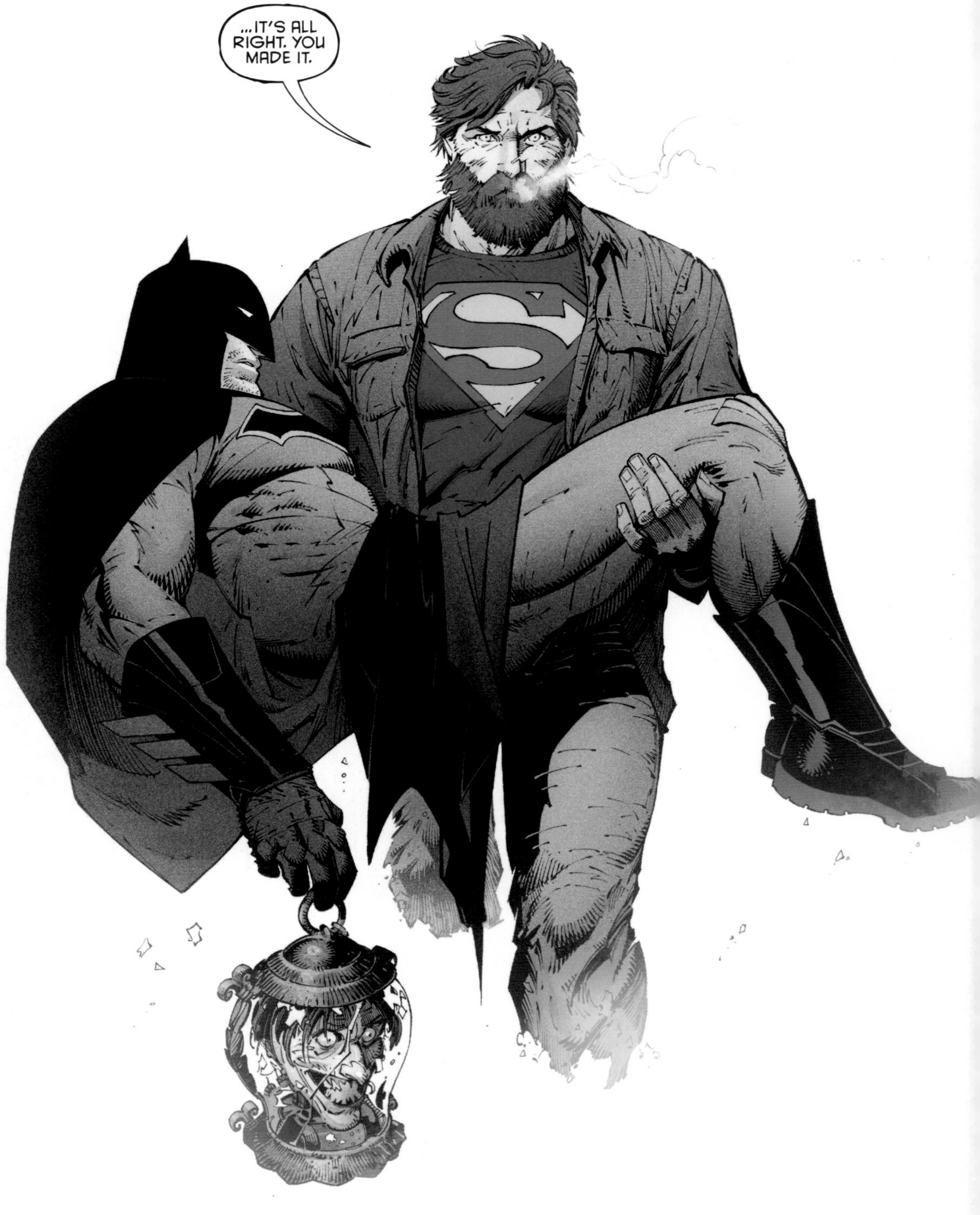
...IT'S ALL RIGHT. YOU MADE IT.

PART SIX:
THE
MIRACLE

I ASKED YOU A **QUESTION!**

WHY ARE YOU HIDING IN SOME **CAVE** UNDER TONS OF CRYSTAL WHILE THE WORLD FALLS APART?

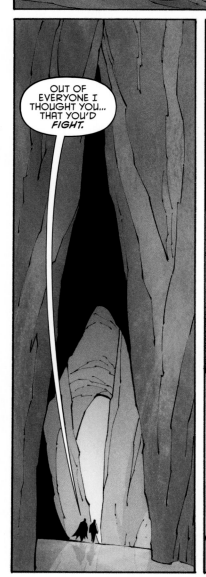

OUT OF EVERYONE I THOUGHT YOU... THAT YOU'D **FIGHT.**

TALK TO ME, DAMMIT!

WHAT IS THIS PLACE?!

HOME.

TAKE A LOOK.

THE FARM? I... I DON'T UNDERSTAND.

THIS WAY.

YOU DUG ALL THIS OUT?

YOU'VE JUST... BEEN *DOWN* HERE?

I SAID THIS WAY.

NO. WHAT'S GOING ON?!

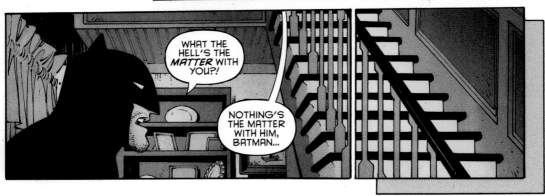

WHAT THE HELL'S THE *MATTER* WITH YOU?!

NOTHING'S THE MATTER WITH HIM, BATMAN...

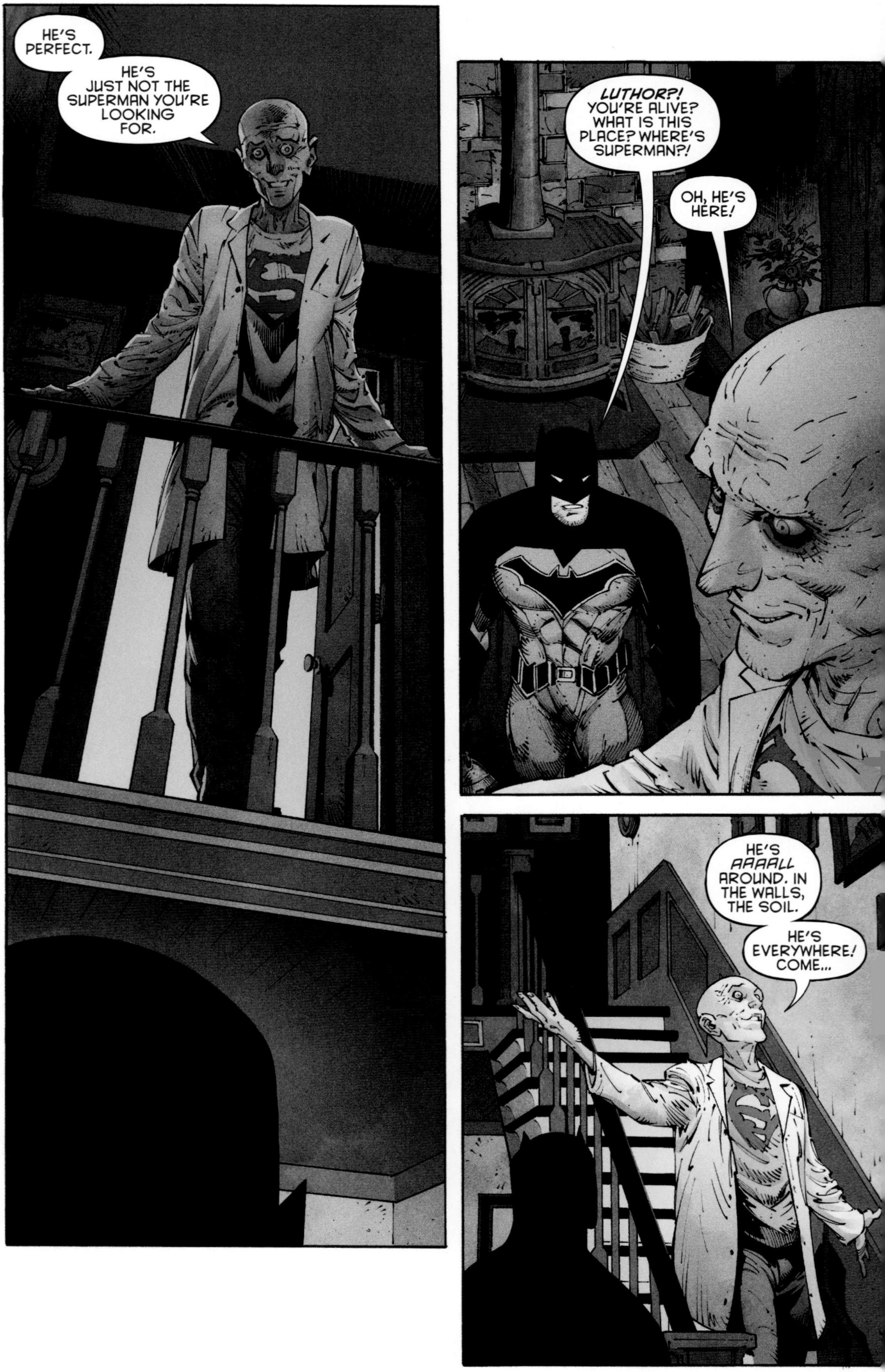
HE'S PERFECT.
HE'S JUST NOT THE SUPERMAN YOU'RE LOOKING FOR.
LUTHOR?! YOU'RE ALIVE? WHAT IS THIS PLACE? WHERE'S SUPERMAN?!
OH, HE'S HERE!
HE'S AAAALL AROUND. IN THE WALLS, THE SOIL.
HE'S EVERYWHERE! COME...

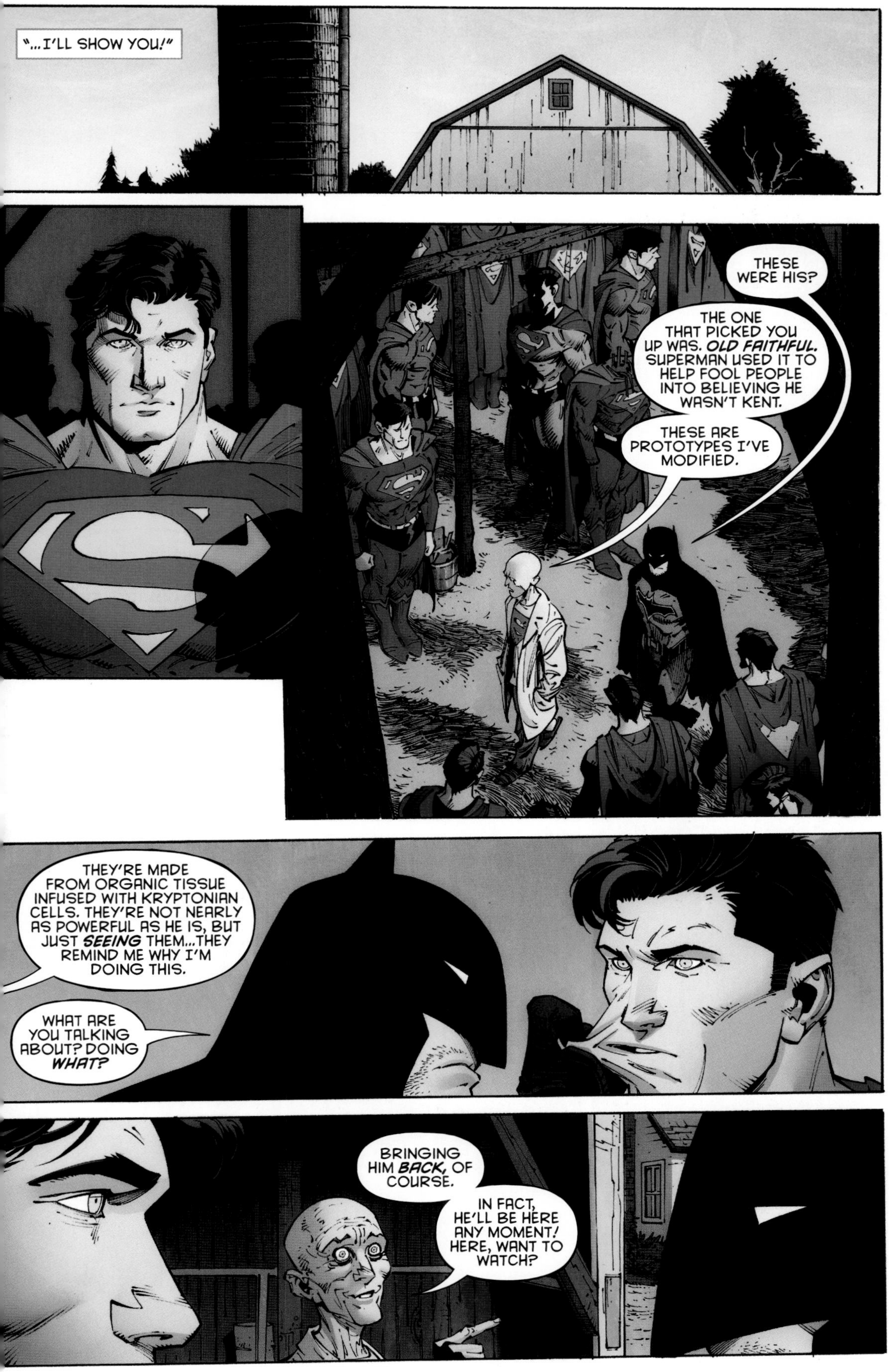
"...I'LL SHOW YOU!"
THESE WERE HIS?
THE ONE THAT PICKED YOU UP WAS. OLD FAITHFUL. SUPERMAN USED IT TO HELP FOOL PEOPLE INTO BELIEVING HE WASN'T KENT.
THESE ARE PROTOTYPES I'VE MODIFIED.
THEY'RE MADE FROM ORGANIC TISSUE INFUSED WITH KRYPTONIAN CELLS. THEY'RE NOT NEARLY AS POWERFUL AS HE IS, BUT JUST SEEING THEM...THEY REMIND ME WHY I'M DOING THIS.
WHAT ARE YOU TALKING ABOUT? DOING WHAT?
BRINGING HIM BACK, OF COURSE.
IN FACT, HE'LL BE HERE ANY MOMENT! HERE, WANT TO WATCH?

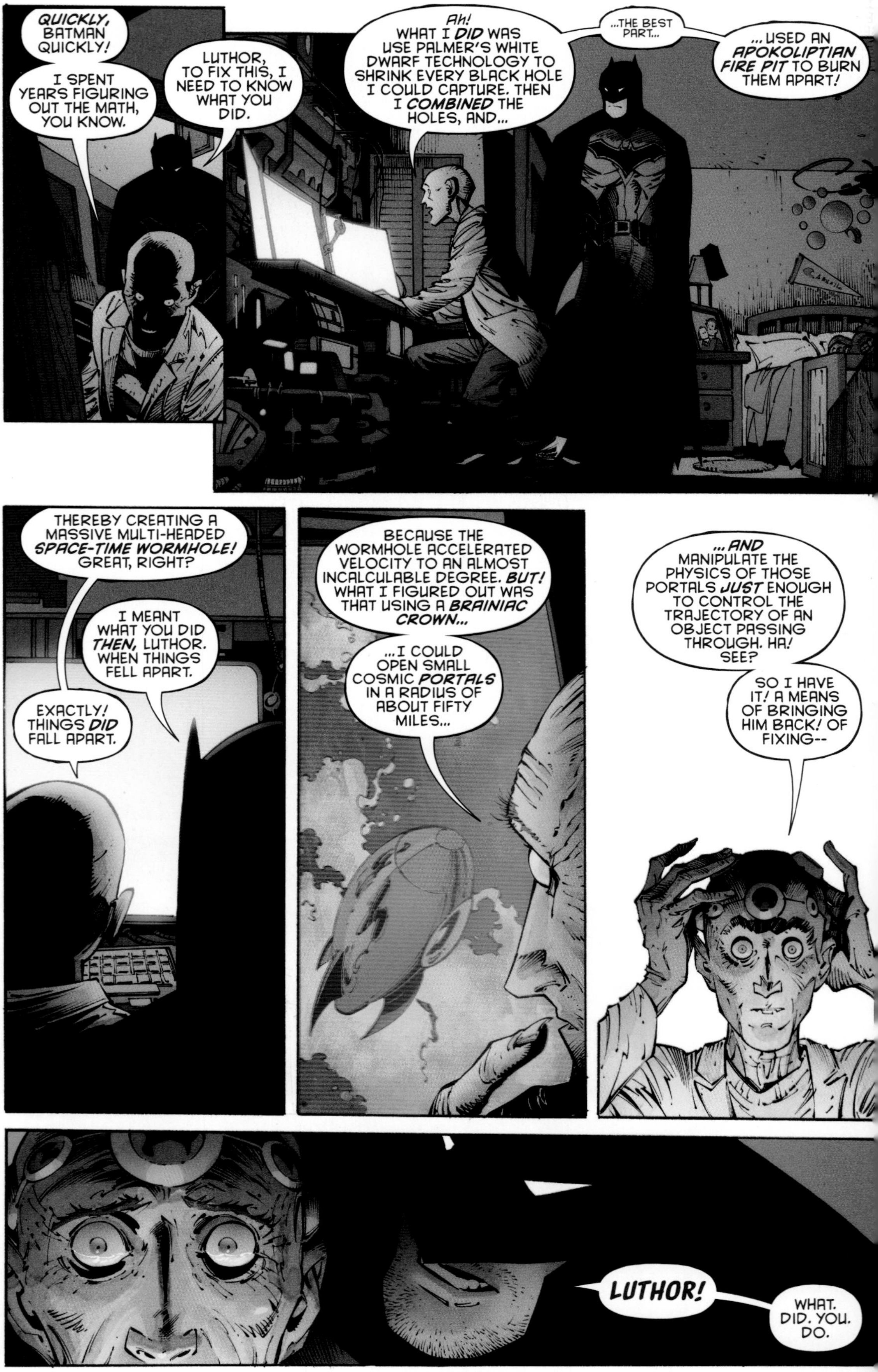
QUICKLY, BATMAN QUICKLY!
I SPENT YEARS FIGURING OUT THE MATH, YOU KNOW.
LUTHOR, TO FIX THIS, I NEED TO KNOW WHAT YOU DID.
AH! WHAT I DID WAS USE PALMER'S WHITE DWARF TECHNOLOGY TO SHRINK EVERY BLACK HOLE I COULD CAPTURE. THEN I COMBINED THE HOLES, AND...
...THE BEST PART...
...USED AN APOKOLIPTIAN FIRE PIT TO BURN THEM APART!
THEREBY CREATING A MASSIVE MULTI-HEADED SPACE-TIME WORMHOLE! GREAT, RIGHT?
I MEANT WHAT YOU DID THEN, LUTHOR. WHEN THINGS FELL APART.
EXACTLY! THINGS DID FALL APART.
BECAUSE THE WORMHOLE ACCELERATED VELOCITY TO AN ALMOST INCALCULABLE DEGREE. BUT! WHAT I FIGURED OUT WAS THAT USING A BRAINIAC CROWN...
...I COULD OPEN SMALL COSMIC PORTALS IN A RADIUS OF ABOUT FIFTY MILES...
...AND MANIPULATE THE PHYSICS OF THOSE PORTALS JUST ENOUGH TO CONTROL THE TRAJECTORY OF AN OBJECT PASSING THROUGH. HA! SEE?
SO I HAVE IT! A MEANS OF BRINGING HIM BACK! OF FIXING--
LUTHOR!
WHAT. DID. YOU. DO.

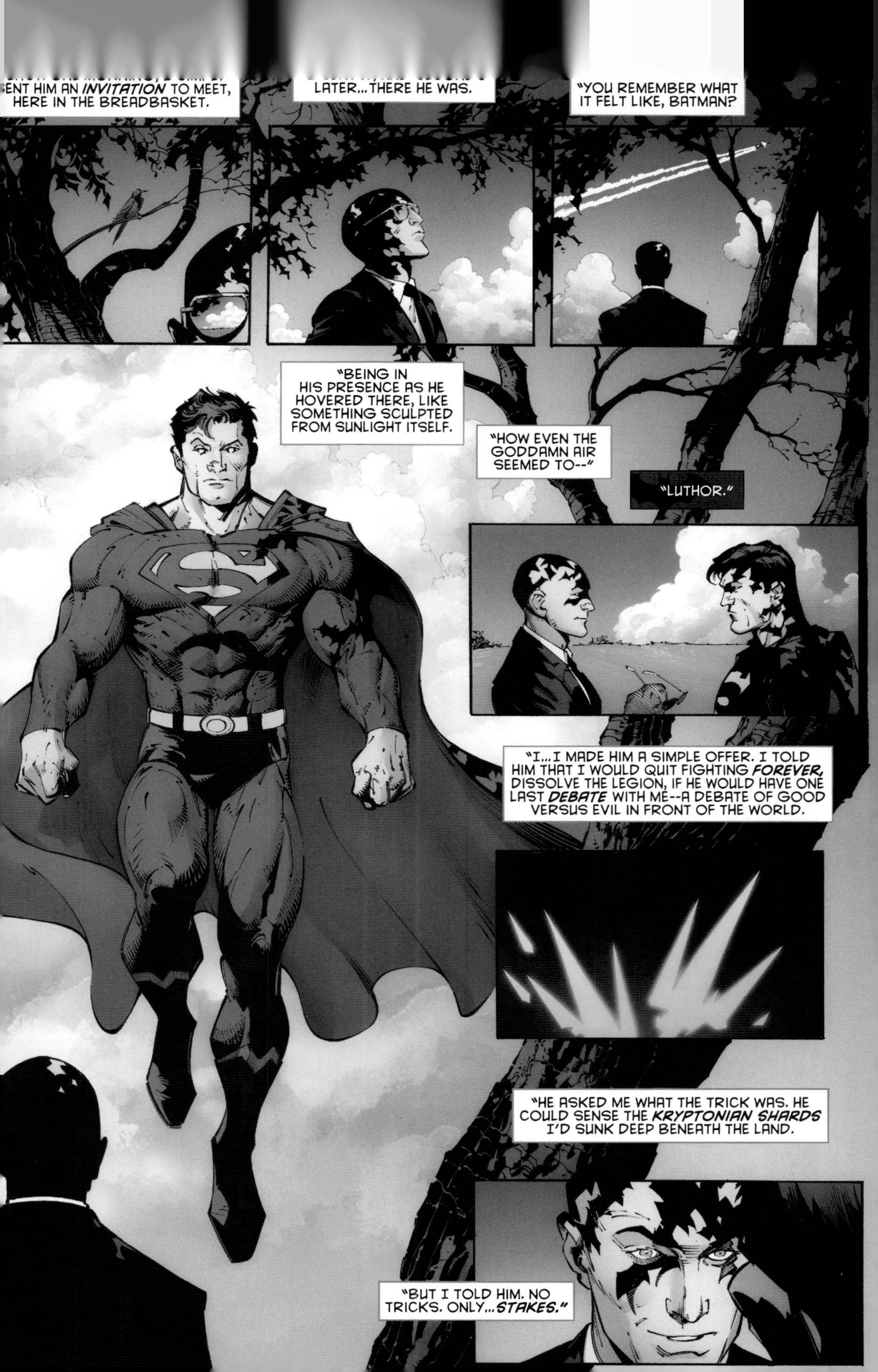

SENT HIM AN *INVITATION* TO MEET, HERE IN THE BREADBASKET.
LATER... THERE HE WAS.
"YOU REMEMBER WHAT IT FELT LIKE, BATMAN?
"BEING IN HIS PRESENCE AS HE HOVERED THERE, LIKE SOMETHING SCULPTED FROM SUNLIGHT ITSELF.
"HOW EVEN THE GODDAMN AIR SEEMED TO--"
"LUTHOR."
"I...I MADE HIM A SIMPLE OFFER. I TOLD HIM THAT I WOULD QUIT FIGHTING ***FOREVER,*** DISSOLVE THE LEGION, IF HE WOULD HAVE ONE LAST ***DEBATE*** WITH ME--A DEBATE OF GOOD VERSUS EVIL IN FRONT OF THE WORLD.
"HE ASKED ME WHAT THE TRICK WAS. HE COULD SENSE THE ***KRYPTONIAN SHARDS*** I'D SUNK DEEP BENEATH THE LAND.
"BUT I TOLD HIM. NO TRICKS. ONLY...***STAKES.***"

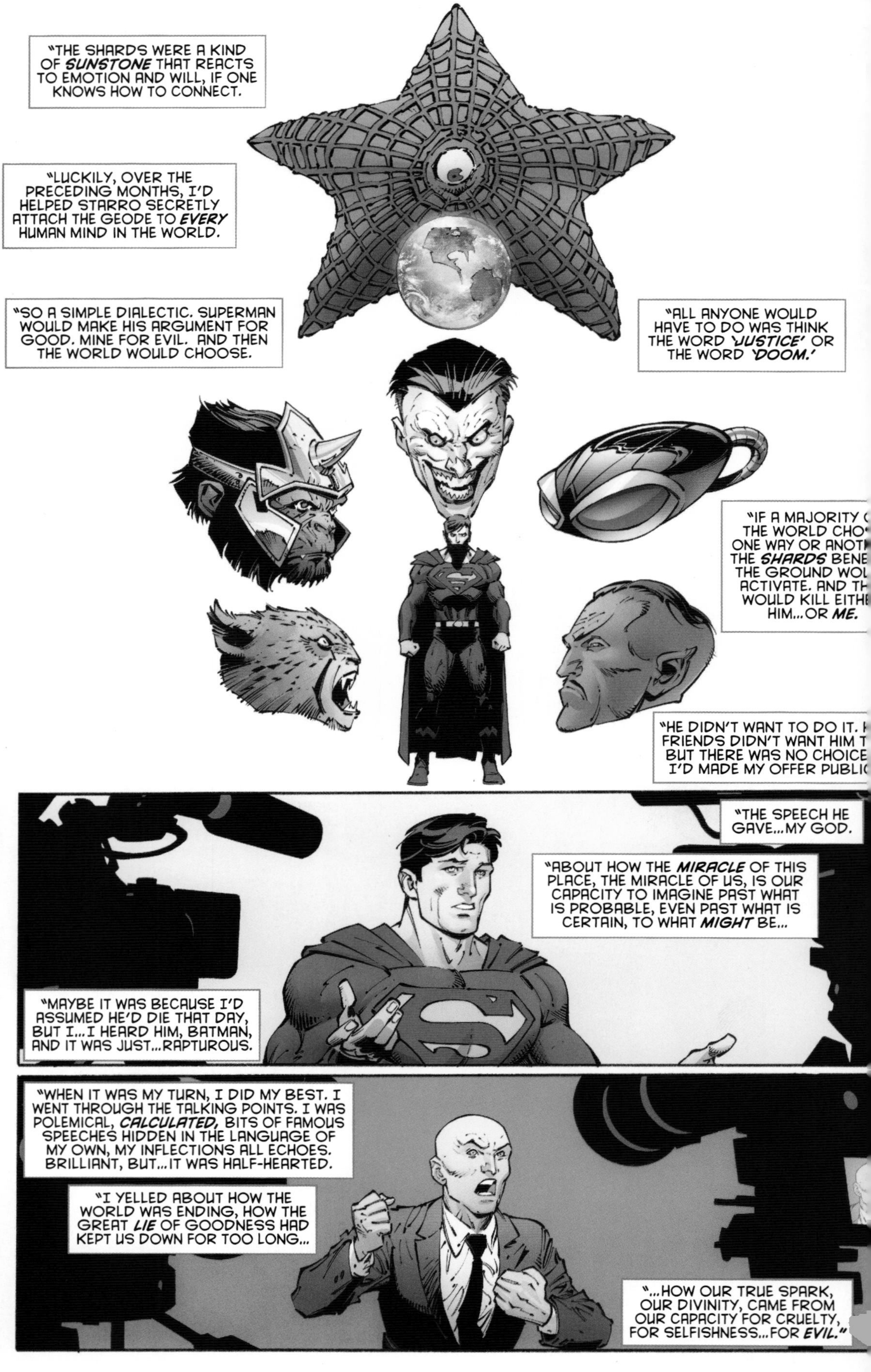
"THE SHARDS WERE A KIND OF SUNSTONE THAT REACTS TO EMOTION AND WILL, IF ONE KNOWS HOW TO CONNECT.
"LUCKILY, OVER THE PRECEDING MONTHS, I'D HELPED STARRO SECRETLY ATTACH THE GEODE TO EVERY HUMAN MIND IN THE WORLD.
"SO A SIMPLE DIALECTIC. SUPERMAN WOULD MAKE HIS ARGUMENT FOR GOOD. MINE FOR EVIL. AND THEN THE WORLD WOULD CHOOSE.
"ALL ANYONE WOULD HAVE TO DO WAS THINK THE WORD 'JUSTICE' OR THE WORD 'DOOM.'
"IF A MAJORITY THE WORLD CHO ONE WAY OR ANOT THE SHARDS BENE THE GROUND WOU ACTIVATE. AND TH WOULD KILL EITHE HIM...OR ME.
"HE DIDN'T WANT TO DO IT. FRIENDS DIDN'T WANT HIM T BUT THERE WAS NO CHOICE I'D MADE MY OFFER PUBLIC
"THE SPEECH HE GAVE... MY GOD.
"ABOUT HOW THE MIRACLE OF THIS PLACE, THE MIRACLE OF US, IS OUR CAPACITY TO IMAGINE PAST WHAT IS PROBABLE, EVEN PAST WHAT IS CERTAIN, TO WHAT MIGHT BE...
"MAYBE IT WAS BECAUSE I'D ASSUMED HE'D DIE THAT DAY, BUT I... I HEARD HIM, BATMAN, AND IT WAS JUST... RAPTUROUS.
"WHEN IT WAS MY TURN, I DID MY BEST. I WENT THROUGH THE TALKING POINTS. I WAS POLEMICAL, CALCULATED, BITS OF FAMOUS SPEECHES HIDDEN IN THE LANGUAGE OF MY OWN, MY INFLECTIONS ALL ECHOES. BRILLIANT, BUT... IT WAS HALF-HEARTED.
"I YELLED ABOUT HOW THE WORLD WAS ENDING, HOW THE GREAT LIE OF GOODNESS HAD KEPT US DOWN FOR TOO LONG...
"...HOW OUR TRUE SPARK, OUR DIVINITY, CAME FROM OUR CAPACITY FOR CRUELTY, FOR SELFISHNESS... FOR EVIL."

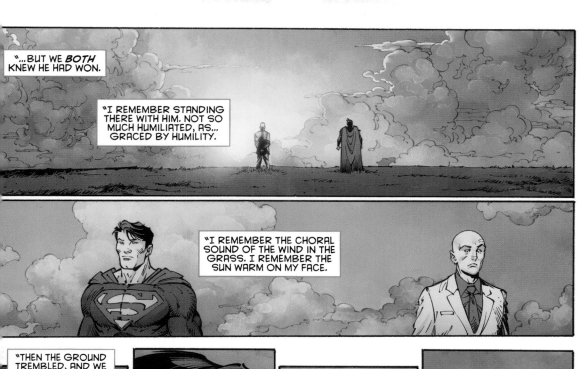

"...BUT WE *BOTH* KNEW HE HAD WON.

"I REMEMBER STANDING THERE WITH HIM. NOT SO MUCH HUMILIATED, AS... GRACED BY HUMILITY.

"I REMEMBER THE CHORAL SOUND OF THE WIND IN THE GRASS. I REMEMBER THE SUN WARM ON MY FACE.

"THEN THE GROUND TREMBLED, AND WE BOTH BRACED FOR WHAT WAS COMING...

SHIK

SHIK

SHIK

"...THE MOMENT HE WOULD SAVE ME FROM THE SHARDS WITH HIS SUPER-SPEED..."

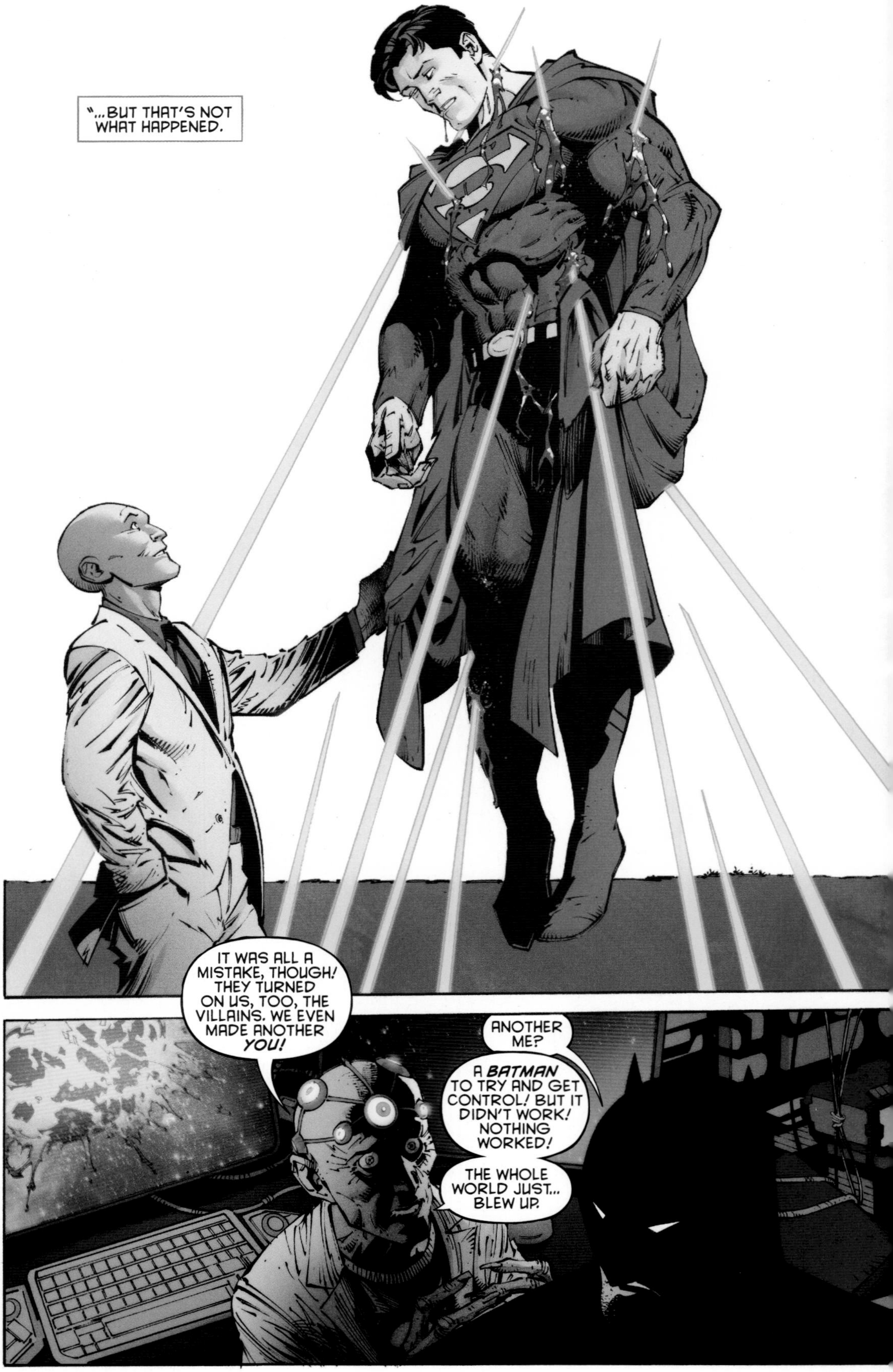
"...BUT THAT'S NOT WHAT HAPPENED.
IT WAS ALL A MISTAKE, THOUGH! THEY TURNED ON US, TOO, THE VILLAINS. WE EVEN MADE ANOTHER *YOU!*
ANOTHER ME?
A *BATMAN* TO TRY AND GET CONTROL! BUT IT DIDN'T WORK! NOTHING WORKED!
THE WHOLE WORLD JUST... BLEW UP.

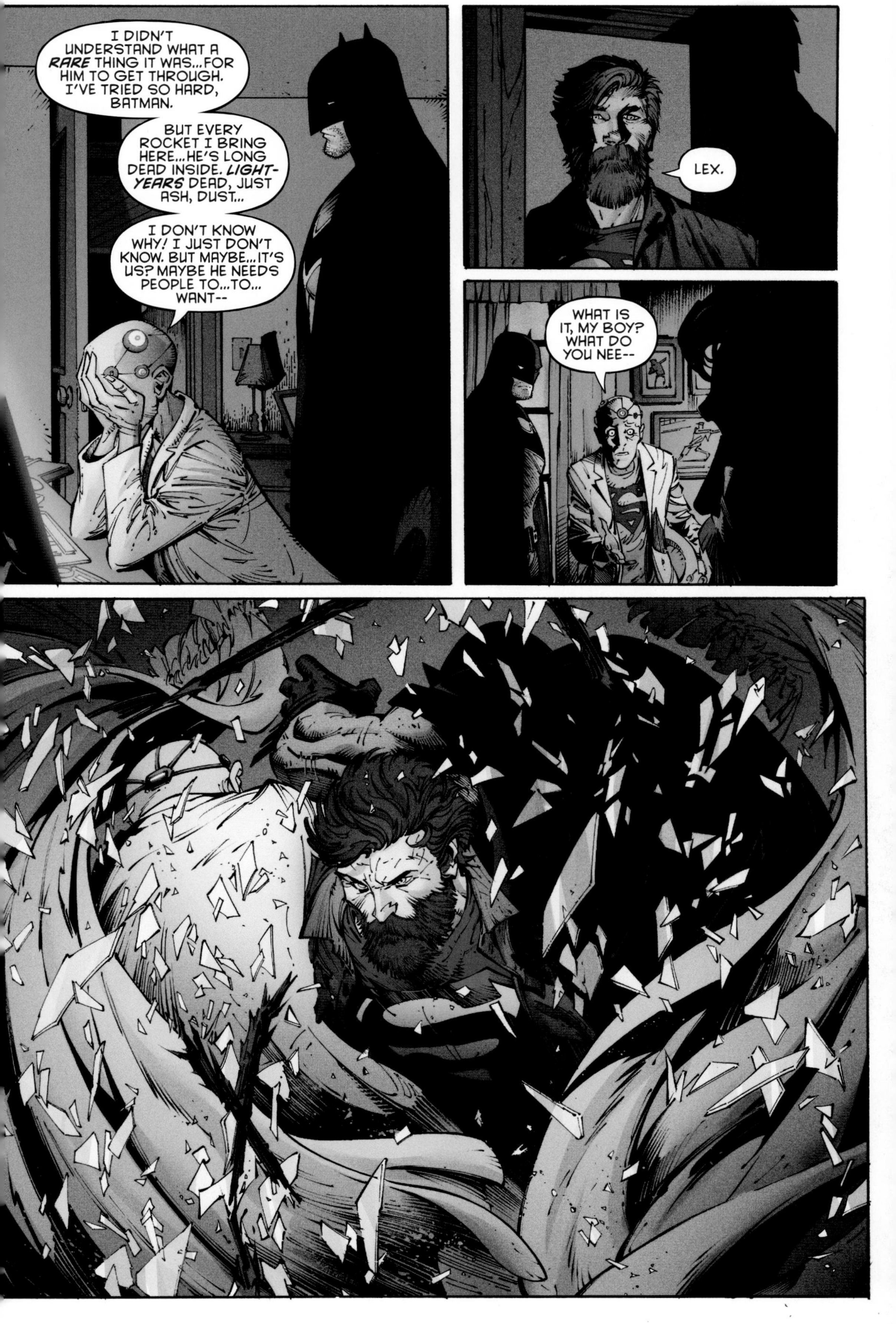
I DIDN'T UNDERSTAND WHAT A RARE THING IT WAS...FOR HIM TO GET THROUGH. I'VE TRIED SO HARD, BATMAN.
BUT EVERY ROCKET HE'S BRING HERE...HE'S LONG DEAD INSIDE. LIGHT-YEARS DEAD, JUST ASH, DUST...
I DON'T KNOW WHY! I JUST DON'T KNOW. BUT MAYBE...IT'S US? MAYBE HE NEEDS PEOPLE TO...TO... WANT--
LEX.
WHAT IS IT, MY BOY? WHAT DO YOU NEE--

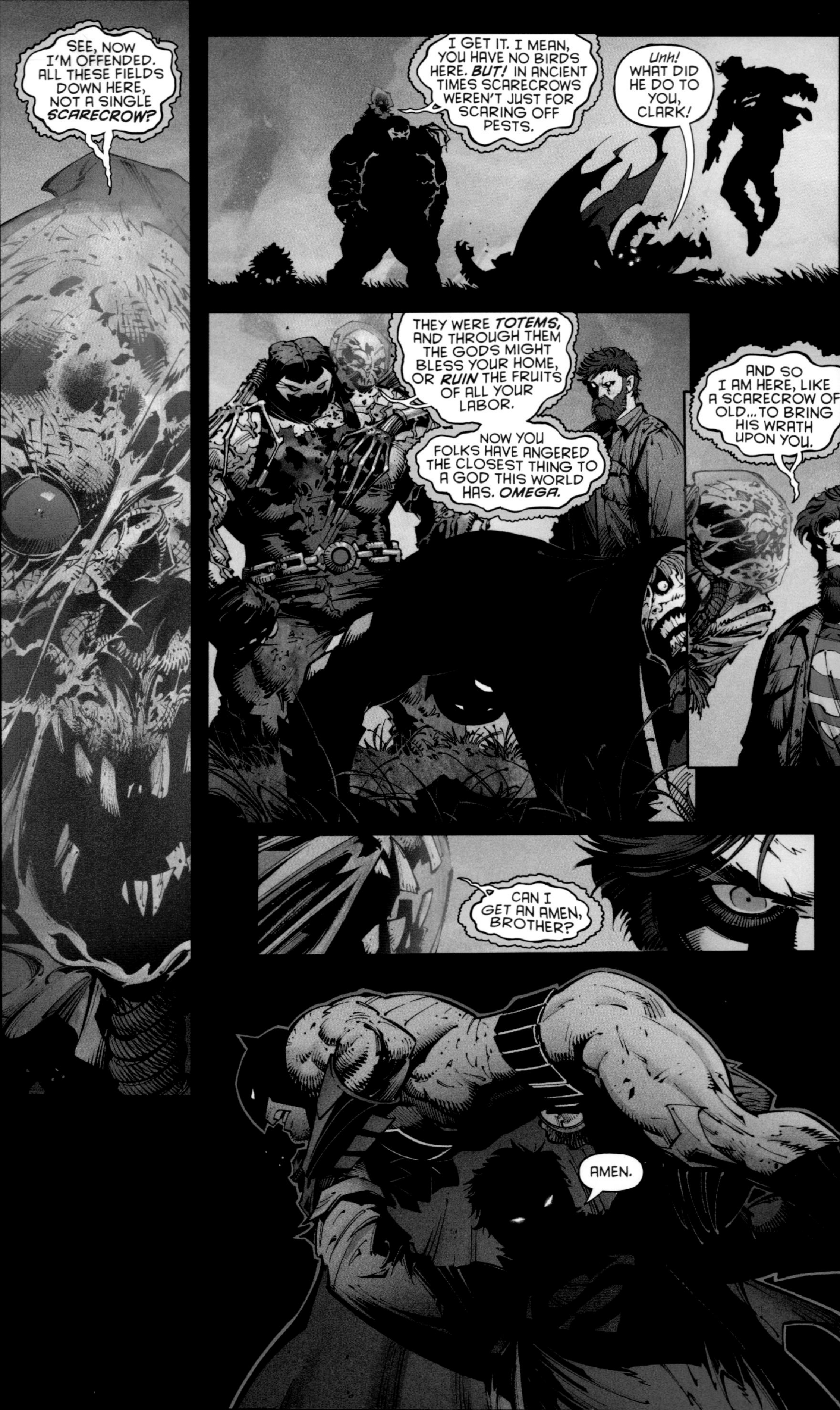
SEE, NOW I'M OFFENDED. ALL THESE FIELDS DOWN HERE, NOT A SINGLE SCARECROW?
I GET IT. I MEAN, YOU HAVE NO BIRDS HERE. BUT! IN ANCIENT TIMES SCARECROWS WEREN'T JUST FOR SCARING OFF PESTS.
Unh! WHAT DID HE DO TO YOU, CLARK!
THEY WERE TOTEMS, AND THROUGH THEM THE GODS MIGHT BLESS YOUR HOME, OR RUIN THE FRUITS OF ALL YOUR LABOR.
NOW YOU FOLKS HAVE ANGERED THE CLOSEST THING TO A GOD THIS WORLD HAS. OMEGA.
AND SO I AM HERE, LIKE A SCARECROW OF OLD...TO BRING HIS WRATH UPON YOU.
CAN I GET AN AMEN, BROTHER?
AMEN.

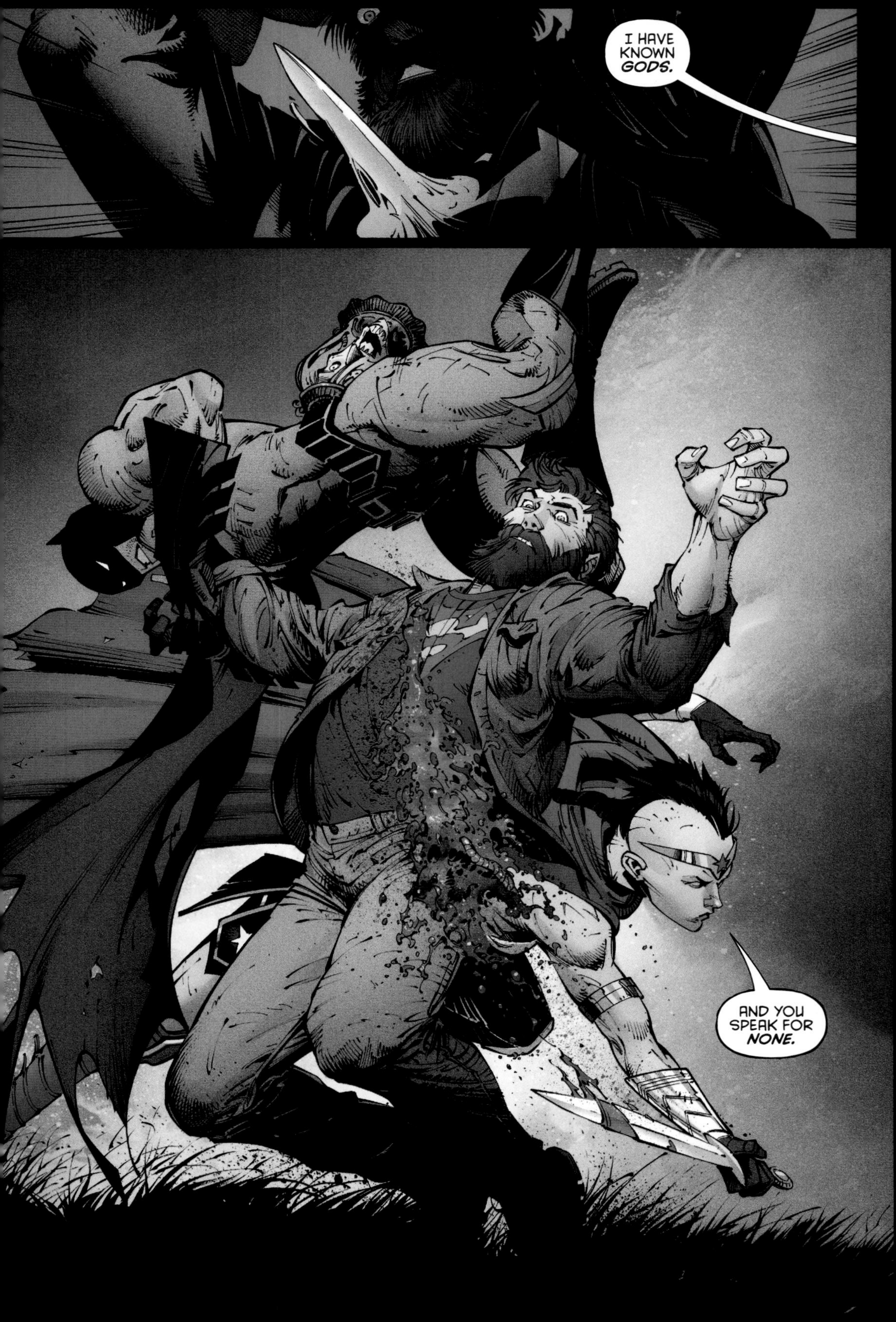
I HAVE KNOWN GODS.
AND YOU SPEAK FOR NONE.

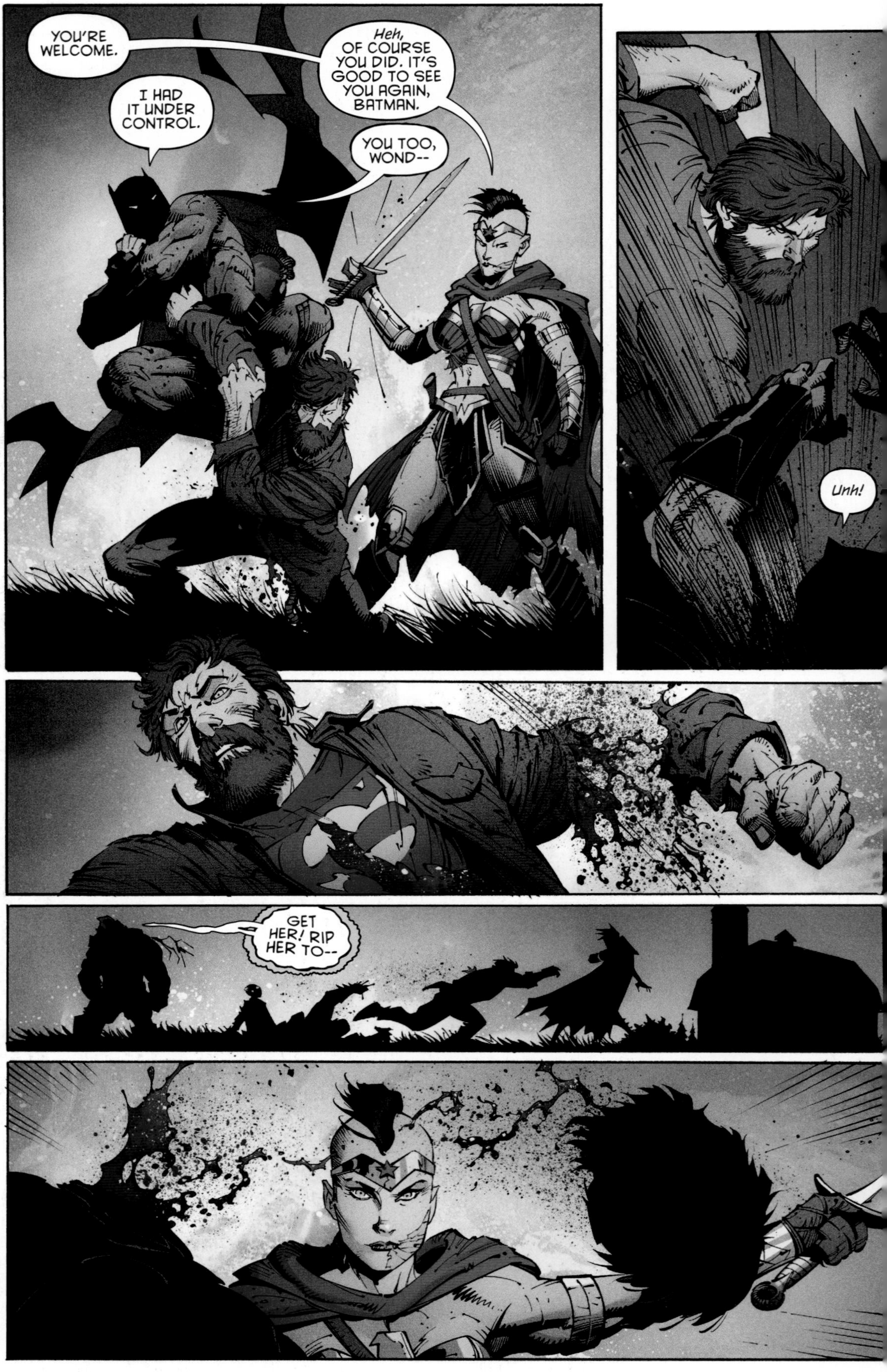
YOU'RE WELCOME.
I HAD IT UNDER CONTROL.
Heh, OF COURSE YOU DID. IT'S GOOD TO SEE YOU AGAIN, BATMAN.
YOU TOO, WOND--
Unh!
GET HER! RIP HER TO--

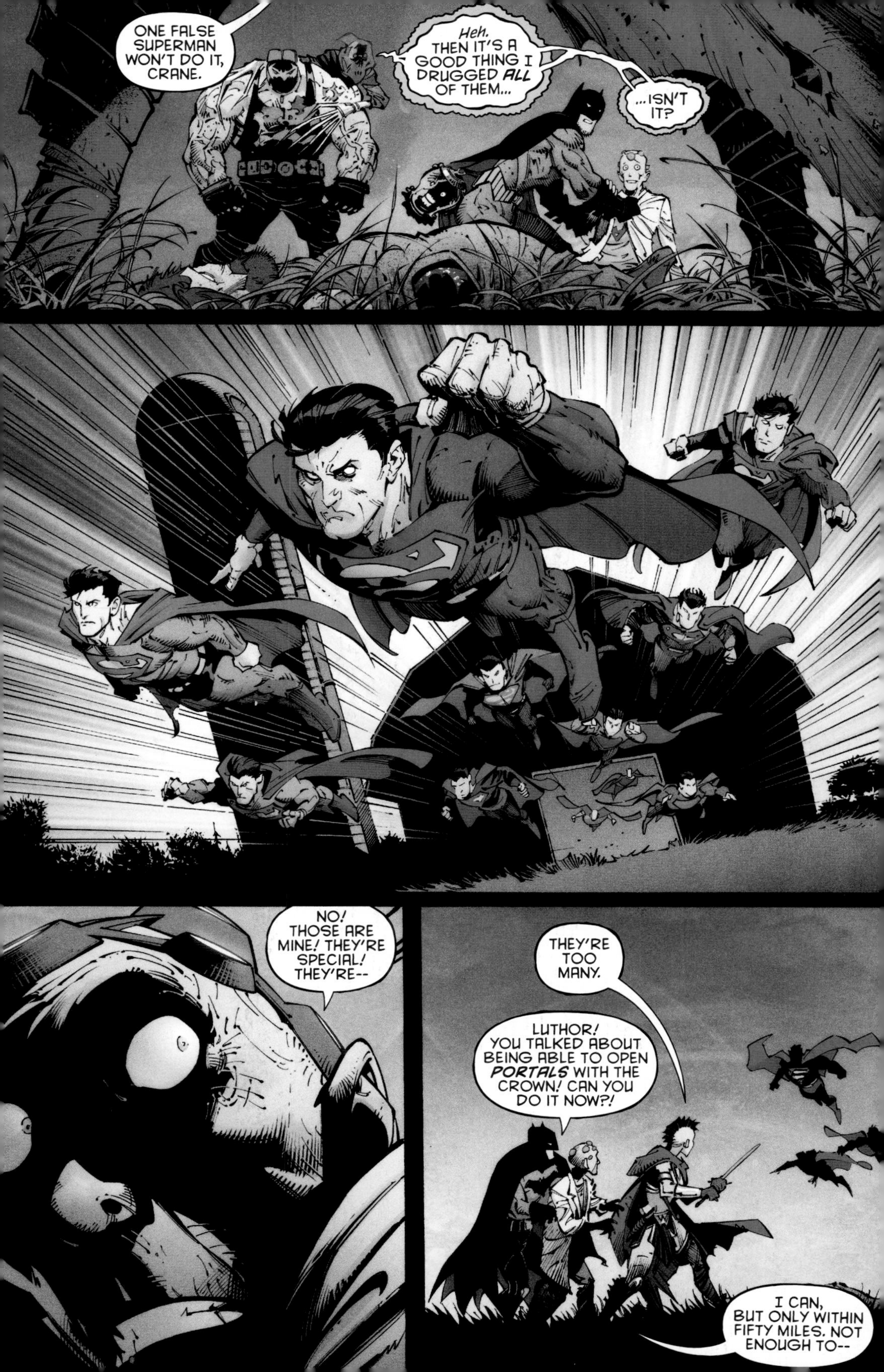
ONE FALSE SUPERMAN WON'T DO IT, CRANE.
Heh. THEN IT'S A GOOD THING I DRUGGED ALL OF THEM...
...ISN'T IT?
NO! THOSE ARE MINE! THEY'RE SPECIAL! THEY'RE--
THEY'RE TOO MANY.
LUTHOR! YOU TALKED ABOUT BEING ABLE TO OPEN PORTALS WITH THE CROWN! CAN YOU DO IT NOW?!
I CAN, BUT ONLY WITHIN FIFTY MILES. NOT ENOUGH TO--

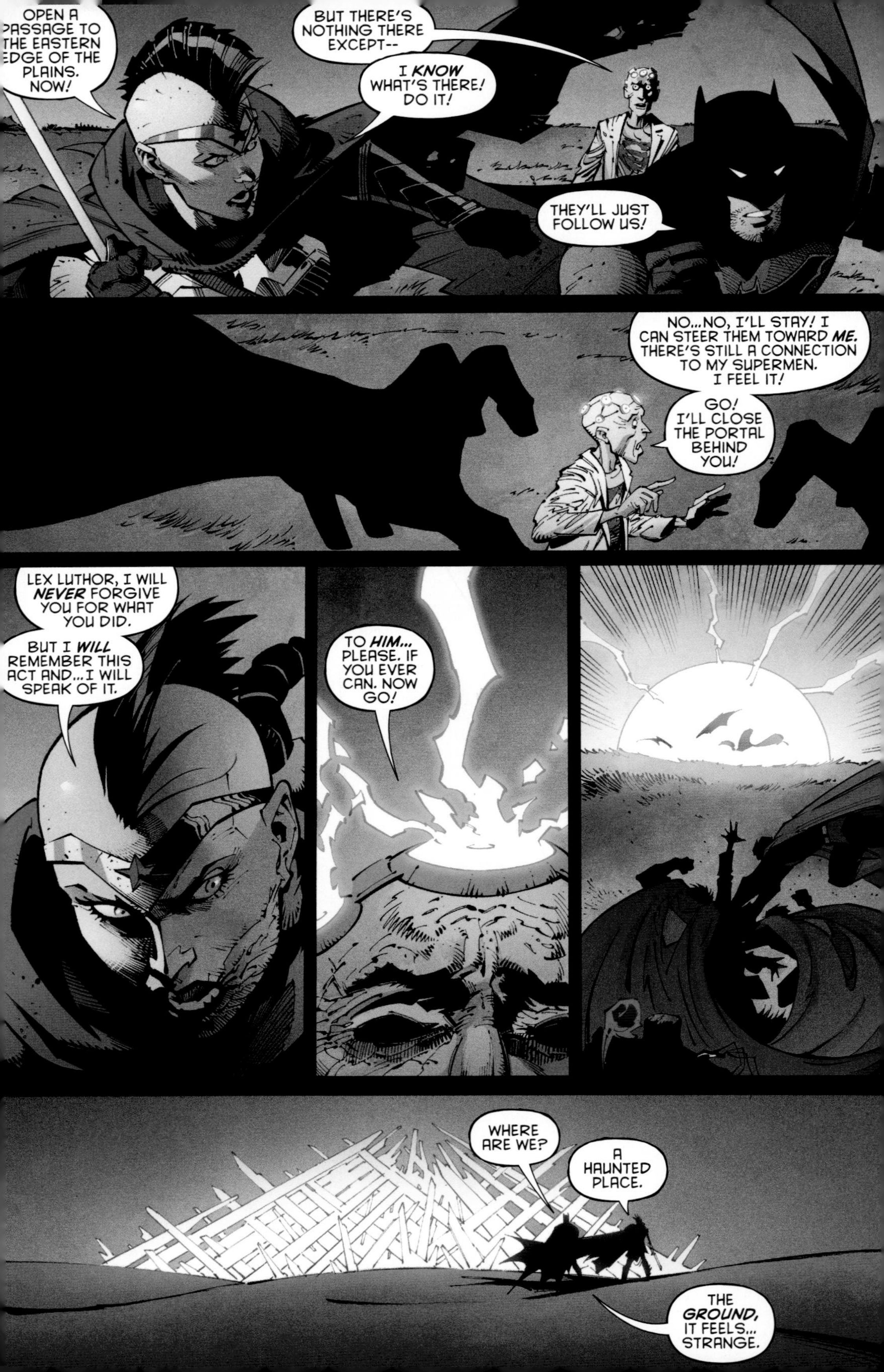
OPEN A PASSAGE TO THE EASTERN EDGE OF THE PLAINS. NOW!
BUT THERE'S NOTHING THERE EXCEPT--
I KNOW WHAT'S THERE! DO IT!
THEY'LL JUST FOLLOW US!
NO...NO, I'LL STAY! I CAN STEER THEM TOWARD ME. THERE'S STILL A CONNECTION TO MY SUPERMEN. I FEEL IT!
GO! I'LL CLOSE THE PORTAL BEHIND YOU!
LEX LUTHOR, I WILL NEVER FORGIVE YOU FOR WHAT YOU DID.
BUT I WILL REMEMBER THIS ACT AND...I WILL SPEAK OF IT.
TO HIM... PLEASE. IF YOU EVER CAN. NOW GO!
WHERE ARE WE?
A HAUNTED PLACE.
THE GROUND, IT FEELS... STRANGE.

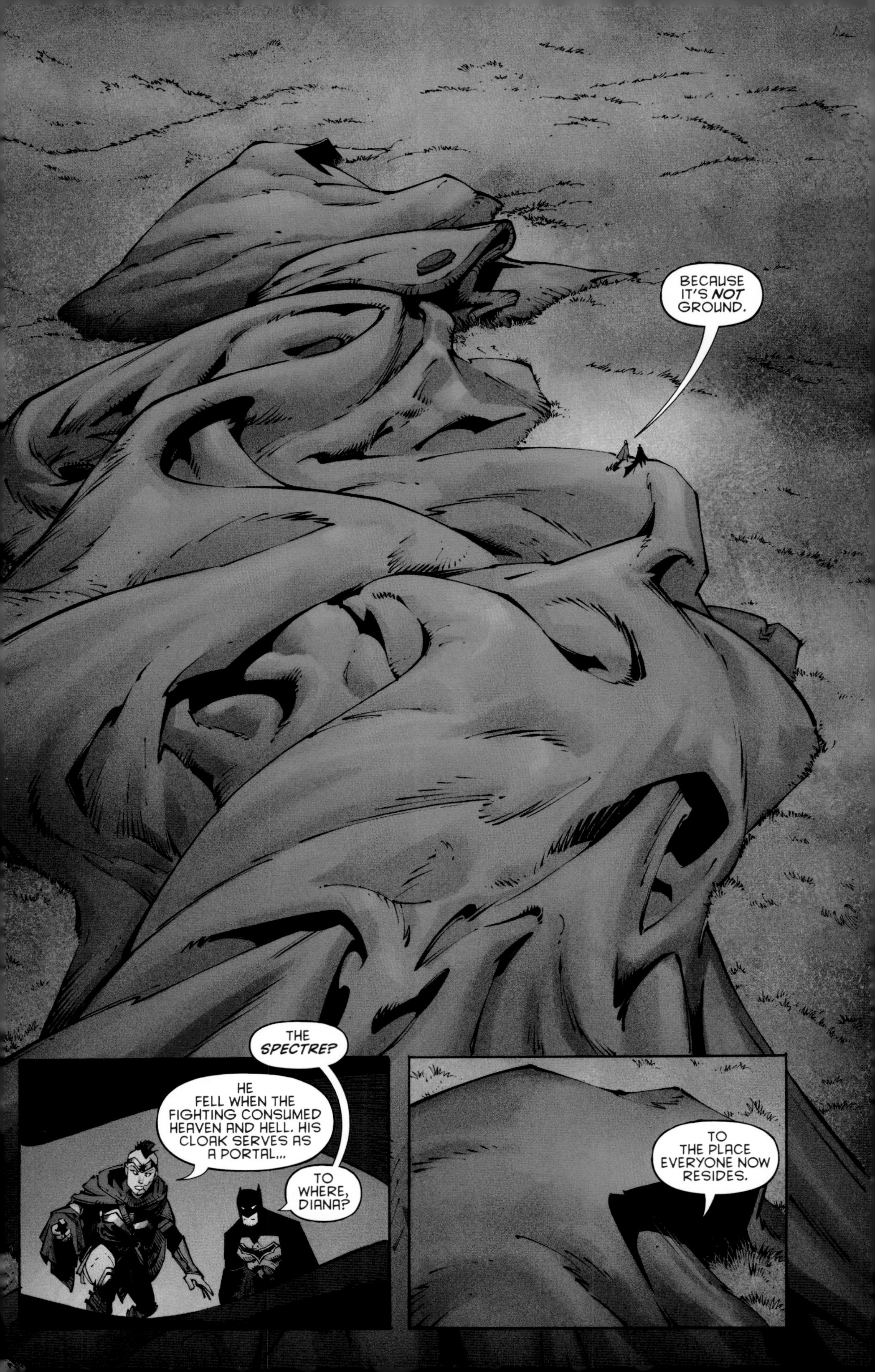

BECAUSE IT'S **NOT** GROUND.
THE ***SPECTRE?***
HE FELL WHEN THE FIGHTING CONSUMED HEAVEN AND HELL. HIS CLOAK SERVES AS A PORTAL...
TO WHERE, DIANA?
TO THE PLACE EVERYONE NOW RESIDES.

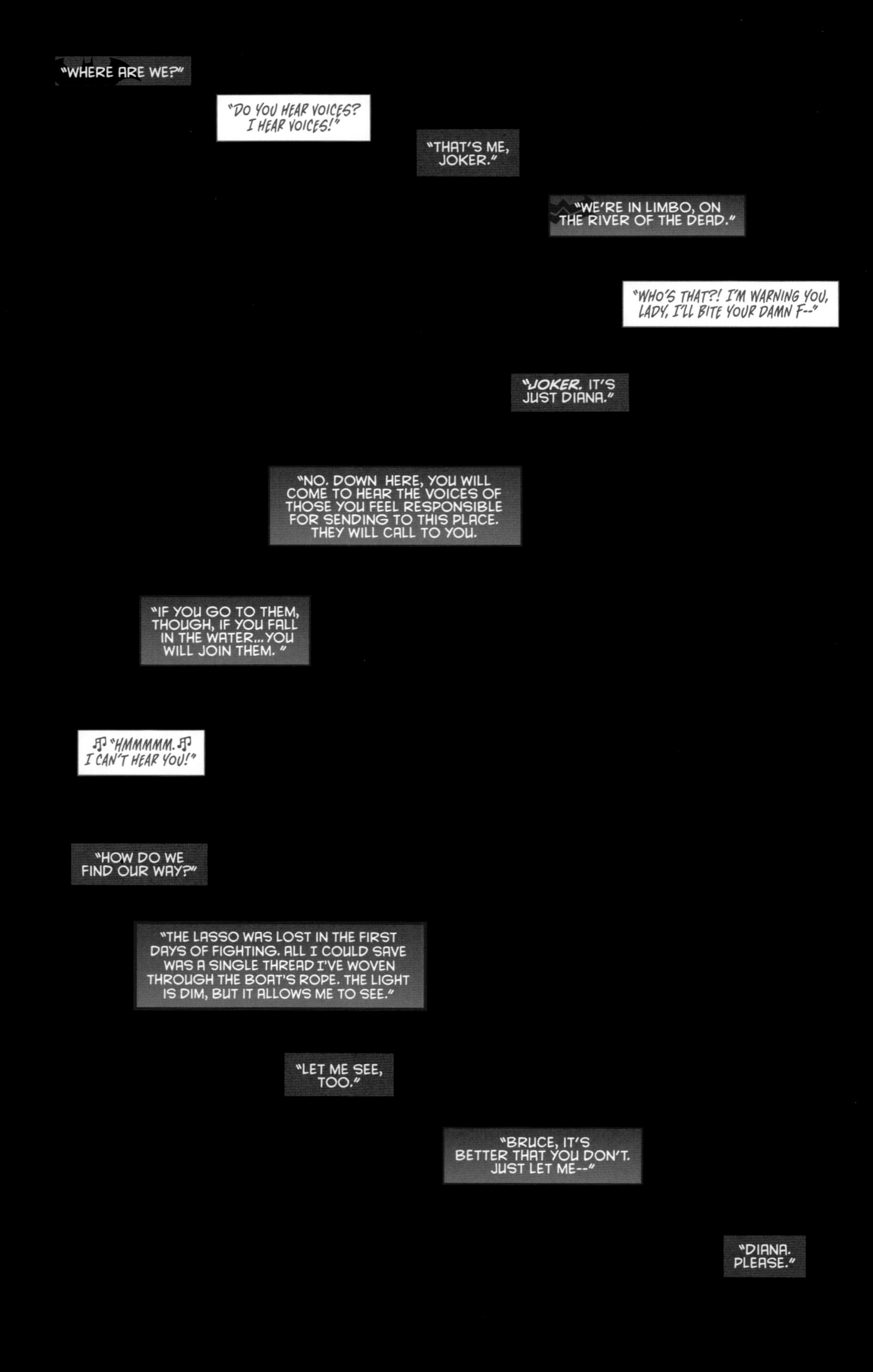
"WHERE ARE WE?"
"DO YOU HEAR VOICES? I HEAR VOICES!"
"THAT'S ME, JOKER."
"WE'RE IN LIMBO, ON THE RIVER OF THE DEAD."
"WHO'S THAT?! I'M WARNING YOU, LADY, I'LL BITE YOUR DAMN F--"
"JOKER. IT'S JUST DIANA."
"NO. DOWN HERE, YOU WILL COME TO HEAR THE VOICES OF THOSE YOU FEEL RESPONSIBLE FOR SENDING TO THIS PLACE. THEY WILL CALL TO YOU.
"IF YOU GO TO THEM, THOUGH, IF YOU FALL IN THE WATER...YOU WILL JOIN THEM."
♫ "HMMMMM. ♫ I CAN'T HEAR YOU!"
"HOW DO WE FIND OUR WAY?"
"THE LASSO WAS LOST IN THE FIRST DAYS OF FIGHTING. ALL I COULD SAVE WAS A SINGLE THREAD I'VE WOVEN THROUGH THE BOAT'S ROPE. THE LIGHT IS DIM, BUT IT ALLOWS ME TO SEE."
"LET ME SEE, TOO."
"BRUCE, IT'S BETTER THAT YOU DON'T. JUST LET ME--"
"DIANA. PLEASE."

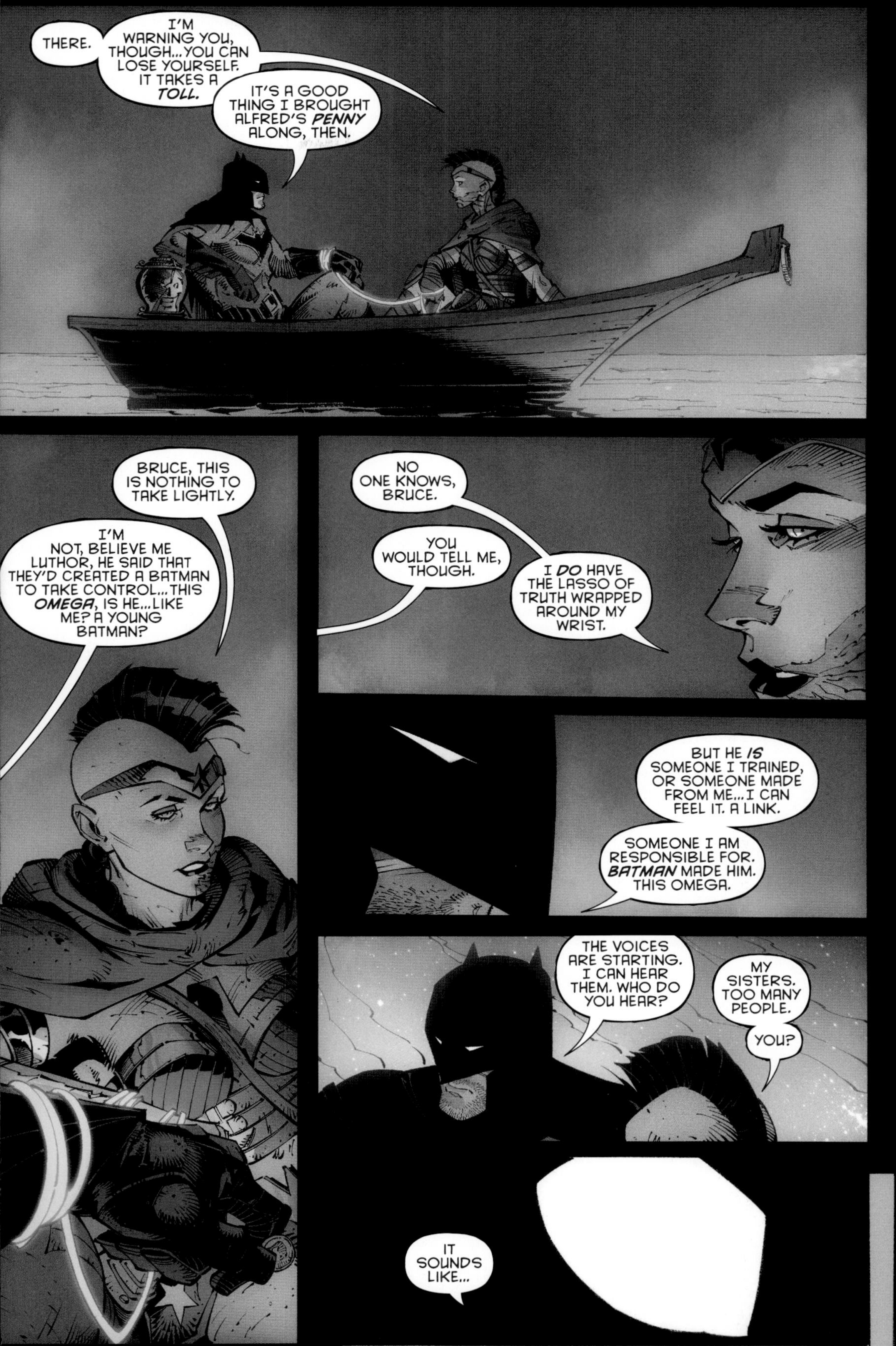

THERE.
I'M WARNING YOU, THOUGH...YOU CAN LOSE YOURSELF. IT TAKES A *TOLL.*
IT'S A GOOD THING I BROUGHT ALFRED'S *PENNY* ALONG, THEN.
BRUCE, THIS IS NOTHING TO TAKE LIGHTLY.
I'M NOT, BELIEVE ME LUTHOR, HE SAID THAT THEY'D CREATED A BATMAN TO TAKE CONTROL...THIS *OMEGA*, IS HE...LIKE ME? A YOUNG BATMAN?
NO ONE KNOWS, BRUCE.
YOU WOULD TELL ME, THOUGH.
I *DO* HAVE THE LASSO OF TRUTH WRAPPED AROUND MY WRIST.
BUT HE *IS* SOMEONE I TRAINED, OR SOMEONE MADE FROM ME...I CAN FEEL IT. A LINK.
SOMEONE I AM RESPONSIBLE FOR. *BATMAN* MADE HIM. THIS OMEGA.
THE VOICES ARE STARTING. I CAN HEAR THEM. WHO DO YOU HEAR?
MY SISTERS. TOO MANY PEOPLE.
YOU?
IT SOUNDS LIKE...

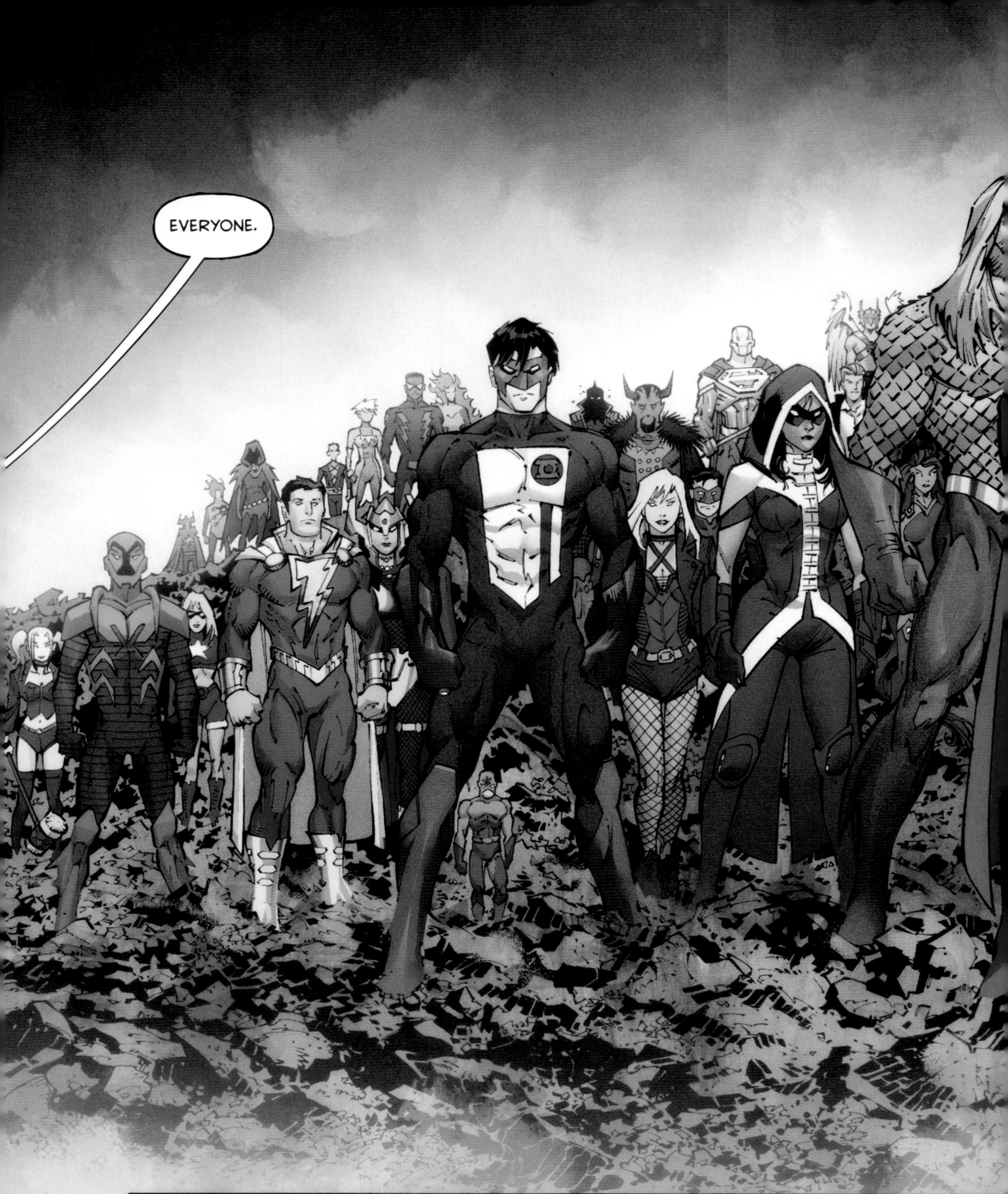
EVERYONE.

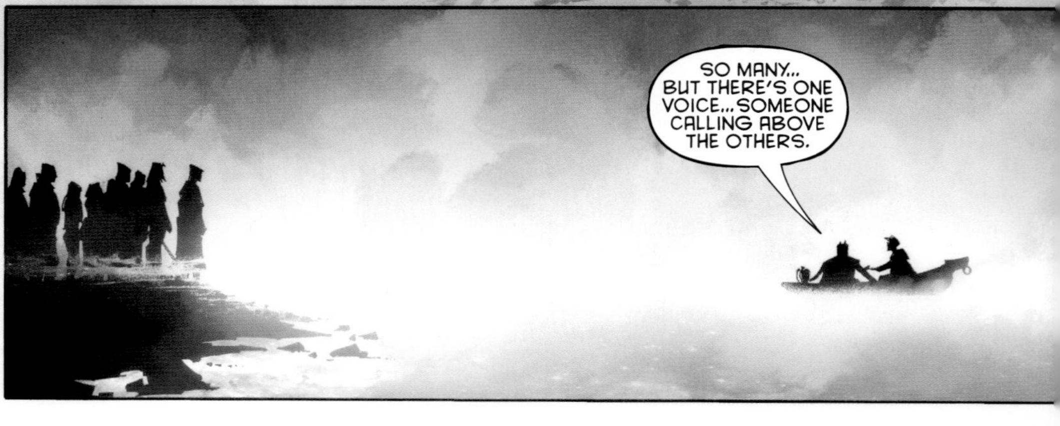
SO MANY... BUT THERE'S ONE VOICE... SOMEONE CALLING ABOVE THE OTHERS.

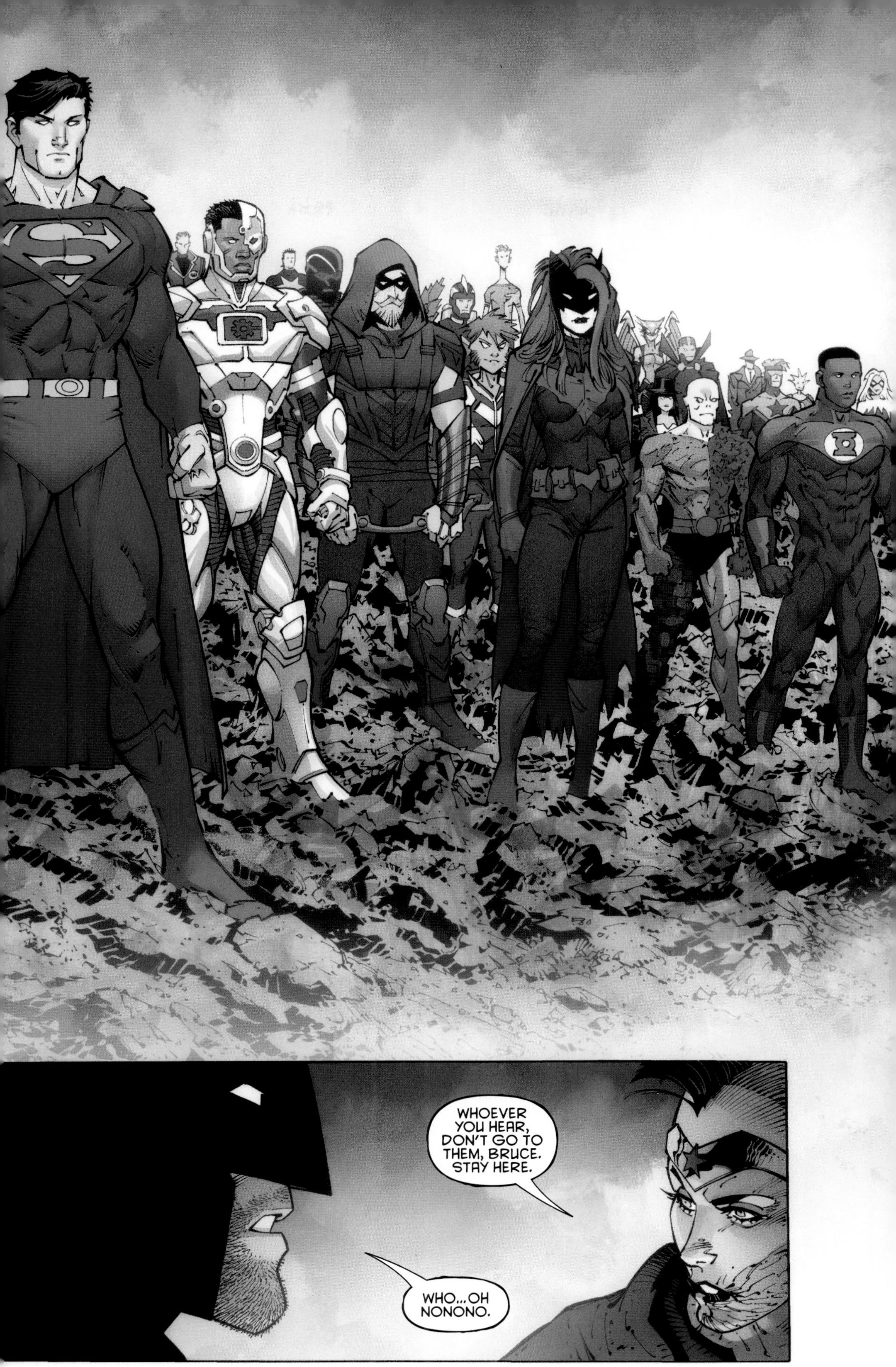
WHOEVER YOU HEAR, DON'T GO TO THEM, BRUCE. STAY HERE.
WHO...OH NONONO.

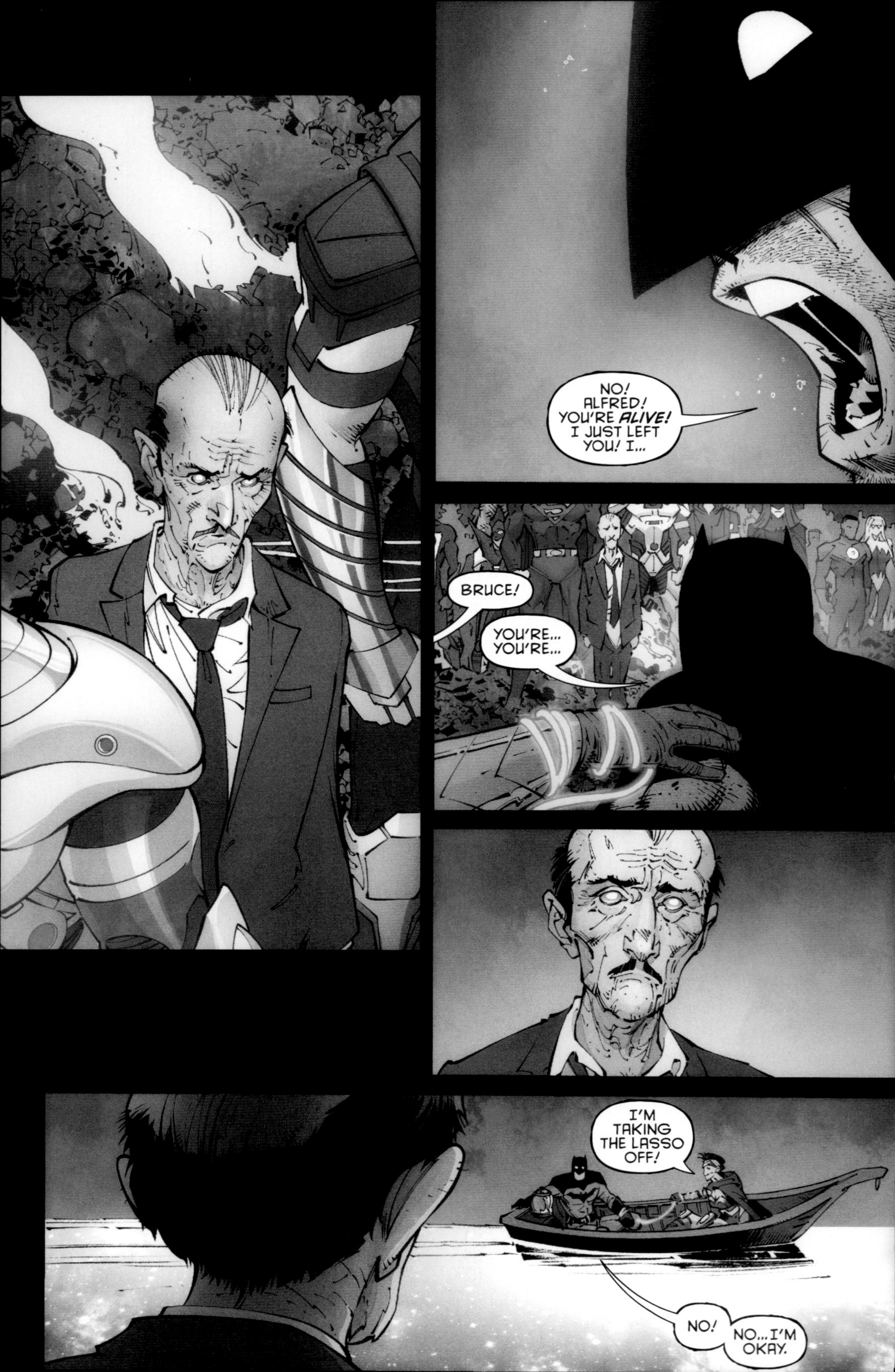
NO! ALFRED! YOU'RE ALIVE! I JUST LEFT YOU! I...
BRUCE!
YOU'RE... YOU'RE...
I'M TAKING THE LASSO OFF!
NO!
NO...I'M OKAY.

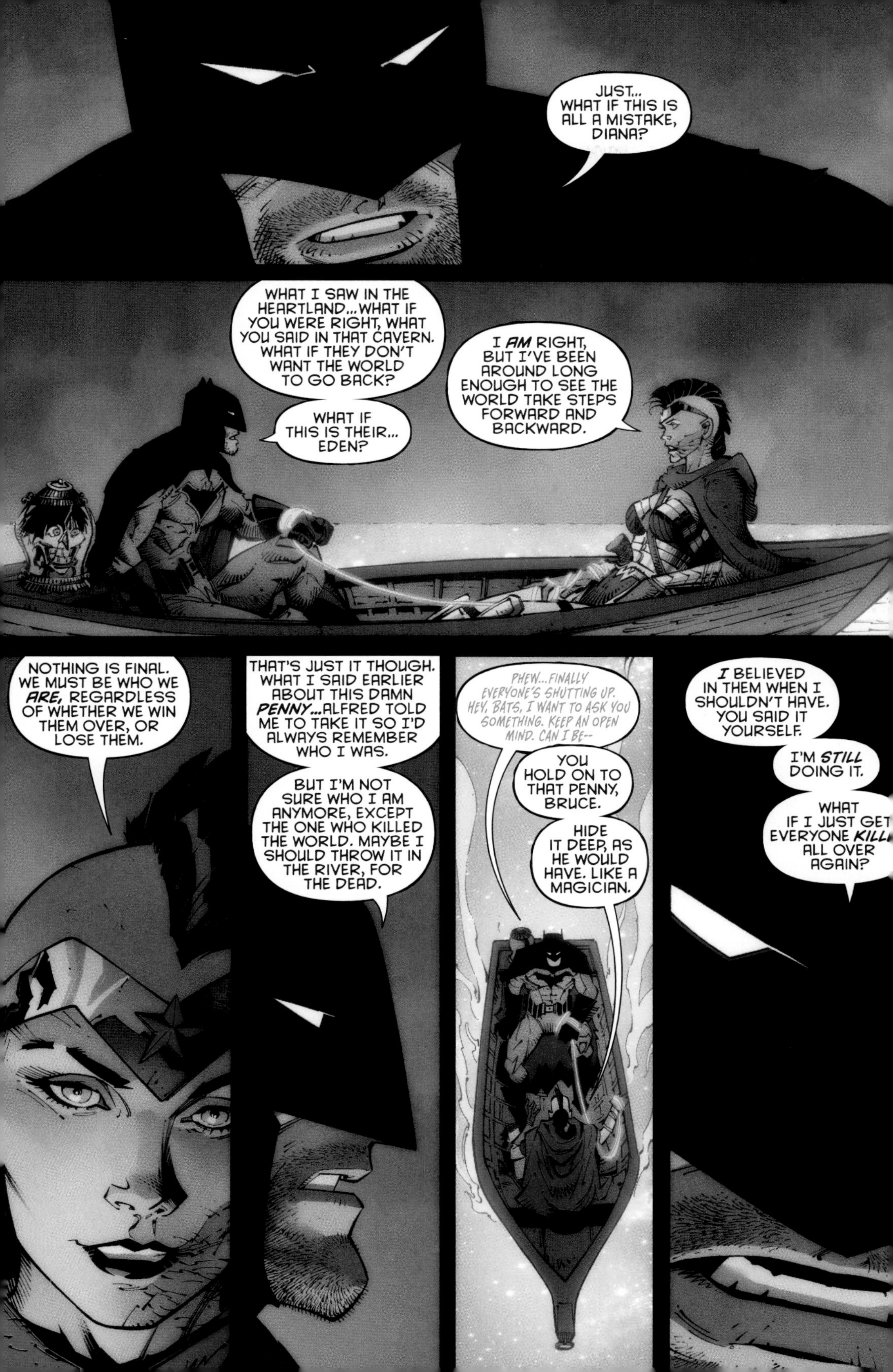
JUST... WHAT IF THIS IS ALL A MISTAKE, DIANA?
WHAT I SAW IN THE HEARTLAND...WHAT IF YOU WERE RIGHT, WHAT YOU SAID IN THAT CAVERN. WHAT IF THEY DON'T WANT THE WORLD TO GO BACK?
WHAT IF THIS IS THEIR... EDEN?
I *AM* RIGHT, BUT I'VE BEEN AROUND LONG ENOUGH TO SEE THE WORLD TAKE STEPS FORWARD AND BACKWARD.
NOTHING IS FINAL. WE MUST BE WHO WE *ARE,* REGARDLESS OF WHETHER WE WIN THEM OVER, OR LOSE THEM.
THAT'S JUST IT THOUGH. WHAT I SAID EARLIER ABOUT THIS DAMN *PENNY*...ALFRED TOLD ME TO TAKE IT SO I'D ALWAYS REMEMBER WHO I WAS.
BUT I'M NOT SURE WHO I AM ANYMORE, EXCEPT THE ONE WHO KILLED THE WORLD. MAYBE I SHOULD THROW IT IN THE RIVER, FOR THE DEAD.
PHEW...FINALLY EVERYONE'S SHUTTING UP. HEY, BATS, I WANT TO ASK YOU SOMETHING. KEEP AN OPEN MIND. CAN I BE--
YOU HOLD ON TO THAT PENNY, BRUCE.
HIDE IT DEEP, AS HE WOULD HAVE. LIKE A MAGICIAN.
I BELIEVED IN THEM WHEN I SHOULDN'T HAVE. YOU SAID IT YOURSELF.
I'M *STILL* DOING IT.
WHAT IF I JUST GET EVERYONE KILL ALL OVER AGAIN?

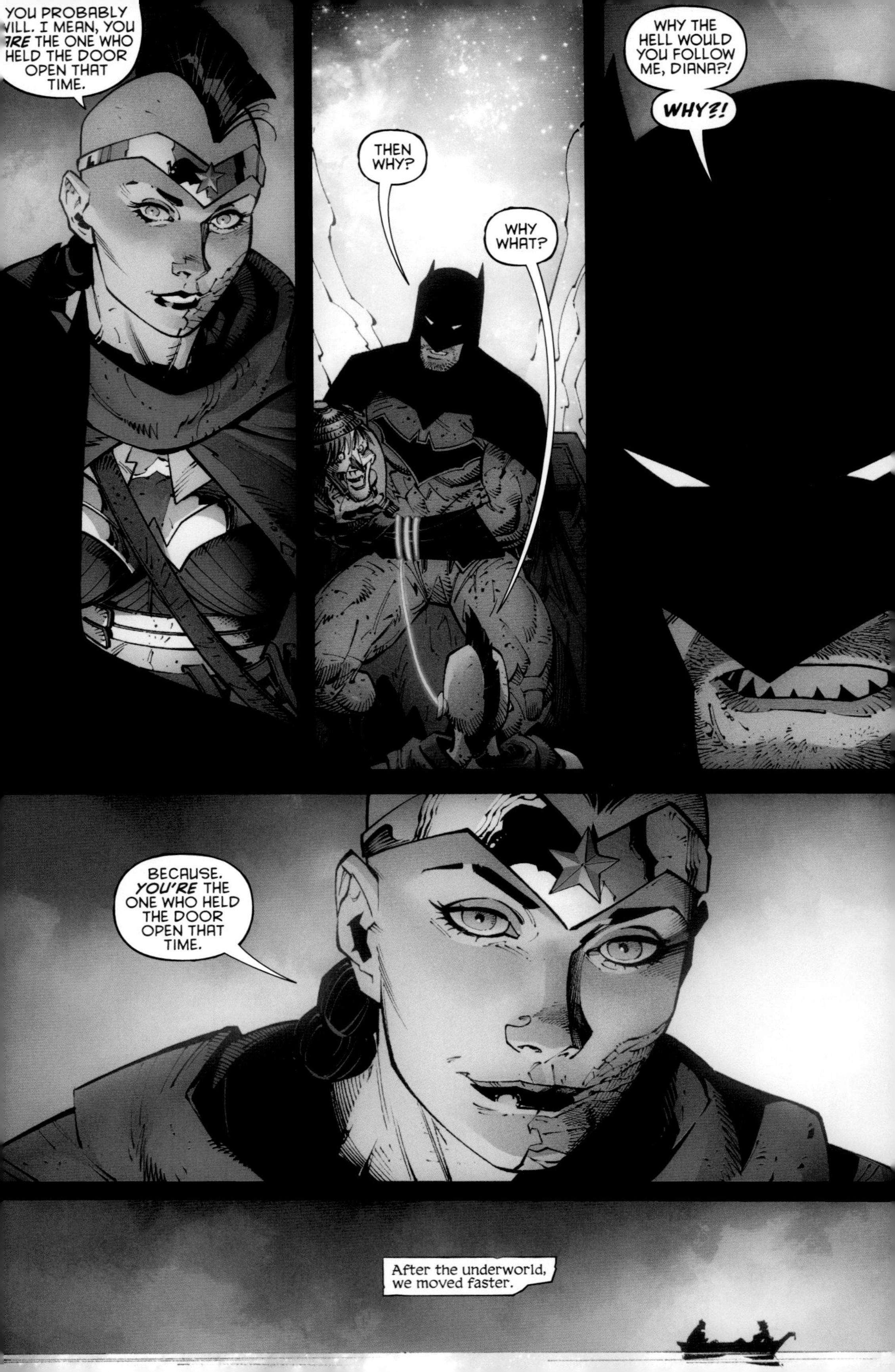
YOU PROBABLY WILL. I MEAN, YOU ARE THE ONE WHO HELD THE DOOR OPEN THAT TIME.
THEN WHY?
WHY WHAT?
WHY THE HELL WOULD YOU FOLLOW ME, DIANA?!
WHY?!
BECAUSE. YOU'RE THE ONE WHO HELD THE DOOR OPEN THAT TIME.
After the underworld, we moved faster.

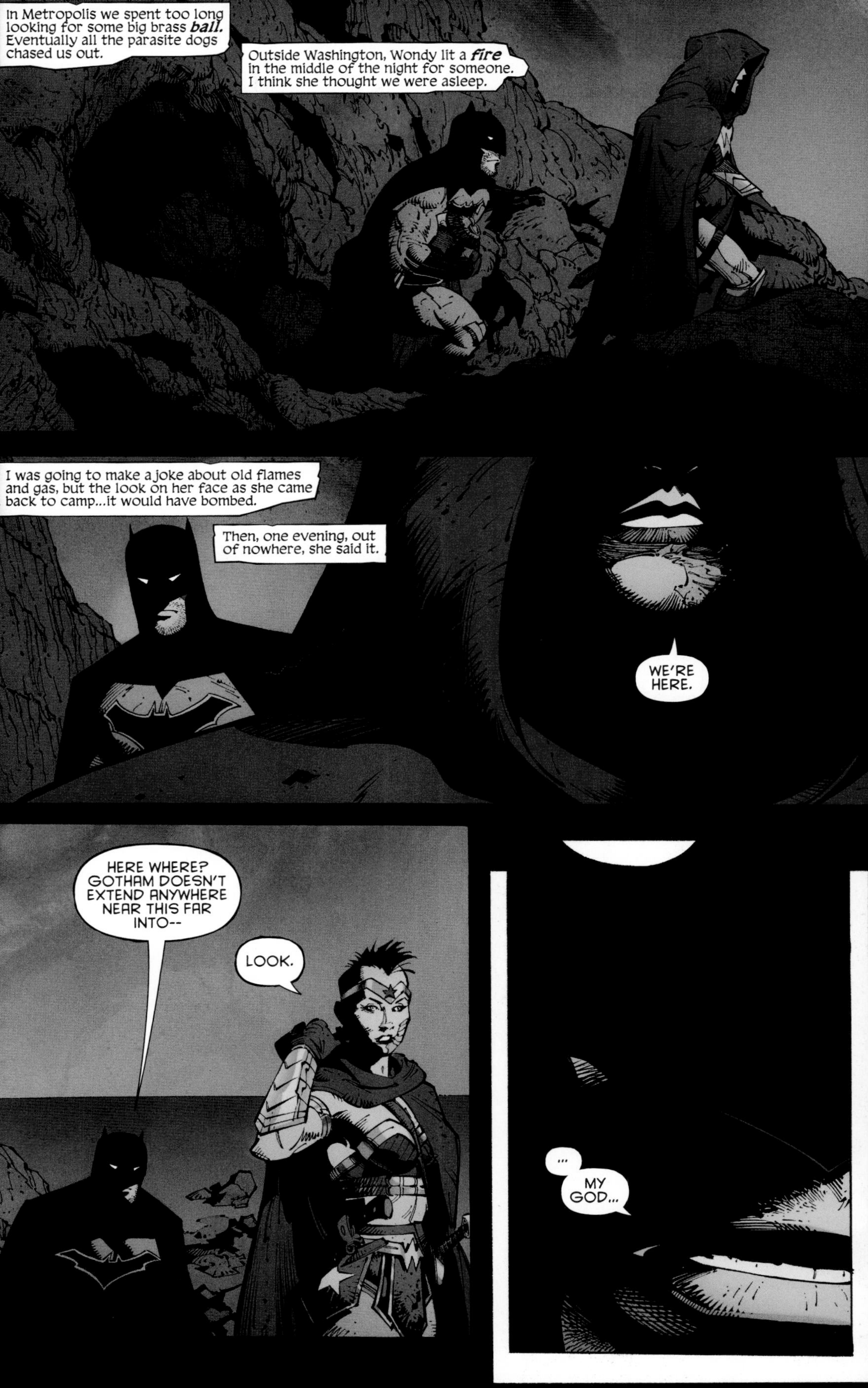
In Metropolis we spent too long looking for some big brass **ball.** Eventually all the parasite dogs chased us out.
Outside Washington, Wondy lit a ***fire*** in the middle of the night for someone. I think she thought we were asleep.
I was going to make a joke about old flames and gas, but the look on her face as she came back to camp...it would have bombed.
Then, one evening, out of nowhere, she said it.
WE'RE HERE.
HERE WHERE? GOTHAM DOESN'T EXTEND ANYWHERE NEAR THIS FAR INTO--
LOOK.
...
MY GOD...

PART SEVEN:
PARADISE

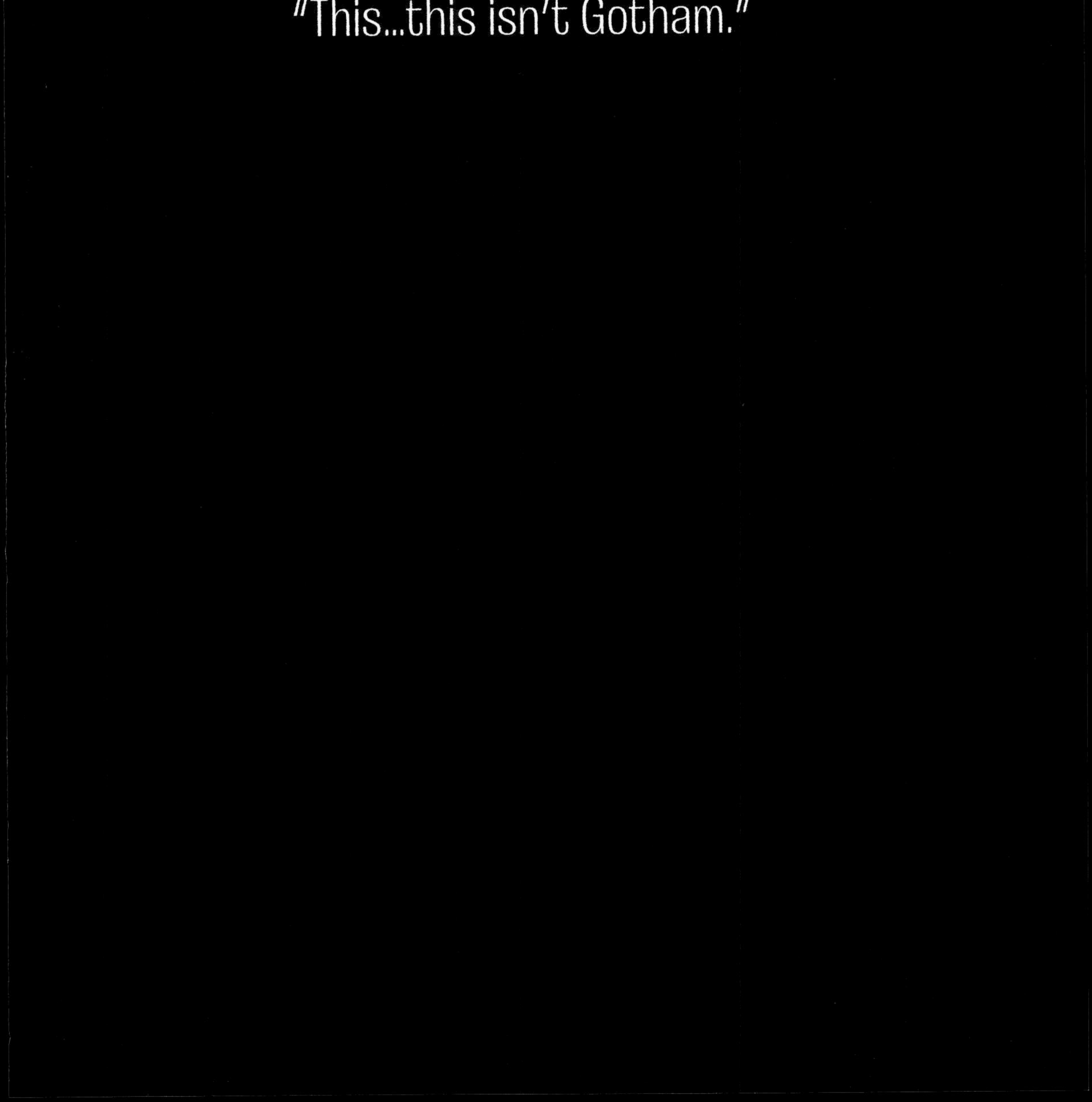
"This...this isn't Gotham."

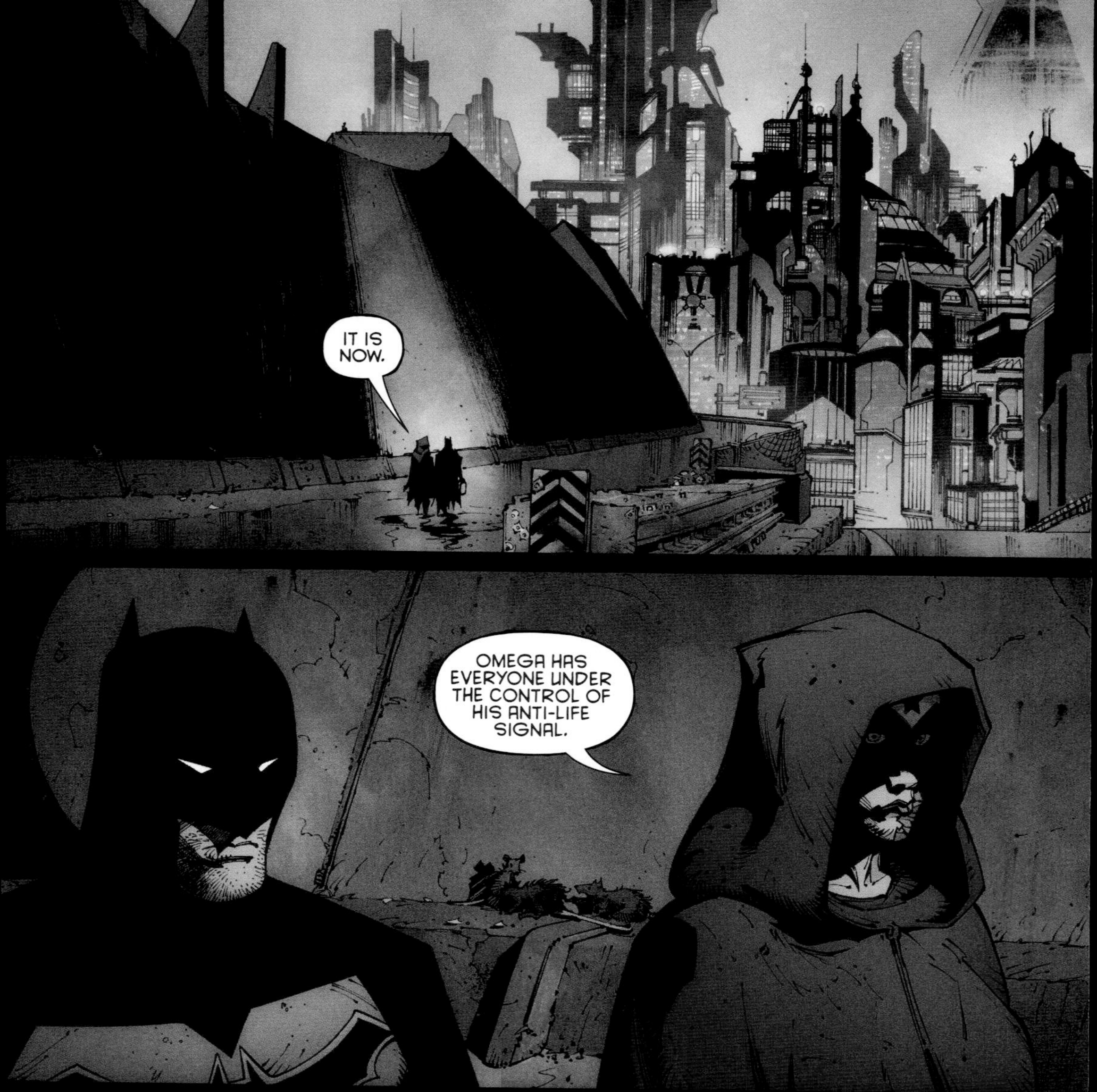
IT IS NOW.
OMEGA HAS EVERYONE UNDER THE CONTROL OF HIS ANTI-LIFE SIGNAL.

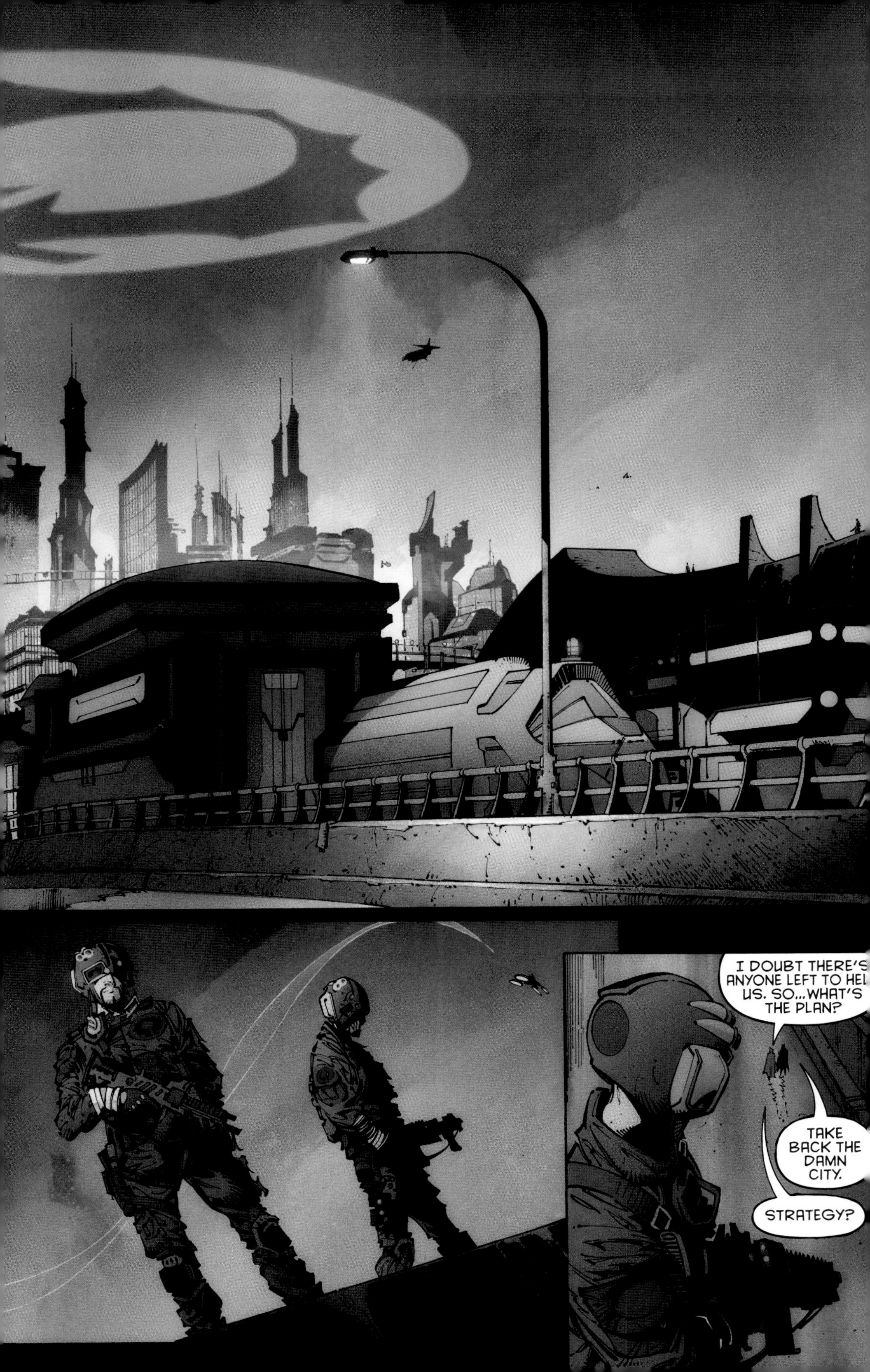
I DOUBT THERE'S ANYONE LEFT TO HEL US. SO...WHAT'S THE PLAN?
TAKE BACK THE DAMN CITY.
STRATEGY?

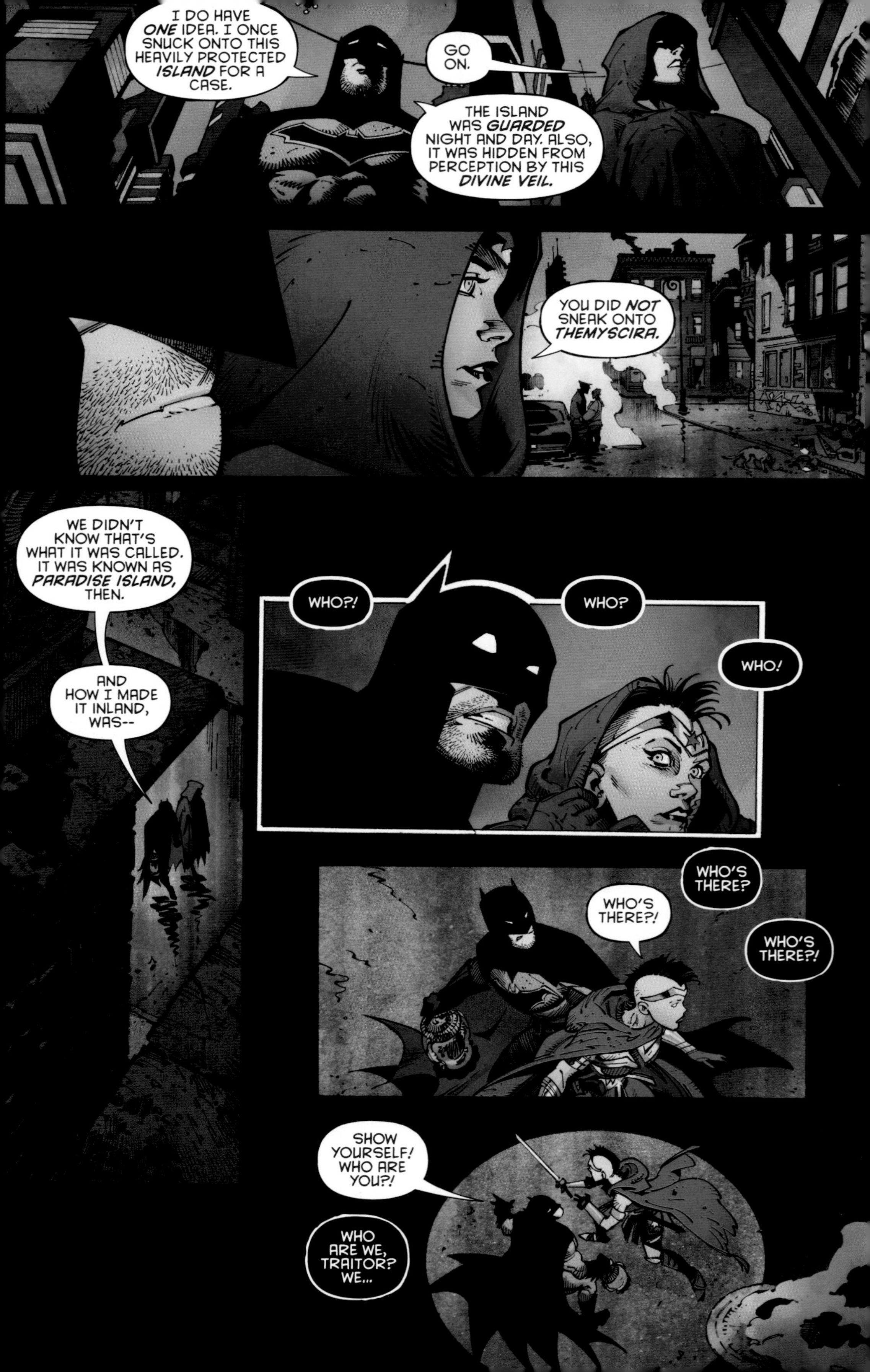
I DO HAVE ONE IDEA. I ONCE SNUCK ONTO THIS HEAVILY PROTECTED ISLAND FOR A CASE.
GO ON.
THE ISLAND WAS GUARDED NIGHT AND DAY. ALSO, IT WAS HIDDEN FROM PERCEPTION BY THIS DIVINE VEIL.
YOU DID NOT SNEAK ONTO THEMYSCIRA.
WE DIDN'T KNOW THAT'S WHAT IT WAS CALLED. IT WAS KNOWN AS PARADISE ISLAND, THEN.
AND HOW I MADE IT INLAND, WAS--
WHO?!
WHO?
WHO!
WHO'S THERE?
WHO'S THERE?!
WHO'S THERE?!
SHOW YOURSELF! WHO ARE YOU?!
WHO ARE WE, TRAITOR? WE...

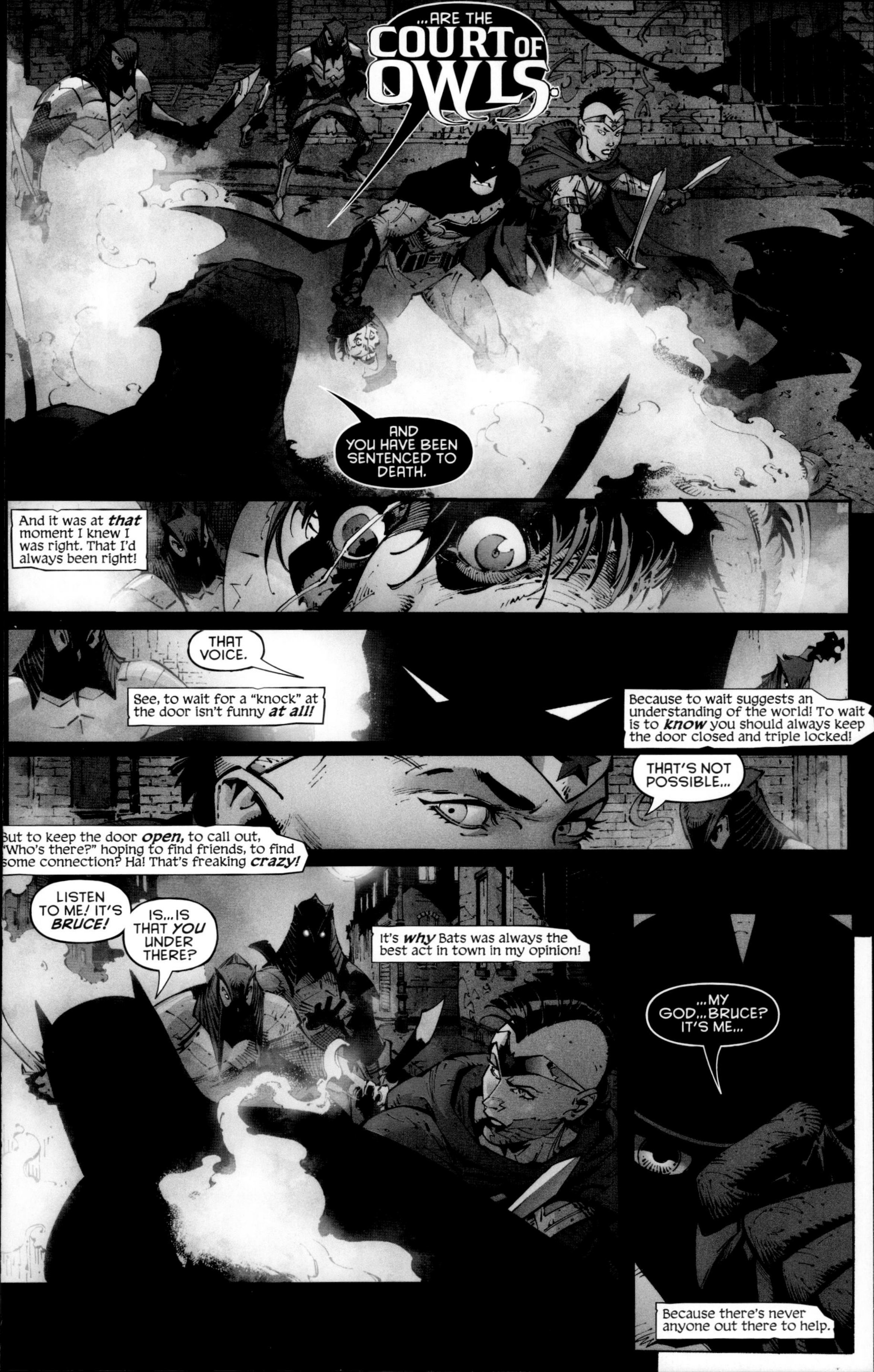
...ARE THE COURT OF OWLS.
AND YOU HAVE BEEN SENTENCED TO DEATH.
And it was at *that* moment I knew I was right. That I'd always been right!
THAT VOICE.
See, to wait for a "knock" at the door isn't funny *at all!*
Because to wait suggests an understanding of the world! To wait is to *know* you should always keep the door closed and triple locked!
THAT'S NOT POSSIBLE...
But to keep the door *open,* to call out, "Who's there?" hoping to find friends, to find some connection? Ha! That's freaking *crazy!*
LISTEN TO ME! IT'S *BRUCE!*
IS...IS THAT *YOU* UNDER THERE?
It's *why* Bats was always the best act in town in my opinion!
...MY GOD...BRUCE? IT'S ME...
Because there's never anyone out there to help.

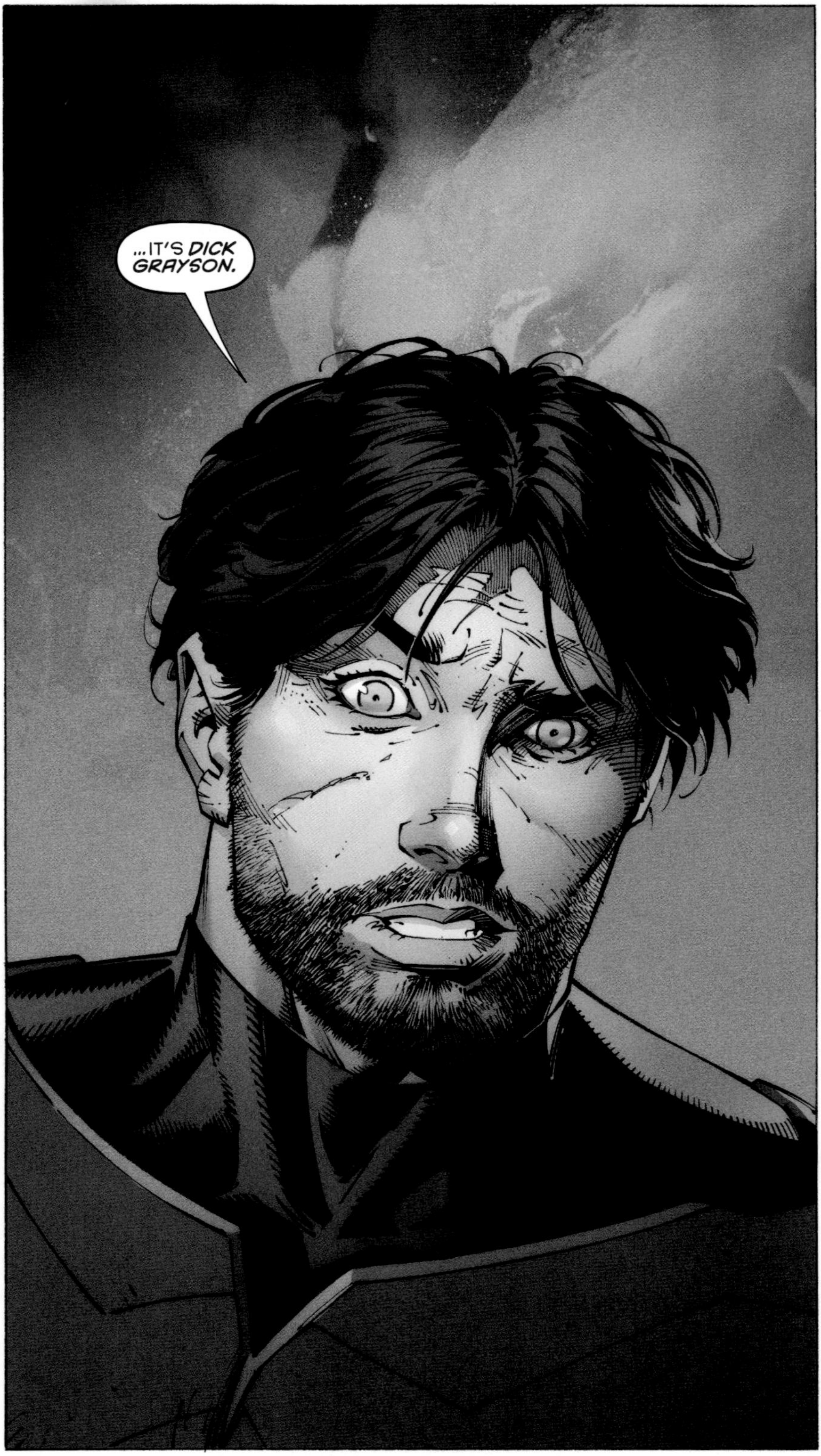
...IT'S DICK GRAYSON.

That's why it's funnier *my* way!

PART EIGHT:
THE SIGNAL

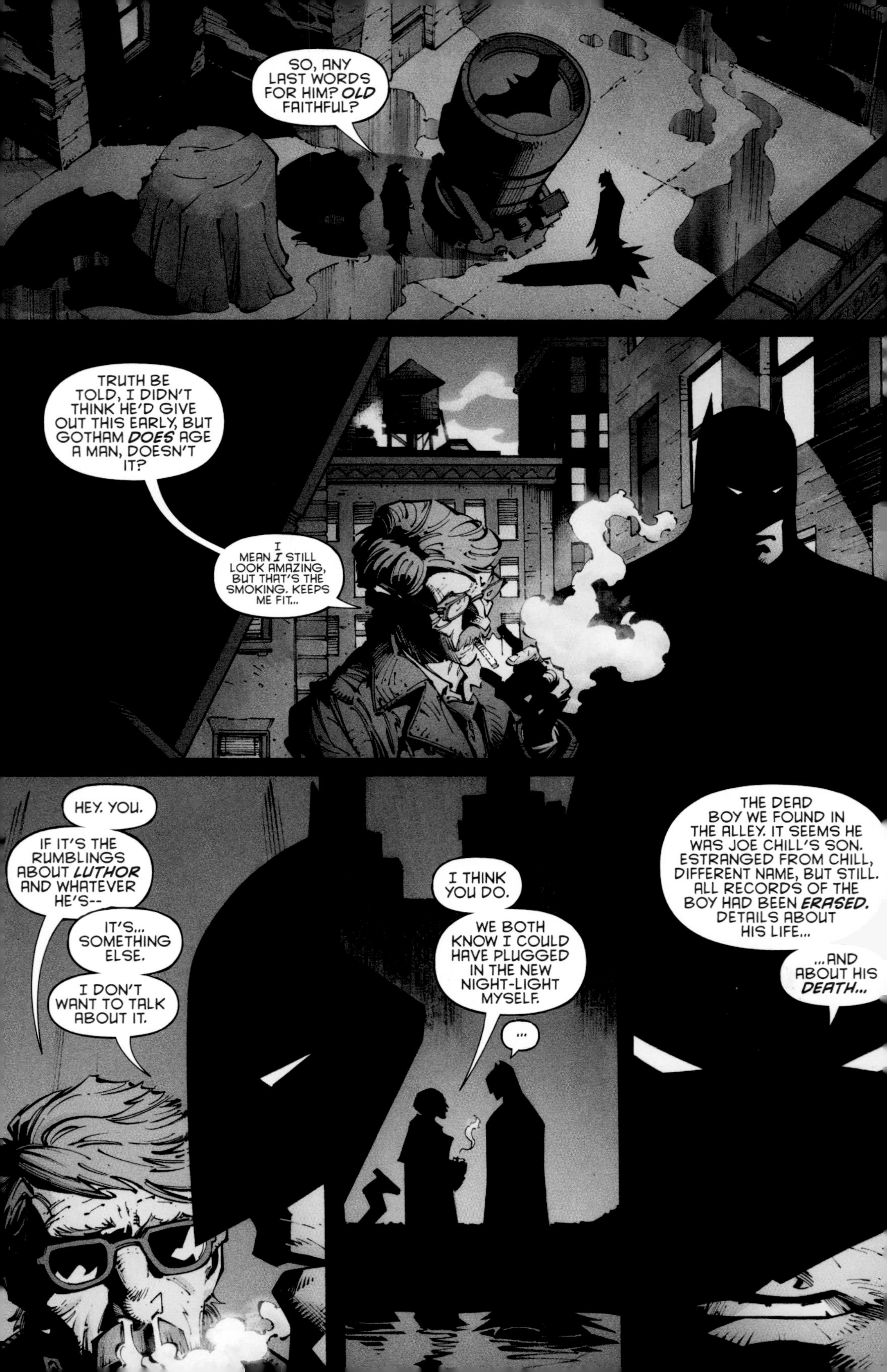
SO, ANY LAST WORDS FOR HIM? OLD FAITHFUL?
TRUTH BE TOLD, I DIDN'T THINK HE'D GIVE OUT THIS EARLY, BUT GOTHAM DOES AGE A MAN, DOESN'T IT?
I MEAN I STILL LOOK AMAZING, BUT THAT'S THE SMOKING. KEEPS ME FIT...
HEY. YOU.
IF IT'S THE RUMBLINGS ABOUT LUTHOR AND WHATEVER HE'S--
IT'S... SOMETHING ELSE.
I DON'T WANT TO TALK ABOUT IT.
I THINK YOU DO.
WE BOTH KNOW I COULD HAVE PLUGGED IN THE NEW NIGHT-LIGHT MYSELF.
...
THE DEAD BOY WE FOUND IN THE ALLEY. IT SEEMS HE WAS JOE CHILL'S SON. ESTRANGED FROM CHILL, DIFFERENT NAME, BUT STILL. ALL RECORDS OF THE BOY HAD BEEN ERASED. DETAILS ABOUT HIS LIFE...
...AND ABOUT HIS DEATH...

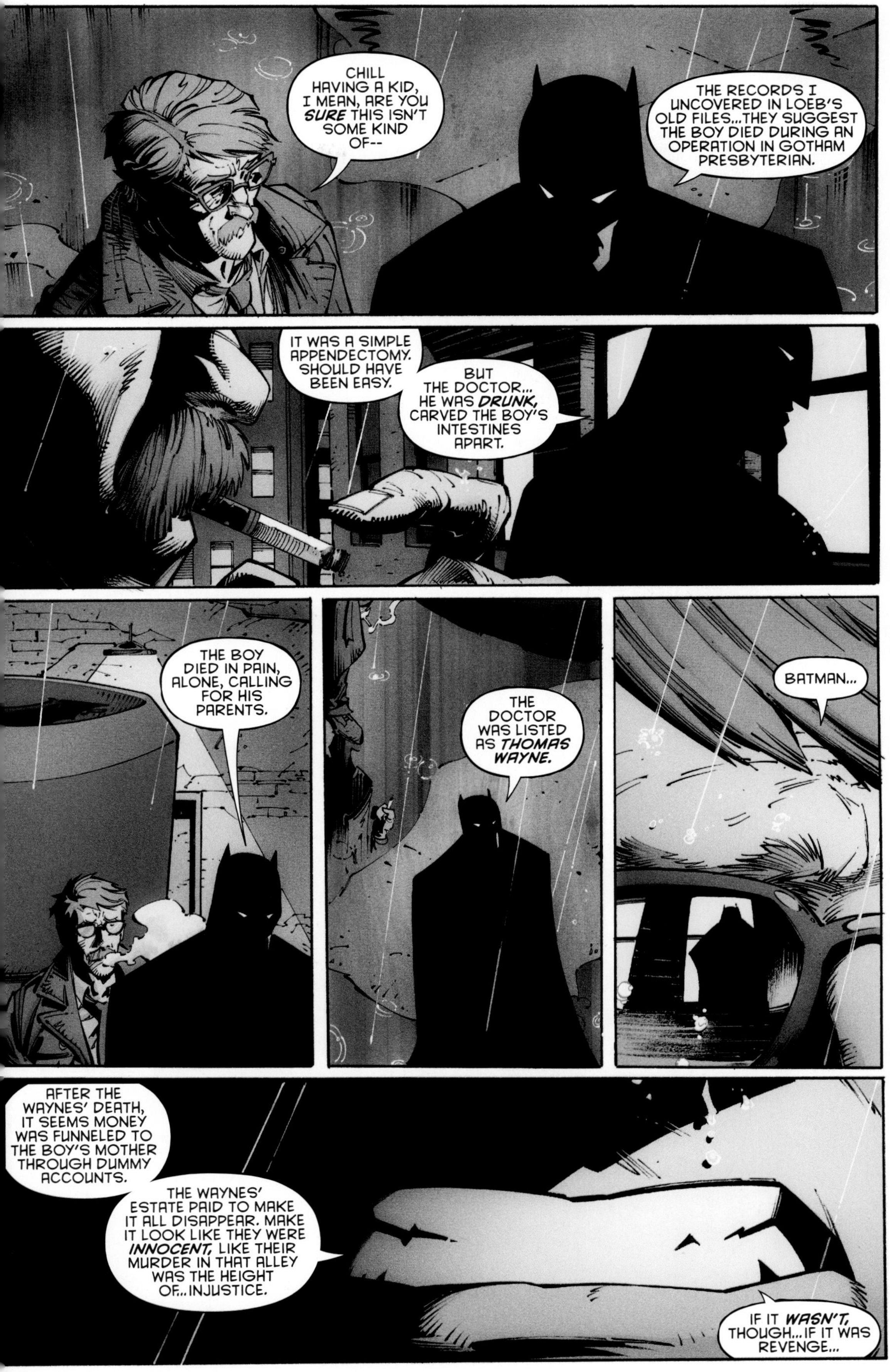
CHILL HAVING A KID, I MEAN, ARE YOU SURE THIS ISN'T SOME KIND OF--
THE RECORDS I UNCOVERED IN LOEB'S OLD FILES...THEY SUGGEST THE BOY DIED DURING AN OPERATION IN GOTHAM PRESBYTERIAN.
IT WAS A SIMPLE APPENDECTOMY. SHOULD HAVE BEEN EASY.
BUT THE DOCTOR... HE WAS DRUNK, CARVED THE BOY'S INTESTINES APART.
THE BOY DIED IN PAIN, ALONE, CALLING FOR HIS PARENTS.
THE DOCTOR WAS LISTED AS THOMAS WAYNE.
BATMAN...
AFTER THE WAYNES' DEATH, IT SEEMS MONEY WAS FUNNELED TO THE BOY'S MOTHER THROUGH DUMMY ACCOUNTS.
THE WAYNES' ESTATE PAID TO MAKE IT ALL DISAPPEAR. MAKE IT LOOK LIKE THEY WERE INNOCENT, LIKE THEIR MURDER IN THAT ALLEY WAS THE HEIGHT OF...INJUSTICE.
IF IT WASN'T, THOUGH...IF IT WAS REVENGE...

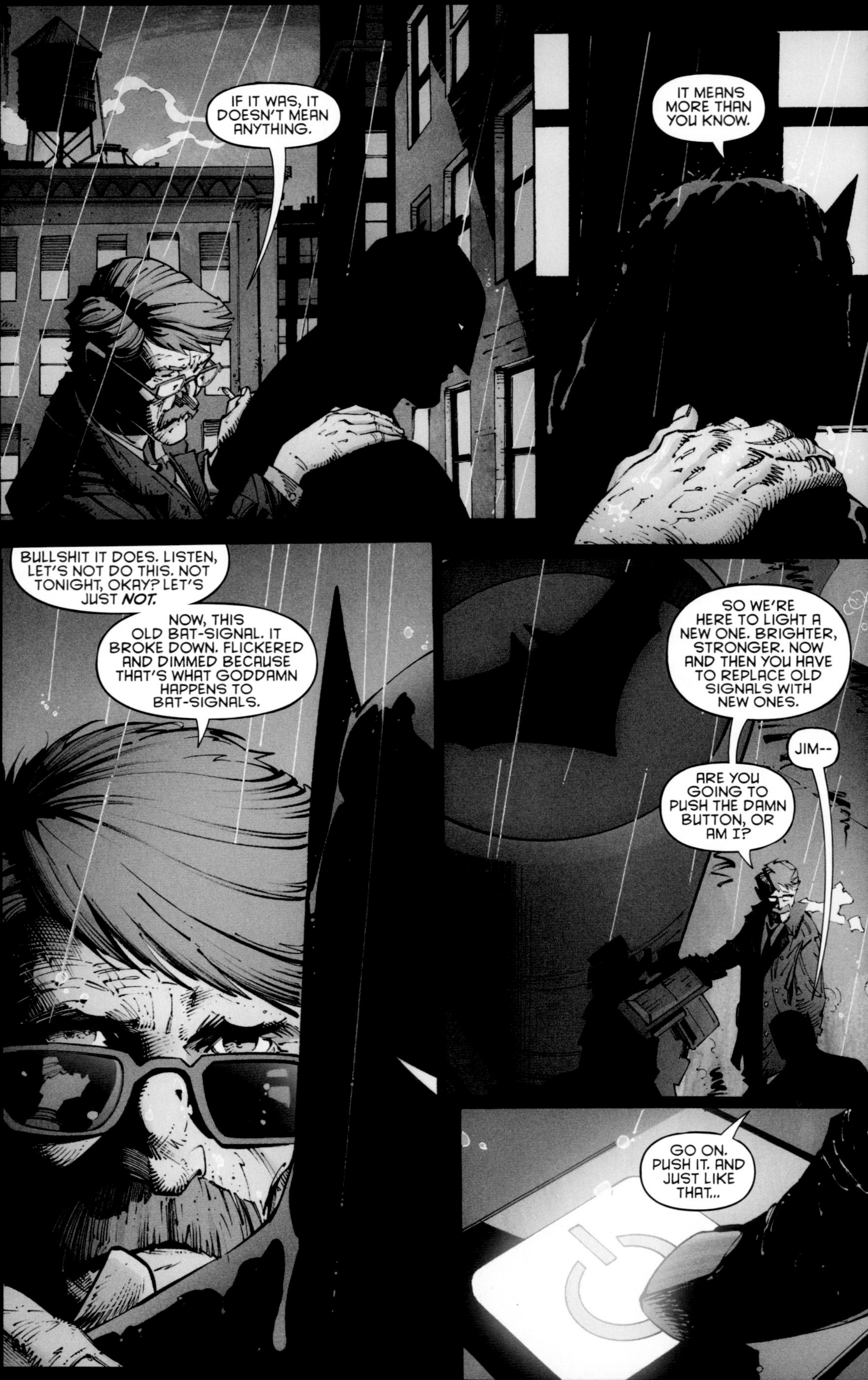
IF IT WAS, IT DOESN'T MEAN ANYTHING.
IT MEANS MORE THAN YOU KNOW.
BULLSHIT IT DOES. LISTEN, LET'S NOT DO THIS. NOT TONIGHT, OKAY? LET'S JUST NOT.
NOW, THIS OLD BAT-SIGNAL. IT BROKE DOWN. FLICKERED AND DIMMED BECAUSE THAT'S WHAT GODDAMN HAPPENS TO BAT-SIGNALS.
SO WE'RE HERE TO LIGHT A NEW ONE. BRIGHTER, STRONGER. NOW AND THEN YOU HAVE TO REPLACE OLD SIGNALS WITH NEW ONES.
JIM--
ARE YOU GOING TO PUSH THE DAMN BUTTON, OR AM I?
GO ON. PUSH IT. AND JUST LIKE THAT...

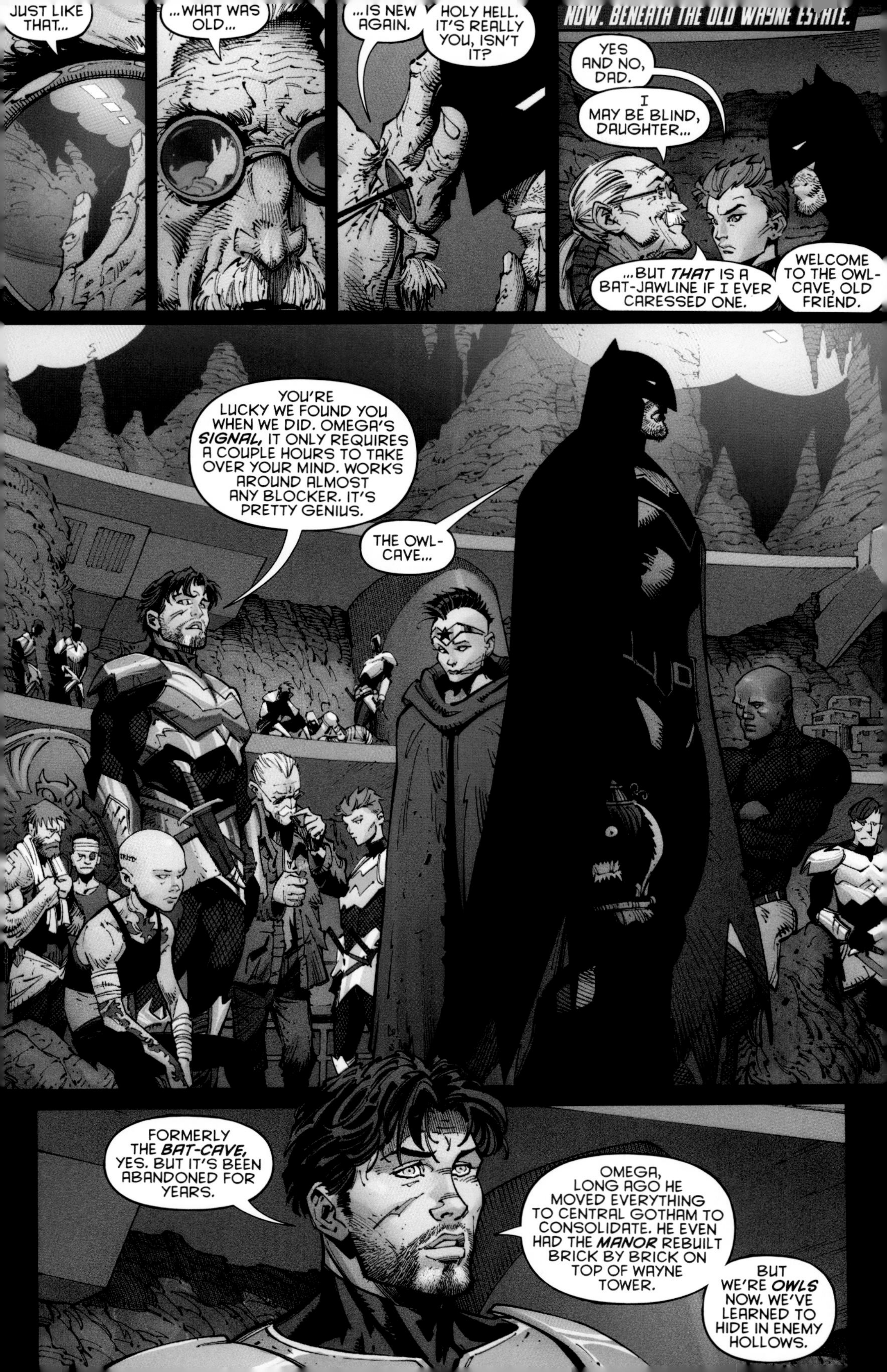
JUST LIKE THAT...
...WHAT WAS OLD...
...IS NEW AGAIN.
HOLY HELL. IT'S REALLY YOU, ISN'T IT?
NOW. BENEATH THE OLD WAYNE ESTATE.
YES AND NO, DAD.
I MAY BE BLIND, DAUGHTER...
...BUT THAT IS A BAT-JAWLINE IF I EVER CARESSED ONE.
WELCOME TO THE OWL-CAVE, OLD FRIEND.
YOU'RE LUCKY WE FOUND YOU WHEN WE DID. OMEGA'S SIGNAL, IT ONLY REQUIRES A COUPLE HOURS TO TAKE OVER YOUR MIND. WORKS AROUND ALMOST ANY BLOCKER. IT'S PRETTY GENIUS.
THE OWL-CAVE...
FORMERLY THE BAT-CAVE, YES. BUT IT'S BEEN ABANDONED FOR YEARS.
OMEGA, LONG AGO HE MOVED EVERYTHING TO CENTRAL GOTHAM TO CONSOLIDATE. HE EVEN HAD THE MANOR REBUILT BRICK BY BRICK ON TOP OF WAYNE TOWER.
BUT WE'RE OWLS NOW. WE'VE LEARNED TO HIDE IN ENEMY HOLLOWS.

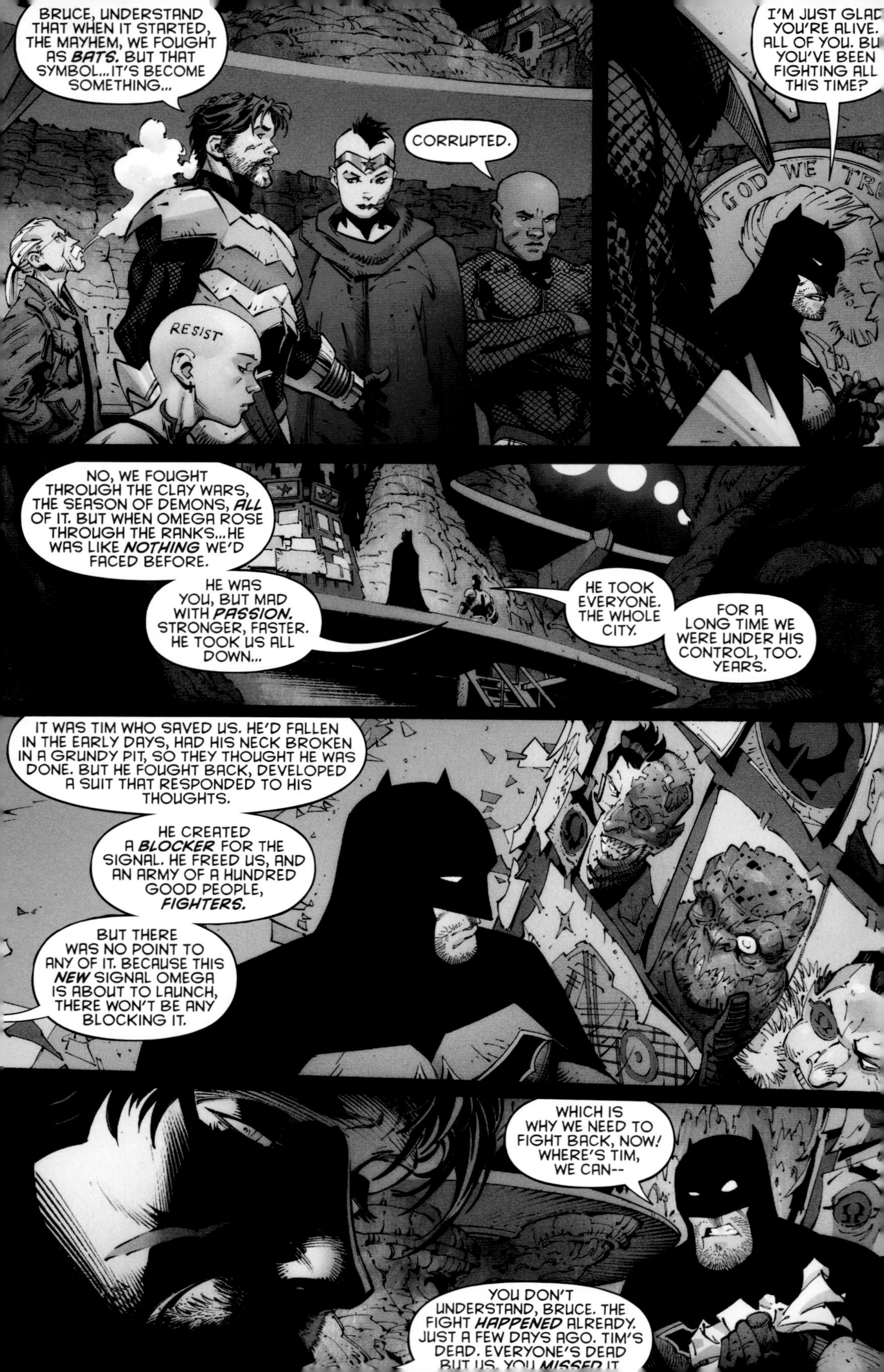
BRUCE, UNDERSTAND THAT WHEN IT STARTED, THE MAYHEM, WE FOUGHT AS *BATS.* BUT THAT SYMBOL...IT'S BECOME SOMETHING...
CORRUPTED.
RESIST
I'M JUST GLAD YOU'RE ALIVE. ALL OF YOU. BU YOU'VE BEEN FIGHTING ALL THIS TIME?
GOD WE
NO, WE FOUGHT THROUGH THE CLAY WARS, THE SEASON OF DEMONS, *ALL* OF IT. BUT WHEN OMEGA ROSE THROUGH THE RANKS...HE WAS LIKE *NOTHING* WE'D FACED BEFORE.
HE WAS YOU, BUT MAD WITH *PASSION.* STRONGER, FASTER. HE TOOK US ALL DOWN...
HE TOOK EVERYONE. THE WHOLE CITY.
FOR A LONG TIME WE WERE UNDER HIS CONTROL, TOO. YEARS.
IT WAS TIM WHO SAVED US. HE'D FALLEN IN THE EARLY DAYS, HAD HIS NECK BROKEN IN A GRUNDY PIT, SO THEY THOUGHT HE WAS DONE. BUT HE FOUGHT BACK, DEVELOPED A SUIT THAT RESPONDED TO HIS THOUGHTS.
HE CREATED A *BLOCKER* FOR THE SIGNAL. HE FREED US, AND AN ARMY OF A HUNDRED GOOD PEOPLE, *FIGHTERS.*
BUT THERE WAS NO POINT TO ANY OF IT. BECAUSE THIS *NEW* SIGNAL OMEGA IS ABOUT TO LAUNCH, THERE WON'T BE ANY BLOCKING IT.
WHICH IS WHY WE NEED TO FIGHT BACK, NOW! WHERE'S TIM, WE CAN--
YOU DON'T UNDERSTAND, BRUCE. THE FIGHT *HAPPENED* ALREADY. JUST A FEW DAYS AGO. TIM'S DEAD. EVERYONE'S DEAD BUT US. YOU *MISSED* IT.

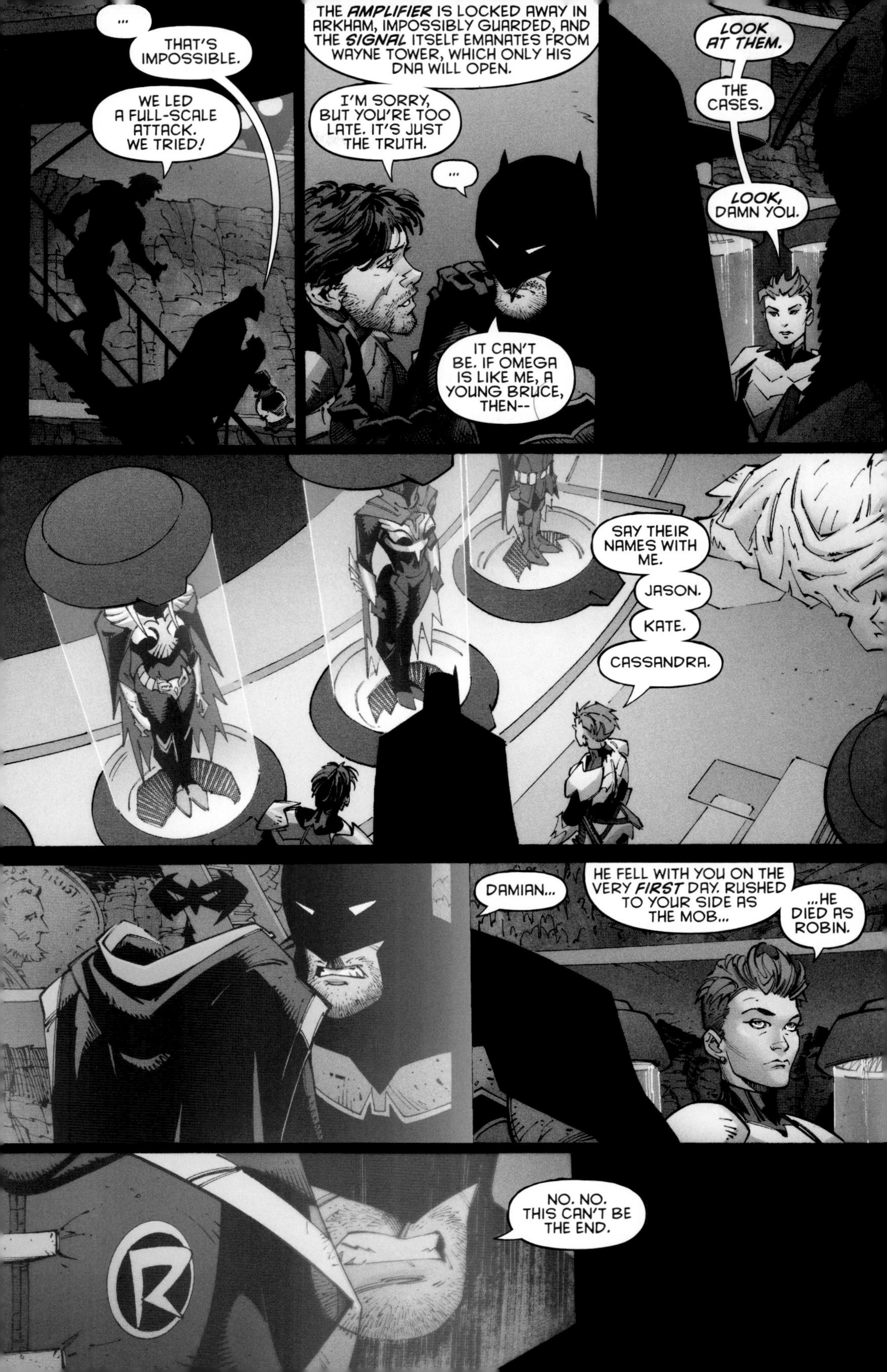
...
THAT'S IMPOSSIBLE.
WE LED A FULL-SCALE ATTACK. WE TRIED!
THE *AMPLIFIER* IS LOCKED AWAY IN ARKHAM, IMPOSSIBLY GUARDED, AND THE *SIGNAL* ITSELF EMANATES FROM WAYNE TOWER, WHICH ONLY HIS DNA WILL OPEN.
I'M SORRY, BUT YOU'RE TOO LATE. IT'S JUST THE TRUTH.
...
IT CAN'T BE. IF OMEGA IS LIKE ME, A YOUNG BRUCE, THEN--
LOOK AT THEM.
THE CASES.
LOOK, DAMN YOU.
SAY THEIR NAMES WITH ME.
JASON.
KATE.
CASSANDRA.
DAMIAN...
HE FELL WITH YOU ON THE VERY *FIRST* DAY. RUSHED TO YOUR SIDE AS THE MOB...
...HE DIED AS ROBIN.
NO. NO. THIS CAN'T BE THE END.

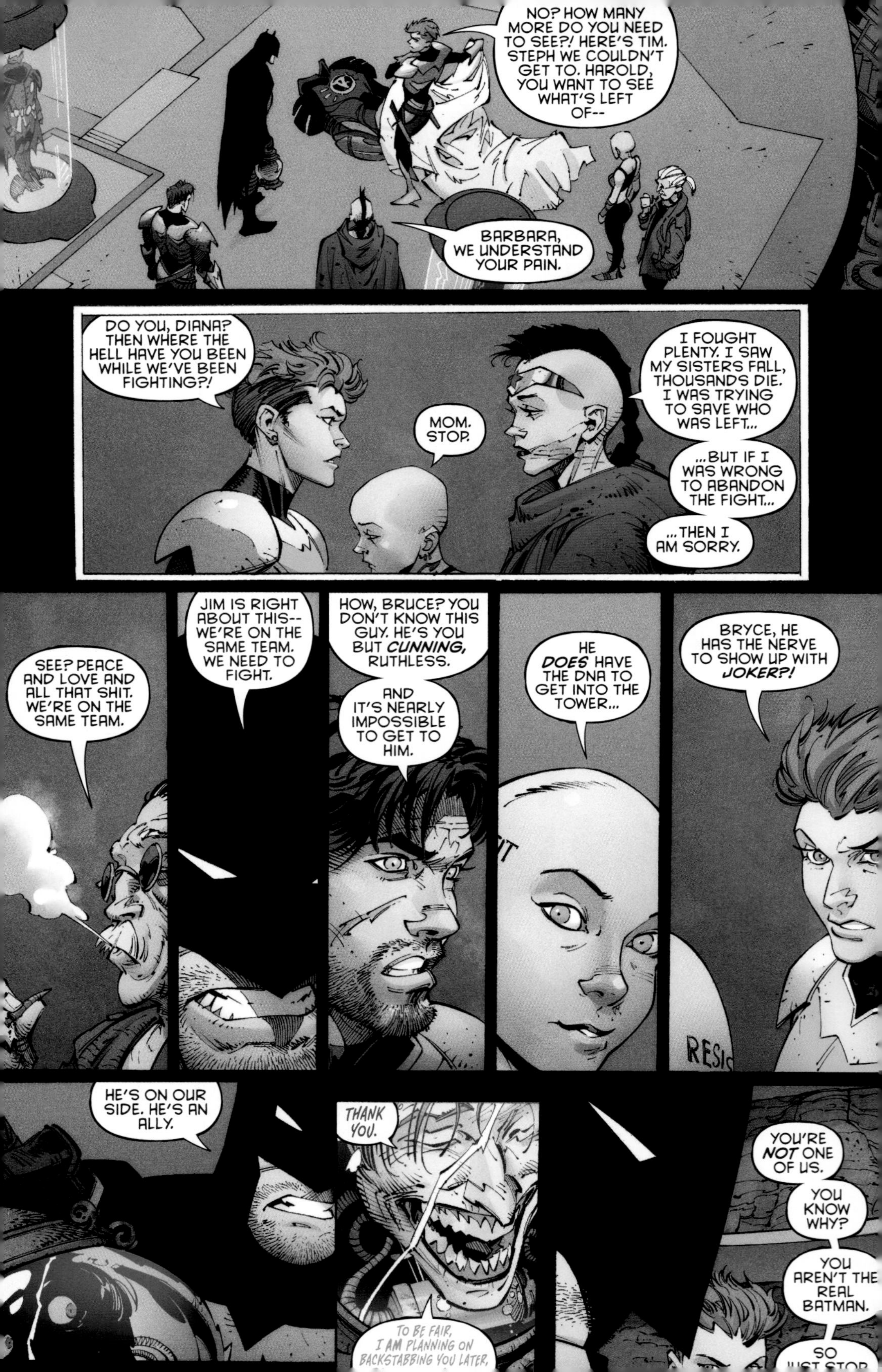
NO? HOW MANY MORE DO YOU NEED TO SEE?! HERE'S TIM. STEPH WE COULDN'T GET TO. HAROLD, YOU WANT TO SEE WHAT'S LEFT OF--
BARBARA, WE UNDERSTAND YOUR PAIN.
DO YOU, DIANA? THEN WHERE THE HELL HAVE YOU BEEN WHILE WE'VE BEEN FIGHTING?!
MOM. STOP.
I FOUGHT PLENTY. I SAW MY SISTERS FALL, THOUSANDS DIE. I WAS TRYING TO SAVE WHO WAS LEFT...
...BUT IF I WAS WRONG TO ABANDON THE FIGHT...
...THEN I AM SORRY.
SEE? PEACE AND LOVE AND ALL THAT SHIT. WE'RE ON THE SAME TEAM.
JIM IS RIGHT ABOUT THIS-- WE'RE ON THE SAME TEAM. WE NEED TO FIGHT.
HOW, BRUCE? YOU DON'T KNOW THIS GUY. HE'S YOU BUT CUNNING, RUTHLESS.
AND IT'S NEARLY IMPOSSIBLE TO GET TO HIM.
HE DOES HAVE THE DNA TO GET INTO THE TOWER...
BRYCE, HE HAS THE NERVE TO SHOW UP WITH JOKER?!
RESIS
HE'S ON OUR SIDE. HE'S AN ALLY.
THANK YOU.
TO BE FAIR, I AM PLANNING ON BACKSTABBING YOU LATER.
YOU'RE NOT ONE OF US.
YOU KNOW WHY?
YOU AREN'T THE REAL BATMAN.
SO

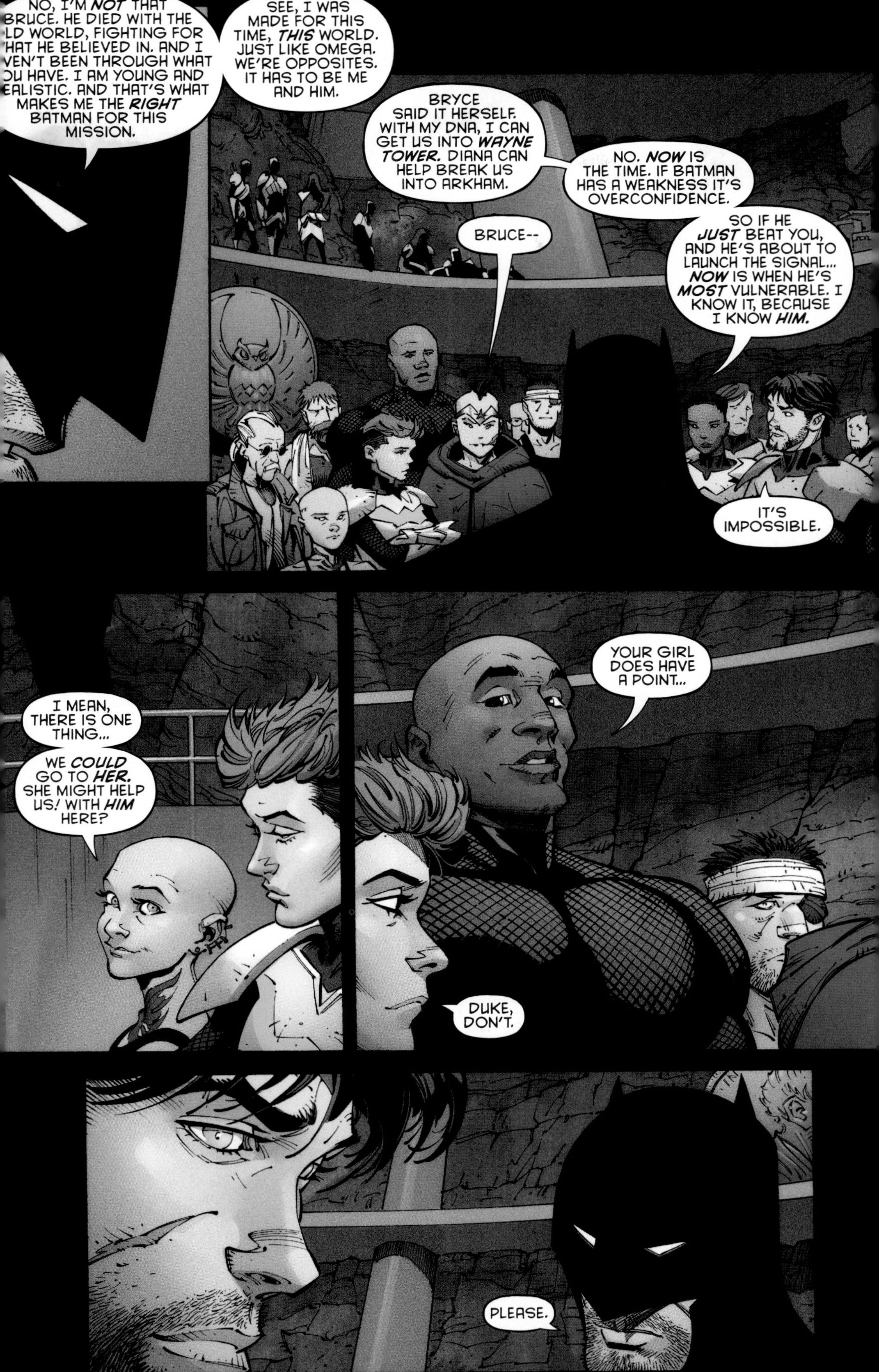

NO, I'M NOT THAT BRUCE. HE DIED WITH THE OLD WORLD, FIGHTING FOR WHAT HE BELIEVED IN. AND I HAVEN'T BEEN THROUGH WHAT YOU HAVE. I AM YOUNG AND REALISTIC. AND THAT'S WHAT MAKES ME THE RIGHT BATMAN FOR THIS MISSION.
SEE, I WAS MADE FOR THIS TIME, THIS WORLD. JUST LIKE OMEGA. WE'RE OPPOSITES. IT HAS TO BE ME AND HIM.
BRYCE SAID IT HERSELF. WITH MY DNA, I CAN GET US INTO WAYNE TOWER. DIANA CAN HELP BREAK US INTO ARKHAM.
NO. NOW IS THE TIME. IF BATMAN HAS A WEAKNESS IT'S OVERCONFIDENCE.
BRUCE--
SO IF HE JUST BEAT YOU, AND HE'S ABOUT TO LAUNCH THE SIGNAL... NOW IS WHEN HE'S MOST VULNERABLE. I KNOW IT, BECAUSE I KNOW HIM.
IT'S IMPOSSIBLE.
I MEAN, THERE IS ONE THING...
WE COULD GO TO HER. SHE MIGHT HELP US! WITH HIM HERE?
YOUR GIRL DOES HAVE A POINT...
DUKE, DON'T.
PLEASE.

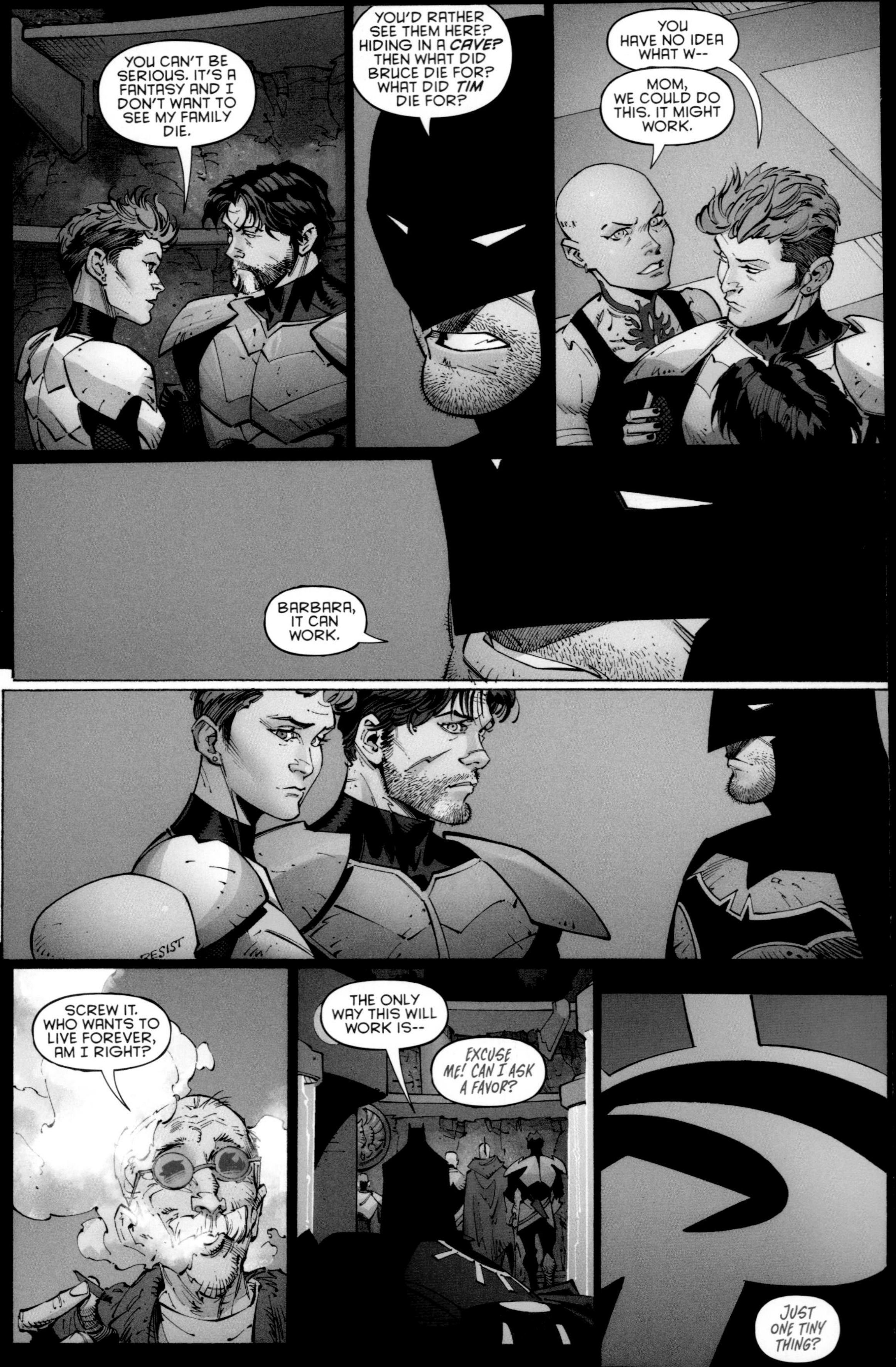
YOU CAN'T BE SERIOUS. IT'S A FANTASY AND I DON'T WANT TO SEE MY FAMILY DIE.
YOU'D RATHER SEE THEM HERE? HIDING IN A *CAVE?* THEN WHAT DID BRUCE DIE FOR? WHAT DID *TIM* DIE FOR?
YOU HAVE NO IDEA WHAT W--
MOM, WE COULD DO THIS. IT MIGHT WORK.
BARBARA, IT CAN WORK.
RESIST
SCREW IT. WHO WANTS TO LIVE FOREVER, AM I RIGHT?
THE ONLY WAY THIS WILL WORK IS--
EXCUSE ME! CAN I ASK A FAVOR?
JUST ONE TINY THING?

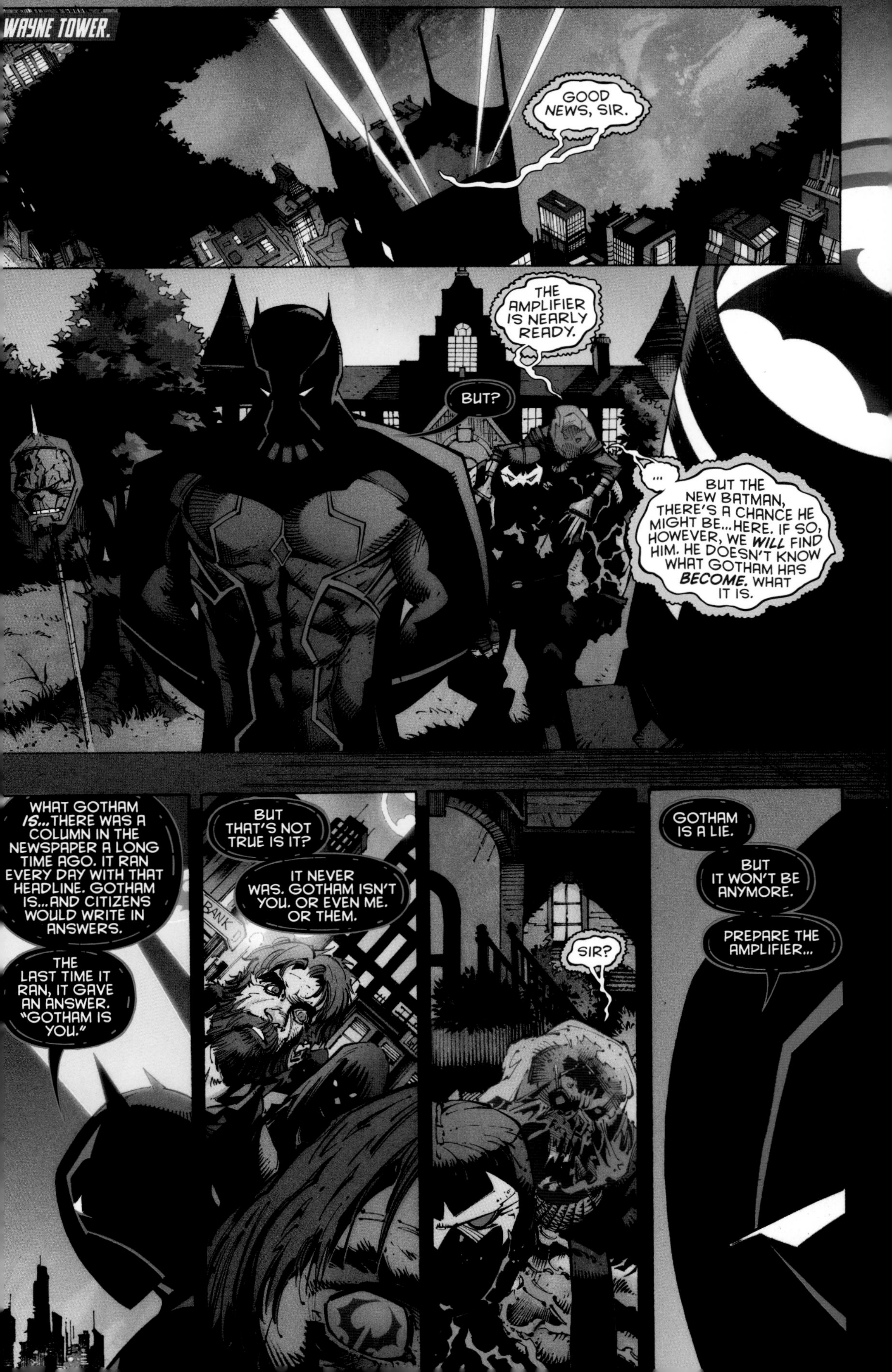
WAYNE TOWER.
GOOD NEWS, SIR.
THE AMPLIFIER IS NEARLY READY.
BUT?
...
BUT THE NEW BATMAN, THERE'S A CHANCE HE MIGHT BE...HERE. IF SO, HOWEVER, WE WILL FIND HIM. HE DOESN'T KNOW WHAT GOTHAM HAS BECOME. WHAT IT IS.
WHAT GOTHAM IS...THERE WAS A COLUMN IN THE NEWSPAPER A LONG TIME AGO. IT RAN EVERY DAY WITH THAT HEADLINE. GOTHAM IS...AND CITIZENS WOULD WRITE IN ANSWERS.
THE LAST TIME IT RAN, IT GAVE AN ANSWER. "GOTHAM IS YOU."
BUT THAT'S NOT TRUE IS IT?
IT NEVER WAS. GOTHAM ISN'T YOU. OR EVEN ME. OR THEM.
BANK
SIR?
GOTHAM IS A LIE.
BUT IT WON'T BE ANYMORE.
PREPARE THE AMPLIFIER...

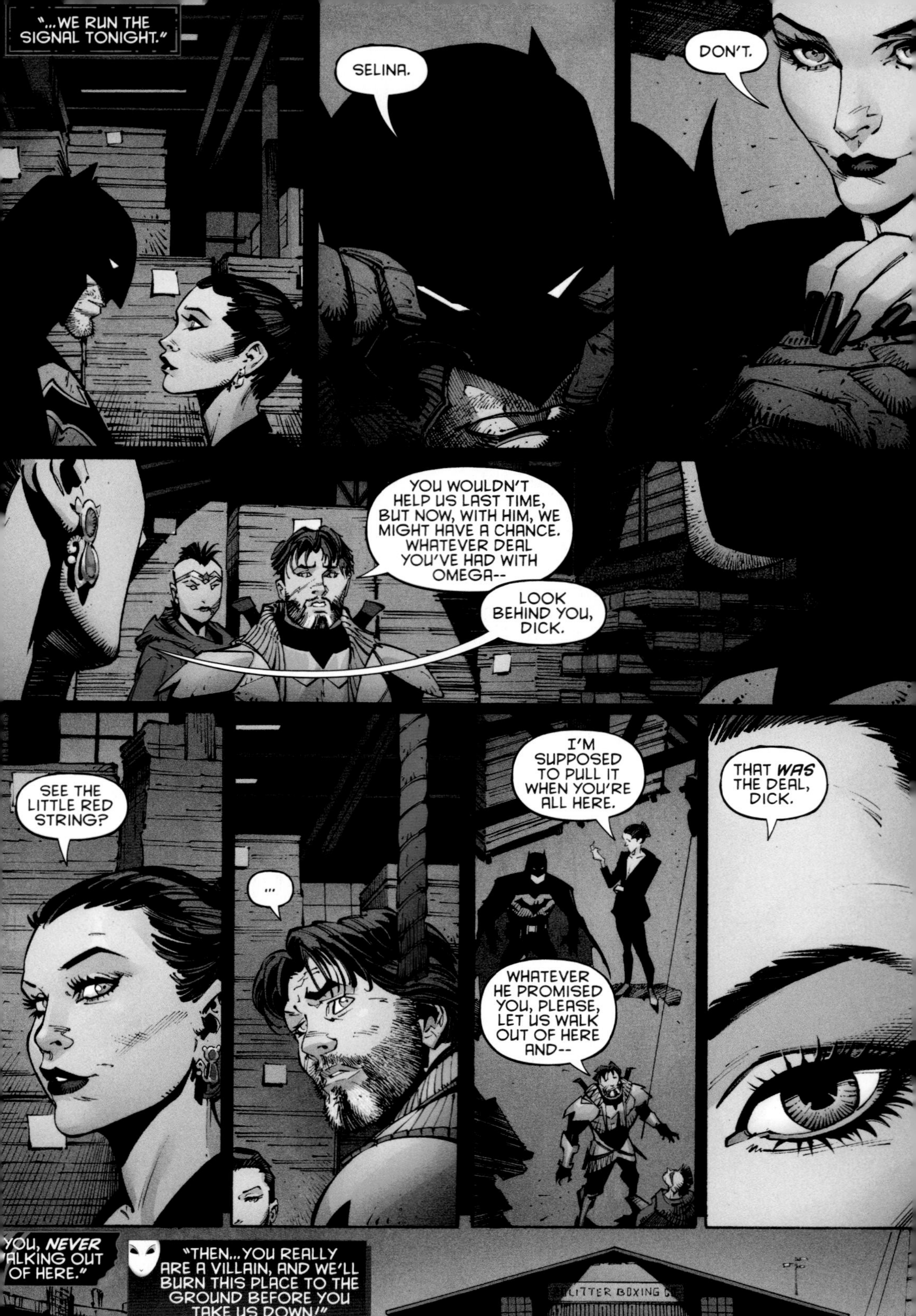
"...WE RUN THE SIGNAL TONIGHT."
SELINA.
DON'T.
YOU WOULDN'T HELP US LAST TIME, BUT NOW, WITH HIM, WE MIGHT HAVE A CHANCE. WHATEVER DEAL YOU'VE HAD WITH OMEGA--
LOOK BEHIND YOU, DICK.
SEE THE LITTLE RED STRING?
...
I'M SUPPOSED TO PULL IT WHEN YOU'RE ALL HERE.
WHATEVER HE PROMISED YOU, PLEASE, LET US WALK OUT OF HERE AND--
THAT *WAS* THE DEAL, DICK.
YOU, *NEVER* WALKING OUT OF HERE."
"THEN...YOU REALLY ARE A VILLAIN, AND WE'LL BURN THIS PLACE TO THE GROUND BEFORE YOU TAKE US DOWN!"
LITTER BOXING

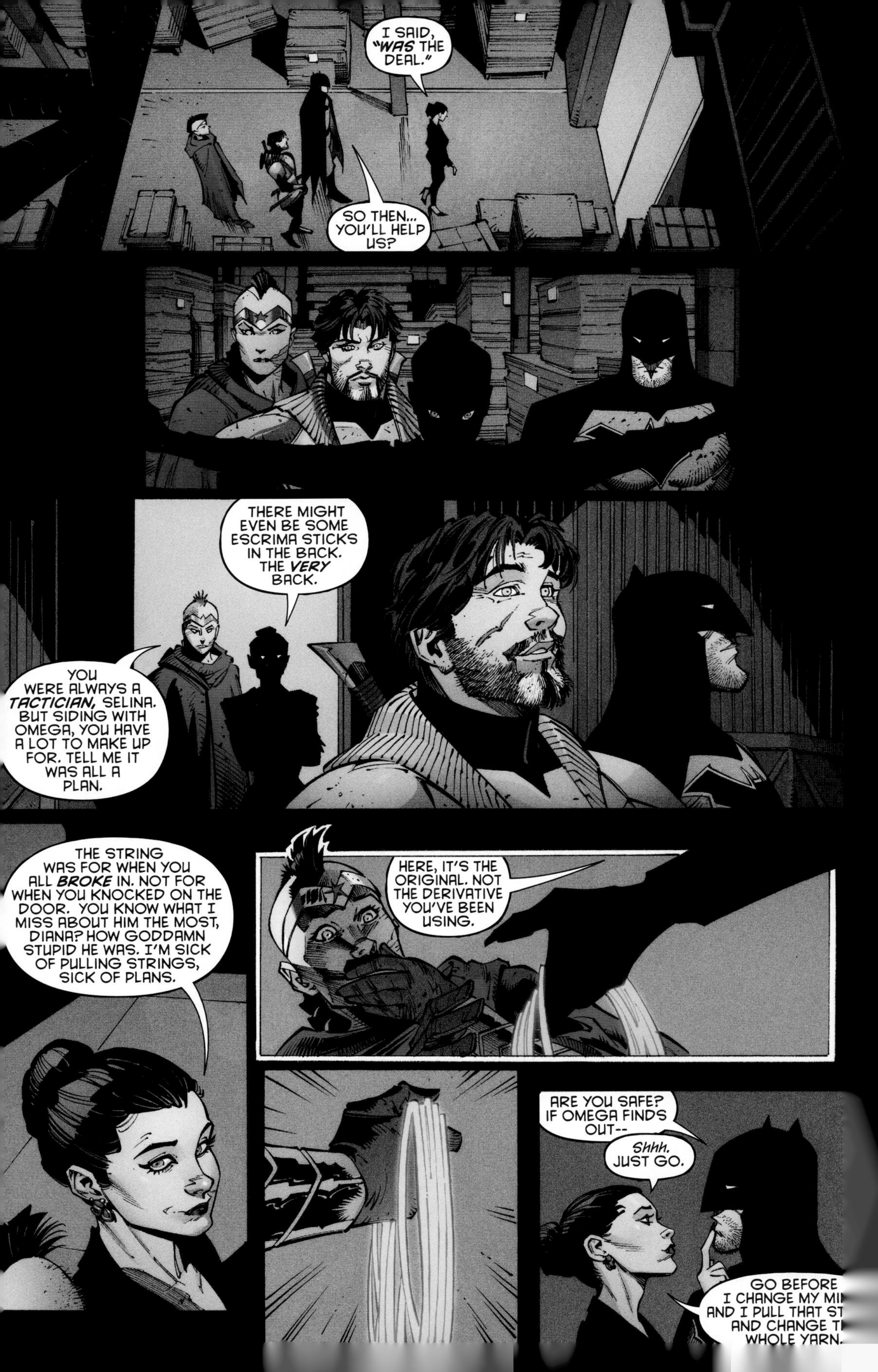
I SAID, "WAS THE DEAL."
SO THEN... YOU'LL HELP US?
THERE MIGHT EVEN BE SOME ESCRIMA STICKS IN THE BACK. THE VERY BACK.
YOU WERE ALWAYS A TACTICIAN, SELINA. BUT SIDING WITH OMEGA, YOU HAVE A LOT TO MAKE UP FOR. TELL ME IT WAS ALL A PLAN.
THE STRING WAS FOR WHEN YOU ALL BROKE IN. NOT FOR WHEN YOU KNOCKED ON THE DOOR. YOU KNOW WHAT I MISS ABOUT HIM THE MOST, DIANA? HOW GODDAMN STUPID HE WAS. I'M SICK OF PULLING STRINGS, SICK OF PLANS.
HERE, IT'S THE ORIGINAL. NOT THE DERIVATIVE YOU'VE BEEN USING.
ARE YOU SAFE? IF OMEGA FINDS OUT--
Shhh. JUST GO.
GO BEFORE I CHANGE MY MI AND I PULL THAT ST AND CHANGE T WHOLE YARN.

PART NINE:
P.O.W.

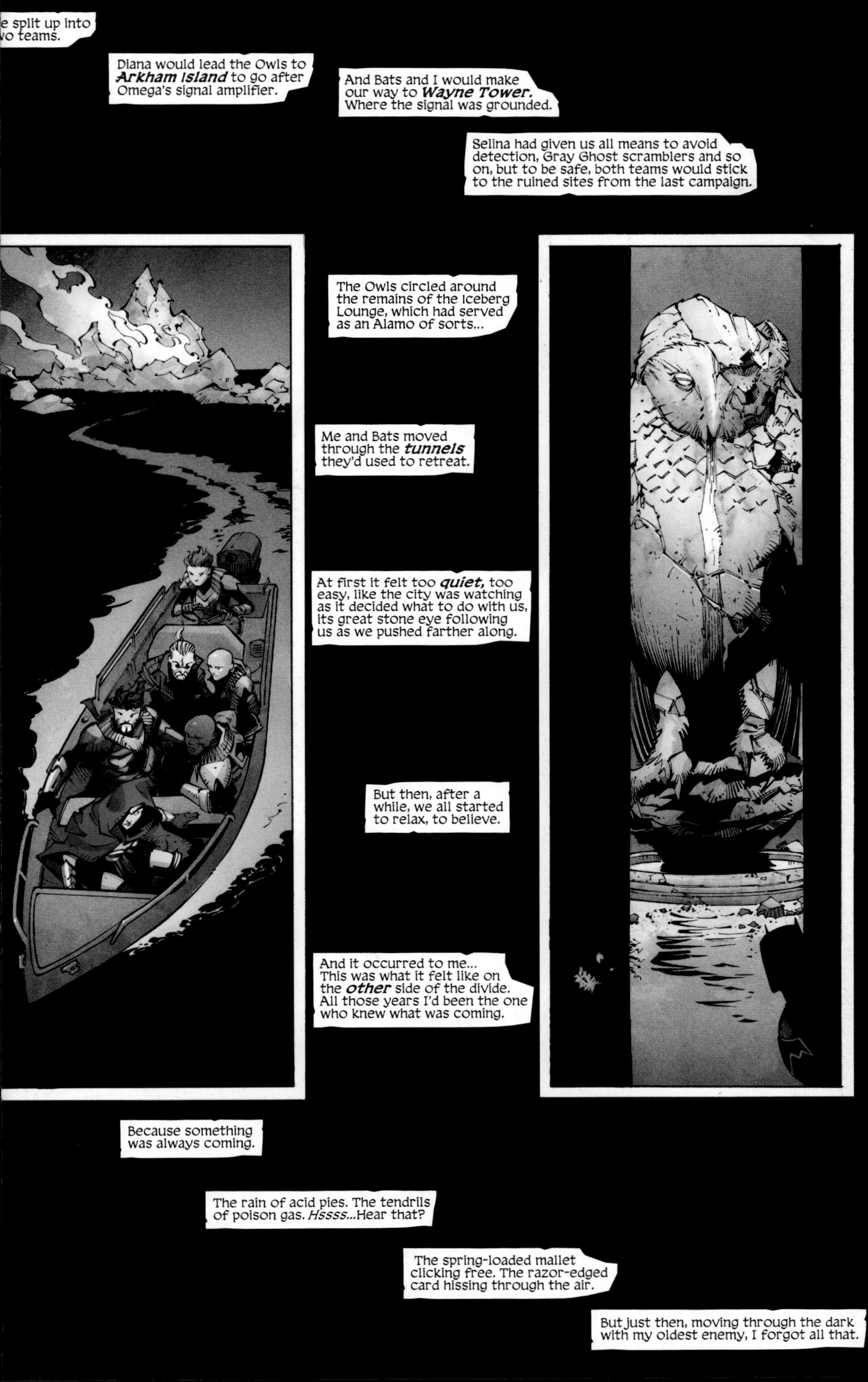
e split up into vo teams.
Diana would lead the Owls to *Arkham Island* to go after Omega's signal amplifier.
And Bats and I would make our way to *Wayne Tower.* Where the signal was grounded.
Selina had given us all means to avoid detection, Gray Ghost scramblers and so on, but to be safe, both teams would stick to the ruined sites from the last campaign.
The Owls circled around the remains of the Iceberg Lounge, which had served as an Alamo of sorts...
Me and Bats moved through the *tunnels* they'd used to retreat.
At first it felt too *quiet,* too easy, like the city was watching as it decided what to do with us, its great stone eye following us as we pushed farther along.
But then, after a while, we all started to relax, to believe.
And it occurred to me... This was what it felt like on the *other* side of the divide. All those years I'd been the one who knew what was coming.
Because something was always coming.
The rain of acid pies. The tendrils of poison gas. *Hssss...*Hear that?
The spring-loaded mallet clicking free. The razor-edged card hissing through the air.
But just then, moving through the dark with my oldest enemy, I forgot all that.

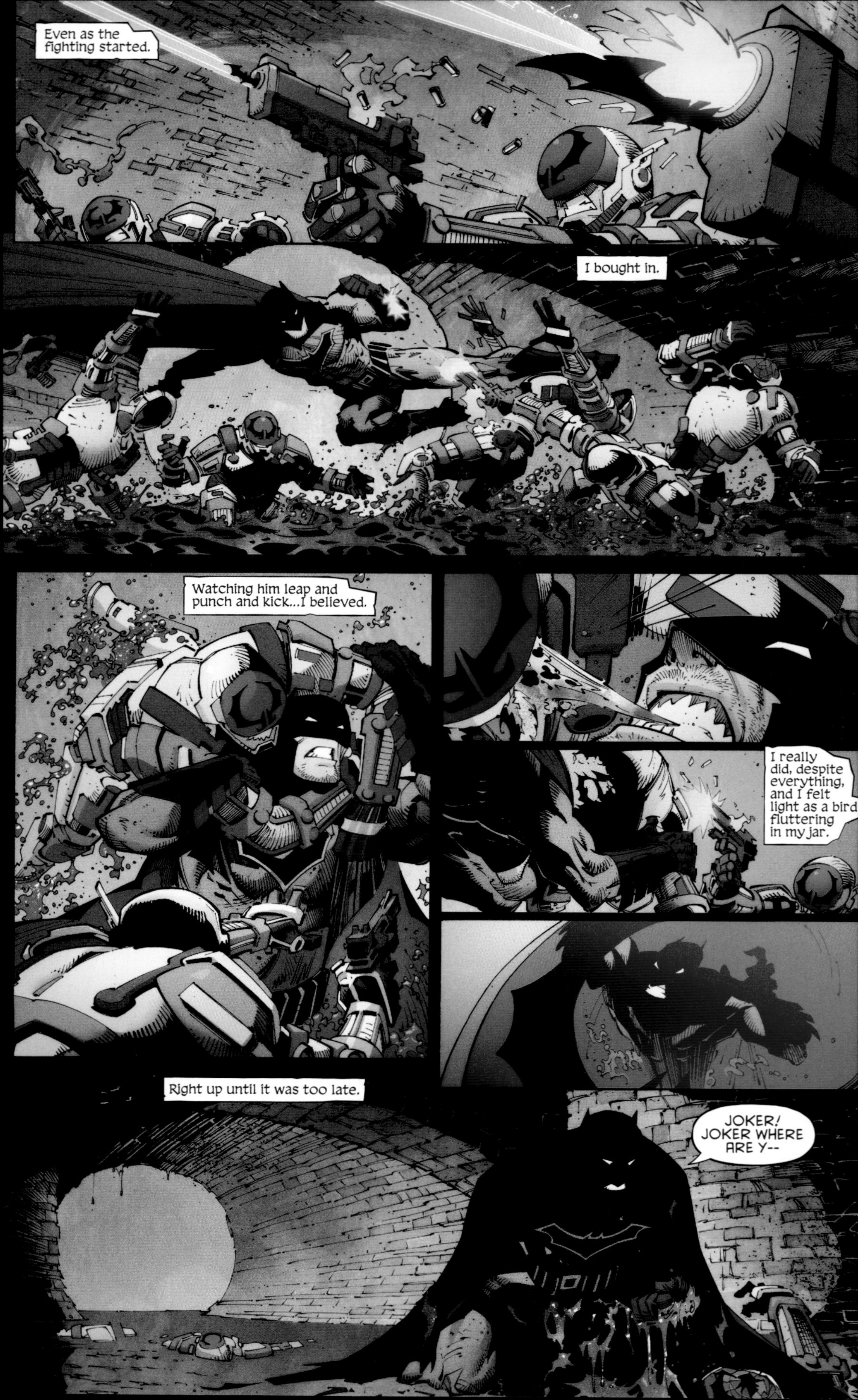
Even as the fighting started.
I bought in.
Watching him leap and punch and kick...I believed.
I really did, despite everything, and I felt light as a bird fluttering in my jar.
Right up until it was too late.
JOKER! JOKER WHERE ARE Y--

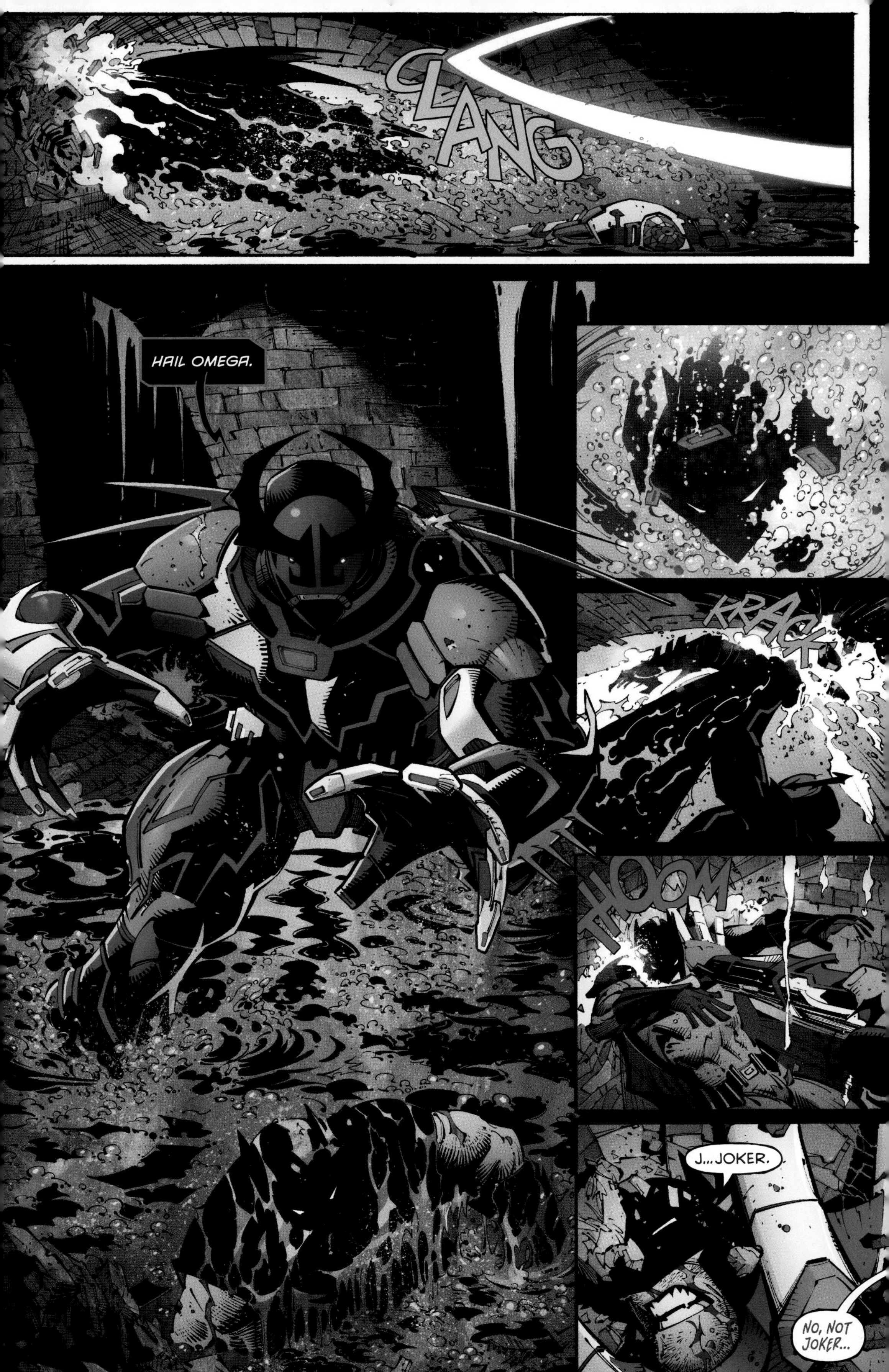
CLANG
HAIL OMEGA.
KRACK
THOOM
J... JOKER.
NO, NOT JOKER...

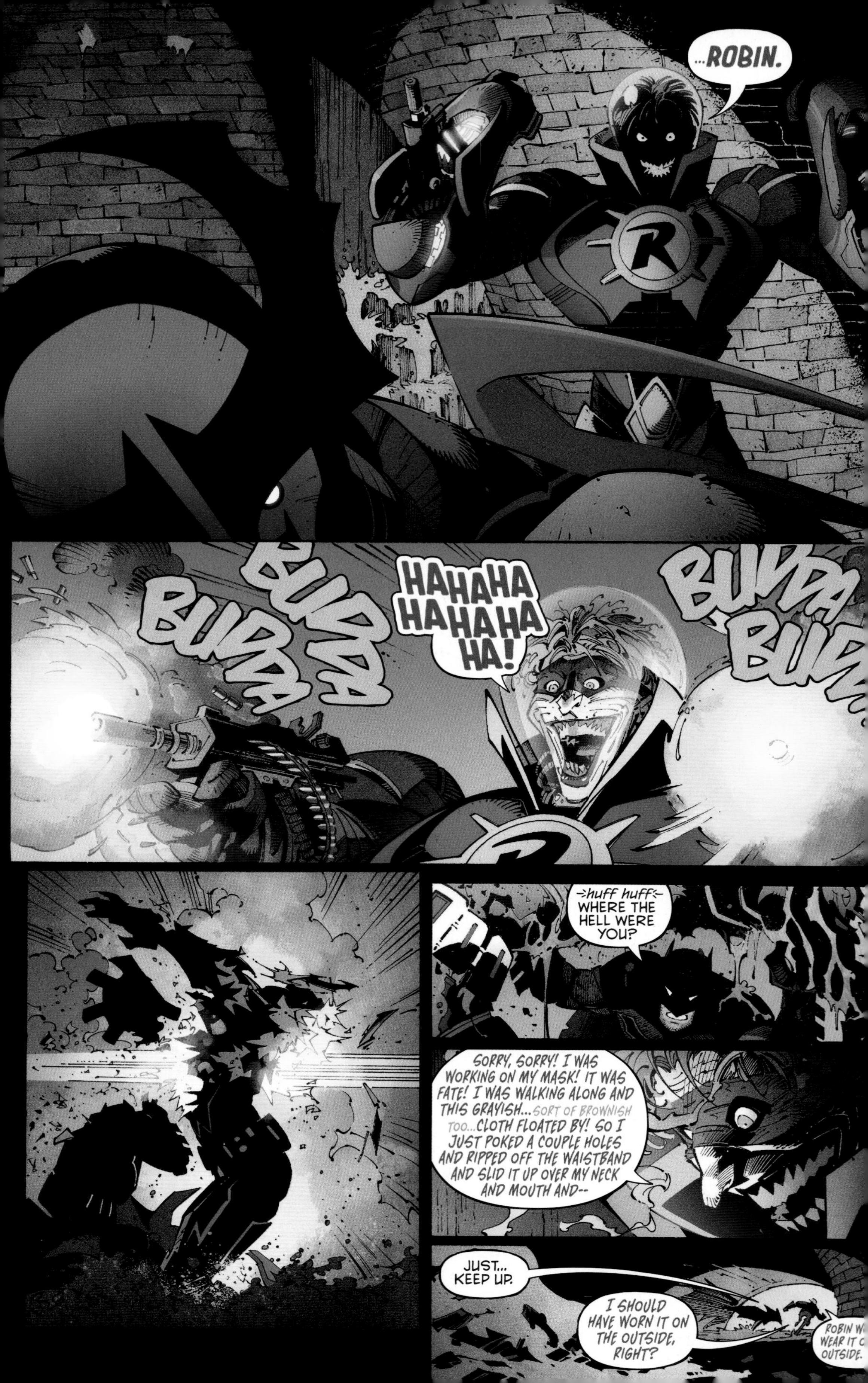
...ROBIN.
BUDDA BUDDA
HAHAHA HAHAHAHA HA!
BUDDA BUDD
-huff huff- WHERE THE HELL WERE YOU?
SORRY, SORRY! I WAS WORKING ON MY MASK! IT WAS FATE! I WAS WALKING ALONG AND THIS GRAYISH... SORT OF BROWNISH TOO... CLOTH FLOATED BY! SO I JUST POKED A COUPLE HOLES AND RIPPED OFF THE WAISTBAND AND SLID IT UP OVER MY NECK AND MOUTH AND--
JUST... KEEP UP.
I SHOULD HAVE WORN IT ON THE OUTSIDE, RIGHT?

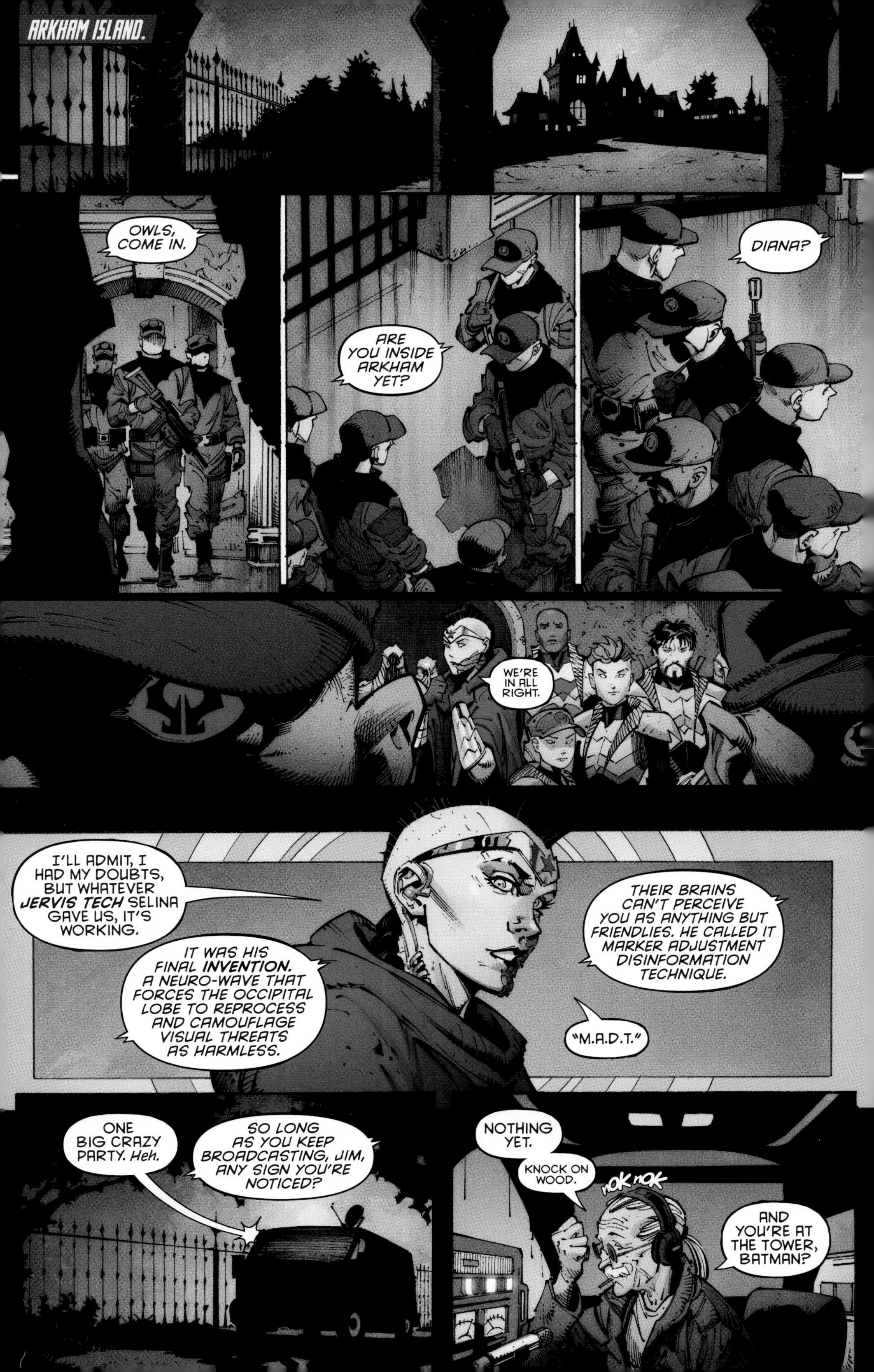
ARKHAM ISLAND.
OWLS, COME IN.
ARE YOU INSIDE ARKHAM YET?
DIANA?
WE'RE IN ALL RIGHT.
I'LL ADMIT, I HAD MY DOUBTS, BUT WHATEVER JERVIS TECH SELINA GAVE US, IT'S WORKING.
IT WAS HIS FINAL INVENTION. A NEURO-WAVE THAT FORCES THE OCCIPITAL LOBE TO REPROCESS AND CAMOUFLAGE VISUAL THREATS AS HARMLESS.
THEIR BRAINS CAN'T PERCEIVE YOU AS ANYTHING BUT FRIENDLIES. HE CALLED IT MARKER ADJUSTMENT DISINFORMATION TECHNIQUE.
"M.A.D.T."
ONE BIG CRAZY PARTY. Heh.
SO LONG AS YOU KEEP BROADCASTING, JIM, ANY SIGN YOU'RE NOTICED?
NOTHING YET.
KNOCK ON WOOD.
NOK NOK
AND YOU'RE AT THE TOWER, BATMAN?

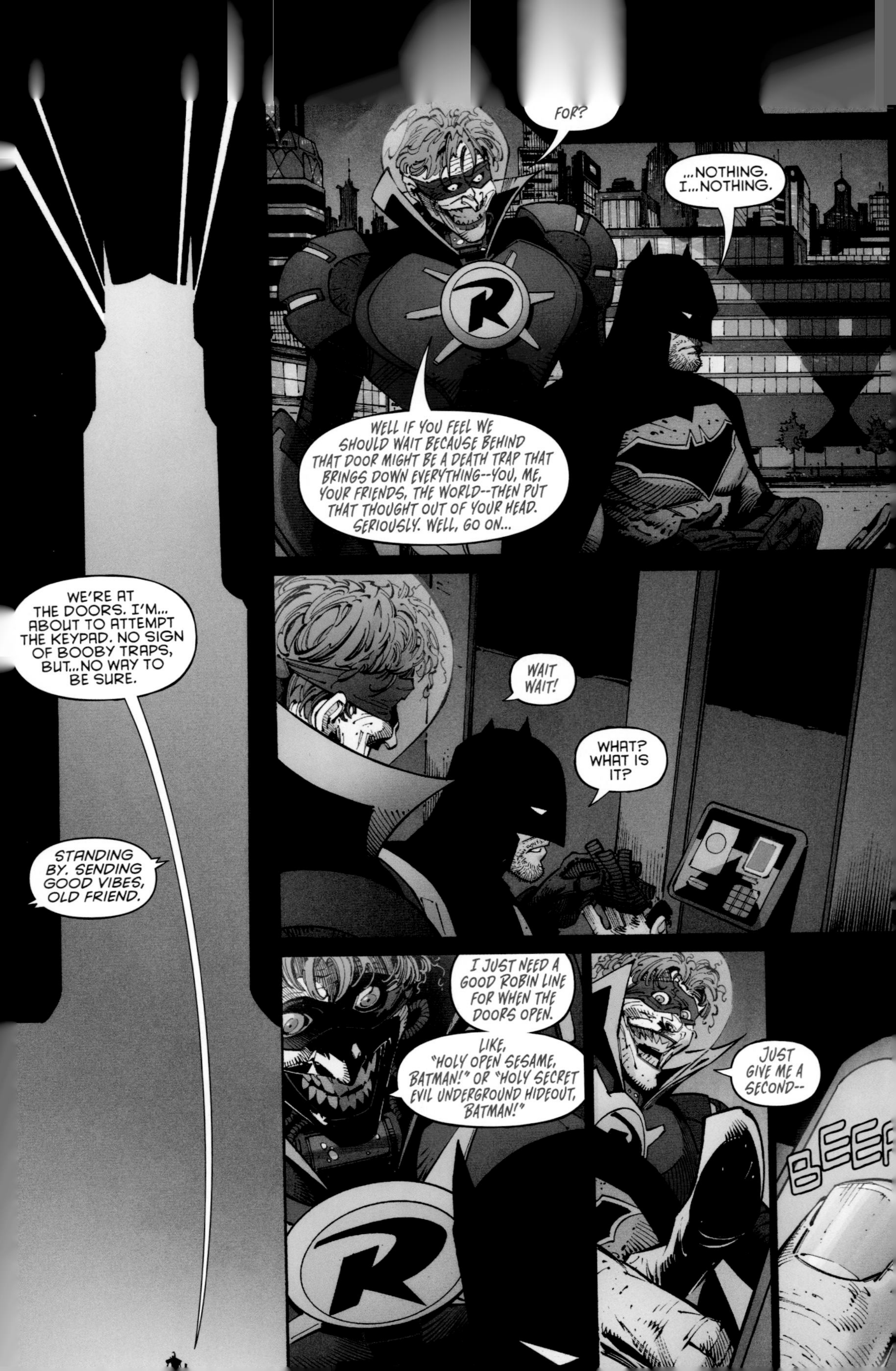
FOR?
...NOTHING. I...NOTHING.
WELL IF YOU FEEL WE SHOULD WAIT BECAUSE BEHIND THAT DOOR MIGHT BE A DEATH TRAP THAT BRINGS DOWN EVERYTHING--YOU, ME, YOUR FRIENDS, THE WORLD--THEN PUT THAT THOUGHT OUT OF YOUR HEAD. SERIOUSLY. WELL, GO ON...
WE'RE AT THE DOORS. I'M... ABOUT TO ATTEMPT THE KEYPAD. NO SIGN OF BOOBY TRAPS, BUT...NO WAY TO BE SURE.
STANDING BY. SENDING GOOD VIBES, OLD FRIEND.
WAIT WAIT!
WHAT? WHAT IS IT?
I JUST NEED A GOOD ROBIN LINE FOR WHEN THE DOORS OPEN.
LIKE, "HOLY OPEN SESAME, BATMAN!" OR "HOLY SECRET EVIL UNDERGROUND HIDEOUT, BATMAN!"
JUST GIVE ME A SECOND--
BEEP

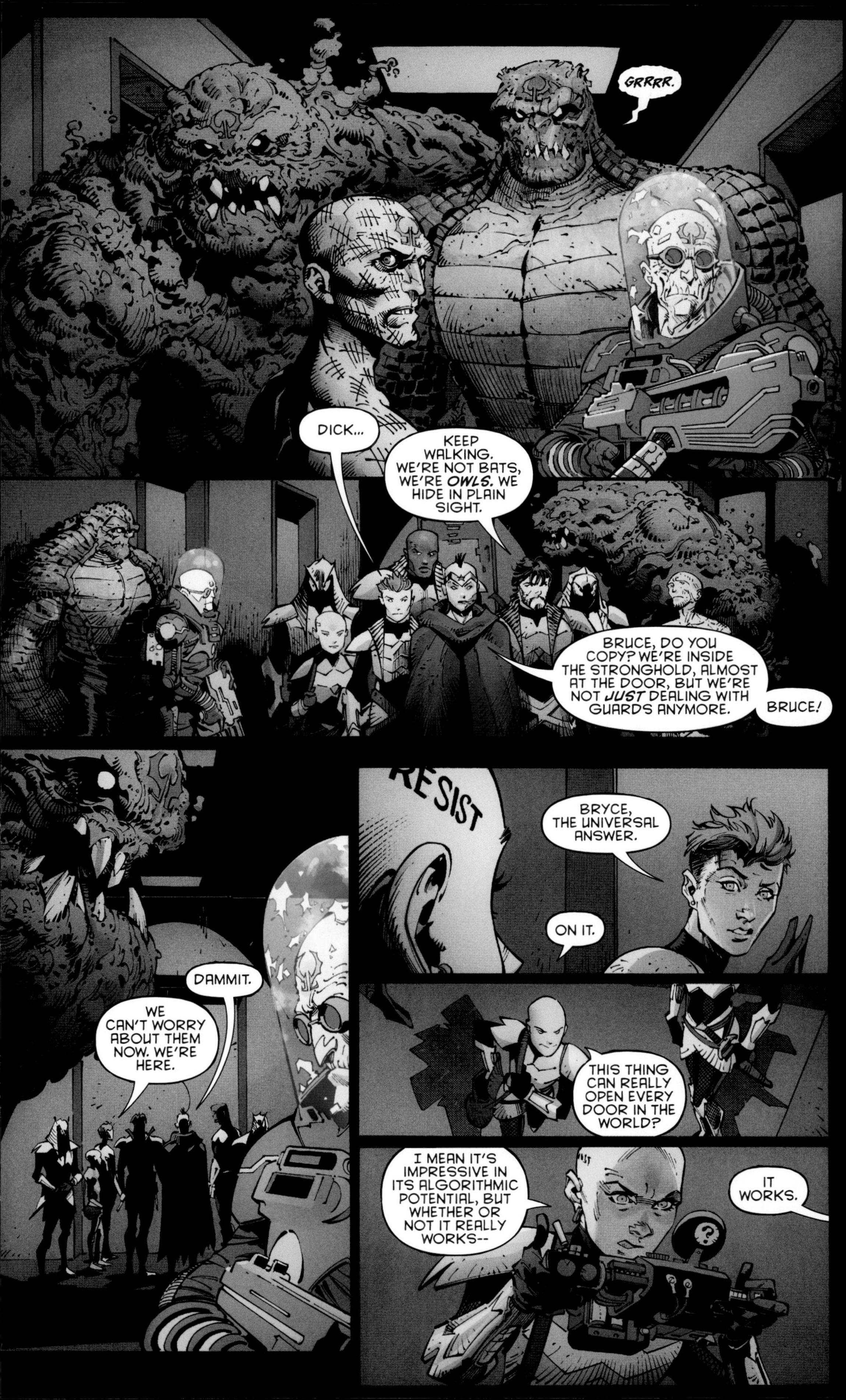
GRRRR.
DICK...
KEEP WALKING. WE'RE NOT BATS, WE'RE OWLS. WE HIDE IN PLAIN SIGHT.
BRUCE, DO YOU COPY? WE'RE INSIDE THE STRONGHOLD, ALMOST AT THE DOOR, BUT WE'RE NOT JUST DEALING WITH GUARDS ANYMORE.
BRUCE!
DAMMIT.
WE CAN'T WORRY ABOUT THEM NOW. WE'RE HERE.
RESIST
BRYCE, THE UNIVERSAL ANSWER.
ON IT.
THIS THING CAN REALLY OPEN EVERY DOOR IN THE WORLD?
I MEAN IT'S IMPRESSIVE IN ITS ALGORITHMIC POTENTIAL, BUT WHETHER OR NOT IT REALLY WORKS--
IT WORKS.

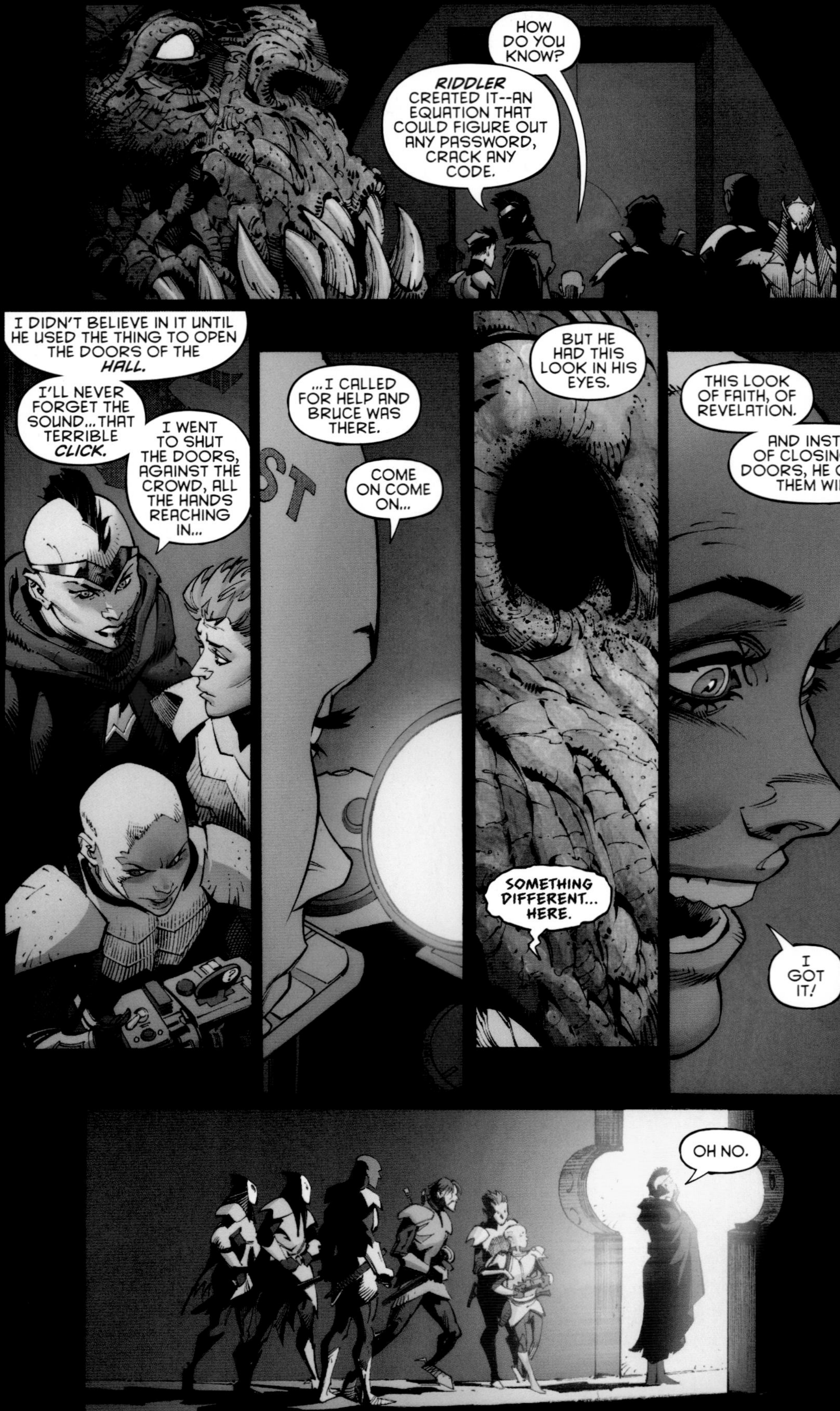
HOW DO YOU KNOW?
RIDDLER CREATED IT--AN EQUATION THAT COULD FIGURE OUT ANY PASSWORD, CRACK ANY CODE.
I DIDN'T BELIEVE IN IT UNTIL HE USED THE THING TO OPEN THE DOORS OF THE HALL.
I'LL NEVER FORGET THE SOUND... THAT TERRIBLE CLICK.
I WENT TO SHUT THE DOORS, AGAINST THE CROWD, ALL THE HANDS REACHING IN...
...I CALLED FOR HELP AND BRUCE WAS THERE.
COME ON COME ON...
BUT HE HAD THIS LOOK IN HIS EYES.
SOMETHING DIFFERENT... HERE.
THIS LOOK OF FAITH, OF REVELATION.
AND INSTEAD OF CLOSING THE DOORS, HE OPENED THEM WIDE.
I GOT IT!
OH NO.

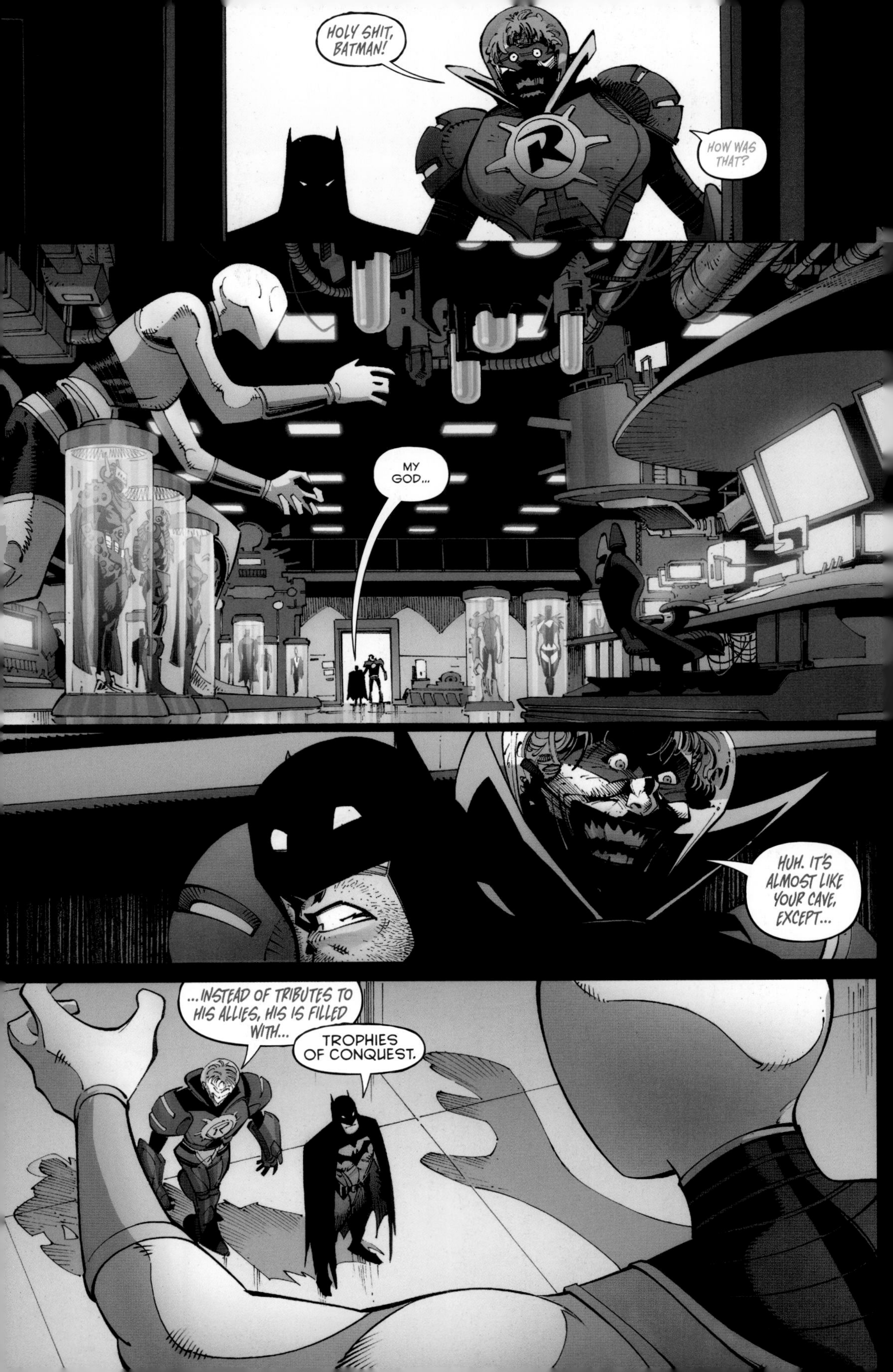

HOLY SHIT, BATMAN!
HOW WAS THAT?
MY GOD...
HUH. IT'S ALMOST LIKE YOUR CAVE, EXCEPT...
...INSTEAD OF TRIBUTES TO HIS ALLIES, HIS IS FILLED WITH...
TROPHIES OF CONQUEST.

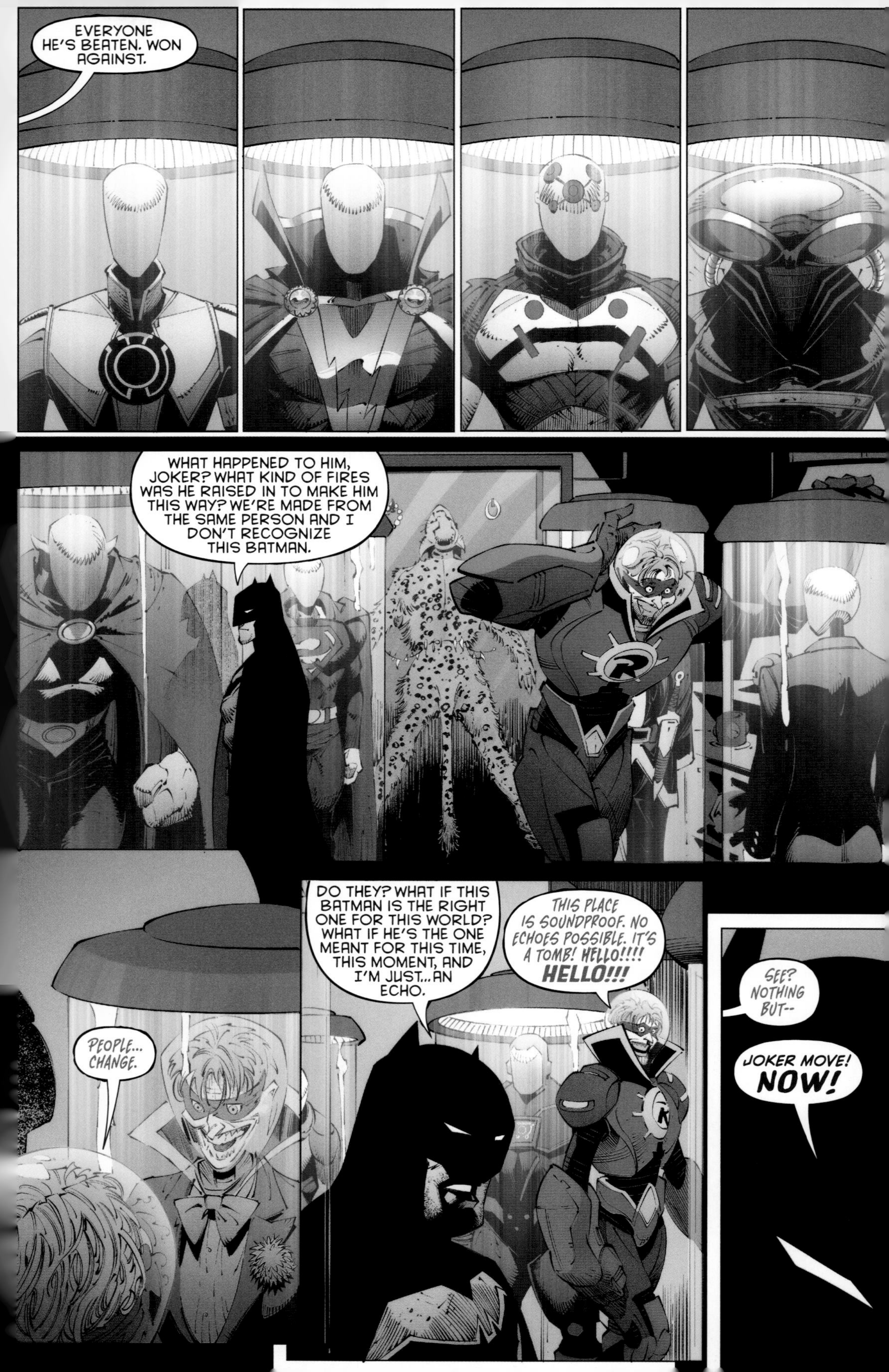

EVERYONE HE'S BEATEN. WON AGAINST.
WHAT HAPPENED TO HIM, JOKER? WHAT KIND OF FIRES WAS HE RAISED IN TO MAKE HIM THIS WAY? WE'RE MADE FROM THE SAME PERSON AND I DON'T RECOGNIZE THIS BATMAN.
PEOPLE... CHANGE.
DO THEY? WHAT IF THIS BATMAN IS THE RIGHT ONE FOR THIS WORLD? WHAT IF HE'S THE ONE MEANT FOR THIS TIME, THIS MOMENT, AND I'M JUST...AN ECHO.
THIS PLACE IS SOUNDPROOF. NO ECHOES POSSIBLE. IT'S A TOMB! HELLO!!!! HELLO!!!
SEE? NOTHING BUT--
JOKER MOVE! NOW!

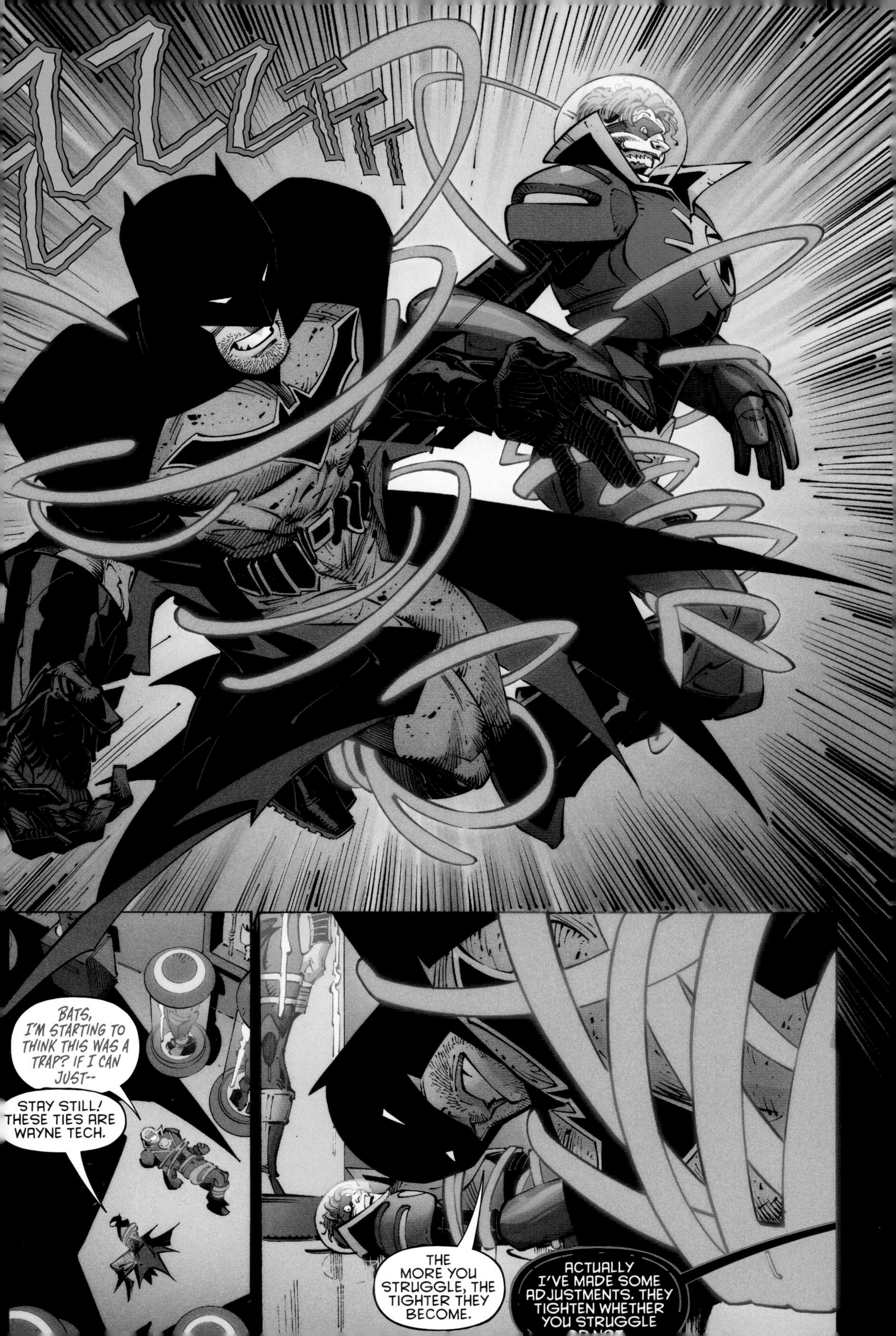
ZZZTTT
BATS, I'M STARTING TO THINK THIS WAS A TRAP? IF I CAN JUST--
STAY STILL! THESE TIES ARE WAYNE TECH.
THE MORE YOU STRUGGLE, THE TIGHTER THEY BECOME.
ACTUALLY I'VE MADE SOME ADJUSTMENTS. THEY TIGHTEN WHETHER YOU STRUGGLE

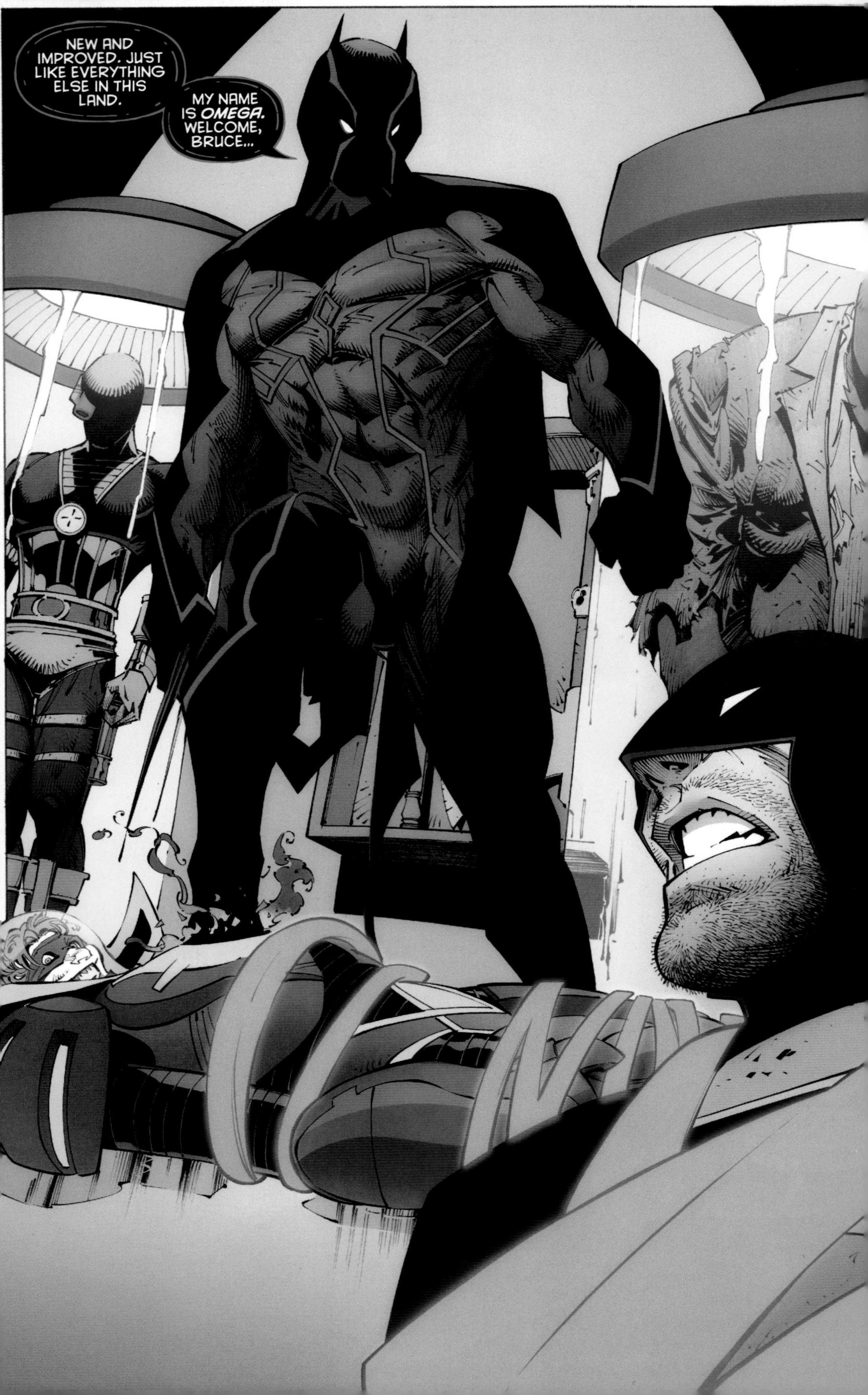
NEW AND IMPROVED. JUST LIKE EVERYTHING ELSE IN THIS LAND.
MY NAME IS OMEGA. WELCOME, BRUCE...

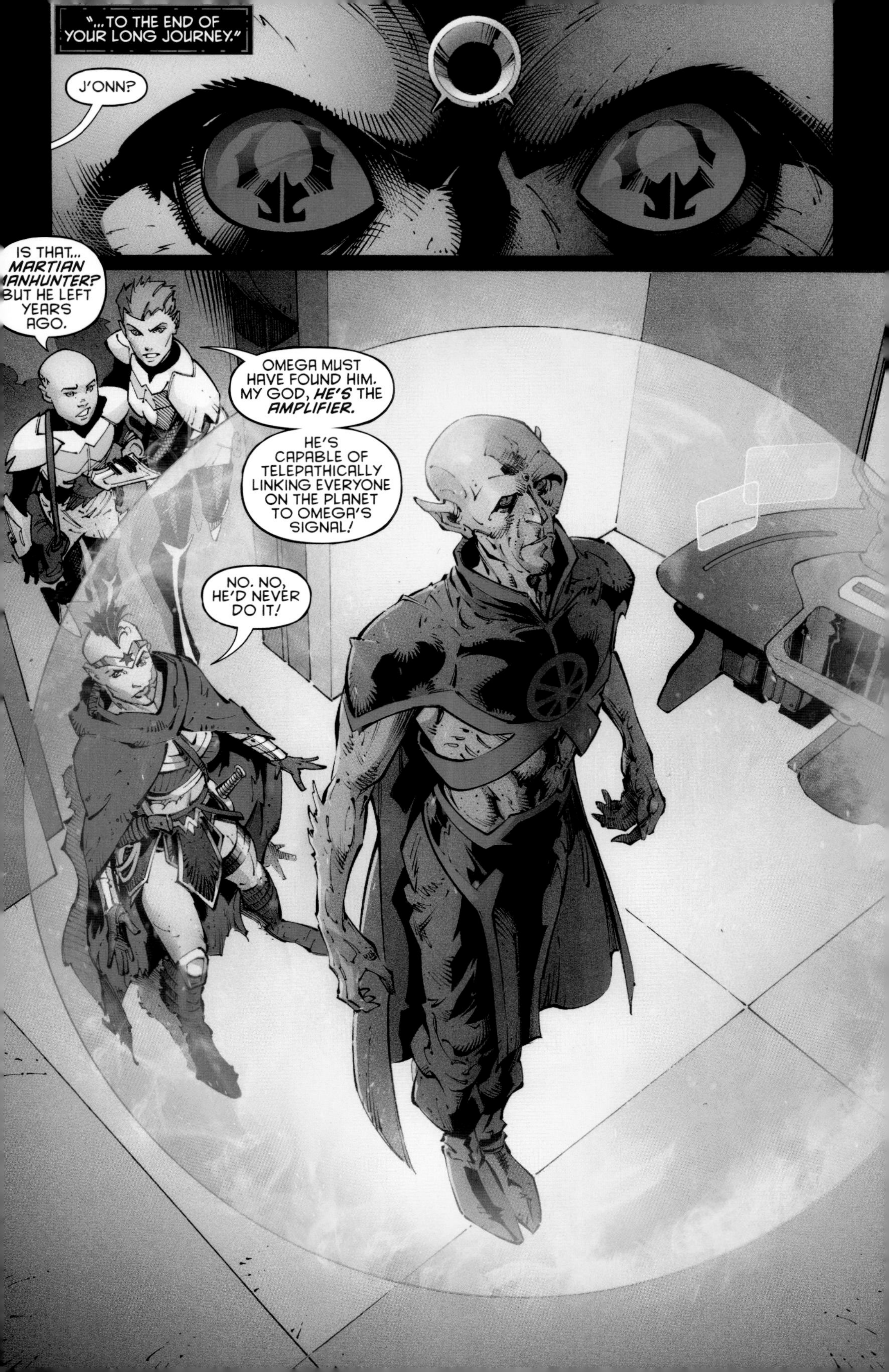
"...TO THE END OF YOUR LONG JOURNEY."
J'ONN?
IS THAT... MARTIAN MANHUNTER? BUT HE LEFT YEARS AGO.
OMEGA MUST HAVE FOUND HIM. MY GOD, HE'S THE AMPLIFIER.
HE'S CAPABLE OF TELEPATHICALLY LINKING EVERYONE ON THE PLANET TO OMEGA'S SIGNAL!
NO. NO, HE'D NEVER DO IT!

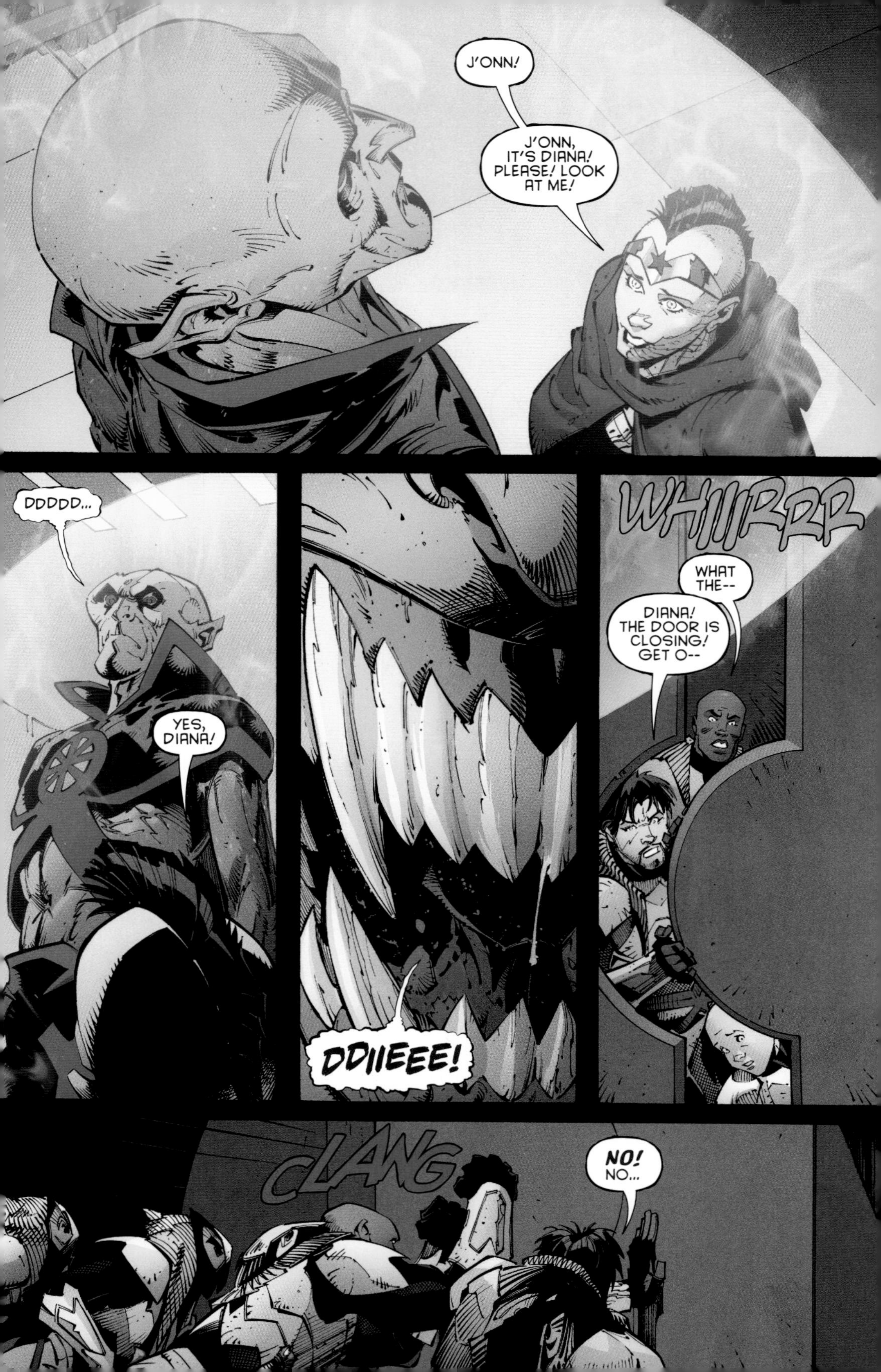

J'ONN!
J'ONN, IT'S DIANA! PLEASE! LOOK AT ME!
DDDDD...
YES, DIANA!
DDIIEEE!
WHIIRRR
WHAT THE--
DIANA! THE DOOR IS CLOSING! GET O--
CLANG
NO! NO...

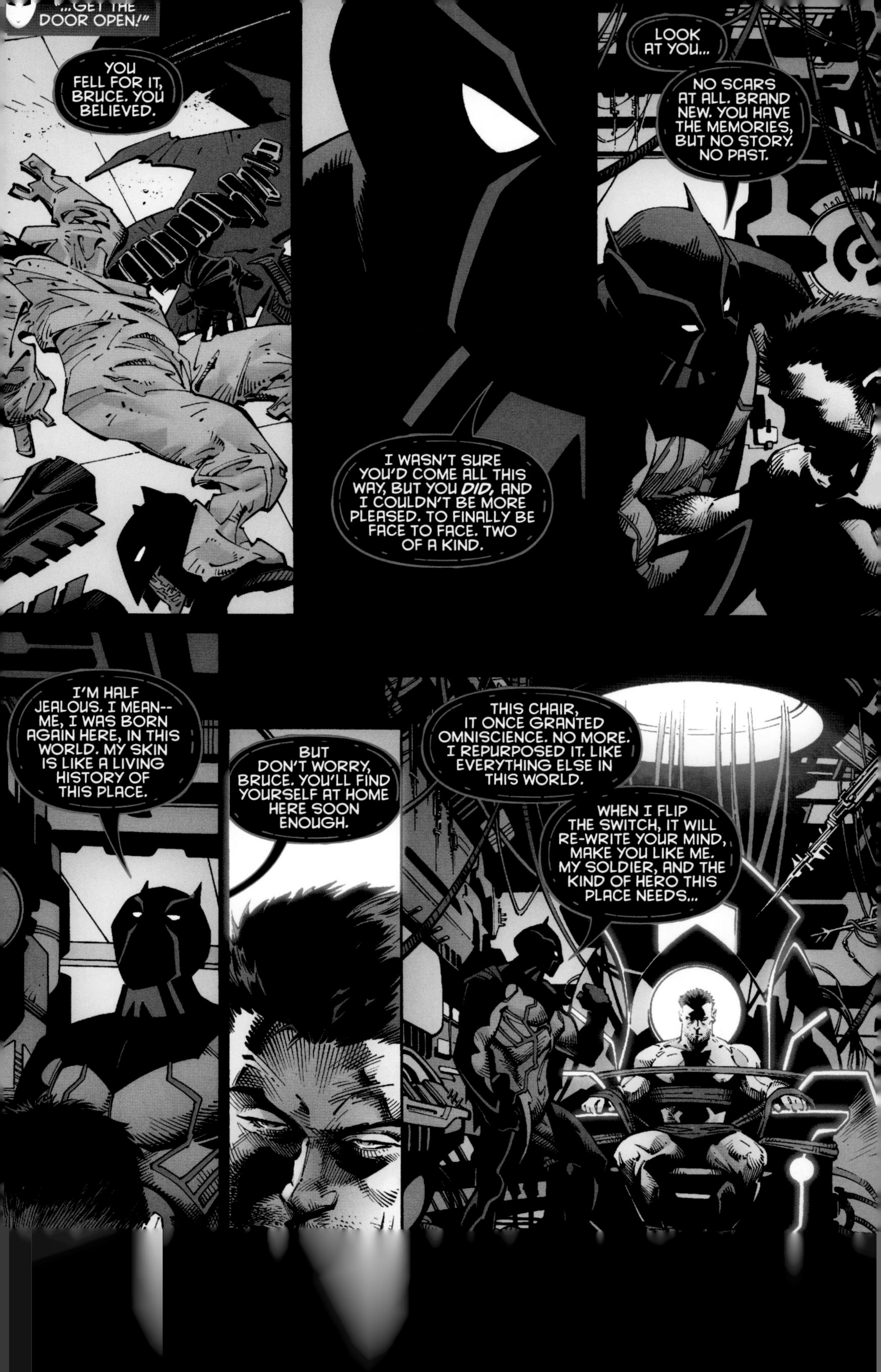
"...GET THE DOOR OPEN!"
YOU FELL FOR IT, BRUCE. YOU BELIEVED.
I WASN'T SURE YOU'D COME ALL THIS WAY, BUT YOU DID, AND I COULDN'T BE MORE PLEASED. TO FINALLY BE FACE TO FACE. TWO OF A KIND.
LOOK AT YOU...
NO SCARS AT ALL. BRAND NEW. YOU HAVE THE MEMORIES, BUT NO STORY. NO PAST.
I'M HALF JEALOUS. I MEAN--ME, I WAS BORN AGAIN HERE, IN THIS WORLD. MY SKIN IS LIKE A LIVING HISTORY OF THIS PLACE.
BUT DON'T WORRY, BRUCE. YOU'LL FIND YOURSELF AT HOME HERE SOON ENOUGH.
THIS CHAIR, IT ONCE GRANTED OMNISCIENCE. NO MORE. I REPURPOSED IT. LIKE EVERYTHING ELSE IN THIS WORLD.
WHEN I FLIP THE SWITCH, IT WILL RE-WRITE YOUR MIND, MAKE YOU LIKE ME. MY SOLDIER, AND THE KIND OF HERO THIS PLACE NEEDS...

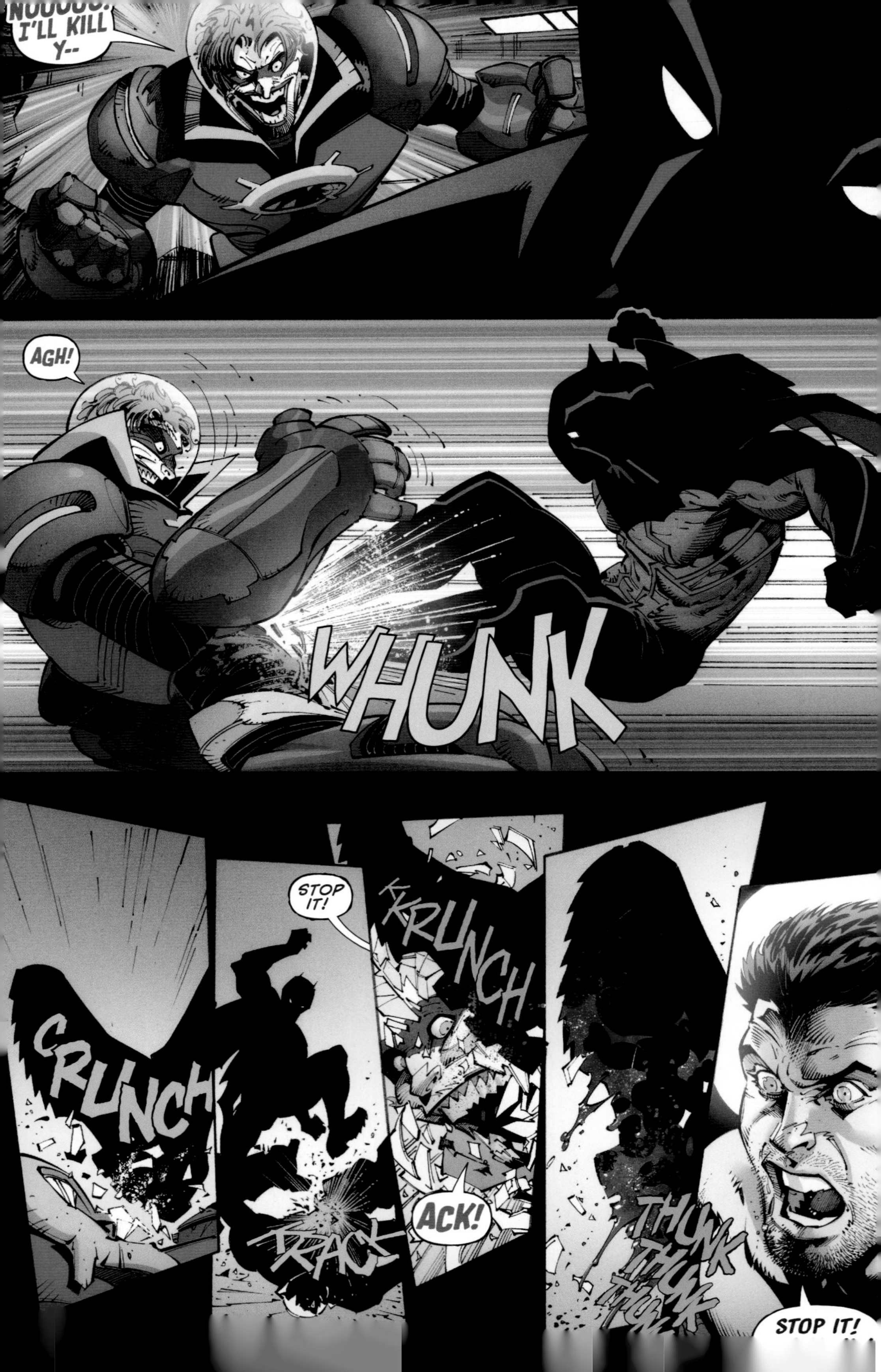
NOOOOO! I'LL KILL Y--
AGH!
WHUNK
CRUNCH
STOP IT!
TRACK
KKRUNCH
ACK!
THUNK THUNK
STOP IT!

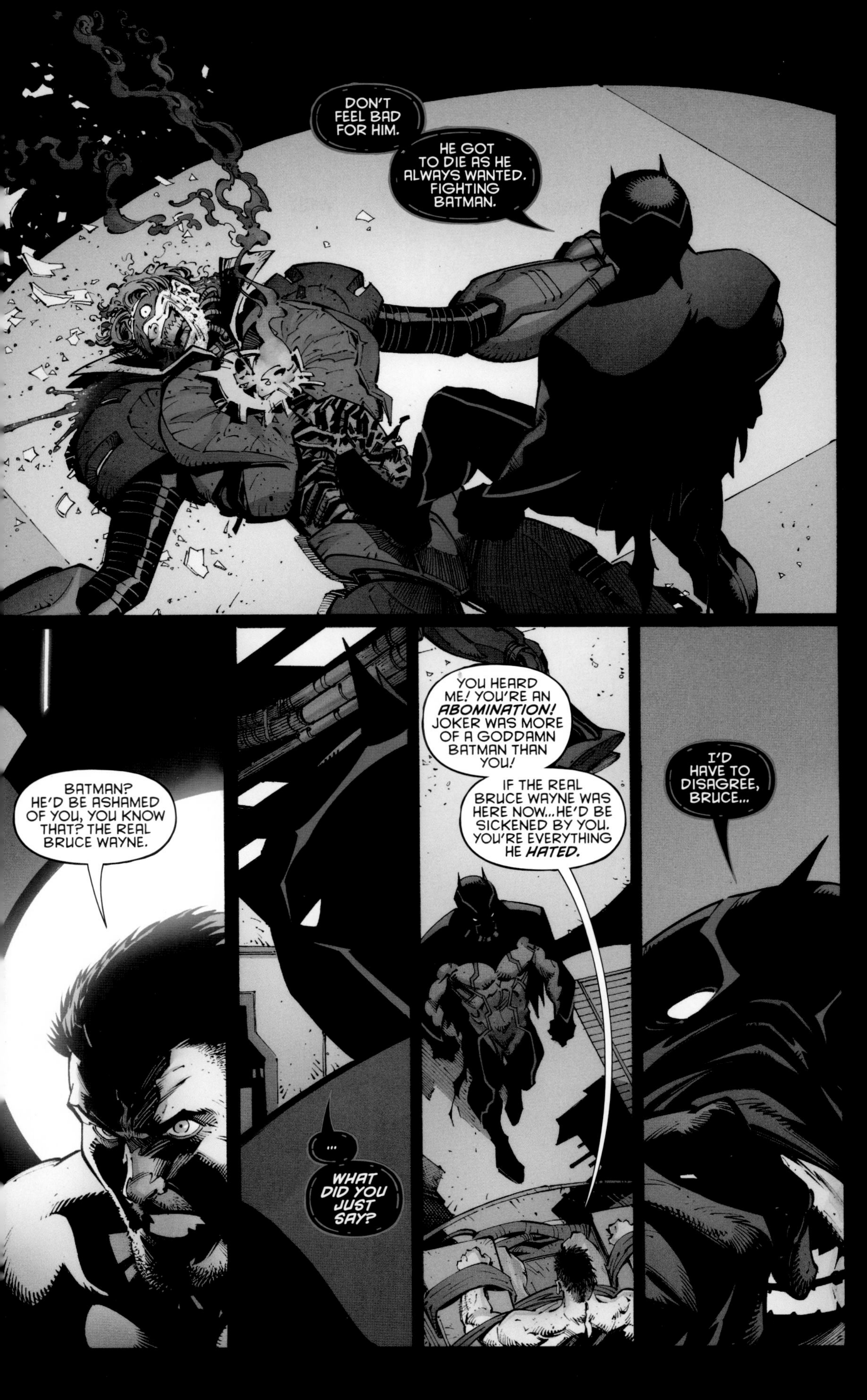
DON'T FEEL BAD FOR HIM.
HE GOT TO DIE AS HE ALWAYS WANTED. FIGHTING BATMAN.
BATMAN? HE'D BE ASHAMED OF YOU, YOU KNOW THAT? THE REAL BRUCE WAYNE.
...
WHAT DID YOU JUST SAY?
YOU HEARD ME! YOU'RE AN ABOMINATION! JOKER WAS MORE OF A GODDAMN BATMAN THAN YOU!
IF THE REAL BRUCE WAYNE WAS HERE NOW...HE'D BE SICKENED BY YOU. YOU'RE EVERYTHING HE HATED.
I'D HAVE TO DISAGREE, BRUCE...

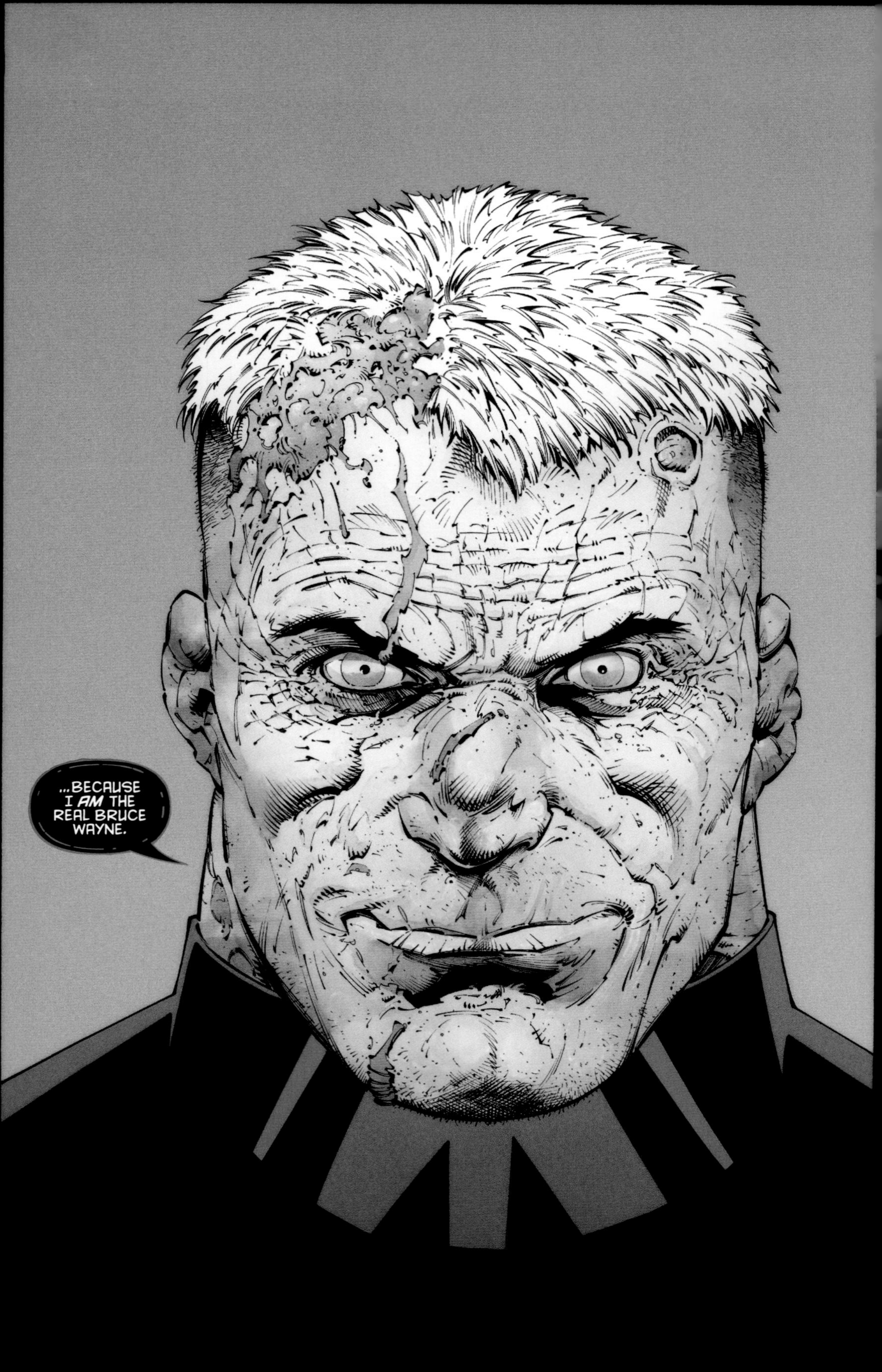
...BECAUSE I **AM** THE REAL BRUCE WAYNE.

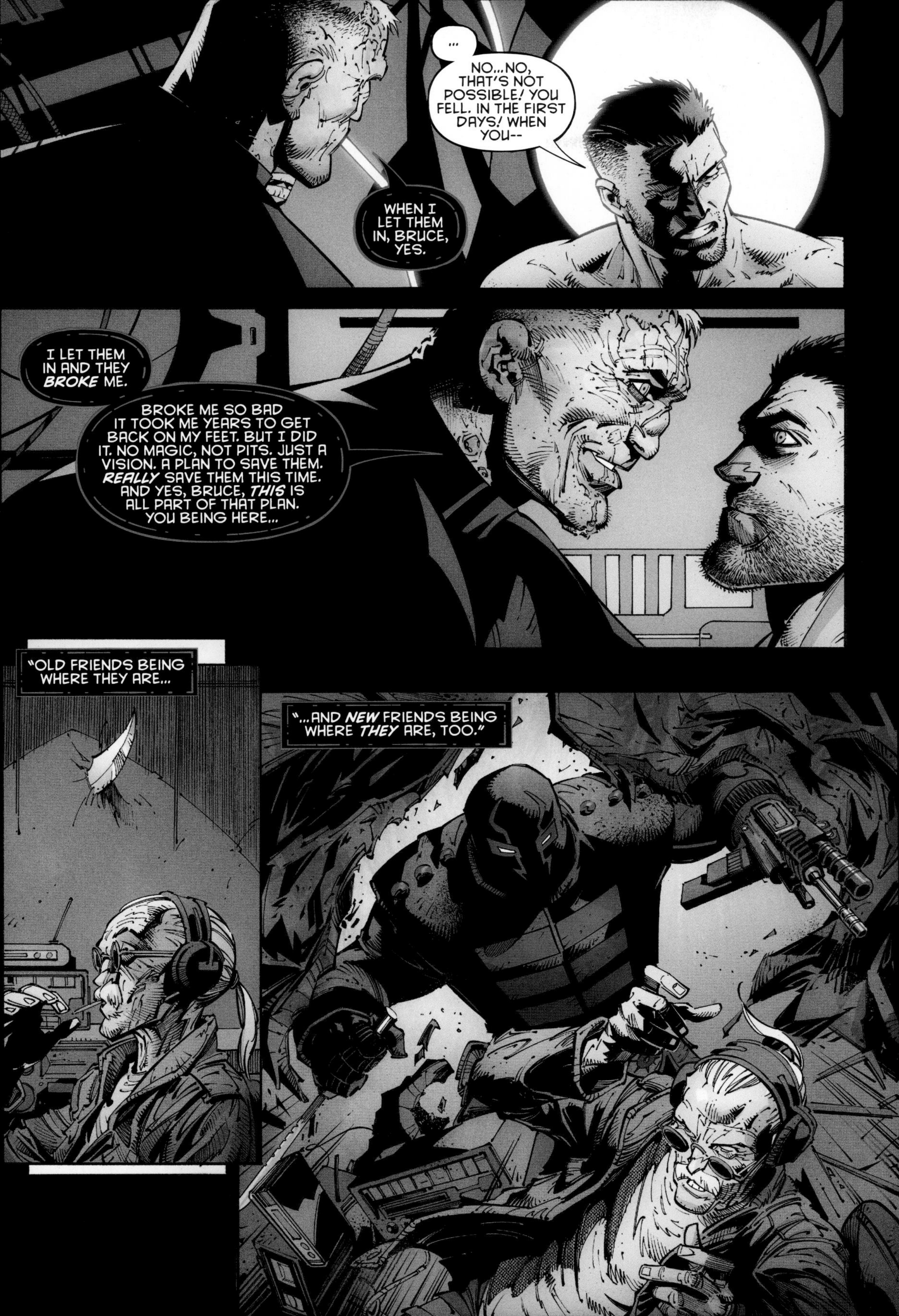

...
NO...NO, THAT'S NOT POSSIBLE! YOU FELL. IN THE FIRST DAYS! WHEN YOU--
WHEN I LET THEM IN, BRUCE, YES.
I LET THEM IN AND THEY *BROKE* ME.
BROKE ME SO BAD IT TOOK ME YEARS TO GET BACK ON MY FEET. BUT I DID IT. NO MAGIC, NOT PITS. JUST A VISION. A PLAN TO SAVE THEM. *REALLY* SAVE THEM THIS TIME. AND YES, BRUCE, *THIS* IS ALL PART OF THAT PLAN. YOU BEING HERE...
"OLD FRIENDS BEING WHERE THEY ARE...
"...AND *NEW* FRIENDS BEING WHERE *THEY* ARE, TOO."

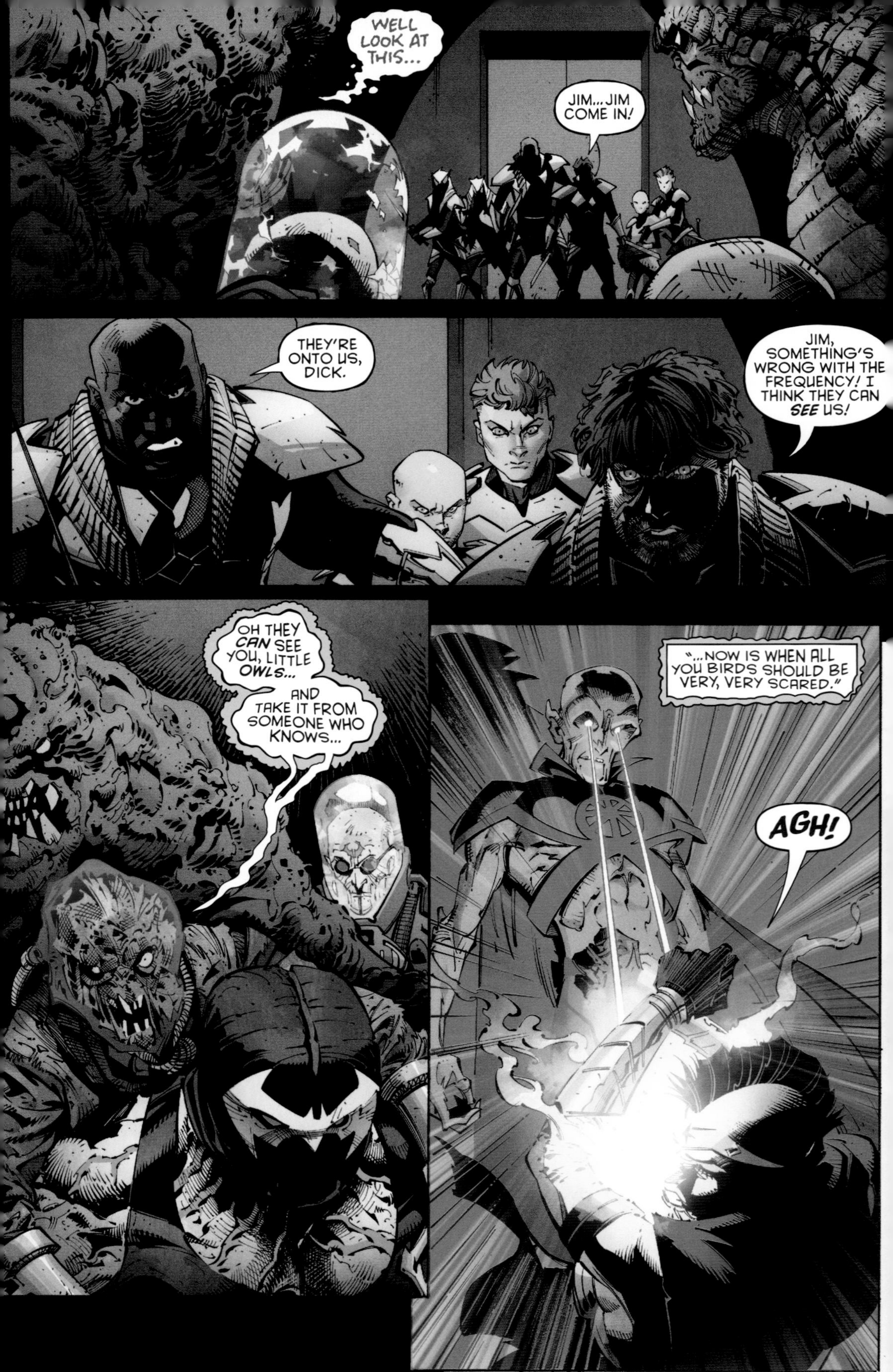
WELL LOOK AT THIS...
JIM...JIM COME IN!
THEY'RE ONTO US, DICK.
JIM, SOMETHING'S WRONG WITH THE FREQUENCY! I THINK THEY CAN SEE US!
OH THEY CAN SEE YOU, LITTLE OWLS...
AND TAKE IT FROM SOMEONE WHO KNOWS...
"...NOW IS WHEN ALL YOU BIRDS SHOULD BE VERY, VERY SCARED."
AGH!

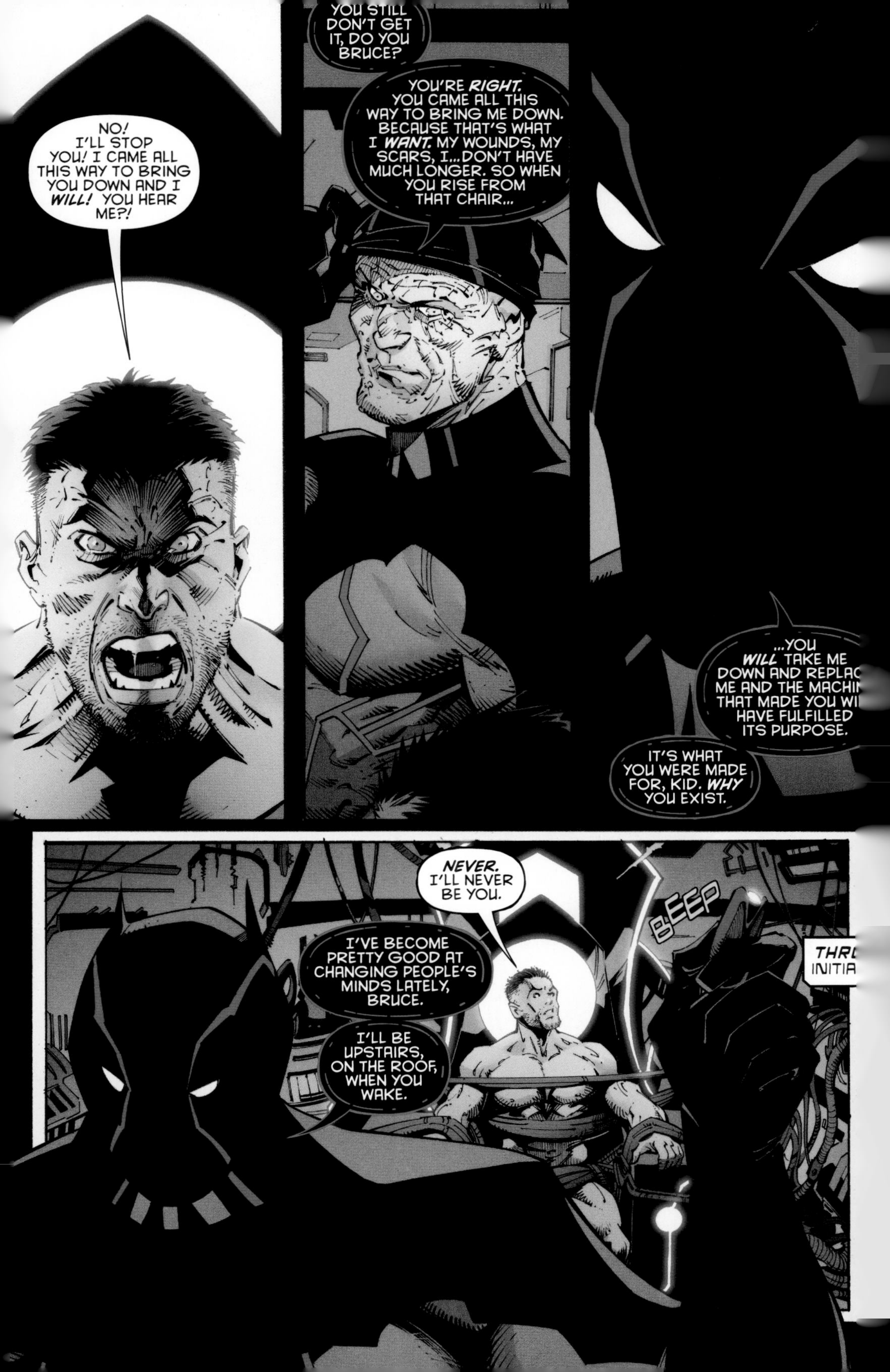
YOU STILL DON'T GET IT, DO YOU BRUCE?
NO! I'LL STOP YOU! I CAME ALL THIS WAY TO BRING YOU DOWN AND I WILL! YOU HEAR ME?!
YOU'RE RIGHT. YOU CAME ALL THIS WAY TO BRING ME DOWN. BECAUSE THAT'S WHAT I WANT. MY WOUNDS, MY SCARS, I...DON'T HAVE MUCH LONGER. SO WHEN YOU RISE FROM THAT CHAIR...
...YOU WILL TAKE ME DOWN AND REPLAC ME AND THE MACHIN THAT MADE YOU WI HAVE FULFILLED ITS PURPOSE.
IT'S WHAT YOU WERE MADE FOR, KID. WHY YOU EXIST.
NEVER. I'LL NEVER BE YOU.
I'VE BECOME PRETTY GOOD AT CHANGING PEOPLE'S MINDS LATELY, BRUCE.
I'LL BE UPSTAIRS, ON THE ROOF, WHEN YOU WAKE.
BEEP
THR
INITIA

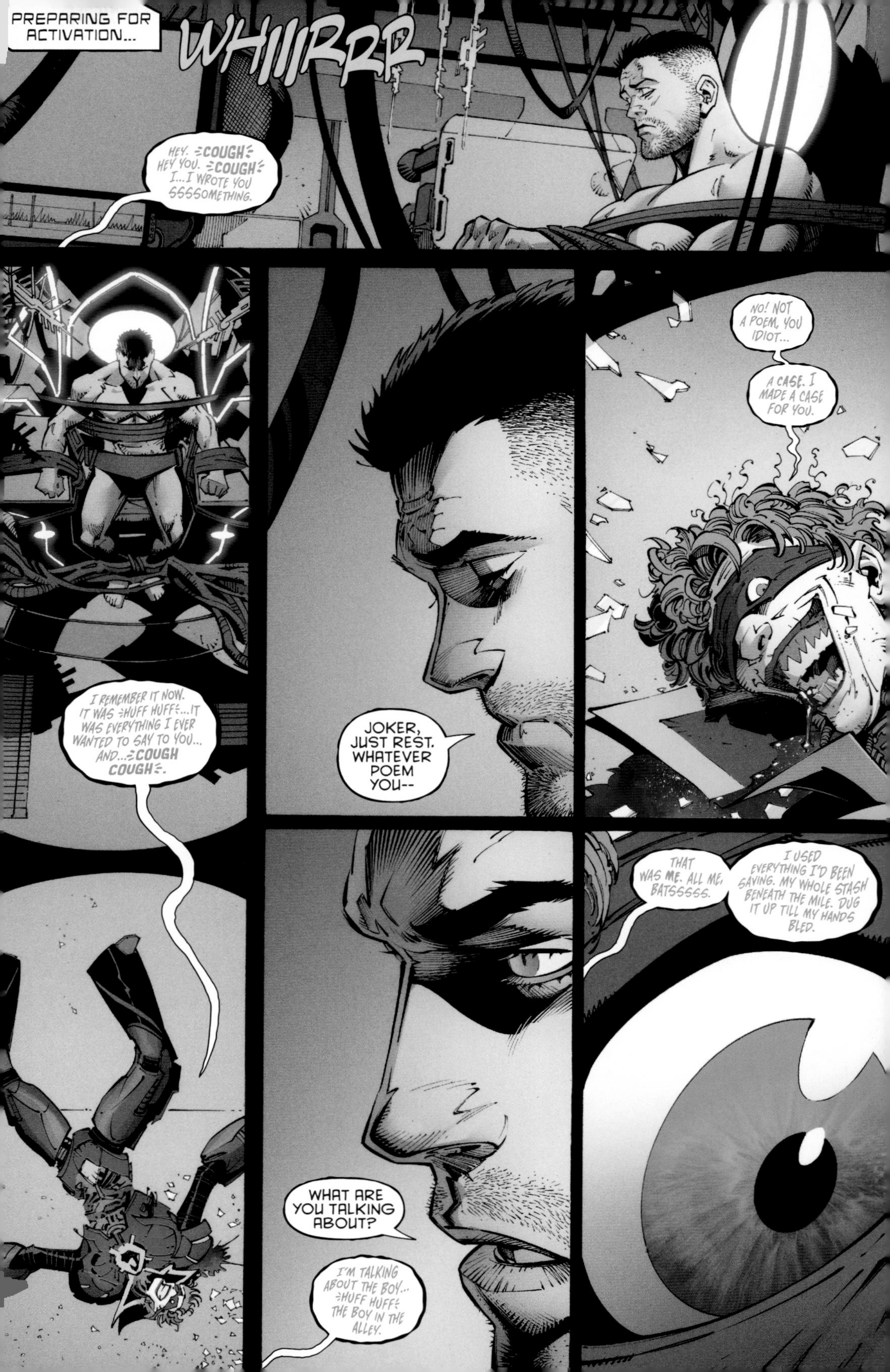
PREPARING FOR ACTIVATION...
WHIIIRRR
HEY. COUGH HEY YOU. COUGH I...I WROTE YOU SSSSOMETHING.
I REMEMBER IT NOW. IT WAS HUFF HUFF ...IT WAS EVERYTHING I EVER WANTED TO SAY TO YOU... AND... COUGH COUGH.
JOKER, JUST REST. WHATEVER POEM YOU--
NO! NOT A POEM, YOU IDIOT...
A CASE. I MADE A CASE FOR YOU.
WHAT ARE YOU TALKING ABOUT?
I'M TALKING ABOUT THE BOY... HUFF HUFF THE BOY IN THE ALLEY.
THAT WAS ME. ALL ME, BATSSSSS.
I USED EVERYTHING I'D BEEN SAVING. MY WHOLE STASH BENEATH THE MILE. DUG IT UP TILL MY HANDS BLED.

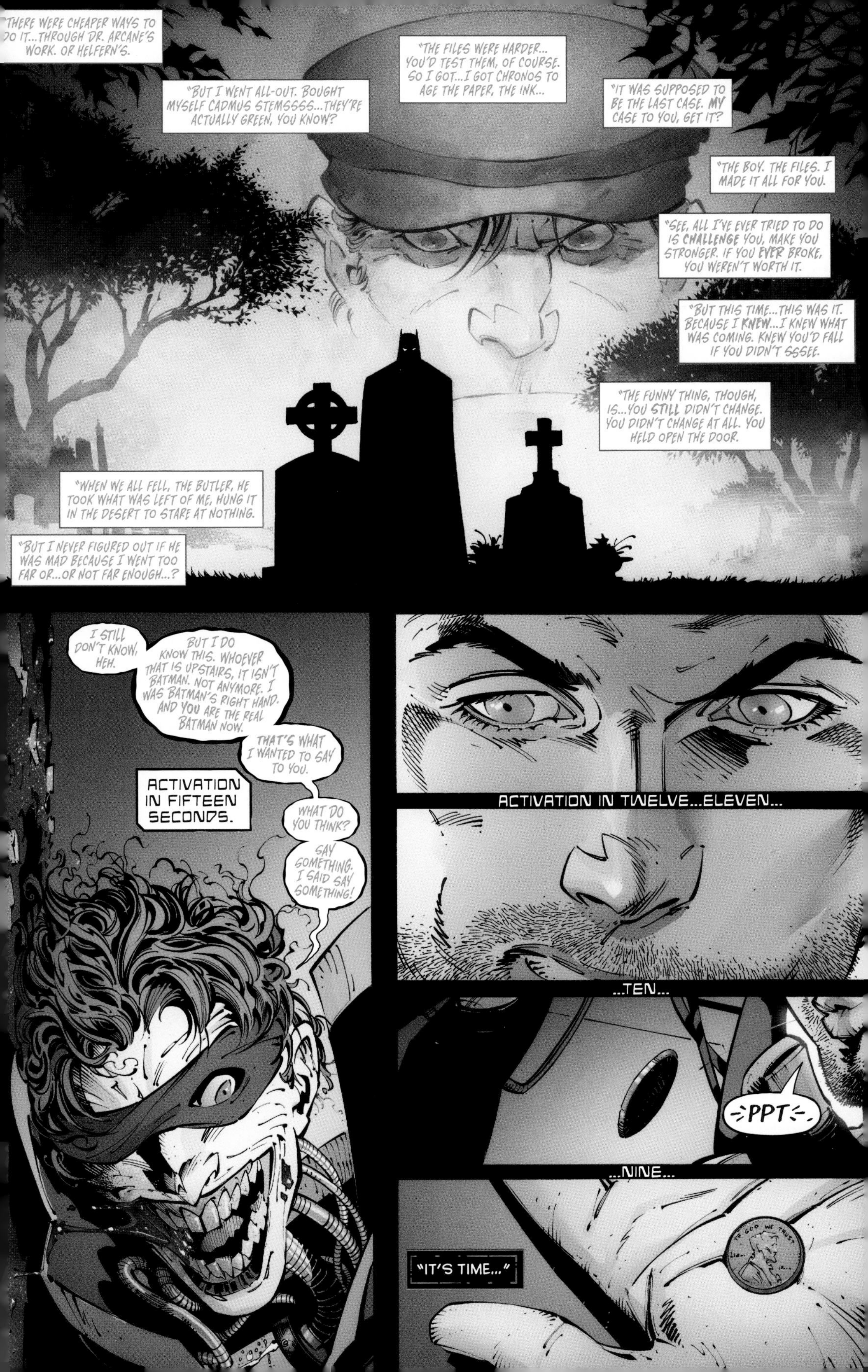
"THERE WERE CHEAPER WAYS TO DO IT...THROUGH DR. ARCANE'S WORK. OR HELFERN'S.
"BUT I WENT ALL-OUT. BOUGHT MYSELF CADMUS STEMSSSS...THEY'RE ACTUALLY GREEN, YOU KNOW?
"THE FILES WERE HARDER... YOU'D TEST THEM, OF COURSE. SO I GOT...I GOT CHRONOS TO AGE THE PAPER, THE INK...
"IT WAS SUPPOSED TO BE THE LAST CASE. MY CASE TO YOU, GET IT?
"THE BOY. THE FILES. I MADE IT ALL FOR YOU.
"SEE, ALL I'VE EVER TRIED TO DO IS CHALLENGE YOU, MAKE YOU STRONGER. IF YOU EVER BROKE, YOU WEREN'T WORTH IT.
"BUT THIS TIME...THIS WAS IT. BECAUSE I KNEW...I KNEW WHAT WAS COMING. KNEW YOU'D FALL IF YOU DIDN'T SSSEE.
"THE FUNNY THING, THOUGH, IS...YOU STILL DIDN'T CHANGE. YOU DIDN'T CHANGE AT ALL. YOU HELD OPEN THE DOOR.
"WHEN WE ALL FELL, THE BUTLER, HE TOOK WHAT WAS LEFT OF ME, HUNG IT IN THE DESERT TO STARE AT NOTHING.
"BUT I NEVER FIGURED OUT IF HE WAS MAD BECAUSE I WENT TOO FAR OR...OR NOT FAR ENOUGH...?
I STILL DON'T KNOW, HEH.
BUT I DO KNOW THIS. WHOEVER THAT IS UPSTAIRS, IT ISN'T BATMAN. NOT ANYMORE. I WAS BATMAN'S RIGHT HAND. AND YOU ARE THE REAL BATMAN NOW.
THAT'S WHAT I WANTED TO SAY TO YOU.
ACTIVATION IN FIFTEEN SECONDS.
WHAT DO YOU THINK?
SAY SOMETHING. I SAID SAY SOMETHING!
ACTIVATION IN TWELVE...ELEVEN...
...TEN...
PPT
...NINE...
"IT'S TIME..."

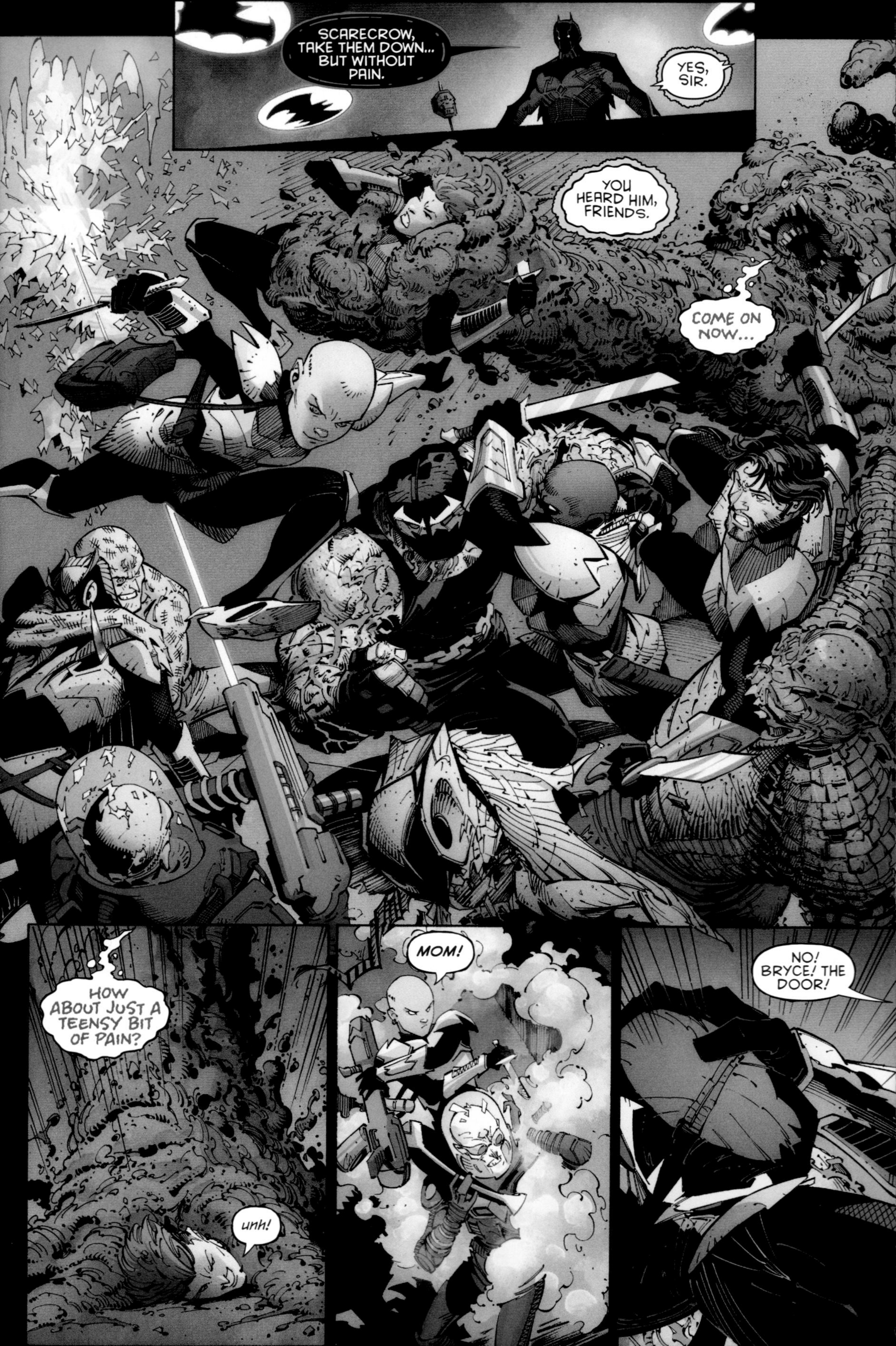
SCARECROW, TAKE THEM DOWN... BUT WITHOUT PAIN.
YES, SIR.
YOU HEARD HIM, FRIENDS.
COME ON NOW...
HOW ABOUT JUST A TEENSY BIT OF PAIN?
unh!
MOM!
NO! BRYCE! THE DOOR!

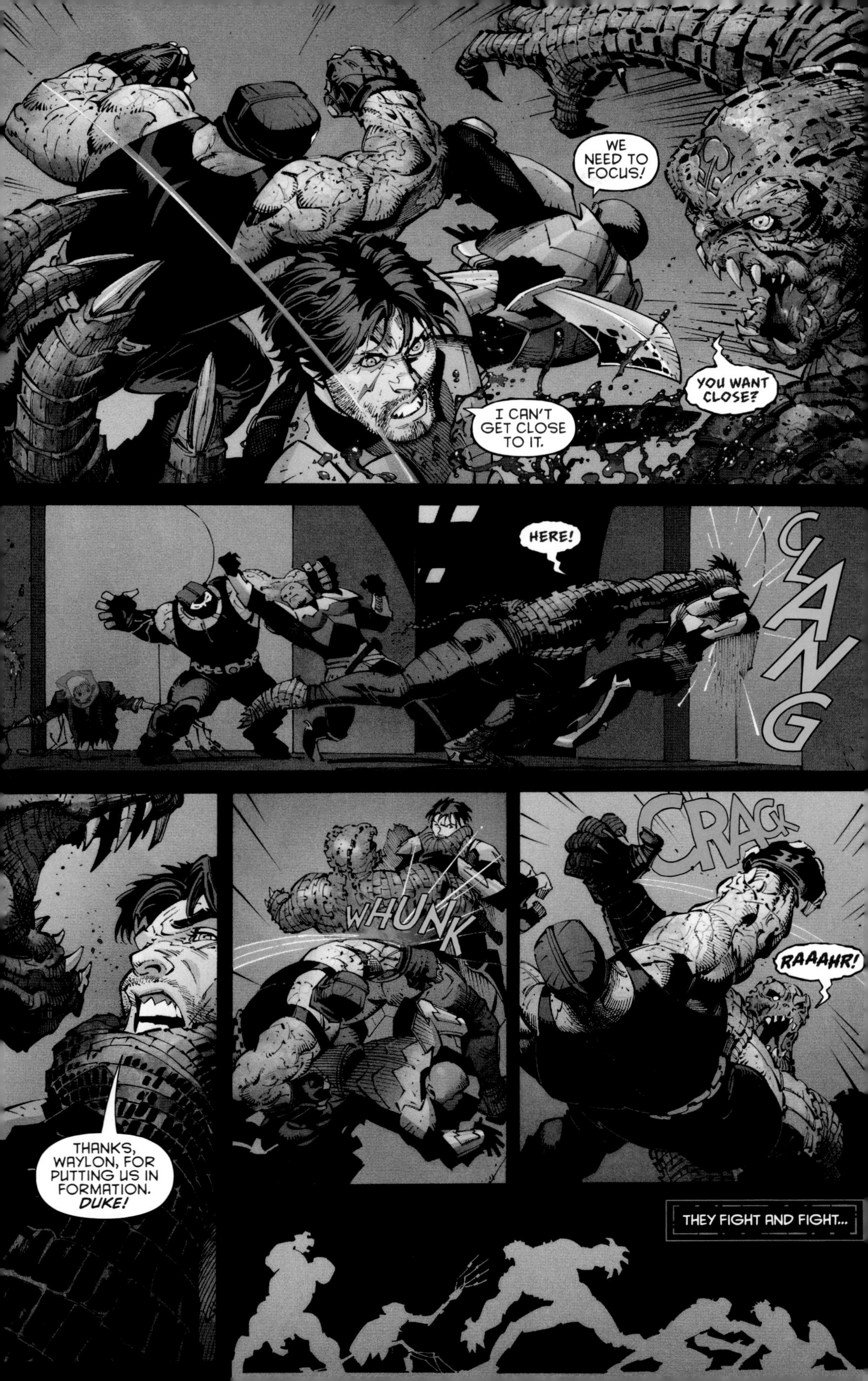
WE NEED TO FOCUS!
I CAN'T GET CLOSE TO IT.
YOU WANT CLOSE?
HERE!
CLANG
THANKS, WAYLON, FOR PUTTING US IN FORMATION. DUKE!
WHUNK
CRACK
RAAAHR!
THEY FIGHT AND FIGHT...

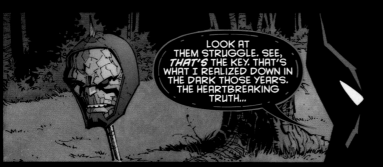

LOOK AT THEM STRUGGLE. SEE, *THAT'S* THE KEY. THAT'S WHAT I REALIZED DOWN IN THE DARK THOSE YEARS. THE HEARTBREAKING TRUTH...

J'ONN, PLEA--

Unh!

AWAITING ORDERS, OMEGA.

"...IS THAT BATS ARE BASICALLY DEAF TO EACH OTHER'S ECHOLOCATION.

"THEY LISTEN AT DIFFERENT FREQUENCIES, EVERYONE HEARING ONLY THEMSELVES.

"AND THAT *WAS* BATMAN. A CALL NO ONE HEARD. A FLIGHT PATH NO ONE FOLLOWED. ONE BAT IN A STORM OF BATS.

"SO NOW, A NEW SIGNAL. THE *REAL* BAT-SIGNAL.

A *CRY* THEY *HAVE* TO HEAR...AND FOLLOW.

RIGHT, BRUCE?

OH, YOU'RE GOING TO *CRY*.

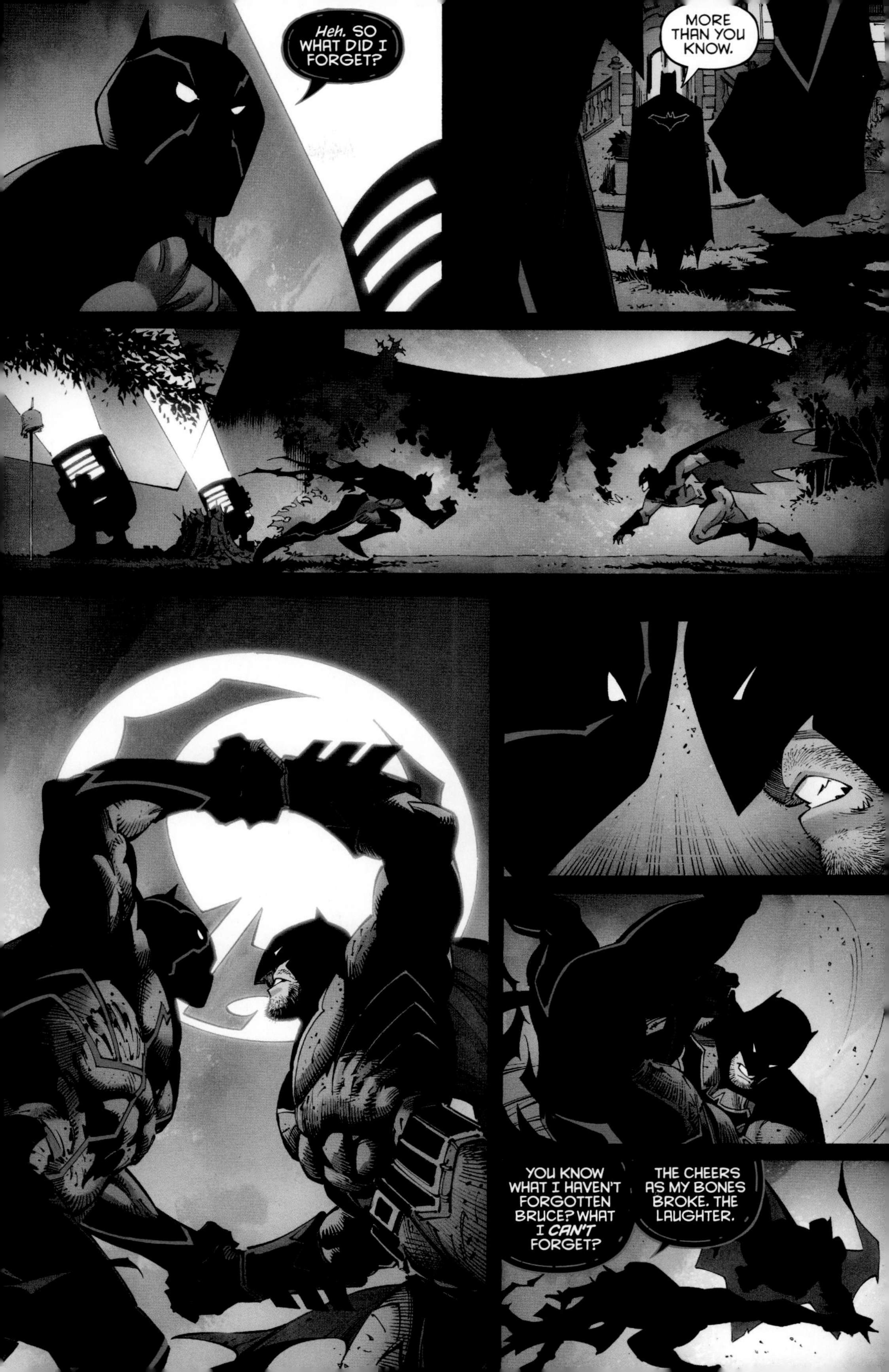
Heh. SO WHAT DID I FORGET?
MORE THAN YOU KNOW.
YOU KNOW WHAT I HAVEN'T FORGOTTEN BRUCE? WHAT I CAN'T FORGET?
THE CHEERS AS MY BONES BROKE. THE LAUGHTER.

I REMEMBER A FATHER HELPING HIS SON CUTPIECES OFF ME TO KEEP.

AND NEAR THE END, I REMEMBER A LITTLE GIRL KNEELING, MAYBE SEVEN YEARS OLD, NEAR ME. I HAD NO TONGUE, NO TEETH, BUT I TRIED TO TELL HER TO GO HIDE...

THWIP

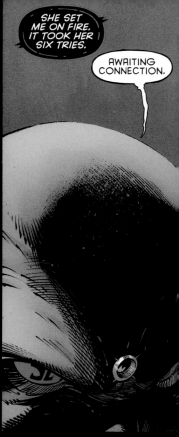

SHE SET ME ON FIRE. IT TOOK HER SIX TRIES.

AWAITING CONNECTION.

I REMEMBER WHAT THEY DID TO MY FRIENDS, MY FAMILY.

IT WON'T BUDGE!

IT ÷UNH÷... IT HAS TO!

ENOUGH! IT'S TIME TO END THIS...WITH A GOOD DEAL OF PAIN.

NOW YOU'RE TALKING.

DICK, HURRY!

"I REMEMBER PLENTY. NOW YOU CAN FIGHT ME ALL YOU WANT, BUT THE TRUTH IS..."

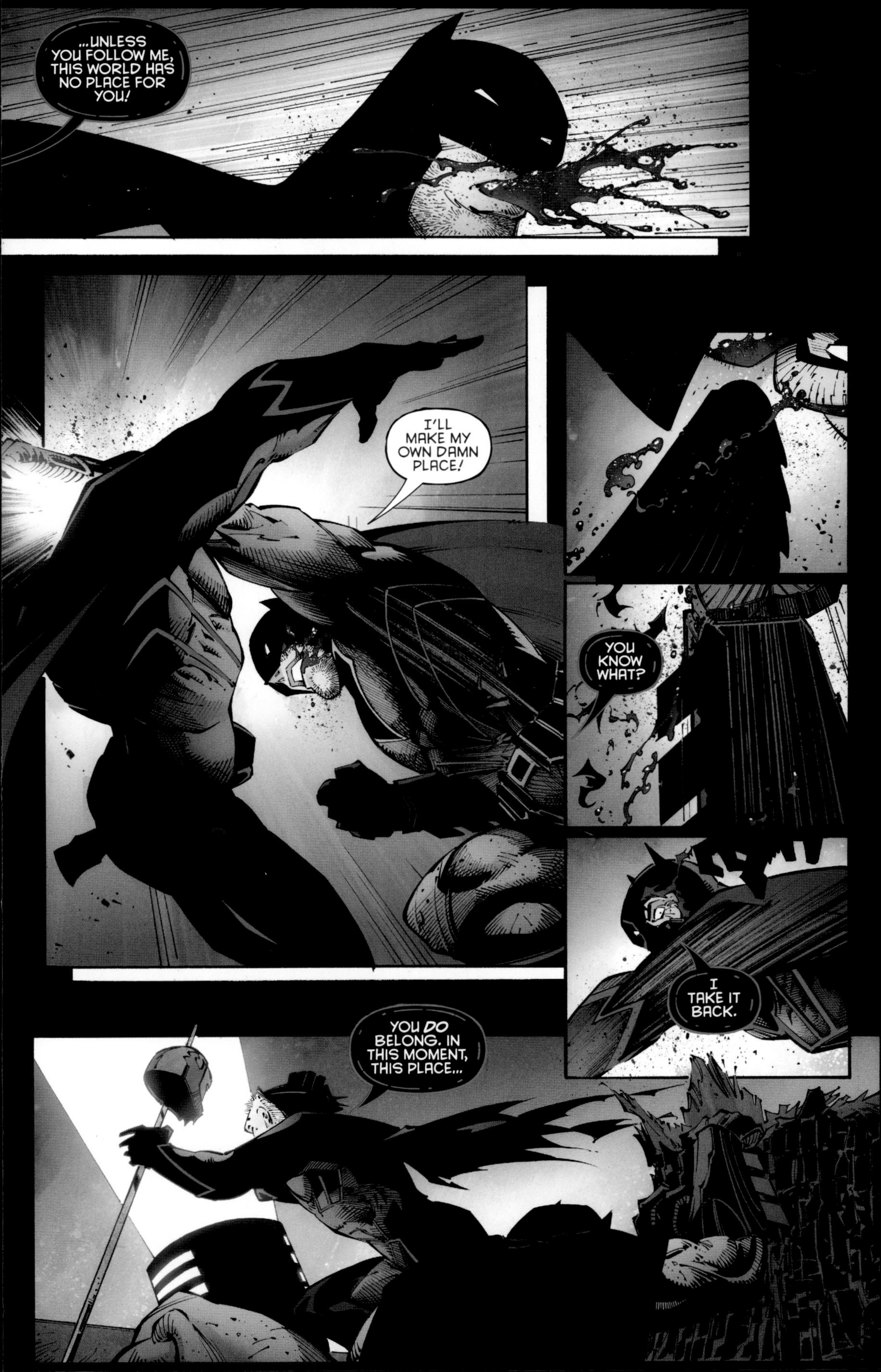
...UNLESS YOU FOLLOW ME, THIS WORLD HAS NO PLACE FOR YOU!
I'LL MAKE MY OWN DAMN PLACE!
YOU KNOW WHAT?
I TAKE IT BACK.
YOU *DO* BELONG. IN THIS MOMENT, THIS PLACE...

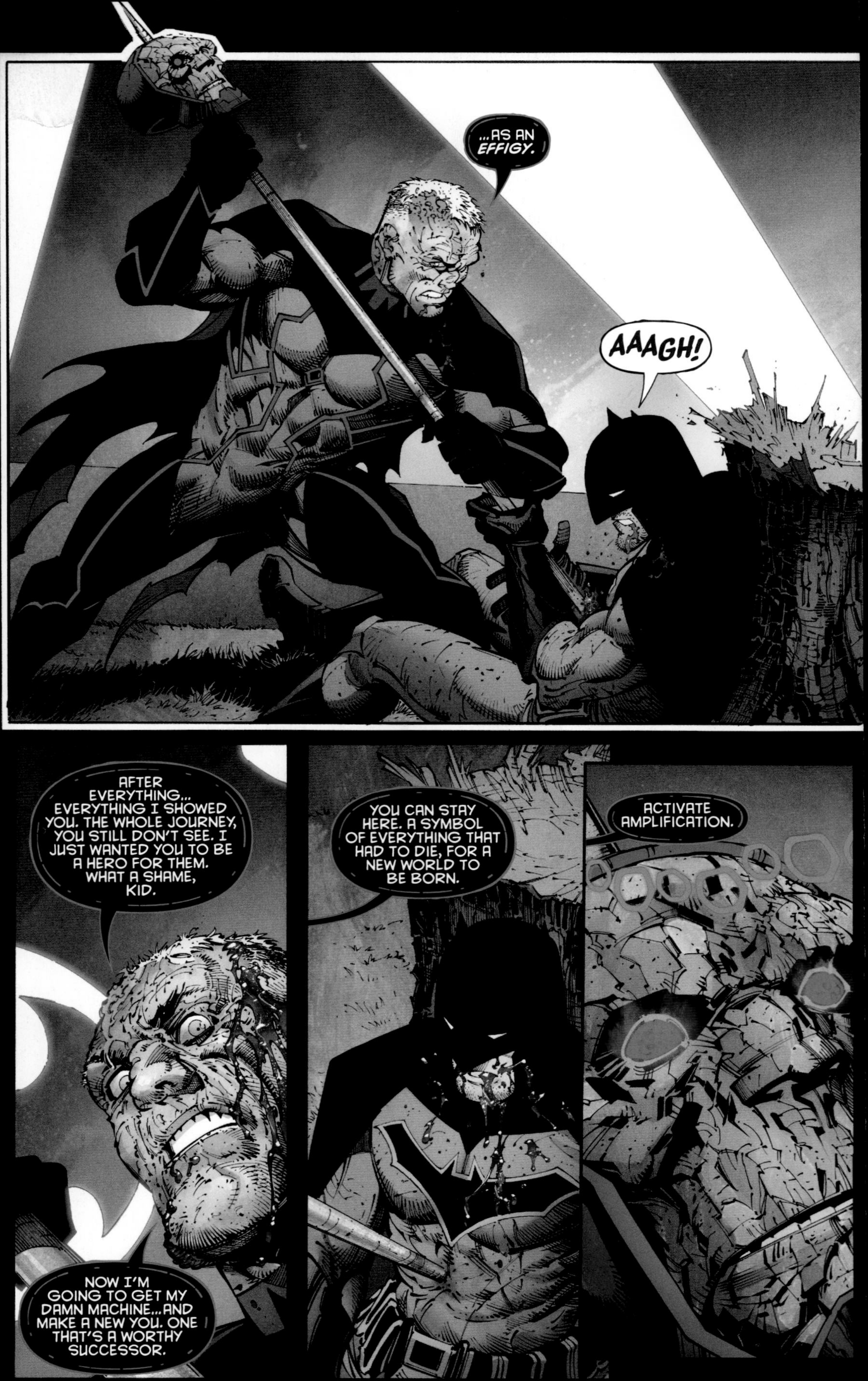
...AS AN EFFIGY.
AAAGH!
AFTER EVERYTHING... EVERYTHING I SHOWED YOU. THE WHOLE JOURNEY, YOU STILL DON'T SEE. I JUST WANTED YOU TO BE A HERO FOR THEM. WHAT A SHAME, KID.
NOW I'M GOING TO GET MY DAMN MACHINE...AND MAKE A NEW YOU. ONE THAT'S A WORTHY SUCCESSOR.
YOU CAN STAY HERE. A SYMBOL OF EVERYTHING THAT HAD TO DIE, FOR A NEW WORLD TO BE BORN.
ACTIVATE AMPLIFICATION.

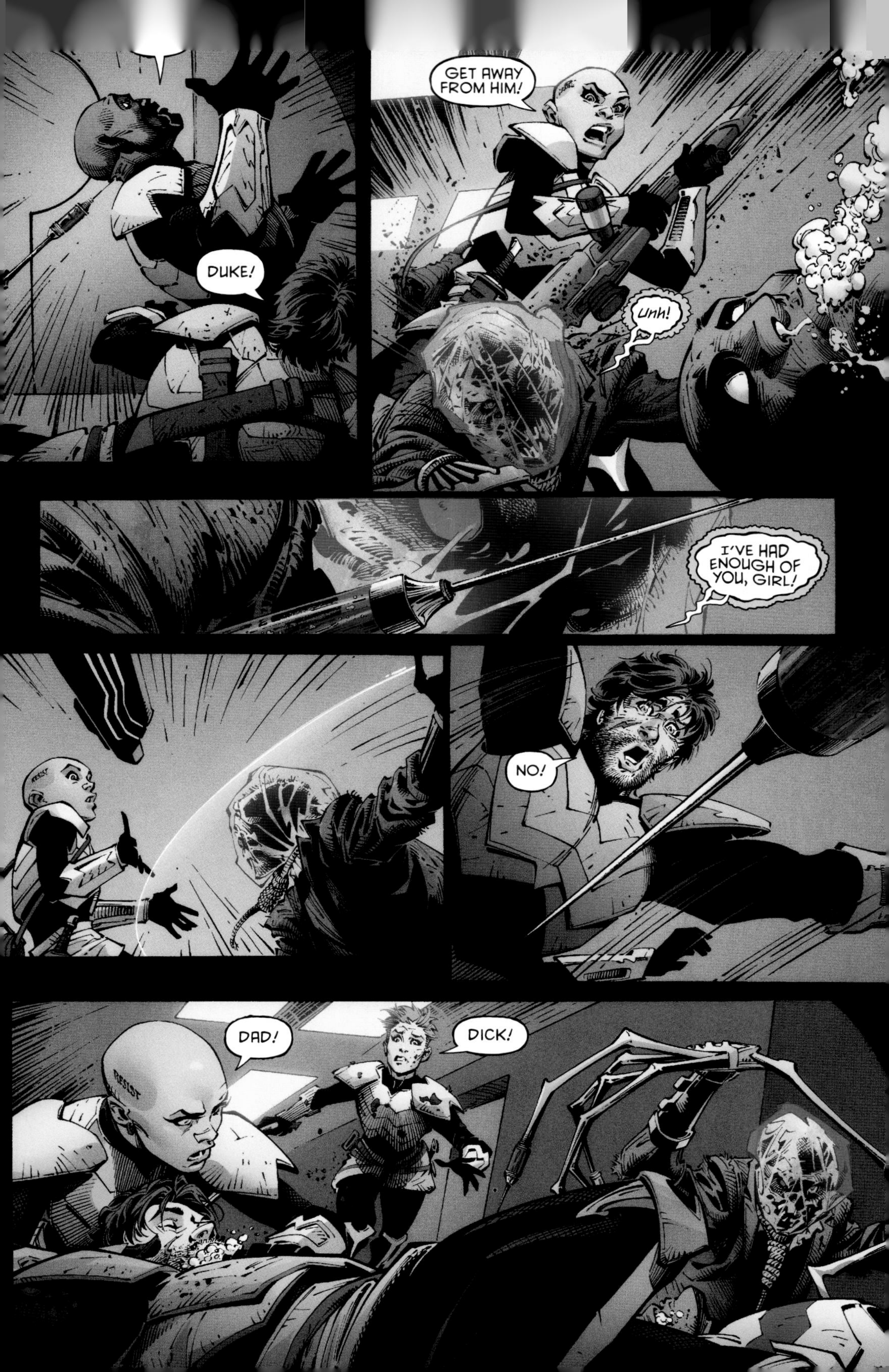
DUKE!
GET AWAY FROM HIM!
Unh!
I'VE HAD ENOUGH OF YOU, GIRL!
NO!
DAD!
DICK!
RESIST
RESIST

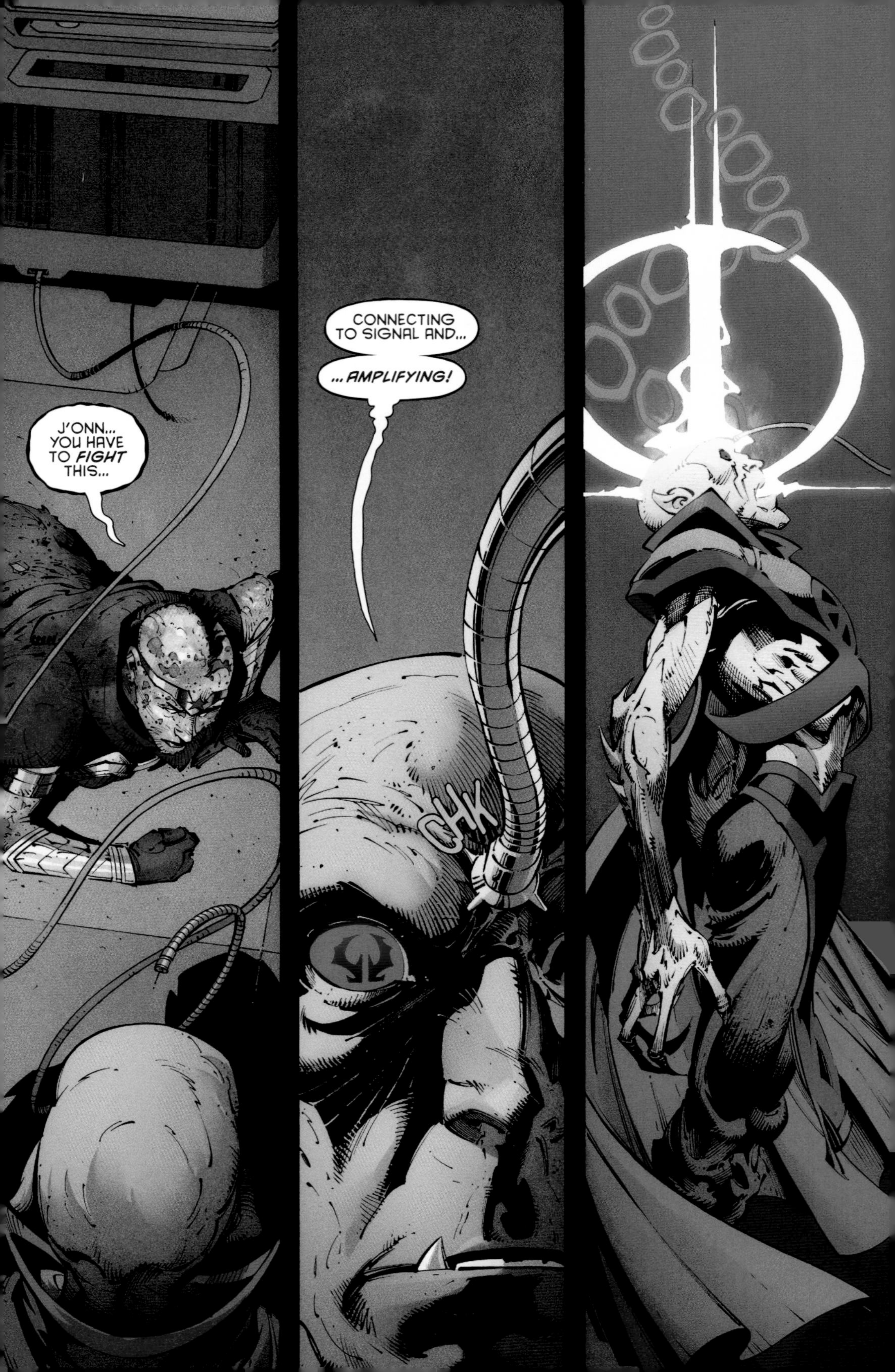
J'ONN... YOU HAVE TO FIGHT THIS...
CONNECTING TO SIGNAL AND...
...AMPLIFYING!
CHK

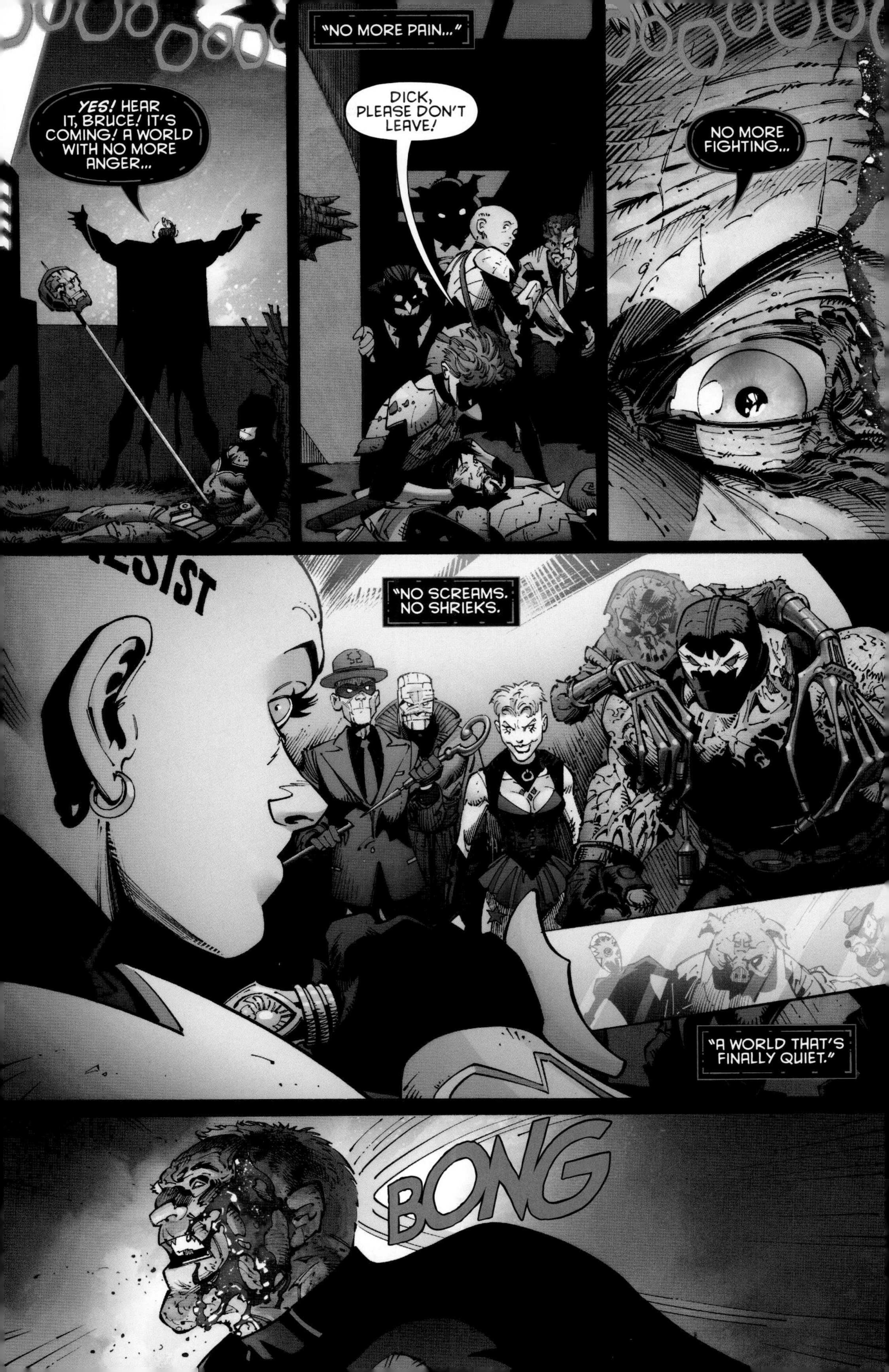

YES! HEAR IT, BRUCE! IT'S COMING! A WORLD WITH NO MORE ANGER...
"NO MORE PAIN..."
DICK, PLEASE DON'T LEAVE!
NO MORE FIGHTING...
RESIST
"NO SCREAMS. NO SHRIEKS.
"A WORLD THAT'S FINALLY QUIET."
BONG

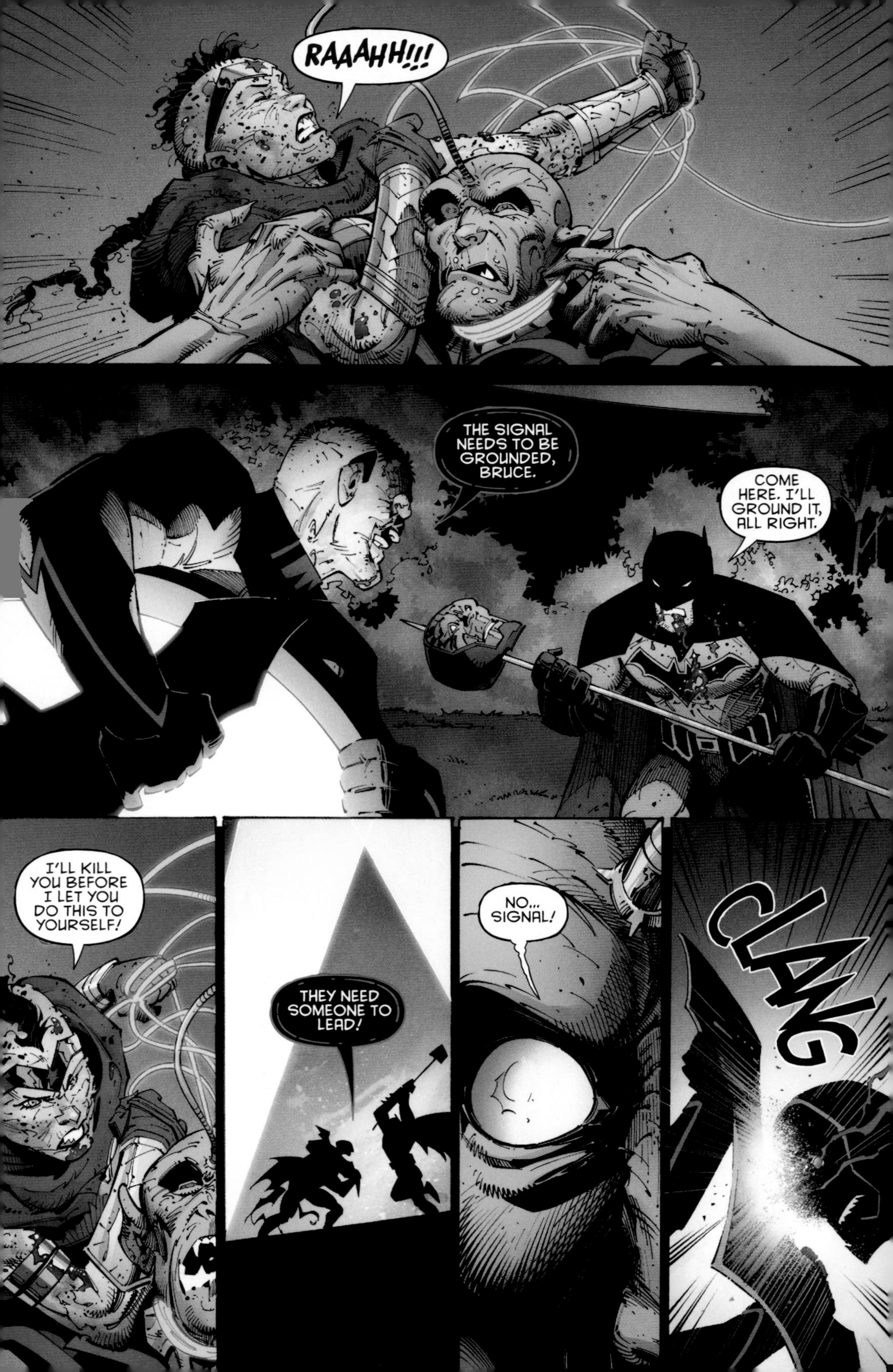
RAAAHH!!!
THE SIGNAL NEEDS TO BE GROUNDED, BRUCE.
COME HERE. I'LL GROUND IT, ALL RIGHT.
I'LL KILL YOU BEFORE I LET YOU DO THIS TO YOURSELF!
THEY NEED SOMEONE TO LEAD!
NO... SIGNAL!
CLANG

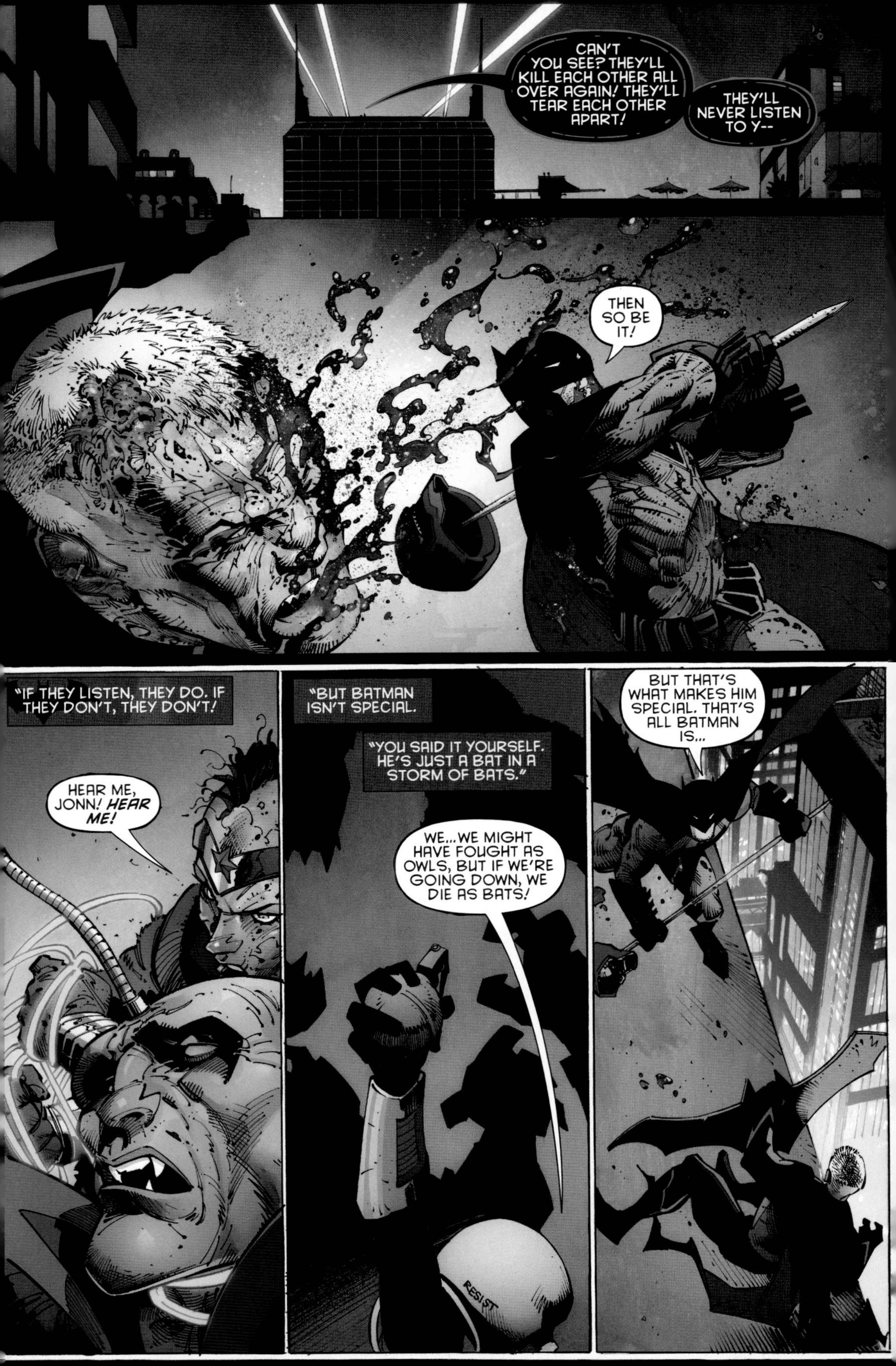
CAN'T YOU SEE? THEY'LL KILL EACH OTHER ALL OVER AGAIN! THEY'LL TEAR EACH OTHER APART!
THEY'LL NEVER LISTEN TO Y--
THEN SO BE IT!
"IF THEY LISTEN, THEY DO. IF THEY DON'T, THEY DON'T!
HEAR ME, JONN! HEAR ME!
"BUT BATMAN ISN'T SPECIAL.
"YOU SAID IT YOURSELF. HE'S JUST A BAT IN A STORM OF BATS."
WE...WE MIGHT HAVE FOUGHT AS OWLS, BUT IF WE'RE GOING DOWN, WE DIE AS BATS!
RESIST
BUT THAT'S WHAT MAKES HIM SPECIAL. THAT'S ALL BATMAN IS...

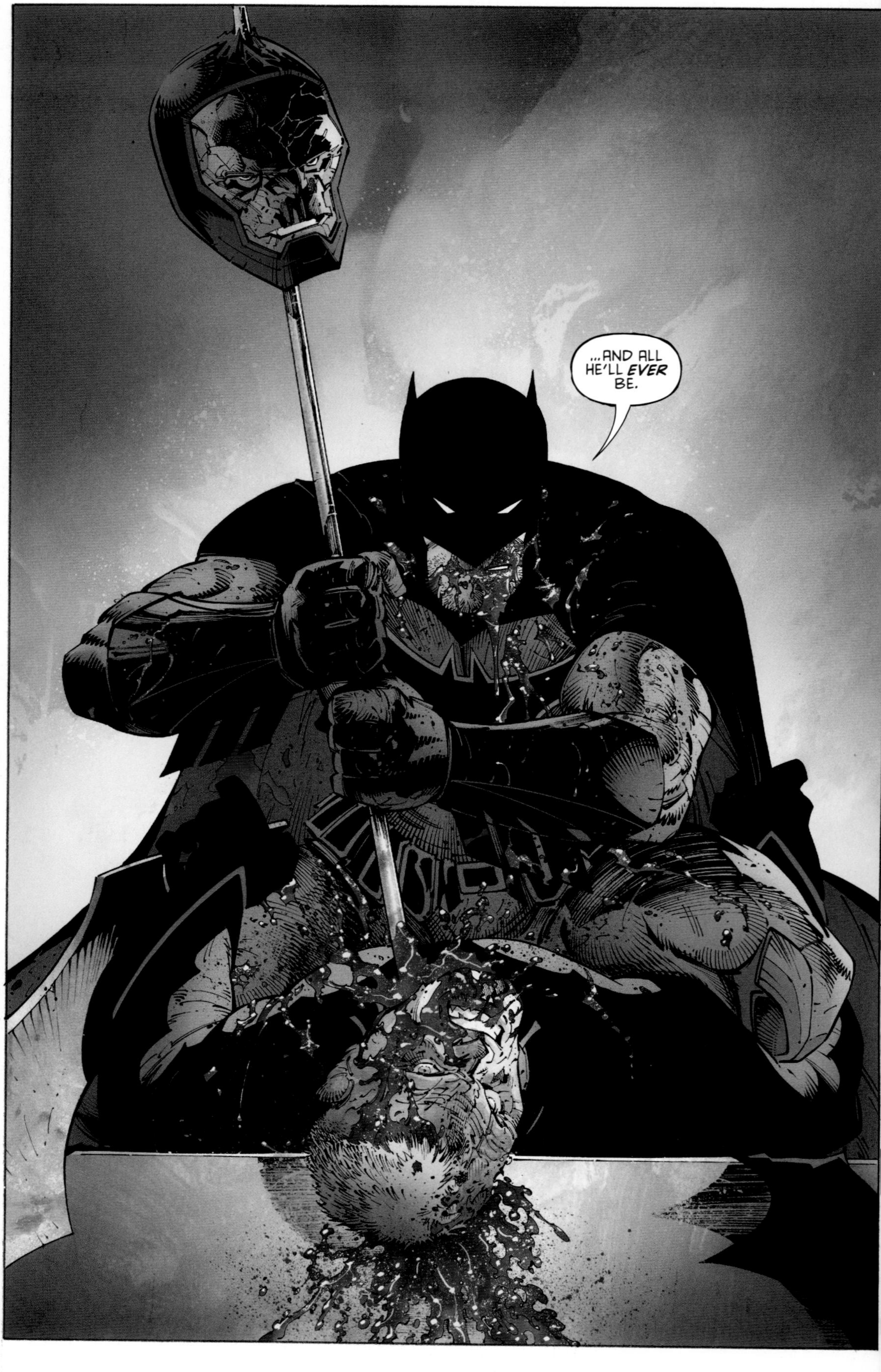
...AND ALL HE'LL EVER BE.

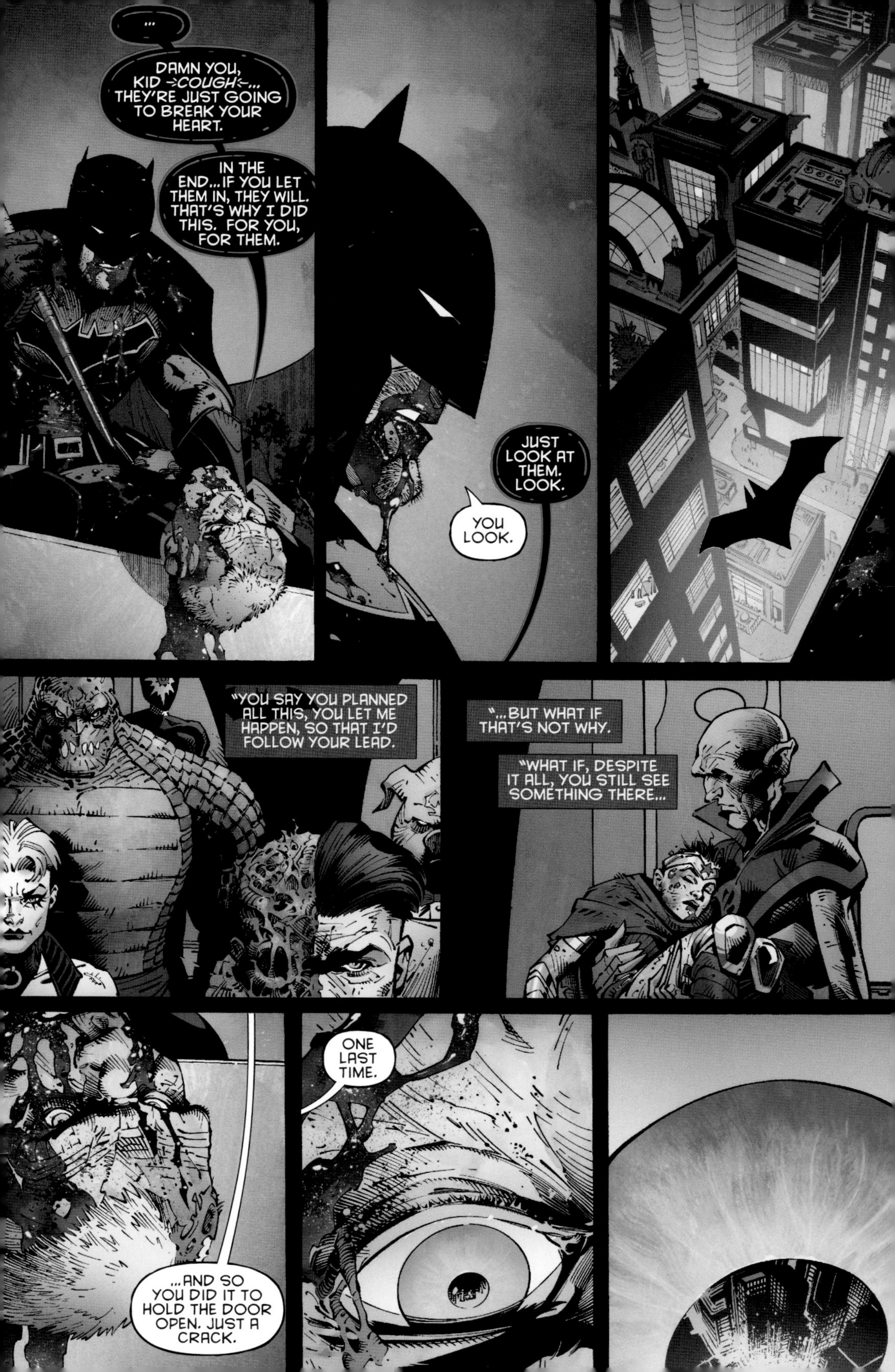
...
DAMN YOU, KID ⇒COUGH⇐... THEY'RE JUST GOING TO BREAK YOUR HEART.
IN THE END... IF YOU LET THEM IN, THEY WILL. THAT'S WHY I DID THIS. FOR YOU, FOR THEM.
JUST LOOK AT THEM. LOOK.
YOU LOOK.
"YOU SAY YOU PLANNED ALL THIS, YOU LET ME HAPPEN, SO THAT I'D FOLLOW YOUR LEAD.
"...BUT WHAT IF THAT'S NOT WHY.
"WHAT IF, DESPITE IT ALL, YOU STILL SEE SOMETHING THERE...
...AND SO YOU DID IT TO HOLD THE DOOR OPEN. JUST A CRACK.
ONE LAST TIME.

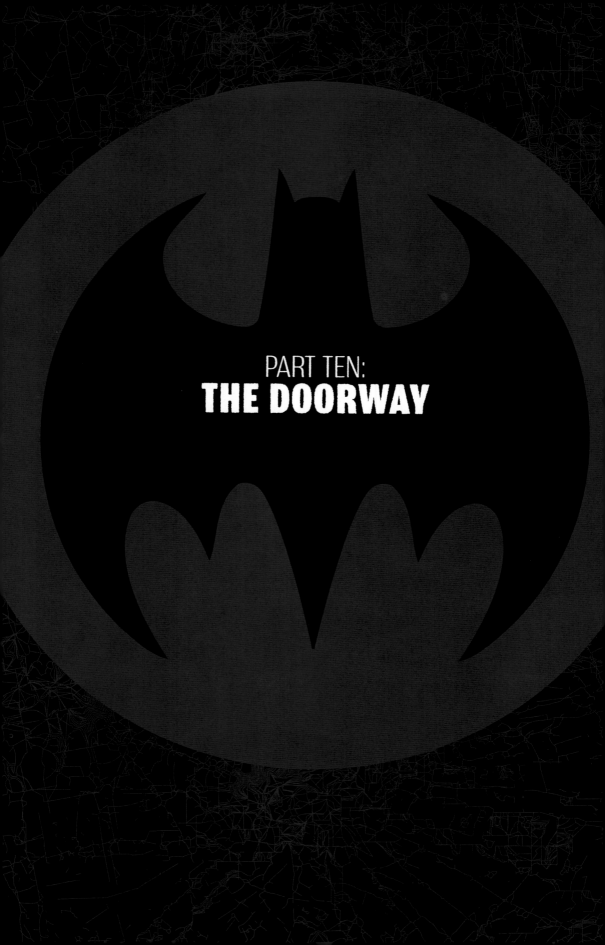

PART TEN:
THE DOORWAY

"We've had many adventures together..."

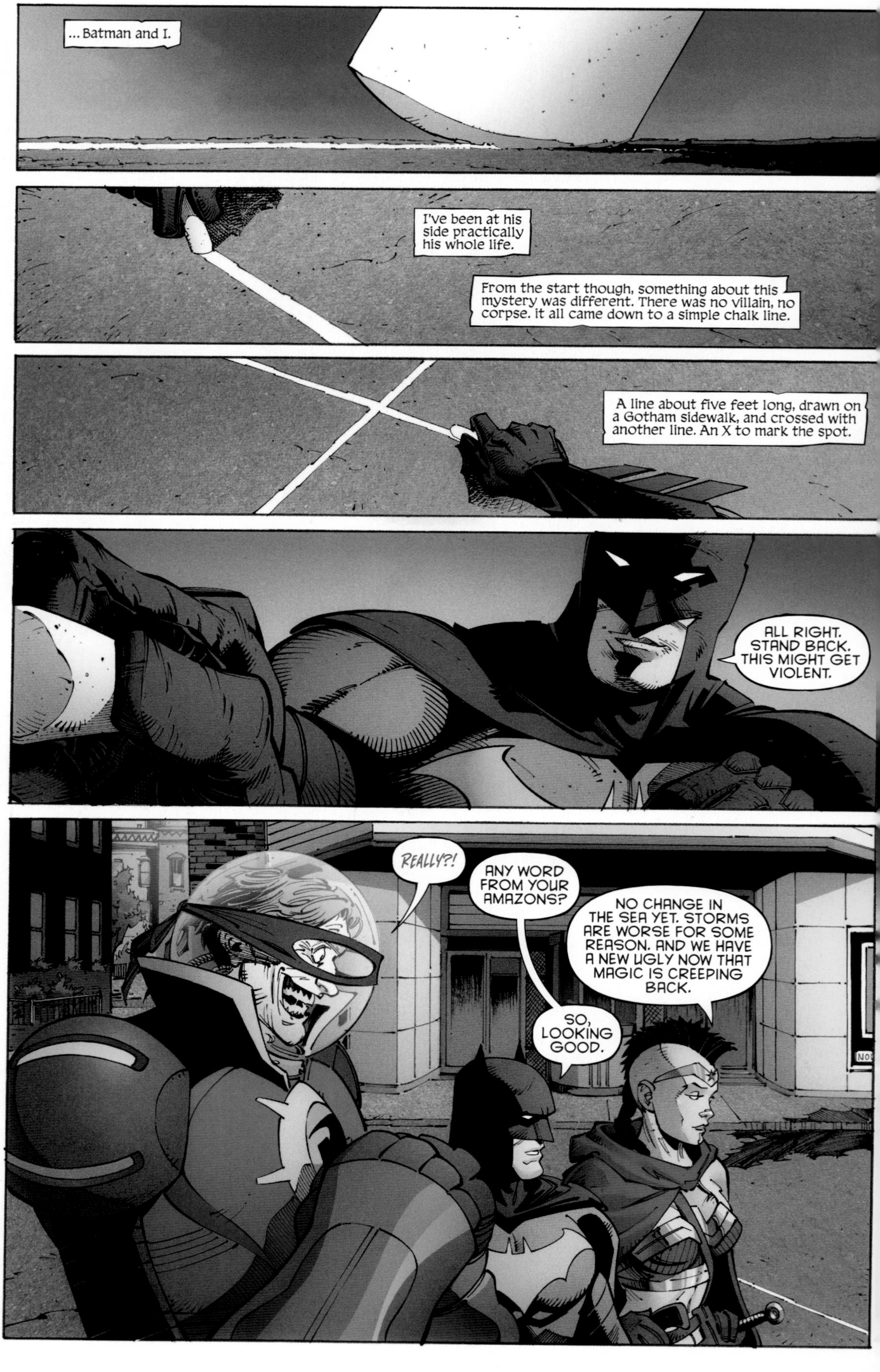
...Batman and I.
I've been at his side practically his whole life.
From the start though, something about this mystery was different. There was no villain, no corpse. it all came down to a simple chalk line.
A line about five feet long, drawn on a Gotham sidewalk, and crossed with another line. An X to mark the spot.
ALL RIGHT. STAND BACK. THIS MIGHT GET VIOLENT.
REALLY?!
ANY WORD FROM YOUR AMAZONS?
NO CHANGE IN THE SEA YET. STORMS ARE WORSE FOR SOME REASON. AND WE HAVE A NEW UGLY NOW THAT MAGIC IS CREEPING BACK.
SO, LOOKING GOOD.

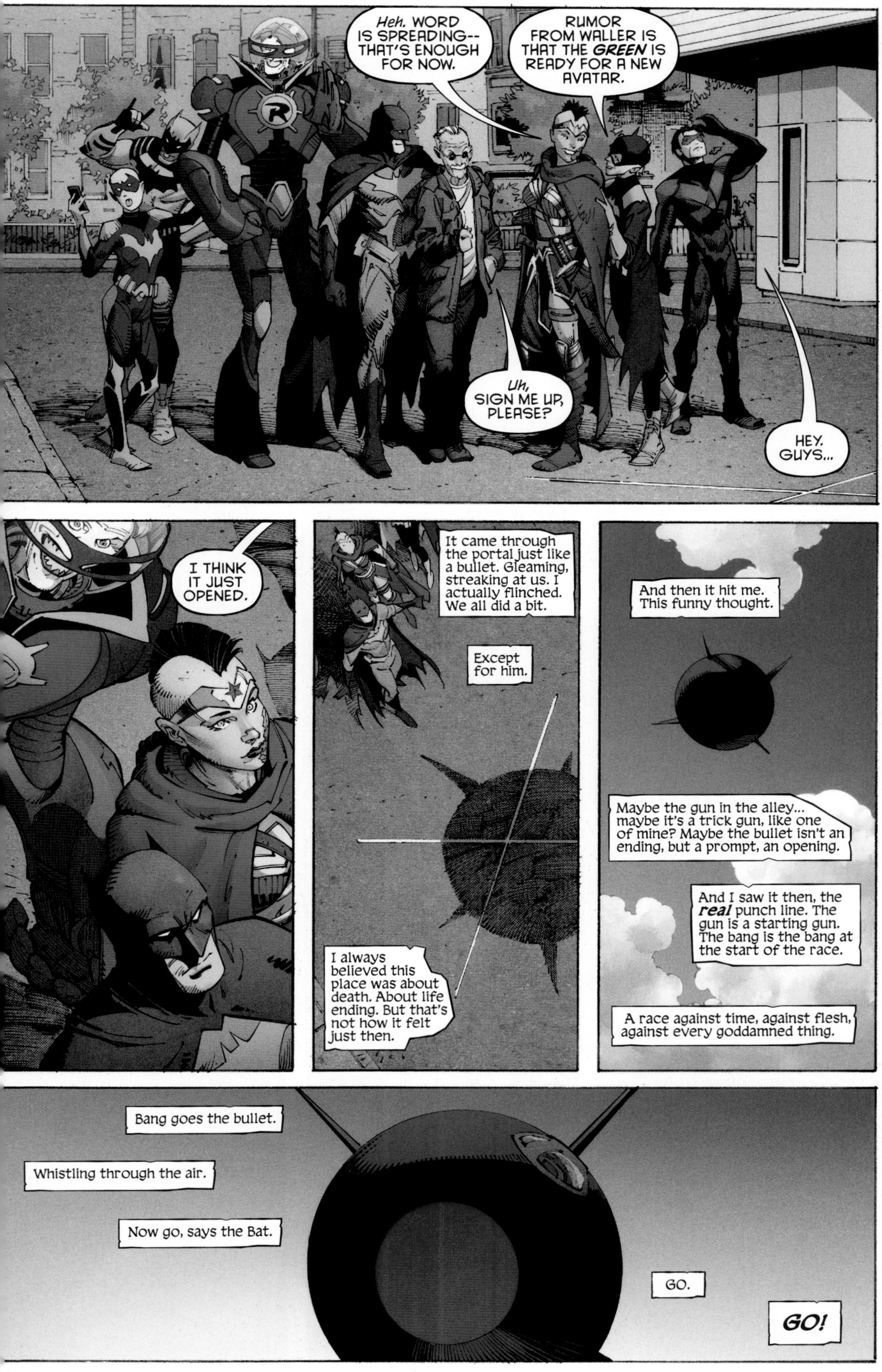

Heh. WORD IS SPREADING-- THAT'S ENOUGH FOR NOW.
RUMOR FROM WALLER IS THAT THE GREEN IS READY FOR A NEW AVATAR.
Uh, SIGN ME UP, PLEASE?
HEY. GUYS...
I THINK IT JUST OPENED.
It came through the portal just like a bullet. Gleaming, streaking at us. I actually flinched. We all did a bit.
Except for him.
I always believed this place was about death. About life ending. But that's not how it felt just then.
And then it hit me. This funny thought.
Maybe the gun in the alley... maybe it's a trick gun, like one of mine? Maybe the bullet isn't an ending, but a prompt, an opening.
And I saw it then, the real punch line. The gun is a starting gun. The bang is the bang at the start of the race.
A race against time, against flesh, against every goddamned thing.
Bang goes the bullet.
Whistling through the air.
Now go, says the Bat.
GO.
GO!

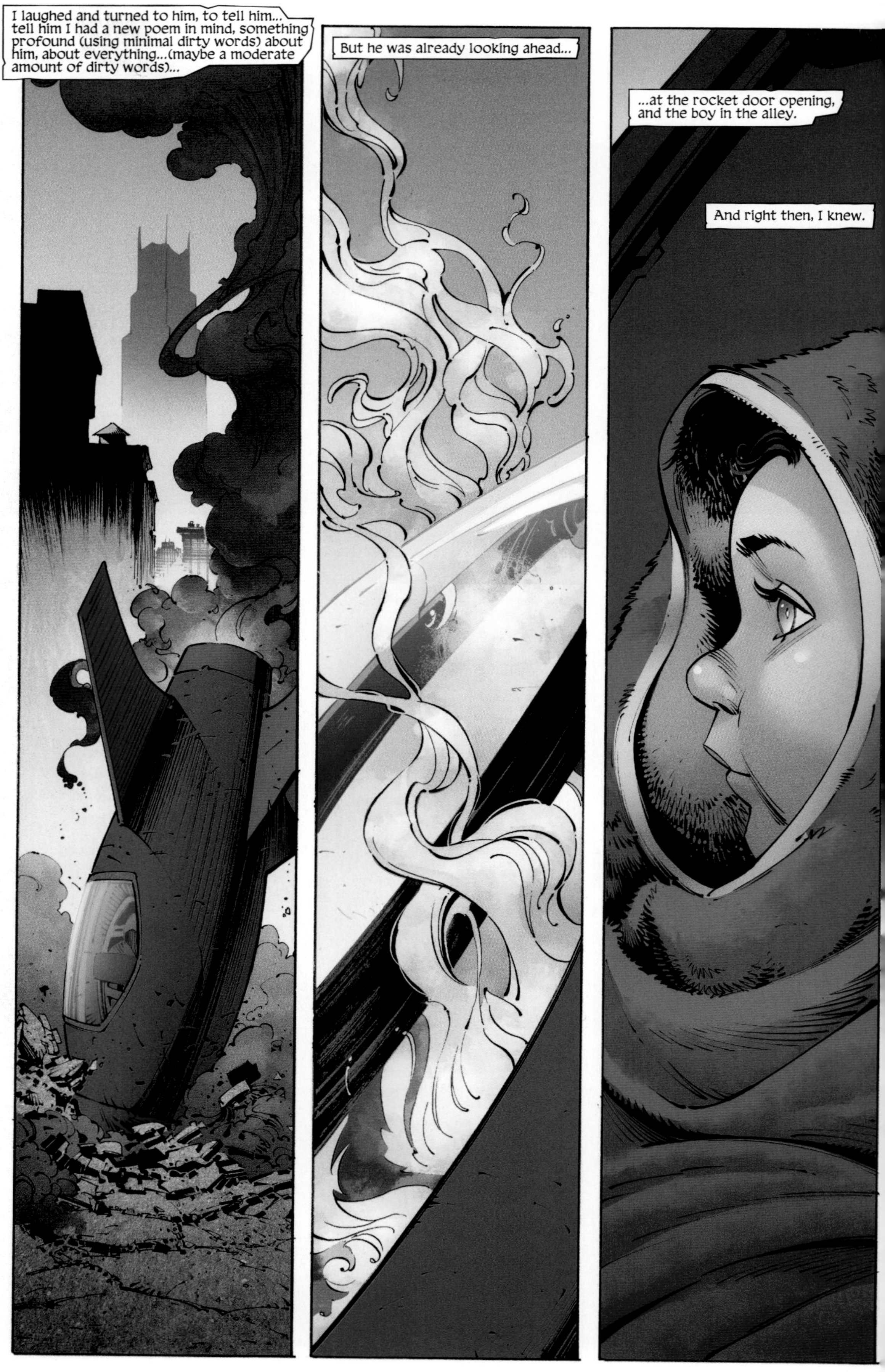
I laughed and turned to him, to tell him... tell him I had a new poem in mind, something profound (using minimal dirty words) about him, about everything...(maybe a moderate amount of dirty words)...
But he was already looking ahead...
...at the rocket door opening, and the boy in the alley.
And right then, I knew.

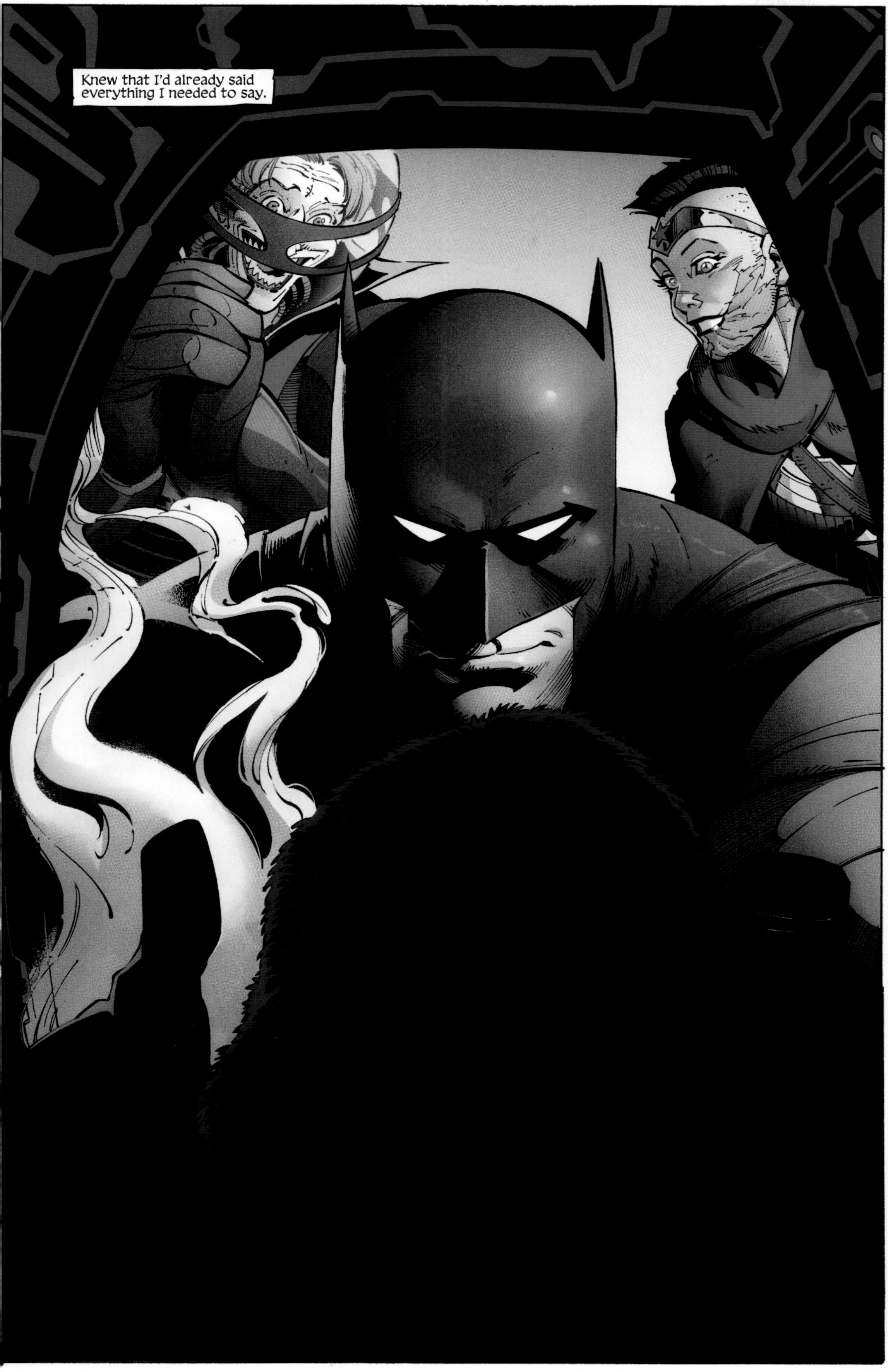
Knew that I'd already said everything I needed to say.

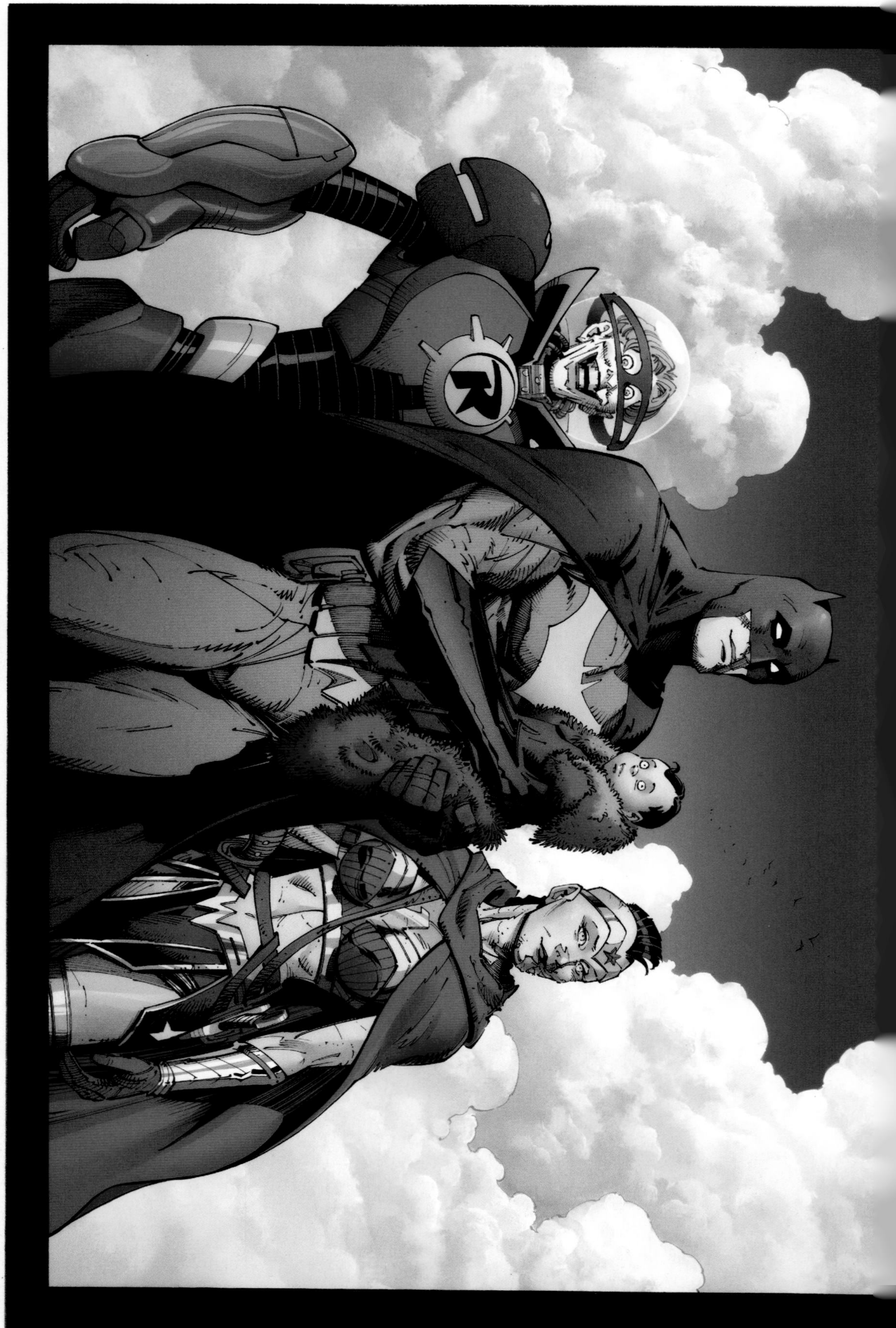

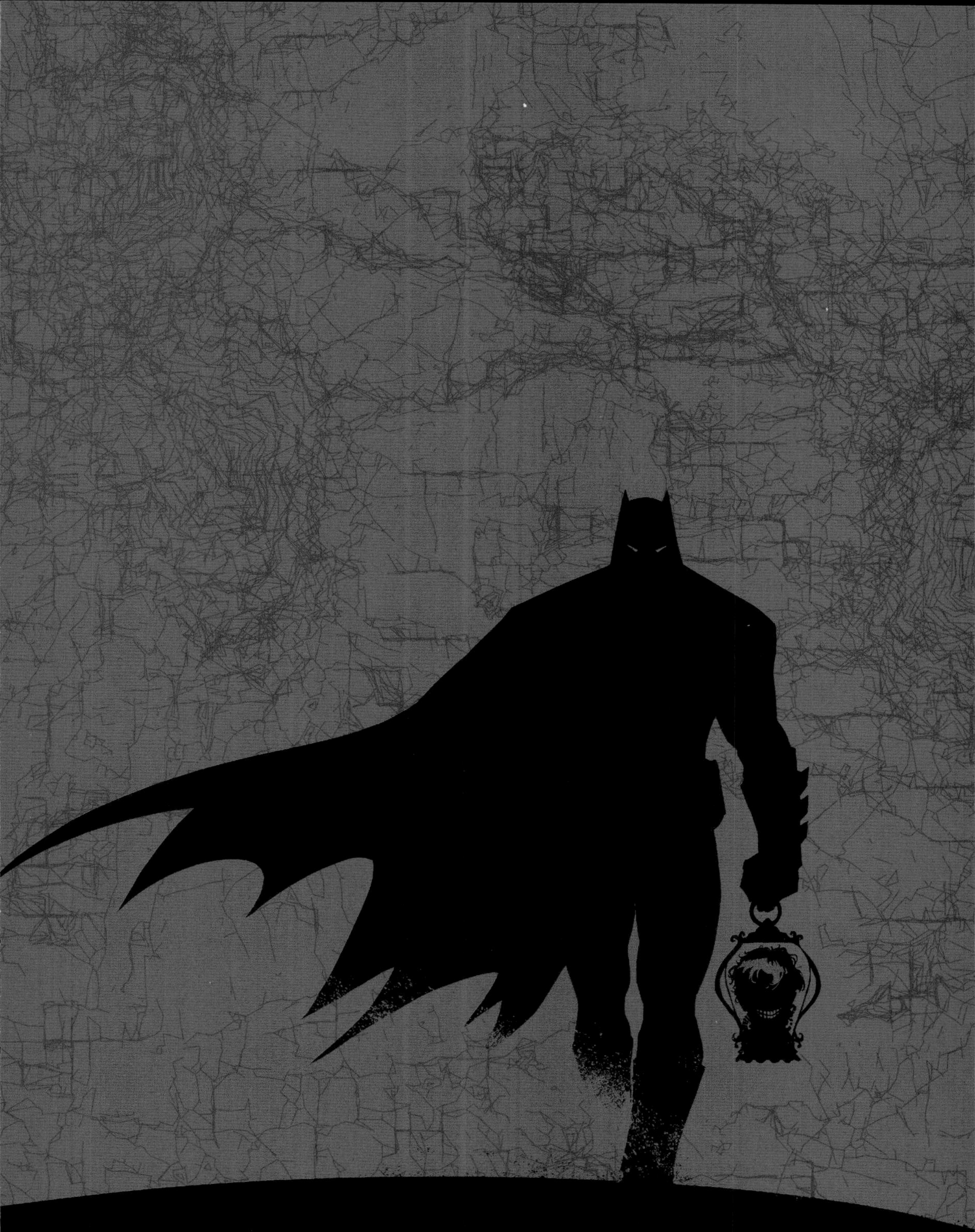

SCOTT SNYDER

has written the bestselling series *American Vampire*, *Batman*, *Swamp Thing*, *Superman Unchained*, and *Dark Nights: Metal*. He is also the author of the story collection *Voodoo Heart* (Dial Press). He teaches writing at Sarah Lawrence College, NYU, and Columbia University. He lives on Long Island with his wife, Jeanie, and his three children. He is a dedicated and unironic fan of Elvis Presley.

GREG CAPULLO

is a comic book artist who has worked on *Batman* and *Dark Nights: Metal* for DC Comics, *Quasar* and *X-Force* for Marvel Comics, and *Spawn*, *Angela*, and *The Haunt* for Image Comics. He has also written and drawn the creator-owned series *The Creech*. Outside of comics, Capullo has worked on CD covers for the bands Disturbed and Korn. Greg has been a regular contributor to *World of Warcraft*, supplying painted art. He was also involved with character design for the animated sequences in the Jodie Foster film *The Dangerous Lives of Altar Boys* and the award-winning HBO animated series *Spawn*, created by Todd McFarlane.

JONATHAN GLAPION

began his comics career in 1998 at Image, where he contributed inks to such titles as *Curse of the Spawn, Sam and Twitch,* and *Universe.* After spending several years at Marvel inking *Elektra: The Hand, Gravity,* and *Ultimate X-Men,* he shifted his focus to their distinguished competition. Since 2007, he has worked on a wide variety of DC titles, including the New 52 *Batman, Batgirl, Suicide Squad, Batman/Superman, New Super-Man,* and *Action Comics* as well as *Wonder Woman.* He is the winner of three Inkwell Awards (the Props Award in 2010, the Most-Adaptable Inker Award in 2013 and the S.P.A.M.I. Award in 2017) and was a Harvey Award nominee for Best Inker in 2013. More recently, Jonathan worked on *Reborn* with Greg Capullo and Millarworld and DC's *Dark Nights: Metal* and *Batman: Last Knight on Earth.*

FCO PLASCENCIA

is a professional comic book colorist based in Mexico. A student of graphic design, he was handpicked by Greg Capullo to collaborate on *Batman* "because he's not your average colorist. His influences are film and fine arts, and he doesn't step on the line work." Plascencia's other works include *Spawn, Invincible, Haunt, Gemini,* and *The Walking Dead,* among others. He enjoys drawing, painting, and playing guitar.

COVER
GALLERY

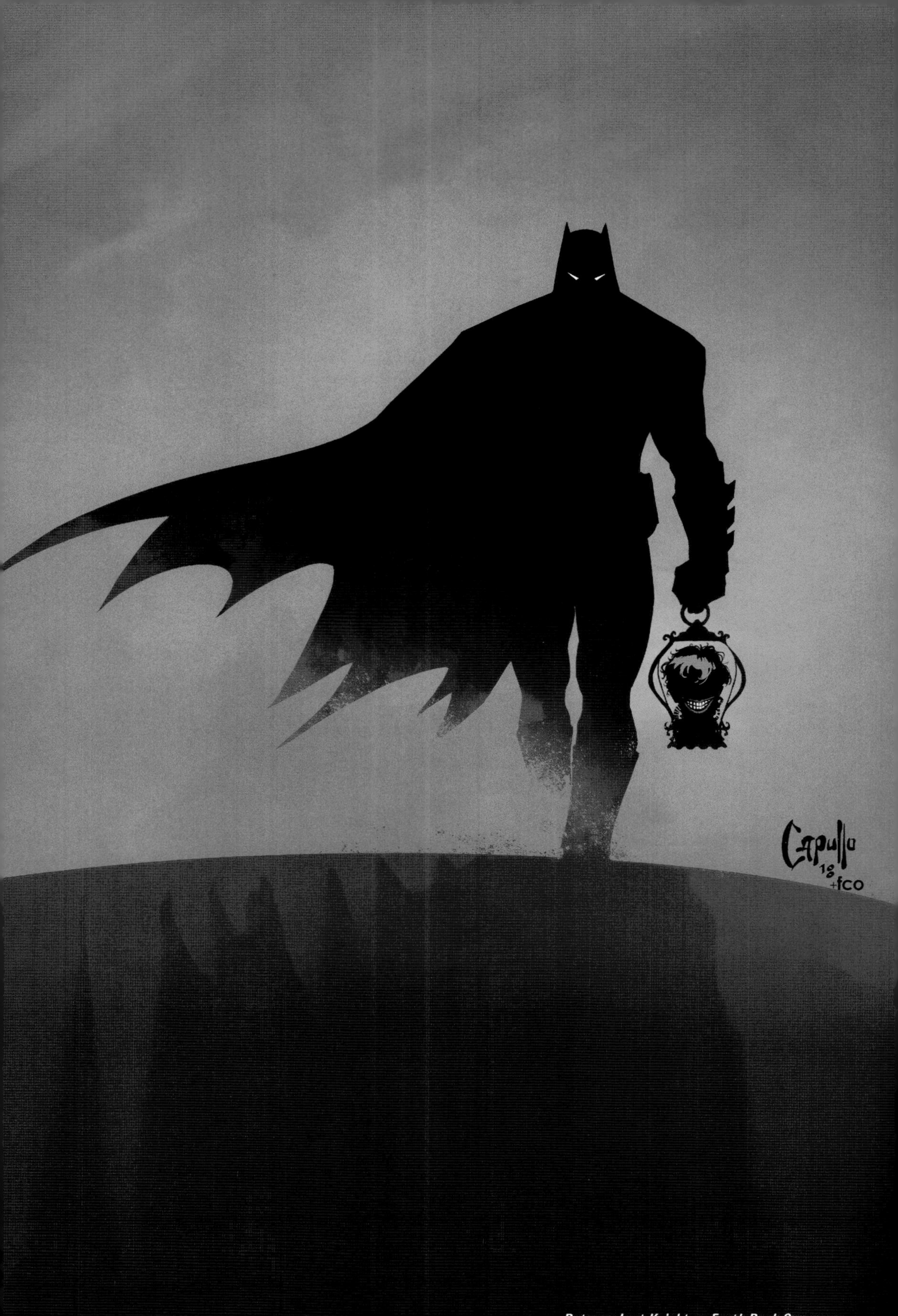
Capullo
18
+fco

Batman: Last Knight on Earth Book One cover
by Greg Capullo and FCO Plascencia

Batman: Last Knight on Earth Book Two cover
by Greg Capullo, Jonathan Glapion, and FCO Plascencia

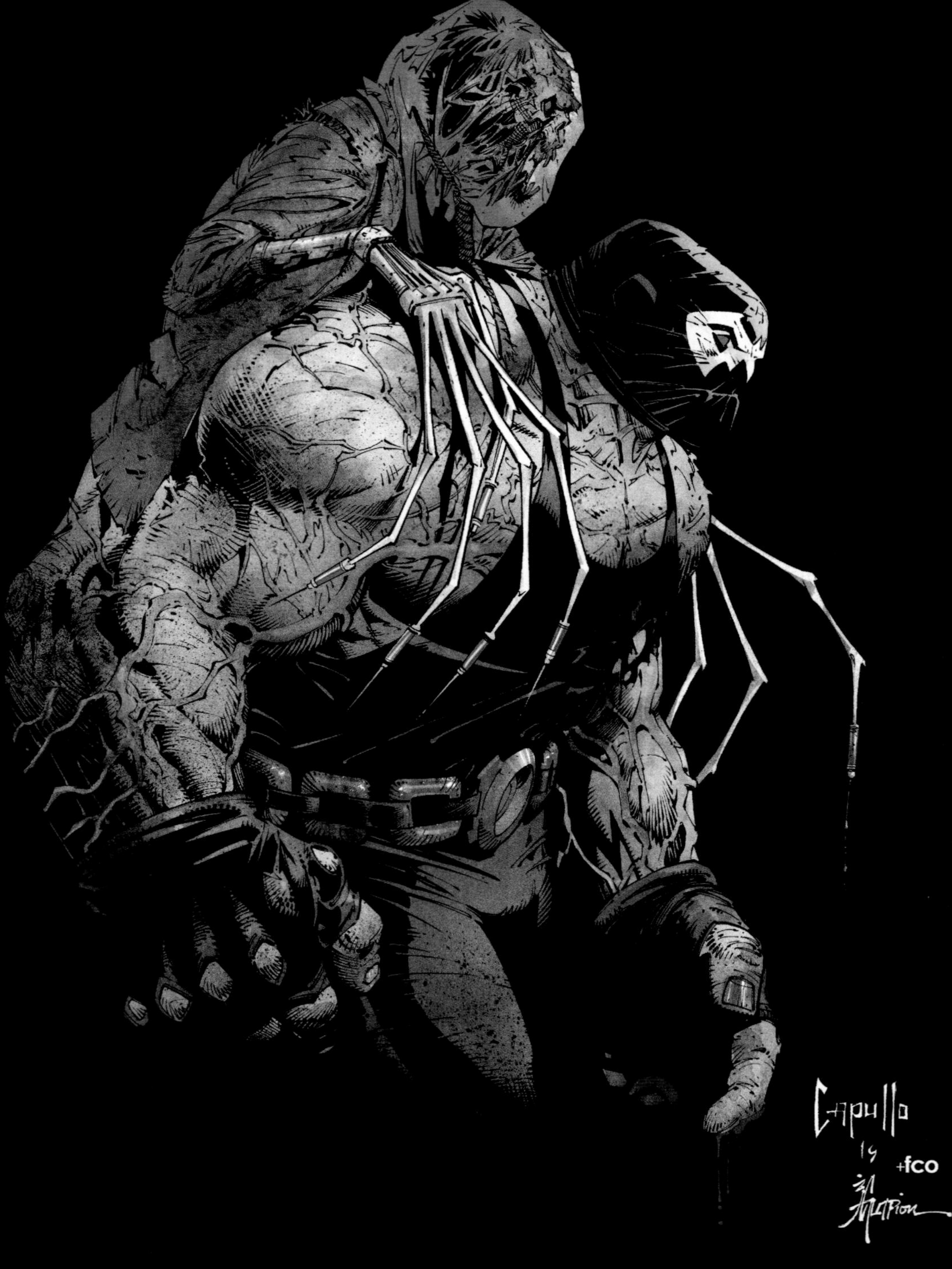
Capullo
19
+fco
Glapion

Batman: Last Knight on Earth Book One
variant cover by Jock

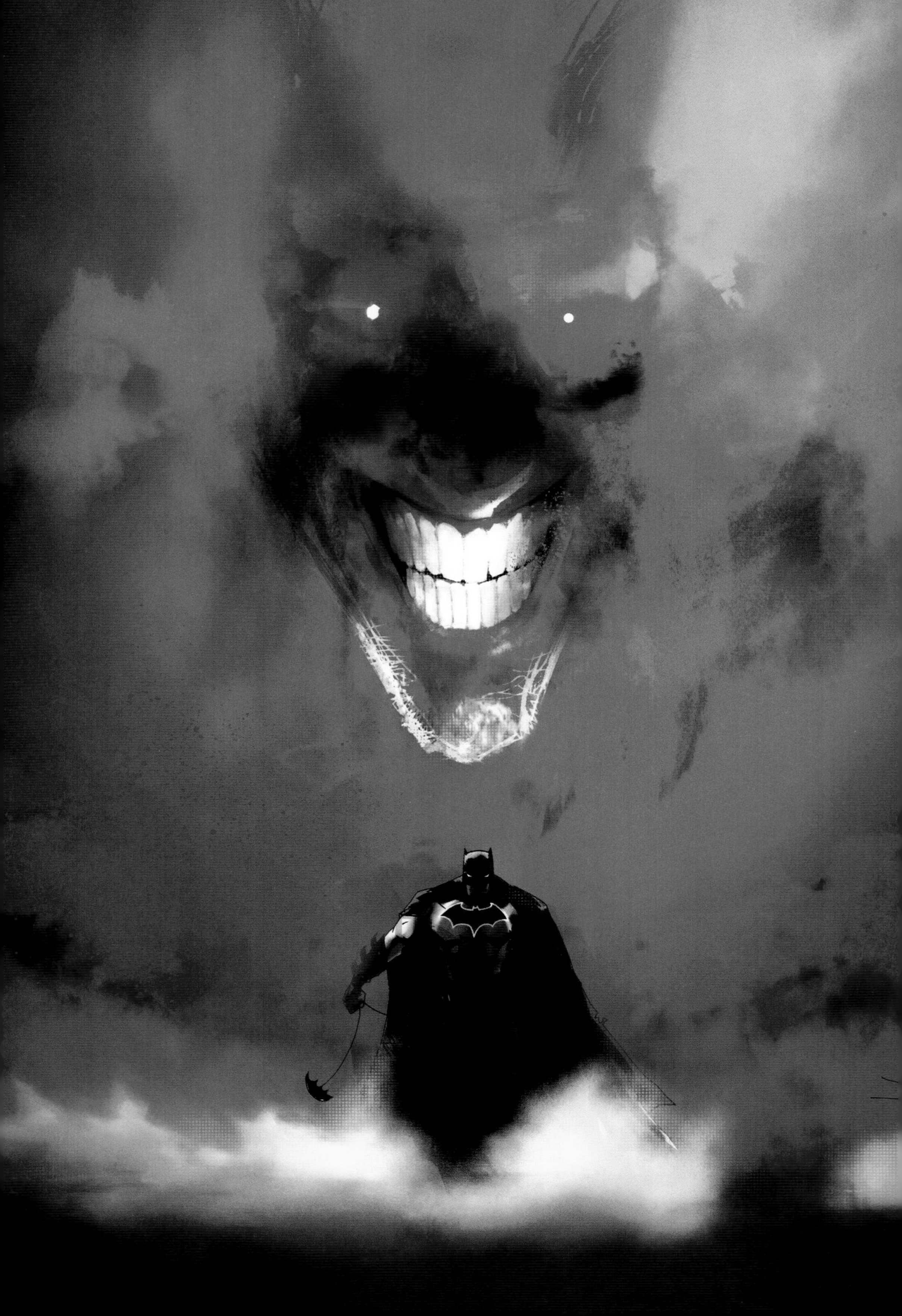

Batman: Last Knight on Earth Book Two variant cover
by John Romita Jr. and Peter Steigerwald

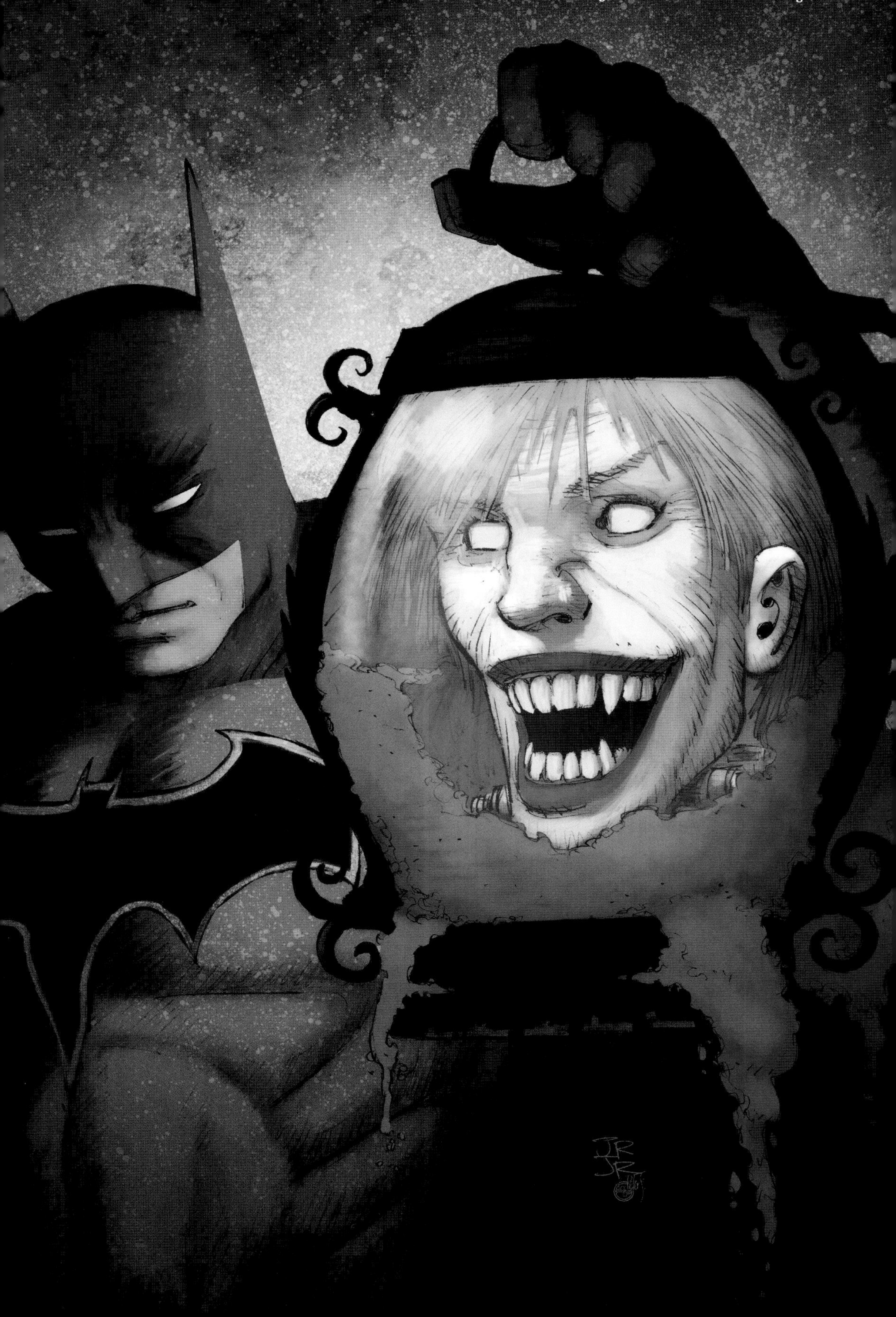

Batman: Last Knight on Earth Book Three
variant cover by Rafael Albuquerque

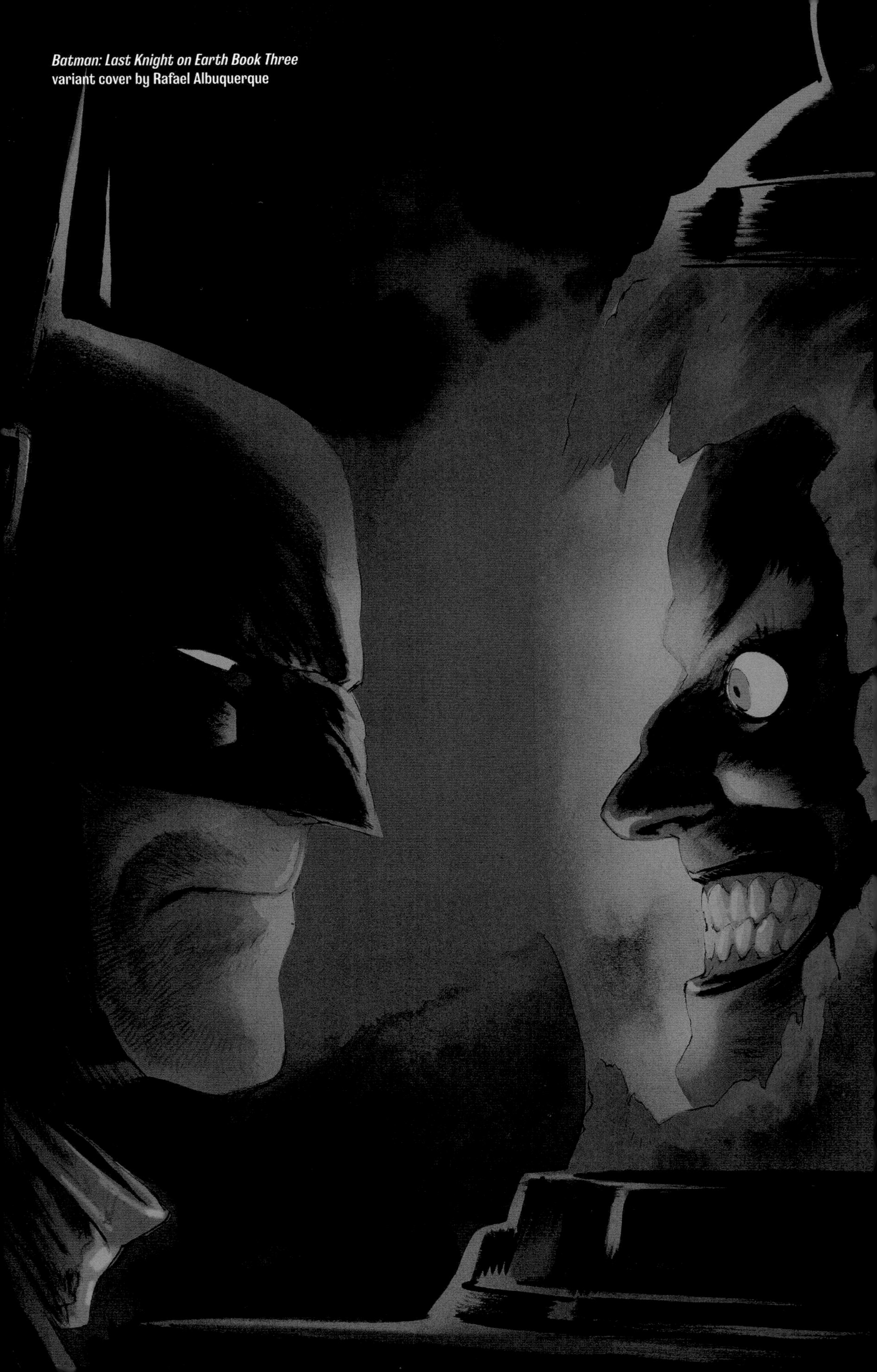

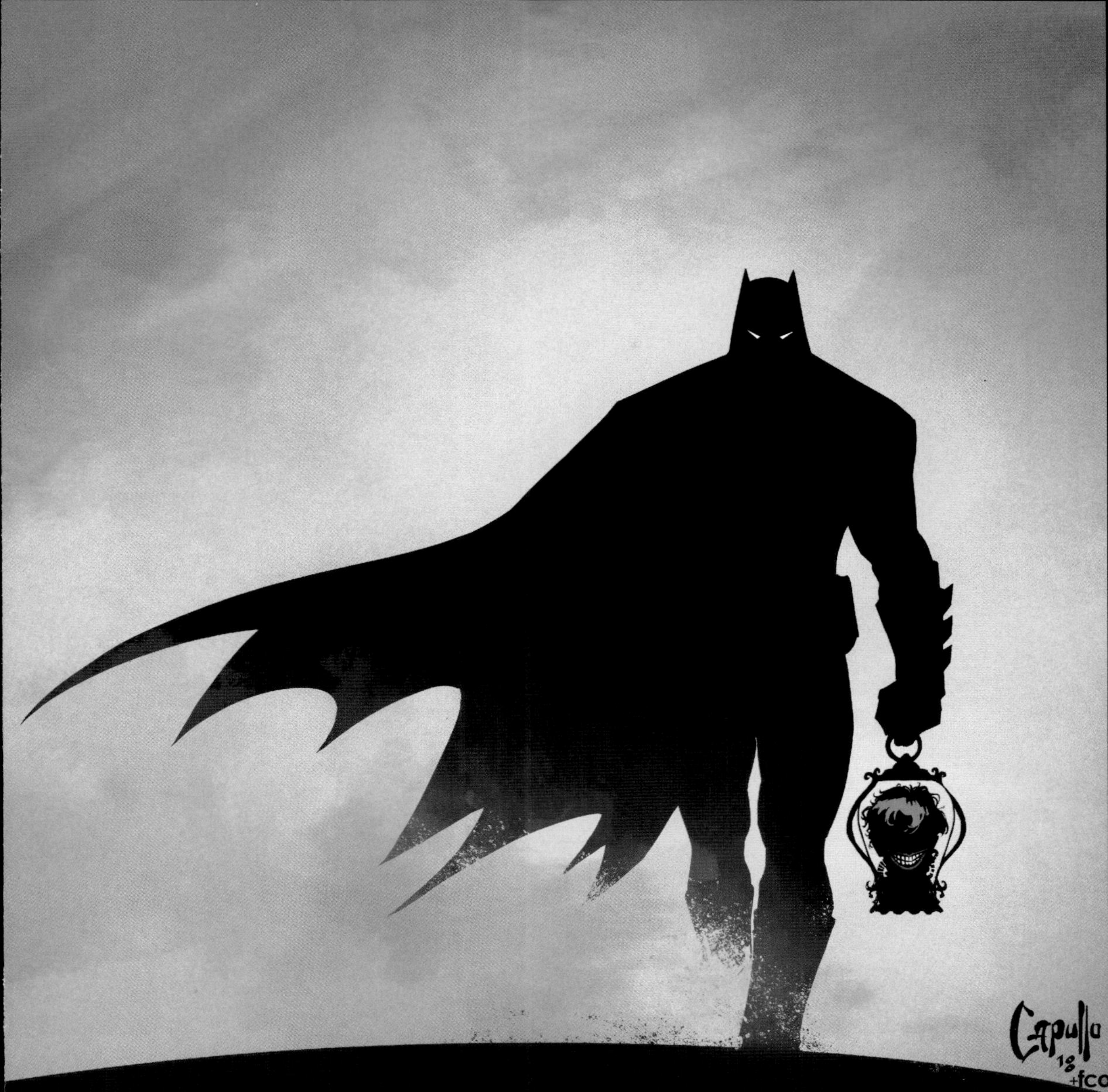
Capullo
18
+fco

Black-and-white art for *Batman: Last Knight on Earth Book Three* cover by Greg Capullo and Jonathan Glapion

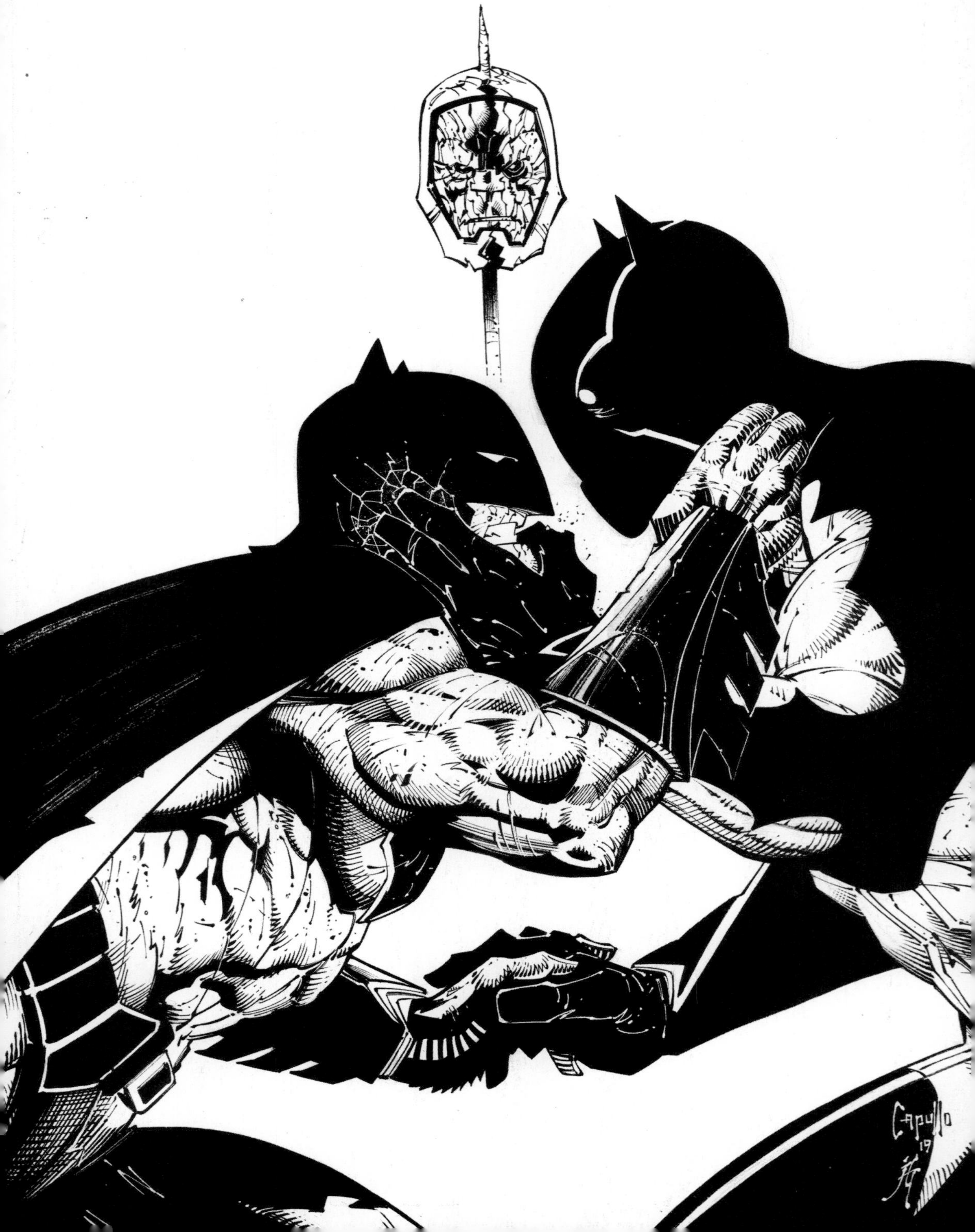
Capullo 19